A MEMOIR OF
THOMAS BEWICK
WRITTEN BY HIMSELF

A MEMOIR OF
THOMAS BEWICK

WRITTEN BY HIMSELF

EDITED WITH
AN INTRODUCTION BY
IAIN BAIN

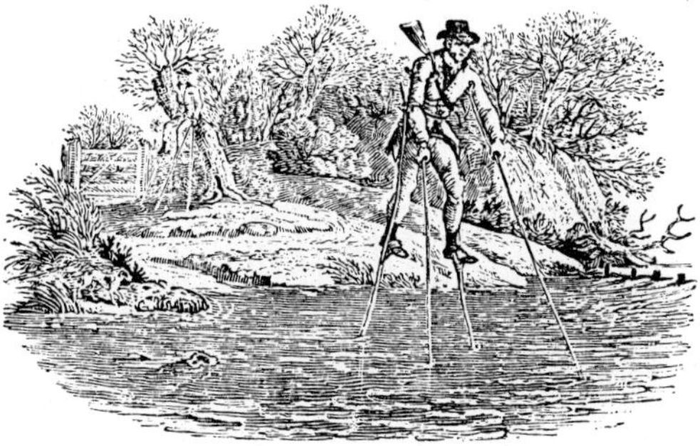

OXFORD UNIVERSITY PRESS
OXFORD NEW YORK TORONTO MELBOURNE
1979

Oxford University Press, Walton Street, Oxford OX2 6DP

OXFORD LONDON GLASGOW
NEW YORK TORONTO MELBOURNE WELLINGTON
KUALA LUMPUR SINGAPORE JAKARTA HONG KONG TOKYO
DELHI BOMBAY CALCUTTA MADRAS KARACHI
NAIROBI DAR ES SALAAM CAPE TOWN

First published 1975
Reprinted with corrections as an Oxford University Press Paperback 1979

ISBN 0 19 281271 8

Printed in Great Britain by
Lowe & Brydone Printers Limited, Thetford, Norfolk

CONTENTS

LIST OF ILLUSTRATIONS

The illustrations appear by kind permission of the following: Bewick aged seventy (detail), and Robert Pollard (detail), National Portrait Gallery, London; Bewick in middle life (detail), and marble bust, Literary and Philosophical Society, Newcastle upon Tyne; John, Jane, Isabella, and Robert Elliot Bewick, Natural History Society of Northumbria; Bewick's workshop, B. Collingwood Stevenson; Tool box, Central Library, Newcastle upon Tyne (Pease Collection); 18th-century printing presses, Science Museum, London, Crown Copyright. The water-colours, the engraved bank note, and the engraved portrait of William Bulmer are in the Editor's collection.

ACKNOWLEDGEMENTS

For assistance and permission to make use of Bewick letters, many of them hitherto unpublished, I am much indebted to several institutions and private owners: Sir Geoffrey Keynes, Mr Hugh Gibson, and Mr John Hack; the Trustees of the British Museum, the Central Library, Newcastle upon Tyne (Pease Collection), the Henry E. Huntington Library and Art Gallery, the Literary and Philosophical Society and the Laing Art Gallery and Museum of Newcastle upon Tyne, the Shropshire Record Office and the Victoria and Albert Museum. Professor J. D. H. Widdess most generously allowed a complete stranger to borrow Jane Bewick's corrected proof sheets of the *Memoir*, and besides those already mentioned, many friends and acquaintances have given much assistance and encouragement, particularly David Chambers, Dr Edward Ford, Bewick Hack, Marshall Hall, Professor Peter Isaac, R. Hunter Middleton, James Mosley, Edmund Poole, John Ryder, Reynolds Stone, Peter Summers, Arthur Wallace, and Gordon Williams.

Since the publication of the first edition, Professor Widdess, with surpassing kindness and generosity, has transferred to my keeping not only the proof sheets of Jane Bewick's edition but also the most extensive collection of Bewick correspondence and other manuscripts now in private hands.

ABBREVIATIONS

BM: British Museum
Huntington MSS: Bewick papers in the collections of the Henry E. Huntington Library & Art Gallery, San Marino, California
Hack MSS: Bewick papers in the possession of John Hack Esq.
Laing MSS: Bewick papers in the collections of the Laing Art Gallery & Museum, Newcastle upon Tyne
V & A MSS: Bewick papers in the collections of the Victoria & Albert Museum National Art Library, London
Pease Collection: The collection of Bewick books, manuscripts, drawings, and wood-blocks assembled by J. W. Pease and now in the Central Library, Newcastle upon Tyne
Brand: John Brand, *The History and Antiquities . . . of Newcastle upon Tyne*, 1789
Dobson: Austin Dobson (ed.) *A Memoir of Thomas Bewick*, 1887
Hugo: The Revd Thomas Hugo, *The Bewick Collector*, 1866
Mackenzie: E. Mackenzie, *A Descriptive and Historical Account of . . . Newcastle upon Tyne*, 1827

INTRODUCTION

Thomas Bewick's autobiographical *Memoir*, written at the end of his life and published posthumously in 1862, thirty-four years after his death, owes its reputation as a minor classic to two principal facts: first, that as a record of a north-country childhood and of a craftsman's life and work in the latter half of the eighteenth century it is unique, and secondly, that the achievement of its author as an artist-engraver on wood had no precedent and remains unequalled. The immediate success of his first major work, *A General History of Quadrupeds*, published in 1790, together with that of Gilbert White's *Natural History and Antiquities of Selborne* which appeared in the previous year, was to contribute much to the remarkable growth of popular interest in natural history. The many successive editions of the *Quadrupeds* and of his even more successful *History of British Birds*, 1797 and 1804, secured his reputation for all time.

In 1838, William Howitt wrote in his *Rural Life of England*: 'I have heard those who loved the country, and loved it because they knew it, say, that the opening of Bewick was a new era in their lives. I have seen how his volumes are loved, and treasured, and reverted to time after time, in many a country house; the more familiar, the more prized; the oftener seen, the oftener desired.'[1] Howitt was not alone in his affection for Bewick. Many others were inspired to praise him, from Wordsworth[2] and Charlotte Brontë,[3] to Carlyle[4] and C. R. Leslie. As did Howitt, Leslie considered him akin to Burns and wrote at length in his *Hand-Book for Young Painters*:

> While speaking of the English School, I must not omit to notice a truly original genius, who, though not a painter, was an artist of the highest order in his way–Thomas Bewick, the admirable designer and engraver on wood. His works, indeed, are of the smallest dimensions, but this

[1] ii. 39. [2] In his verse 'The Two Thieves'. [3] In the opening pages of *Jane Eyre*.
[4] In a letter of 20 December 1865 to Ruskin, who had persuaded him to read the *Memoir*.

makes it only the more surprising that so much of interest could be comprised within such little spaces. The wood-cuts that illustrate his books of natural history may be studied with advantage by the most ambitious votary of the highest classes of Art–filled as they are by the truest feeling for Nature, and though often representing the most ordinary objects, yet never, in a single instance, degenerating into common-place. . . . The student of Landscape can never consult the works of Bewick without improvement. The backgrounds to the figures of his Quadrupeds and his Birds, and his vignettes, have a charm of Nature quite his own. He gives us, in these, every season of the year; and his trees, whether in the clothing of summer, or in the nakedness of winter, are the trees of an artist bred in the country. He is equally true in his little home scenes, his farm-yards and cottages, as in his wild coast scenery, with flocks of sea-birds wheeling round the rocks. . . .[1]

John Ruskin spoke of Bewick's 'magnificent artistic virtue' and 'the flawless virtue, veracity, tenderness, the infinite humour of the man', and he considered his subtlety of drawing second only to Holbein and Turner.[2] The entrancing vignettes and tail-pieces with which Bewick illustrated his major works are a never-ending source of delight to this day and they continue to be used to decorate books, newspaper articles, ephemeral printing of every class, and even china. Many of them are true *tale*-pieces in their narrative portrayal of rural incident, and many point a moral with pathos and humour. The view they give of the countryside and manners of Georgian England has no equal, and their detailed backgrounds are masterpieces of compression and atmosphere.

The circumstances of Bewick's birth and early upbringing at Eltringham and Ovingham, villages on the Tyne some twelve miles west of Newcastle, are recorded in his *Memoir* with a direct and appealing freshness quite without sentimentality, and we are soon made aware of his early spontaneous talent for drawing and of his natural sympathy for wild and domestic animals. His vivid descriptions of the Northumberland countryside, of winter cold on the fell-side, and fishing on summer evenings, of the singing of border songs and ballads, cock-fighting, coursing, ghosts and superstition–all a background to his father's occupation as farmer and tenant collier–go far to explain their lasting influence throughout his life and their constant portrayal in his work. It was and still is

1 *Hand-Book for Young Painters*, 1855, pp. 144–6.

2 *Ariadne Florentina*, 1876, pp. 86 and 88. In his *Aratra Pentelici*, 1872, Ruskin advised his students to acquire and profit by TB's *Memoir*.

a lovely countryside. The last fragment of Bewick's old home, Cherryburn, perched on a high bank above the Tyne, remains as part of the farmyard of the larger house built by the family not long after he died.[1] It looks out over the still unspoilt rolling country of the Roman Wall and although modern development approaches one can still sense something of the atmosphere of earlier days.

As was Bewick's declared intention, the *Memoir* is a much peopled book. It is far from introspective, being rather more concerned with his 'observations made on men and things in passing through a long life.'[2] Of his first thirty pages he wrote to a correspondent: 'even this contains a good deal of biographical matter concerning the Characters of the people I knew–I intend as I go on to notice others, who I deem deserving notice, and none more so than your grandfather, & your uncle, & my plan is to continue my observations of men & things in the same kind of way– . . . These will be (if I live) interlarded with moral remarks as to character, those I can say no good of will be short, & I hope *pithy*, but without ever mentioning their names.'[3] Thus from the early pages we are given delightful portraits of the worthies and characters–old soldiers, farmers, schoolmasters, beekeepers, colliers–who inhabited the countryside of his childhood. His telling of their stories reflects a keen sense of the past and the social background to their lives. It is very evident that the homiletic nature of his parents and his parson-schoolmaster had the most powerful effect on him. For in spite of a sometimes unruly and high-spirited boyhood, his disciplined and rigorous apprenticeship to Ralph Beilby, a twenty-four-year-old 'engraver-in-general' in Newcastle, produced a quite positive reaction: the young Bewick proceeded to flourish under a self-imposed régime based on the principles laid out in Luigi Cornaro's manual of *Sure and Certain Methods of Attaining a Long and Healthful Life.*[4] No doubt the

[1] On 13 June 1828 TB wrote to J. F. M. Dovaston: 'I have lately been spending a few days in visiting the place of my nativity & the scenes of many happy days (but the House, in which I was born is I fear *agoing* to be pulled down–it is very old)' (BM Egerton MS 3147).

[2] TB to Henry Hole, 11 October 1826 (Hack MSS).

[3] TB to – Gray, probably grandson of Gilbert Gray the bookbinder (see pp. 43ff), 14 December 1822 (Laing MSS).

[4] Fourth edition of the English translation, 1724. A copy of this edition was in the Bewick family sale of 1884, item 129.

recollection of old age over-emphasized the amount of time he devoted to 'plans for conducting himself in life',[1] but there is also no doubt that the independent and resourceful nature of his character won through. From the account of Bewick's apprenticeship with its lack of sophisticated training, early self-taught draughtsmanship and hard discipline in metal engraving techniques, we realize very clearly the degree of his originality as an artist and the tenacity of his purpose.

Newcastle in the 1760s retained much of its medieval character. It was a town of less than 25,000 inhabitants,[2] still with its walls and gatehouses and its ancient house-bearing bridge across the Tyne. Its growth was accelerating with the prosperity of the coal trade which generated the greater part of its wealth, and yet the influence of the countryside was still close at hand. Bewick was fortunate in the fact that his master had the only workshop of its kind in the town and that the demand for its services from the expanding commercial interests brought engraving work of every sort to his door. He was also greatly fortunate in the wide range of his acquaintance–silversmiths, printers, bookbinders, glass painters, musicians, engineers, artists, and scholars–all of whom widened his experience, brought him to books and learning, and by their example encouraged him to excel in his craft. His debt to them is repaid in his shrewd and affectionate record of their lives.

With the end of apprenticeship came an interlude of three years during which Bewick worked at home at Cherryburn, took a 350–mile walk into Scotland, and spent nine months in London. The Scotch tour provided further material for his observant eye and inspired a delightful passage of descriptive writing. After his experience of the simple and hospitable ways of the Highlanders, the first contact with southern manners in London came as a severe contrast and provoked his Cobbett-like nature into vigorous outburst. In later years he wrote to a friend: 'I would rather be herding sheep on Mickley bank top than remain in London, although for doing so I was to be made Premier of England'.[3] These same sentiments were more extensively expressed in the

[1] p. 50.
[2] S. Middlebrook, *Newcastle upon Tyne, Its Growth and Achievement*, 1950, p. 321.
[3] TB to Christopher Gregson, 18 April 1803 (Pease Collection, 371).

record Dr Robert Blakey preserved in his *Memoirs*: 'Bewick often dwelt upon his trip to London, and, with facetious wit and great drollery . . . "I was", said he, "quite overpowered by the coldness and selfishness of everything I witnessed. . . . I never saw a single recognition of acquaintanceship or friendship in the streets; . . . in London life is cheap; the hearts of even good men get hardened; and that mutual regard and sympathy, which are the real balsams of life, are seldom tasted. I was delighted beyond measure when I turned my back on the place." '[1]

After his return from London, Bewick settled down to a twenty-year partnership with his former master, which brought long hours at the bench of the general engraving shop, with work on his natural histories kept for the quiet of uninterrupted evenings. Apart from the occasional walking tour, and family visits to the seaside at Tynemouth, there was little movement or drama in his life; and this to some extent explains the difficulty Bewick may have felt in putting together any account of his middle and later years.

That the *Memoir* is uneven in quality and construction cannot be denied. Some of the reasons for this will perhaps be understood from the following account of its composition. Bewick achieved fame in his lifetime and his success prompted the enquiries of several would-be biographers. In 1815 he prepared a 1900-word biographical note for one John Chambers who intended to write 'the lives of all the Artists now practising in this Country'. An account of his 'professional career' was all he was prepared and had time to give, referring to others who had 'picked up' a history of his life, a Mr Oxley and Sir Richard Phillips among them.[2] By 1822, when he was 69, his family had persuaded him to write the full account himself. '. . . this I was urged to do for various reasons & not the least of which was my knowing that more than one literary character was taking every pains to collect materials for that purpose, but lest as was likely such accounts might be filled with untruths–I thought it best write it myself &

[1] Revd H. Miller (ed.) *Memoirs of Dr. Robert Blakey*, 1879, pp. 36–7.

[2] TB to John Chambers, 10 March 1815 (Collection of Sir Geoffrey Keynes). E. Oxley of Hull was a surgeon and amateur of natural history: several of his letters to TB are in the V & A MSS (L.3528). Sir Richard Phillips, publisher and bookseller in London was one of TB's customers and failed to pay him the balance due for the work on his edition of Thornton's *Herbal*, 1810.

I have by correspondents & friends been put in mind of various desiderata tending to make this account as full and perfect as possible . . .'[1] In November and December of that year he completed the first thirty-four pages of the manuscript while away at Tynemouth.[2] As so often when old age recollects early youth, the task was not so hard: on 12 December he wrote to his old friend, Thomas Ranson, the engraver: 'I feel it to be quite an easy job–I have no author to consult on the business–& it flows upon me', comparing it at the same time with the writing of his *Fables of Aesop* which took him 'a deal of consideration'.[3] A further sixty-six pages were completed between 29 May and 24 June of 1823 while Bewick was 'confined by a fit of gout at home',[4] and by 18 November he had written twenty pages more.[5] These passages deal with his apprenticeship and his early years in business until the death of his parents in 1785. From here on the continuous narrative comes to an end and the writing begins to lose shape: it was 'committed to paper by fits and starts' during the following three years, and 221 of the 241 pages had been completed by 20 January 1827.[6] Although a certain number of drafts on rough slips have survived, there seems to be no evidence that any outline plan was prepared. The second half of the book becomes more haphazard and the concentration of homily and political observation increases.

Bewick clearly wrote with publication in mind,[7] although he said to his friend John Dovaston in November 1827: '. . . the manuscript copy is hers [Jane Bewick's], and she seems very unwilling that I should publish it *in my life time*–I think her wrong in this, for several reasons–but as I feel indifferent about it I can easily be put off'.[8] Jane won the day, presumably much embarrassed by references to friends and acquaintances still living, and so it was that the *Memoir* rambled to a stop with its many alternatives of word and phrase undecided. '. . . the Memoir wants only summing up to bring it to a close' Bewick wrote to

[1] TB to Henry Hole, 11 October 1826 (Hack MSS).
[2] Note in the *Memoir*, p. 29.
[3] TB to Thomas Ranson, 12 December 1822 (Huntington MSS).
[4] Note in the *Memoir*, p. 95.
[5] TB to J. F. M. Dovaston, 18 November 1823 (Shropshire Record Office).
[6] TB to Henry Hole, 20 January 1827 (Hack MSS).
[7] p. 195.
[8] TB to J. F. M. Dovaston, 23 November 1827 (BM Egerton MS 3147).

Dovaston in October 1828, 'yet I have not set about doing so, with the usual energy.'[1] Although he planned to keep it up to date (he told Dovaston that he had not yet included the account of their visit to Buxton in 1826),[2] in the later pages his growing concern with the hereafter kept out any references to his daily activities.

Several critics have deplored the later sections of the *Memoir*. The Revd Thomas Hugo remarked: 'I think that most readers of the "Memoir" will agree with me in regretting that the chapters on religious and political matters were not omitted. It is the artist-life of Thomas Bewick which one desires to possess, not his opinions about subjects on which he was and could be no authority.'[3] This is far from just, for though the balance of the work may be disturbed, what he wrote was of deep concern to him and unquestionably it portrays the man. Contrary to the generality of men, who in his view 'do not reason–they only ruminate',[4] such topics were long and seriously discussed when he met his cronies at Swarley's Club and at the Blue Bell inn. There is in fact a deal of good sense in what he wrote. Hugo no doubt disapproved of Bewick's wry view of organized religion, the 'chaos of what is called religious works' and the 'waggon loads of sermons'[5] with which he tells us his youthful mind was confused. His impatience with sectarian nonsense and his very modern ecumenical sentiments would likewise have offended Hugo. On the Enclosure Acts, on rich and reckless landowners, on Pitt and the war against France, and on the education of children, he has much to say that to present day opinion is wholly sensible. As Dr Robert Blakey remarked, Bewick 'could not be considered a learned man, but he possessed a more than usual share of common sense; and this generally conducted him to safe and judicious conclusions on most subjects in which he felt any interest. He was a keen observer of the world, yet his shrewdness was entirely devoid of cunning and ill-nature.'[6]

The extensive collections of letters and other papers still surviving are essential for the rounding out of our view of Bewick's character and for the detail of his daily activities. We have little

[1] Ibid., 14 October 1828.
[2] Ibid., 20 September 1826.
[3] *The Bewick Collector*, 1866, p. xiii.
[4] TB to J. F. M. Dovaston, 9 February 1825 (BM Egerton MS 3147).
[5] p. 48. [6] Revd H. Miller (ed.), *Memoirs of Dr. Robert Blakey*, 1879, p. 36.

of the family man in the *Memoir* but many letters survive which were written to his wife and children when he or they were away from home, and which display an admonitory, yet essentially kindly and loving manner towards them: 'I am affraid *you* will never be enabled to make amends to the kind folks in South Shields for their Hot Breakfasts, their Tea & Spice Cakes', he wrote to his nine-year-old Jane, 'unless you can prevail upon your Mother & Father to assist you in your endeavours to be grateful . . . I hope you will treat her [Mrs Molly Hencles], while she remains with you, with great kindness, remembering, that tho' she is but simple, yet she is our honest Servant at command. . . .'[1] His loving concern for his children–and a delightful glimpse of the convivial, cheerful, fire-side man–appears again in a charming letter he wrote to his wife in July 1791 while at Wycliffe preparing drawings for his *History of British Birds*:

> The Stewart, Mr Collier is as civil to me as possible–and so is Mrs Newcomb, the Housekeeper–but there is no drinking–no excess–a single glass of Wine or so is all–I believe I shall be *quite weaned* by the time that I return to NC again–but I believe if I was at home, again it wou'd not be long before I shou'd have a wetting of *nebs* with my hearty friend Mr Joseph Bell,[2] who I often think about–when I am surrounded *with Buckram Canvass & Stay tape*— . . . —how anxiously desirous am I to hear as good an Account of you & how glad wou'd I be to hear that all were as well with my treasures at home–let me know as soon as you can, exactly, how you all are, my dear little Boy–I wou'd fain hope is better–let me once more beg that you wou'd be attentive to his health–let him lie cool & take him often to play at the sea side–I hope also that my little darlings are well. . . .[3]

From the *Memoir* we can see something of the affection Bewick had for his brother John who had been his first apprentice and who, with a still maturing talent as an engraver, died so young. John's blithe nature, free of his brother's not infrequent earnestness, flourished in London–no doubt partly a result of being away

[1] TB to Jane Bewick, 2 July 1796 (Huntington MSS).

[2] 'He was fond of porter, and I have known him sit from seven o'clock in the evening till eleven, sipping his favourite beverage to the tune of five or six pints. It did not seem to produce any muddling or stupefying effect upon him whatever. He was always clear, collected, humorous, and pleasant. Custom, I have no doubt, had rendered this indulgence quite innoxuous and harmless both to his body and mind.' *Memoirs of Dr. Robert Blakey*, 1879, p. 35.

[3] TB to Mrs Isabella Bewick, 22 July 1791 (Literary and Philosophical Society of Newcastle upon Tyne).

from elder-brotherly restraints. His letters home are colourful and lively; they contain much of interest relating to printing and publishing trade practice and there is frequent concern at his brother's reluctance to come south to promote the sale of his books. His respect for Thomas did not prevent him from speaking his mind:

I should be glad if you could inform me in your next when your History may be expected,[1] I think you are very delatory with it,––I am perfectly of your opinion with regard to the Sky in your Upsaal view,[2] I did not wish to say much in my last but I think the Clouds are badly fancied and rather School-boyish if I may use the expression, . . .[3] . . . I return you my sincear & hearty thanks for your very kind offer to serve me, but your opinion & good advice is quite sufficient, & shall allways be strictly adhear'd to & thankfully rec'd, & shall make it my peculiar study to merit the Characture you so anciously wish to hear of me, . . . I do assure you I have not eat much Idle Bread.[4]

The reflective and sometimes morbid aspect of Bewick's nature was not reserved for his formal writing alone, nor was it simply a condition of his old age: several letters to his friends were written in this vein, but with, at the same time, a touch of domestic colour: 'I then took a long walk, backward & forward at the end of the burial ground–listing to the roars of the dashing surge below –this on the one side & the frail memorials of the silent dead on the other–disposed the mind to contemplation & solemn meditation –after this I went home & was sure to meet with what I *call a scold at home* "now Thomas what can you mean by walking among gravestones in the dark night alone I'm sure it is an odd fancy" &c . . .'.[5] The north country preoccupation with death and the accepted brevity of life is often reflected in Bewick's art and writing. One of his letters to Robert Pollard, a friend from boyhood days, tells of a bizarre graveside scene in the most matter of fact way: '. . . –To see our old friend Mr Chris^r^ Gregson put into his Fathers Grave, in Octr last at Ovingham, & to have the Scull of my old preceptor pointed out to me, upon the occasion, raked up in my mind such a croud–such a load of reflections, as greatly overfilled my mind–but indeed the Scull of my own Father, only

[1] *A General History of Quadrupeds*, first published 1790.

[2] A copper engraving etched in line and aquatint for Consett's *Tour in Sweden, Swedish-Lapland, Finland and Denmark*, 1789.

[3] John Bewick to TB, 30 September 1788 (Hack MSS).

[4] Ibid., 9 April 1788.

[5] TB to Robert Pollard, 3 February 1823 (Laing MSS).

a few months before, was turned out of his Grave & gave rise in my mind to a similar glut of reflections–In the latter case I had some hours to spare to examine it & to turn it over & over & talk to it, all alone, I knew it so well that I cou'd pick it out from among 10,000–'[1]

Bewick did not suffer fools gladly and was quite uncompromising in his dealings. He would stand for ever on a small matter of principle, and would be prepared to let a small difference mushroom into an agony of protracted dissension and bitterness. Behind the relatively brief reference in the *Memoir* to the dispute with the widow of his friend and printer, Solomon Hodgson, there is a mound of surviving material from both sides of the argument.[2] The whole affair blew up from a small discrepancy in Hodgson's account for the printing of the first volume of the *Birds*. Because Bewick would not compromise, and because Sarah Hodgson was not without her own awkwardness, they conducted a bitter dispute which lasted many months and which involved scores of letters and expensive litigation. Yet Bewick could still write to her: 'I must beg that you will be so good as to blot out the last mentioned Article [an engraving of a memorial to Solomon Hodgson], in my note against you–I once on a time never meant to charge you any thing for it, and now, notwithstanding our late squabbles, I repent that I have done so . . . in charging you with the scabey expence of it I have done wrong–I have forgot myself . . .'.[3] Of the dispute, one of Mrs Hodgson's acquaintances wrote to her: '. . . Having exhausted all my *Wonder* on the Subject of *Tommy Bewick's* Cession from your House,[4] I have not a Word to say on that very extraordinary business; the thing in Question (which ever Party were right, or wrong) not being of Importance sufficient to have required an Hour's Conference . . .'.[5]

Bewick was always quick to suspect an injury or to imagine that someone was taking advantage of him. He writes in the *Memoir*: 'I am conscious that I never sought a quarrel with any one, but when insulted I found it very bad to bear and mostly in the most

1 Ibid., 29 January 1816.

2 The two principal collections of papers relating to the dispute are in the V & A (L3527) and BM (Add. MSS 50240–2). See p. 125.

3 TB to Mrs Sarah Hodgson, 25 January 1805 (BM Add. MSS 50240–2).

4 A reference to TB's having taken the printing of the fifth edition of the *Quadrupeds* from Hodgson's to Walker's printing office.

5 John Ware to Mrs Sarah Hodgson, 23 November 1802 (BM Add. MSS 50240–2).

secret or hidden manner contrived *to fight it out*.'[1] This was of his youth, but the characteristic continued into later life. He was little inclined to give the benefit of the doubt in his suspicions. His boyhood friend, William Bulmer, who went south to London and became the most celebrated printer of his day, was a careful business man. His unwillingness to pay more than Bewick had originally quoted for his work on Bulmer's grand edition of the *Poems by Goldsmith and Parnell* was perfectly fair, but the fact that Bulmer quickly took £1500 in the sale of the book was long resented by the family. The payment of £36. 15*s*. for the drawings and blocks which had been the principal means of its success was felt to be mean.[2] (Bulmer's introduction said of the blocks: 'they form the most extraordinary effort of the art of engraving upon wood, that ever was produced in any age, or any country . . .'. Although Bulmer wanted to continue with other similar productions,[3] the association ceased: Bewick apparently felt he was taking liberties, and his daughter Jane later somewhat unjustly remarked that if the printer 'had not suffered his grasping greediness to rule him–in all likelihood–other works of equal excellence might have appeared embellished by T.B.'[4] Happily in old age they were reconciled and there was a warm reunion in London in 1828.

Bewick's important relationship with his partner and former master Ralph Beilby, as shown in the *Memoir*, is only a partial view. We read of their differences and of the basic affection and respect they had for one another, but apart from what Bewick himself writes,[5] there is other evidence that the talented Beilby family always held themselves superior and that their condescension long rankled with him. The multifarious skills of Ralph, Mary, and William–children of a jeweller and silversmith–in metal engraving, enamel painting on glass, and in drawing, gave them a social standing of which they appear to have been somewhat conscious, and by it their country-boy apprentice was made to feel an inferiority. In later years Jane Bewick, far from impartial, wrote of Ralph Beilby:

[1] p. 14.
[2] Jane Bewick's MS memoranda relating to her father's correspondents (Laing MSS).
[3] '–Have you yet thought of any little Poem or Poems, that you would wish to engrave some blocks for . . .'. William Bulmer to TB, 21 July 1802 (Pease Collection 178).
[4] Jane Bewick's MS memoranda (Laing MSS). [5] p. 124.

. . . My grand mother said 'he was a cunning man', but my father did not, or would not see it, till too late.–My father could not bear the thought of setting up in opposition to his Master–which was one cause of the unfortunate connection betwixt them, which lasted from 1777 to 1797–he shared my good fathers labors, & no man ever labored harder– . . . I have never seen in the engraving books any acc^{t} of division of moneys, but have heard my Mother say that it was never done–My Father would say to her 'Beilby has had a rapid call for Money'–His Letters paint his character (see one recommending TB to settle in Sheffield)–a pecksniffish[1]–far better than I can depicture him–His wife was worse than he–they had no children but assumed to be very *genteel people* & lived in good style. His letters to my Father urging him to *closer attention* to the business of the Shop while the writer was pursuing his own profitable business elsewhere–appears to me as worthy of a place in Dickens . . . –In his last illness–my Father called to see him, till the wife w^{d} no longer admit him–he, TB, heard Beilby on the stairs say–'I *will* see him'–but he was always *hen*-pecked–his conscience had pricked him & she Mrs B might be afraid of a meeting–My F^{r} was not invited to his funeral.[2]

Jane Bewick's reference to her father's seeming lack of concern for money and his freedom with it, is confirmed both in his own record[3] and in a letter he wrote in 1827 to his former apprentice Henry Hole: '. . . my publications have left me a small independancy which with great oeconomy I trust will do–notwithstanding the many heavy losses I have met with and but for these I might have been in very easy circumstances–but you may perhaps know that while I was in my prime I was more liberal than prudent in *giving away* as fast as I got it this was succeeded by my lending people in need almost without end and last and worst was that of being bound for others who I now know to my cost never meant to be honest–if I had my life to lead over again I would do very differently.'[4]

As he writes of it, the dispute between Bewick and his partner over the credit for the authorship of the *Birds* gives the impression that Beilby was making quite unjust claims. Yet the letters Beilby wrote to Bewick, to friends, and to the referees in the dispute, show that it would have been fair to have given Beilby's name a

[1] A reference to Mr Pecksniff the arch-hypocrite in Dickens's *Martin Chuzzlewit*. Very few of Beilby's letters to TB have yet been traced, but one dealing with business matters here referred to and only partially confirming Jane Bewick's view, is now in the Editor's possession.

[2] Jane Bewick's MS memoranda (Laing MSS).

[3] p. 125.

[4] TB to Henry Hole, 20 January 1827 (Hack MSS). See also p. 199, n. 4.

little more notice: to have described themselves as joint editors on the title-page would have been more reasonable. Out of this came the letter from Beilby, written on 7 September 1797, which began the proceedings for their final separation:

If I had insisted that my name should have been joined with yours in the title page, as the joint executor of the cuts, you might have justly considered it as an arrogant presumption. But why I should be denied the *little* merit of putting together the pages which accompany your works, Why *I* am to be rudely thrust aside & set in a corner as your Amanuensis, that *you* may appear sole, both as artist and author, is more than I can conceive. Indeed I cannot help thinking that it is a most indecent violation of propriety and good manners to *strike my name* out, & alter & mutilate my preface in the manner you have done without my consent *first had & obtained* especially as I read it to you with all the offensive parts in it, in my own house, just before it had received its final correction & with your seeming approbation. what has induced you to take so violent a turn you best know. You seem to have forgot your own principles & have committed an act of the purest *despotism*, you have dragged me before a tribunal of your own erecting, where you have judged me to Death, & were to be your own executioner –. . . As the measure of a separation has become absolutely necessary to my own peace of mind, I wish you to consider about it & I will meet you any evening this week at our own Shop to settle matters which I hope may still [be] done in an amicable way . . .[1]

But having made his stand, Bewick was not one to compromise and give ground, and one can sense that here there was more than authorship at stake: with his own reputation in the ascendant the opportunity had come to make even with the slights and condescensions–no doubt a good many of them imagined–of former years. The watch glass business was a very sore matter and when the time came for the division of assets, Bewick asked his lawyer to consider how much he should apply for on account of his extra attendance at the workshop while his partner was otherwise occupied.[2] While the difference in age between them was only ten years, no doubt there was always something remaining of the master and apprentice relationship, and Beilby probably had no difficulty in justifying to himself his pursuit of other enterprises.

Apart from the additional view we can get of Bewick from his surviving papers, several accounts were written of him which had

[1] Collection of Sir Geoffrey Keynes.
[2] TB to John Kirsopp, Solicitor (Draft, n.d. V & A MSS L. 3252).

the advantage of a personal acquaintance. Two of the most attractive of these were written by John Dovaston and by the American artist and naturalist Audubon. Audubon's description, based on visits to Bewick's house in Gateshead during April 1827, is full of atmosphere and gives a most engaging portrait of the man and his hearthside:

At length we reached the dwelling of the Engraver, and I was at once shewn his workshop. There I met the old man, who, coming towards me, welcomed me with a hearty shake of the hand, and for a moment took off a cotton night-cap, somewhat soiled by the smoke of the place. He was a tall stout man, with a large head, and with eyes placed farther apart than those of any man that I have ever seen:–a perfect old Englishman, full of life, although seventy-four years of age, active and prompt in his labours. Presently he proposed shewing me the work he was at, and went on with his tools. It was a small vignette, cut on a block of boxwood not more than three by two inches in surface, and represented a dog frightened at night by what he fancied to be living objects, but which were actually roots and branches of trees, rocks and other objects bearing the semblance of men. This curious piece of art, like all his works, was exquisite. . . . The old gentleman and I stuck to each other, he talking of my drawings, I of his wood cuts. Now and then he would take off his cap, and draw up his grey worsted stockings to his nether clothes; but whenever our conversation became animated, the replaced cap was left sticking as if by magic to the hind part of his head, the neglected hose resumed their downward journey, his fine eyes sparkled, and he delivered his sentiments with a freedom and vivacity which afforded me great pleasure. . . . The tea drinking having in due time come to an end, young Bewick, to amuse me, brought a bagpipe of a new construction, called the Durham Pipe,[1] and played some simple Scotch, English and Irish airs, all sweet and pleasing to my taste . . . The company dispersed at an early hour, and when I parted from Bewick that night, I parted from a friend. . . . I revisited him . . . on the 16th April, and found the whole family so kind and attentive that I felt quite at home. The good gentleman, after breakfast, soon betook himself to his labours, and began to shew me, as he laughingly said, how easy it was to cut wood; but I soon saw that cutting wood in his style and manner was no joke, although to him it seemed indeed easy. His delicate and beautiful tools were all made by himself, and I may with truth say that his shop was the only artist's 'shop' that I ever found perfectly clean and tidy.[2]

[1] A confusion of counties: Audubon meant the Northumbrian pipes, the 'new construction' being a reference to the key-work on the pipe chanter which at that time had not long been introduced. See p. 97 and n. 1.

[2] J. J. Audubon, *Ornithological Biography*, 1831.

John Dovaston, a native of Shropshire, trained as a barrister and of independent means, devoted much of his time to the study of natural history and many of his observations were original and valuable.[1] He twice visited Bewick in Newcastle during the 1820s[2] and became not a little enamoured of his daughter Jane. Dovaston was good company. His additional interest in music and literature and his sometimes rabelaisian sense of humour appealed to the older man and they wrote to one another regularly during the last five years of Bewick's life. In 1827 when Bewick was taking a cure at Buxton Spa he was accompanied by Dovaston and the following lively anecdote of their stay appeared in the memoir Dovaston wrote of him for Loudon's *Magazine of Natural History*:

In my haste to find his lodging, I passed it; but stumping behind, with his great cudgel, he seized me ardently by the arm before I was aware, exclaiming, 'I seed ye from tha window, and kenned yer back and gait, my kind friend'. I found him in very good lodgings . . . there were three windows in the front room, the ledges and shutters whereof he had pencilled all over with funny characters, as he saw them pass to and fro, visiting the well. These people were the source of great amusement: the probable histories of whom, and how they came by their ailings, he would humourously narrate, and sketch their figures and features in one instant of time. I have seen him draw a striking likeness on his thumb-nail, in one moment; wipe it off with his tongue, and instantly draw another. He told me that, at watering places, if his name were known, he was pestered with people staring at him, and inflicting foolish questions; and he cautioned me always in public to call him the 'old gentleman'. We dined occasionally at the public table; and one day, over the wine, a dispute arose between two gentlemen about a bird; but was soon terminated by the one affirming he had compared it with the figure and description of Bewick, to which the other replied that Bewick was next to Nature. Here the old gentleman seized me by the thigh with his very hand-vice of a grasp; and I contrived to keep up the shuttlecock of conversation playfully to his highest satisfaction, though they who praised him so ardently, little imagined whose ears imbibed all their honest incense. . . . Of mornings he walked out before the gnats and butterflies (as he called the company) began to frisk. . . . and as he always rose very early to 'waak oot', one morning . . . I walked after him, and found him in a place they call the grove . . . playing with a group of curly rosy children, for whom he was drawing funny

[1] See D. E. Allen, 'J. F. M. Dovaston, An Overlooked Pioneer of Field Ornithology', *Journal of the Society for the Bibliography of Natural History*, July 1967, pp. 277–83.
[2] Dovaston's two manuscript journals of his north-country and Scottish tours and which describe his visits are now in the collections of Ohio State University (1823) and the Editor (1825).

figures on a painted bench, and telling them the names of birds, insects, and plants. . . .[1]

Dovaston had tried to get Jane Bewick to let him edit her father's *Memoir*,[2] which he had been allowed to read in manuscript on one of his visits, but she was not to be persuaded. So he wrote his own account of his friend, and it appeared in four successive issues of Loudon's journal. The family obviously disliked it and wished it had not been published,[3] but although florid in style, it has the ring of truth. Perhaps his recounting of some of their broader jokes and the rather too Scotch representation of the north-country dialect did not suit their own view of the celebrated public figure, and certainly Jane Bewick was much embarrassed by the too fulsome references to herself.[4]

Many likenesses of Bewick were painted and engraved in his lifetime. The engraving most liked by the family was that of 1817 by John Burnett after James Ramsay.[5] Another fine oil by Ramsay of Bewick aged seventy, here faces p. 2. Bewick himself said: '. . . I think Mr Ramsay's Portraits *one & all* are *the best* that *ever were done*–he gives the Character as well as the likeness so correctly, that they look like the person alive–they ought indeed not to be called likenesses, but *Fac similes*. Mr Ramsay is also a very agreeable, kind, good man, as well as a first rate painter–'.[6] The cheerful fireside crony is perhaps best seen in the unsigned portrait now in the collection of the Literary and Philosophical Society of Newcastle and here reproduced facing p. 2. The marble bust by E. H. Bailey commissioned by subscription for the same society in 1826 is probably the most faithful likeness in that it was based on a life mask. Two views of this can be seen facing p. 211: it shows very clearly the long head and strong features, and particularly the wide-set eyes observed by Audubon. It is a face full of subtleties and the bust

[1] March 1830, p. 98.
[2] Jane Bewick to J. F. M. Dovaston, 28 November 1829 (Shropshire Record Office).
[3] MS memorandum of Jane Bewick on a letter from J. Adamson to Robert Bewick, 2 February 1830 (V & A MSS L.3254).
[4] Jane Bewick to J. F. M. Dovaston, 20 June 1830 (Shropshire Record Office).
[5] 'The likeness of me in Mr Charnley's Edition of the old Fables [*Select Fables*, 1820], I consider not worth a Pin the only one worth any notice is the one done from Ramsay's painting . . .'. TB to J. F. M. Dovaston, 18 November 1823 (Shropshire Record Office).
[6] TB to Thomas Ranson, 12 December 1815 (Pease Collection, 178).

well displays the fascinating variety of his character, a character most neatly summed up by a contemporary:

. . . his personal appearance was rustic; he was tall and powerfully formed, a quality which he was fond of displaying in his prime. His manners were somewhat rustic too, but he was shrewd, and disdained to ape the gentleman. His countenance was open and expressive, with a capacious forehead, strongly indicating intellect; his dark eyes beamed with the fire of genius. He was a man of strong passions–strong in his affections, and equally strong in his dislikes, the latter sometimes exposed him to the charge of illiberality, but the former and kinder feeling greatly predominated. True he was–as most men are–jealous of his fame, and had not much affection for rival artists, but they seldom crossed his path. His resentment, when once excited, was not easily allayed, but there was much warmth in his friendship. Strictly honourable was he in his dealings; and to his friends there never was a more sincere or kind-hearted man than Thomas Bewick.[1]

But perhaps the final word should be left to Audubon:

My opinion of this remarkable man is, that he was purely a son of nature, to whom alone he owed nearly all that characterized him as an artist and a man. Warm in his affections, of deep feeling, and possessed of a vigorous imagination, with correct and penetrating observation, he needed little extraneous aid to make him what he became, the first engraver on wood that England has produced. Look at his tail-pieces, Reader, and say if you ever saw so much life represented before, . . . As you turn each successive leaf, from beginning to end of his admirable books, scenes calculated to excite your admiration everywhere present themselves. Assuredly you will agree with me in thinking that in his peculiar path none has equalled him. There may be men now, or some may in after years appear, whose works may in some respects rival or even excel his, but not the less must Thomas Bewick of Newcastle-on-Tyne be considered in the art of engraving on wood what Linnaeus will ever be in natural history, though not the founder, yet the enlightened improver and illustrious promoter.[2]

[1] From a single sheet obituary notice published and possibly written by John Sykes, a Newcastle bookseller, *c.* 1829.

[2] *Ornithological Biography*, 1831.

A CHRONOLOGY OF THOMAS BEWICK

	aged
1753 10 or 12 August, born at Cherryburn, Eltringham, Northumberland, eldest son of John Bewick (1715–85), farmer and tenant of land-sale colliery. Baptized Ovingham 19 August	
1760 Brother John born at Cherryburn. Baptized 30 March	7
*c*1763–7 Attends school of Revd Christopher Gregson at Ovingham Parsonage	10–14
1767 1 October, apprenticed to Ralph Beilby (1743–1817), engraver in Newcastle upon Tyne	14
1768 Charles Hutton's *Mensuration* commences part publication: the first work for which Bewick engraves on wood	15
1774 Apprenticeship ends 1 October. Returns to Cherryburn for two years	21
1776 4 January, receives premium from Society for the Encouragement of Arts for engravings for fable illustrations June to August walks to and round Scotland. 1 October travels to seek work in London. T. Saint's *Select Fables* with Bewick's engravings published	23
1777 22 June, returns to Newcastle. Joins Ralph Beilby in Partnership. John Bewick becomes his apprentice	24
1778 17 October, elected a member of Swarley's Club at the Black Boy Inn	25
1779 Publication of *Fables by the late Mr Gay*, and *Tommy Trip's History of Beasts and Birds*, T. Saint, Newcastle	26
1781 Takes over tenancy of Dr Hutton's house in Circus Lane at the Forth, Newcastle, in October	28
1782 18 December, joins Brotherly Society at Whitfield's Golden Lion, Newcastle. John Bewick's indentures cancelled after five years; he removes to London	29

1784 *Select Fables* published by T. Saint incorporating designs from edition of 1776 and some by John Bewick 31

1785 Begins work on cutting blocks for *A General History of Quadrupeds* 15 November, on which day his father dies. Mother, Jane Wilson, dies 20 February 32

1786 20 April, marries Isabella Elliot of Ovingham at St John's Newcastle 33

1787 Eldest child Jane born 29 April. John Bewick commences business at Clerkenwell Green 15 October 34

1788 Son Robert Elliot Bewick born 26 April 35

1789 Engraving of the Chillingham Bull for Marmaduke Tunstall of Wycliffe completed. Consett's *A Tour through Sweden, Swedish-Lapland, Finland and Denmark*, published with Bewick's copper engravings 36

1790 Publication of *A General History of Quadrupeds* 27 April. Considers dissolving partnership with Beilby. Daughter Isabella born 14 January 37

1791 16 July, visits Wycliffe Museum for two months to commence drawings for *A History of British Birds*. Second edition *Quadrupeds* published 38

1792 Third edition *Quadrupeds* published 39

1793 Daughter Elizabeth born 7 March 40

1795 *Poems of Goldsmith and Parnell* printed and published by William Bulmer with engravings by Thomas and John Bewick. Brother John dies aged 35, 5 December. Moves to new engraving shop in south-east corner of St Nicholas's Church Yard 42

1796 Somervile's *Chase* with engravings by Bewick and brother John printed and published by William Bulmer. Le Grand's *Fabliaux* published privately by Gregory Way and printed by Bulmer with engravings by Bewick, John Bewick, and Charlton Nesbit 43

1797 First volume of *British Birds*, Land Birds, published. Partnership with Ralph Beilby dissolved. Beilby continues in watch-glass and clock manufactory 44

1799 Second edition *Land Birds* published 45

1800 Fourth edition *Quadrupeds* published 47

1804 Publication of first edition of the *Water Birds*. Son Robert apprenticed for seven years, 26 May 51

1805 Third edition *Land Birds* and second edition of *Water Birds* published 52

1807 Fifth edition *Quadrupeds* published 54

1809 Fourth edition *Land Birds* and third edition *Water Birds* published. His schoolmaster the Revd Christopher Gregson dies aged 71 56

1811 Son Robert out of apprenticeship 26 May. Sixth edition of *Quadrupeds* published 85

1812 Seriously ill in April. Son Robert into partnership 1 January. Moves to 19 West Street, Gateshead, early September. Begins work on drawings for *Fables of Aesop* 59

1814 Fifth edition *Land Birds* published 61

1815 10 March, writes short autobiographical memoir for John Chambers 62

1816 Sixth edition *Land Birds* and fourth edition *Water Birds* published 63

1817 Ralph Beilby dies 4 January, aged 74 64

1818 *Fables of Aesop* published. Elected member Society of Dilettanti of Edinburgh, 4 May 65

1820 Seventh edition *Quadrupeds* published. Charnley's edition of the *Select Fables* published 67

1821 Seventh edition *Land Birds* and fifth edition *Water Birds* published 68

1822 Begins writing *Memoir*, November 69

1823 Visits Edinburgh and executes first and only lithographic drawing: 'The Cadger's Trot'. Second edition *Fables of Aesop* published 70

1824 Eighth edition *Quadrupeds* published 71

1826 Wife Isabella dies 1 February. Marble bust by E. H. Bailey completed for Literary & Philosophical Society of Newcastle. Eighth edition *Land Birds* and sixth edition *Water Birds* published 73

1827 Visited by Audubon. Completes 221 pages of *Memoir* 74

1828 Visits London for second time. Dies 8 November 75

A MEMOIR OF
THOMAS BEWICK
WRITTEN BY HIMSELF

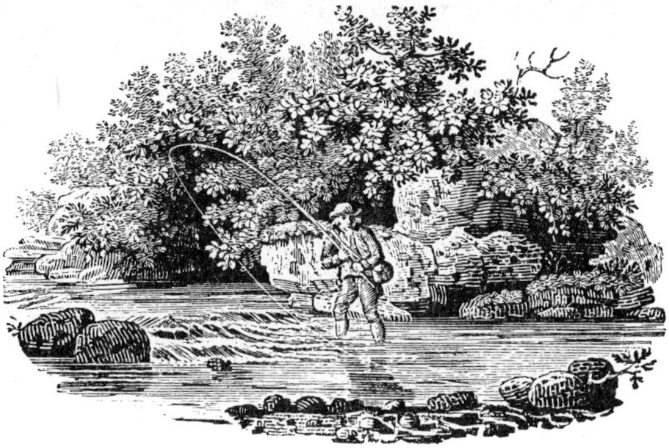

[1]

Tynemouth Nov[r] 1822

My dear Jane

It is in compliance with your wishes, that I have after much hesitation and delay, made up my mind to give you some account of my life, as it may at a future day amuse you & your Brother & Sisters in your passage through its crooked, as well as its pleasant paths; and as it may also satisfy your curiosity to know something about your Pedigree, I will inform you of what I have been told respecting it, as far back as I can.–

My Grandfather, Thomas Bewick, farmed the Lands of Painshaw field and Burches Neuk, near Bywell, and also the Colliery on Mickley Bank or Mickley Common–how long since I know not, but it might probably be about the year 1700—He had the Character of being one of the most intelligent, active & best Farmers on Tyneside, and it was said, that by his good management & great industry, he got to be very rich–and excepting his being an expert or a great Angler, I know little more about him. My Grandmother's maiden Name was Agnes Arthur, the Daughter of a Laird of that name at Kirkheaton, where my Father was born in the year 1715, while his Mother was there (I believe) on a visit to her friends.

My maternal Grandfather, Thomas Wilson & my Grandmother, whose maiden Name was Hannah Thompson, lived at Ainstable in

Cumberland; but whether he was Curate of the Parish of that place, or Parish Clerk I do not know–it is certain however that he was one or the other, and that he taught a School there,–and from the circumstance of his teaching his Sons, and some of his Daughters Latin, I conclude he taught some of his Scholars the same Language.

When he died his Eldest Son, Christopher, became possessed of his Freehold property, consisting of a House &c. and a few Fields adjoining it—The rest of his Family were left little besides a good Education, and were spread abroad in the World to do the best they could for themselves.—In this state of their Affairs, my Mother, Jane, and her youngest Sister Hannah, were taken by a distant relation–a Mrs Gregson of Appleby, & remained with her untill she could get them places to live at.

About this time the Revd Chrisr Gregson had been appointed to the Curacy of Ovingham, and wanted a Housekeeper, and my Mother, 'tho young, was thought able to undertake that Office and accordingly engaged to perform it.

Your maternal Grandfathers name was Robert Elliot and your Grandmother's Jane Forster—He farmed the land of Woodgate near Bill Quay, where your Mother was born; he afterwards removed to a farm at Ovingham, where he died in 1777, leaving the Character of a sensible honest & industrious Man.–

How long my Mother lived in Mr Gregson's place before her Marriage I know not, but from him, I afterwards learned that she was a valuable Servant to him, both with respect to the management in his Housekeeping concerns, and also for the occasional assistance she afforded him in hearing his Pupils their latin Tasks. —From this place, in the year 1752, she married my Father & went to live with him at Cherry-burn House, near the small Village or Hamlet of Eltringham, where all their Family, of which I was the Eldest, were born.—The Family consisting of myself & Brothers John & William & my Sisters Hannah, Agnes, Ann, Sarah & Jane–Sarah died at the Age of 16–the rest were reared to maturity or were sent off one way or another into the World.

In August 1753 I was born[1] and was mostly intrusted to the care of my Aunt Hannah (my Mother's sister) & my Grandmother Agnes Bewick–and the first thing I can remember was that the latter indulged me in every thing I had a wish for, or in other Words made me a great *Pet*–I was not to be snubbed (as it was

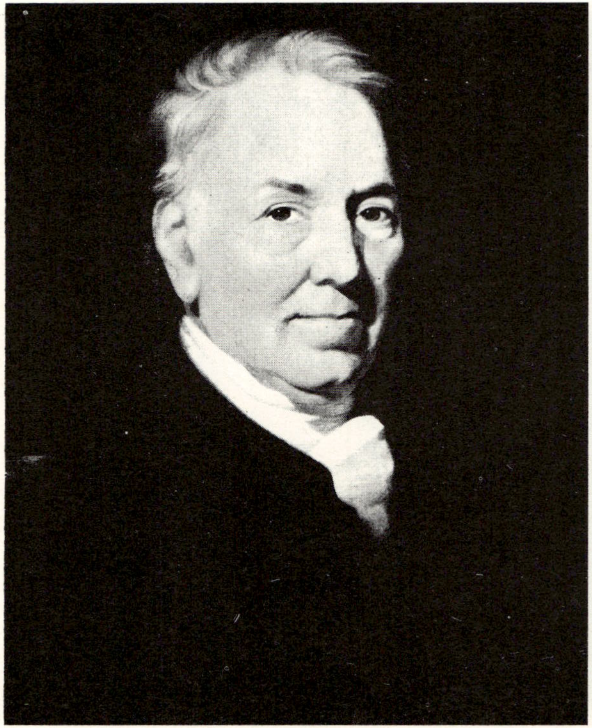

Thomas Bewick aged 70 by James Ramsay

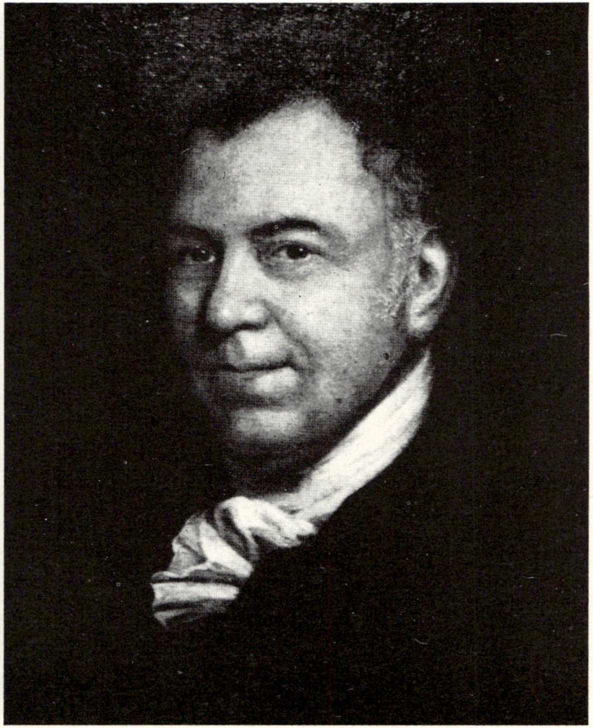

Thomas Bewick in middle life, unsigned

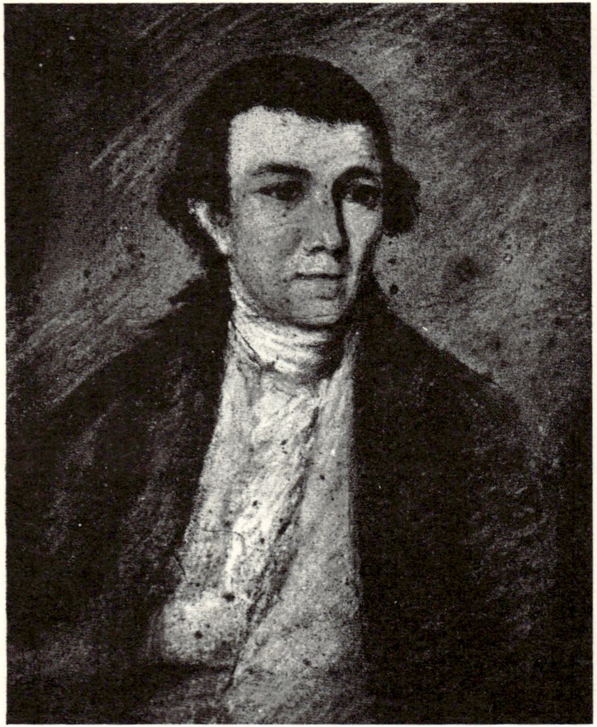

Bewick's brother John, by George Gray

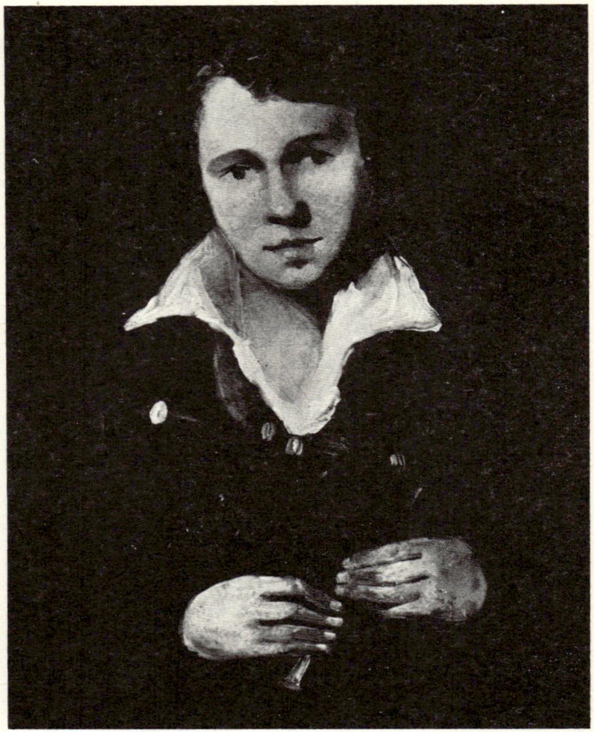

Bewick's son Robert as a boy, playing an early form of the Northumbrian small-pipes, by John Bell

called) do what I would and in consequence of my being thus suffered to have my own way, I was often scalded & burnt, or put in danger of breaking my bones by falls from heights I had clambered up to.

The next circumstance, which I well remember, was that of my being put to Mickley school, when very young, and this was not done so much with a view to my learning, as it was to keep me out of "*harm's way*".—I was sometime at this School without making much progress, in learning my letters & spelling small words–the Master perhaps was instructed not to keep me very close at my book, but in process of time he began to be more & more severe upon me, and I see clearly at this day, that he frequently beat me, when faultless and also for not learning what it was not in my power to comprehend–others suffered in the same way, for he was looked upon as a severe or cross man & did not spare his Rod–his name I do not recollect but he was nicknamed *Shabby Rowns*[1]–he was a tall thin Man, and with a countenance severe & grim he walked about the School Room with the Taws or a switch in his hand, and he no doubt thought he was keeping the Boys to their Lessons. While the gabbering & noise they made was enough to stun any one, and impressed the people passing by, with the Idea that Bedlam was let loose. How long he went on in this way I do not recollect–but like many others, of his profession, who were at that time, appointed to fulfill that most important of all offices, no pains was taken to enquire into the requisite qualifications befitting them for it.–and this Teacher was one of that stamp,–he went on with a senseless System of severity, where ignorance & arrogance were equally conspicuous,–conduct like this sours the minds of some Boys–renders others stupid & serves to make all, more or less disgusted with Learning.

–Upon some occasion or other, he ordered me to be flogged–and this was to be done, by what was called hugging, that is by mounting me upon the back of a stout Boy, who kept hold of my hands over his Shoulders, while the Posteriors was laid bare, & where he supposed he could do the business freely;–in this instance however he was mistaken, for, with a most indignant rage I sprawled, kickt & flung, and as I was told, bit the innocent Boy on the Neck, when he instantly roared out & flung me down, and on my being seized, again by the old man, I rebelled & broke his

Shins with my Iron hooped cloggs & ran off—By this time, the Boy's Mother, who was a spirited Woman, & lived close by attracted by the ferment that was raized, flew (I understood) into the School Room, when a fierce scold ensued between the Master & her.—After this I went no more to his School, but played the Truant every day, and amused myself by making Dams & swimming Boats in a small Bourne which ran through a Place then called the "Colliers-close-Wood", 'till the Evening, when I returned home with my more fortunate or more obedient School Fellows—How long it was before my abscense from School was discovered I know not, but I got many severe beatings from my father and Mother, in the interval between my utterly leaving the School & the old Masters death—As soon as another School Master (James Burn) was appointed, I was sent to him & he happened to be of a directly opposite character to the late one–with him I was quite happy, and learned as fast as any other of the Boys and with as great pleasure. After the death of this much respected young man, who lived only a very few years after his being appointed schoolmaster, my learning any more at Mickley School was at an End.

Sometime after this, my Father put me to school under the care of the Rev[d] C Gregson of Ovingham & well do I remember the conversation that passed between them on the occasion–it was little to my credit, for my Father begun by telling him that I was so very unguideable, that he could not do it, & begged of my new master that he would undertake that Task and they both agreed that to "spare the Rod was to spoil the Child"–and this system was I think too severely acted upon, sometimes upon trivial occasions, & sometimes otherwise.

–After being sometime kept at reading, writing & figures, how long I know not, but I know that as soon as my question was done upon my Slate, I spent as much time as I could find, in filling, with my pencil, all the other spaces of it, with representation of such objects as had struck my fancy, and these were rubbed out (for fear of a beating) before my question was given in. After learning figures as far as Fractions & Decimals &c, I was then put to learn Latin and in this I was for sometime complimented by my Master for the great progress I was making–but as I never knew for what purpose it was that I was put to learn it, & was wearied out with getting off long Tasks, I rather flagged in this department of my

Education, and the margins of my Books and every space of spare & blank paper became filled with various kinds of devices or scenes I had met with & these were often accompanied with wretched Rhymes explanatory of them; but as I soon filled all the blank spaces in my Books, I had recourse, at all spare times to the Grave Stones & the Floor of the Church Porch, with a bit of Chalk to give vent to this propensity of mind of figuring whatever I had seen–at that time I had never heard of the word "drawing" being made use of, nor did I know of any other paintings, besides the Kings Arms in the Church, & the Signs in Ovingham of the Black Bull, the White Horse, the Salmon & the Hounds & Hare–I always thought I could make a far better hunting Scene than the latter, the others were bejond my hand–I remember once of my Master's overlooking me while I was very busy with my chalk in the Porch, and of his putting me greatly to the blush, by ridiculing & calling me a conjurer–My Father also found a deal of fault for "misspending my time in such idle pursuits", but my propensity to drawing was so routed, that nothing could deter me from persevering in it–and many of my evenings at home, were spent in filling the flags of the Floor & the hearth stone with my chalky designs—After I had long scorched my face, in this way, a friend, in compassion, furnished me with a lot of paper, upon which to execute my designs–here I had more scope–pen & Ink and the juice of the Brambleberry made a *grand change*–These were succeeded by a Camel hair pencil & Shells of colours & thus supplied I became completely set up–but of Patterns or drawings I had none–the Beasts & Birds which enlivened the beautiful Scenery of Woods & Wilds, surrounding my native Hamlet, furnished me with an endless supply of Subjects. I now, in the estimation of my rustic Neighbours became an eminent Painter, and the Walls of their Houses were ornamented with an abundance of my rude productions, at a very cheap rate–These chiefly consisted of particular Hunting scenes, in which the portraits of the Hunters, the Horses & of every Dog in the Pack, were in their opinion, as *well as my own*, faithfully delineated.—But while I was proceeding in this way, I was at the same time deeply engaged in matters nearly allied to this propensity for drawing–for I early became acquainted, not only with the History & the character of the domestic Animals, but also with those which roamed at large.

The conversations of the *Nimrods* of that day, in which the instincts & peculiar properties of the various wild animals were described, in such glowing terms, attracted my keenest attention & to their rude & lengthened narratives, I listened with extreme delight–with me they made a winters evening fly fast away—At Hollyday times & at other times, when prevented by the Floods of the Tyne from getting across it to School[1] I was sure, with the most ardent glee, to make one of the number, in the Hunting parties, which frequently took place at that time, whether it might be in the chase of the Fox or the Hare–or in tracing the Foumart[2] in the Snow, or hunting the Badger at midnight.

The pursuing, baiting or killing these animals, never at that time struck me as being cruel,–the mind had not yet been impressed with the feelings of humanity—This however came upon me at last, and the first time I felt the change, happened by my having (in hunting) caught the Hare in my Arms, while surrounded by the Dogs & the Hunters, when the poor terrified creature screemed out so pitiously, like a child, that I would have given any thing to save its life; in this however I was prevented, for a Farmer, well known to me, who stood close by, pressed upon me & desired I would give her to him, & from his being better able (as I thought) to save its life, I complied with his wishes; this was no sooner done than he proposed, to those about him to have a "bit more sport with her" and this was to be done by his first breaking one of its legs, and then again setting the poor Animal off, a little before the Dogs—I wandered off to a little distance, oppressed by my own feelings, & could not join the Crew again, but learned with pleasure that their intended victim had made its escape.

The "Musical din" of the Hounds still continued to have its charms & I still continued to follow them,–but from that day forward I have ever wished that this poor persecuted innocent creature might escape with its life.—The worrying of Foxes, the baiting of Foumarts, Otters & Badgers &c did not awaken in me similar feelings; for in the fierce conflicts between them & the Dogs, there was, something like an exchange of retaliation and not unfrequently the agressors were beaten–and I have with pleasure seen that wonderfully courageous Animal the Badger (with fair play) beat all the Dogs, of a whole Neighbourhood (one after another) completely off.

In some of the vermin hunting excursions, in the depth of Winter while the whole face of nature was bound in frost & covered with deep snow, in traversing through Bogs amidst Reeds & Rushes I have often felt charmed with the sight of Birds flushed & sometimes caught by the Terrier Dogs, which I had never seen or heard of before, and I am still in doubt, whether some of them have not escaped being noticed as British Birds. There were the diversions of the Winter months, which I enjoyed the pleasure [of] in an extreme degree amidst the storm & the tempest.

In that Season, I was also sometimes better employed, by my attentions being engaged in looking after a small Flock of Sheep on the Fell, a part of which flock, was my own—The extremity of the weather had taught them to seek a place of shelter & this was under a steep but low Brea[1] overhung with Whins,[2] under which, in such weather I was almost sure to find them and their Associates all huddled together. To this place through wreaths of Snow, I early bent my way, with a Bundle of Hay on my back & my Pockets sometimes filled with Oats, which I distributed amongst them–upon these occasions, 'tho at other times extremely wild, they were quite tame & seemed to know me*—They were of the long legged, black faced kind, which were almost the only sort at that time kept in this part of the Country–the *improved Breed* with their fatting qualities, were then not known–The Mutton of the former eat like dark juicy Venison, while that of the latter puts one in mind of blubber.—At that time of life every Season had its charms, and I recollect well of listing with delight, from the little window at my bed head, the murmuring or the roaring of the flooded Burn, which passed my Father's house & sometimes roused me from my bed to see what it was like–on such occasions sometimes I would have cut a *shive*[3] from the *black sour rye Loaf* & gone

* From my Sheep, thus drawing into shelter, gave rise to an opinion, I formed and which has been rendered more & more feasible, from long reflection, that much may yet be done to protect the largest flocks from being overblown & lost, on the bleak moors, in great snow storms.—Were long avenues, made by double rows of whin hedges, planted parallel to each other at about six feet asunder, & continued in the form of two sides of a square, with the whins of each side drawn together & to grow interplatted at the tops, so as to form an arched kind of roof–the Sheep would, on instinctively seeing the coming storm, immediately avail themselves of such assylums & particularly in the lambing season–In the corner of the angle of this square, the Shepherd might have his hovel, thatched with heather & ling, and his beds for himself & his dogs, made of the same materials–and the whole of this *beild*[4] rendered so snug as greatly to defy the severity of the winte's drifting blasts & wreaths of snow.

to bed again to eat it—After this, my first & common employment was to Muck the Byer,[1] & when the Servant Girl did not come soon enough I frequently tried my hand at Milking the Cows & I was always particularly keen of being there in snow storms. When this was the case, within the Byer Door I snugly watched the appearance of various Birds, which passed the little dean below, & which the severity of the Weather drove from place to place in search of shelter—With the sight of my intimate Acquaintances, the Robins, the Wrens, Blackbirds, Sparrows, & a solitary Crow & some others, I was not much attracted, but always felt an extreme pleasure & curiosity in seeing the more rare visitants, such as the Woodcock, the Snipe & other Waders, with the Redwings & Fieldfares &c make their appearance.—The Winter evenings were often spent in listning to the traditionary Tales & Songs, relating to Men who had been eminent for their prowess & bravery in the Border Wars, and of others who had been esteemed for better & milder qualities, such as their having been good Landlords, kind Neighbours, and otherwise in every respect being bold independant & honest Men. —I used to be particularly struck or affected with the Warlike music & the Songs relative to the former description of Characters, but with those regarding the latter, a different kind of feeling was drawn forth, and I was often greatly distressed & often gave vent to it in ⟨a flood of⟩ tears.

These Songs & *laments*, were commemorative of many worthies, but the most particular ones that I now remember were those respecting the Earl of Derwent-Water,[2] who was beheaded in the year 1715, and who was looked upon, as ⟨having been⟩ a Victim to the cruelty of the Reigning Family, and was a young man of a remarkably good character, & who was also venerated as a Saint upon Earth–It was said that the light from Heaven attended his Corpse to the Vault, in Dilston Hall,[3] and that prosperity would shine no more upon Tyneside–then followed the sorrowful remembrances of those who were dead & gone–to sigh over them was unavailing–they had filled the space allotted to them on this side of time & the winds have blown over their silent Graves for Ages past. The predictions that the Mansions of those who remained, would soon for want of Heirs, become desolate–these and such like melancholly reflections made a deep impression on my Mind –& I have often since with feelings of extreme regret beheld these

Mansions, once the seats of hospitality, delapidated, & the Families which occupied them now become extinct & forgot.

When the Winter began somewhat to abate of its rigours–or in the early Spring, it was a common job for me, before setting off to school, to rise betimes in the Morning, as indeed I was always accustomed to do, and equipt with an Apron, an old Dyking Mitten,[1] and a sharpened broken sickle, to set off among the Whin Bushes, which were near at hand, to cut off their last years sprouts –these were laid into a corner 'till the Evening, when I stripped & fell to work to *cree*[2] them with a Wooden Mall[3] in a Stone trough, untill these tops of the Whins were beaten to the consistancy of soft wet grass, & with this mess I fed the Horses before I went to bed, or in the morning, as occasion might require—they were shy about eating this kind of provinder at first & I was obliged to mix oats with it, but they soon became so fond of it alone, that there was no nead of any mixture.–I know not whether a scarcity of Fodder, first gave rise to the suggestion of using this expedient, or that it was tried as an experiment, but certain it is that this kind of food agreed so well with the Horses that they became soon very sleek, and cast their winter coat of hair, long before other Horses that were fed in the common way.–Cows would not eat the Whin tops thus prepared (I did not indeed persist in pressing them to do so) but in a Winter of scarcity I have known all hands at work in cutting Ivey from the trees & even small Ash twiggs, to be given to the Cattle as fodder.

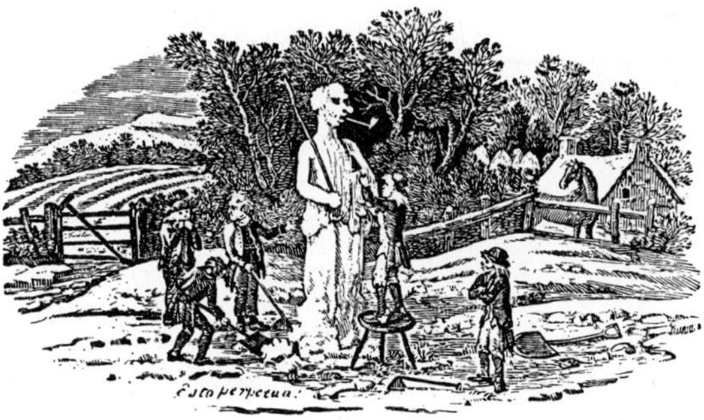

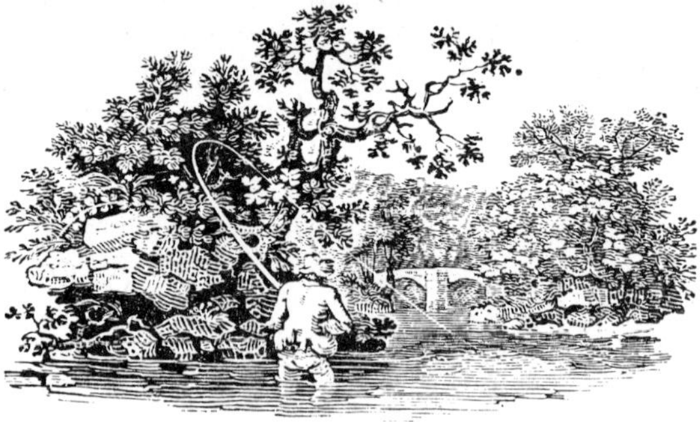

[2]

—From the little Window at my bed head[1] I noticed all the varying seasons of the year, and when the Spring put in, I felt charmed with the music of Birds, which strained their little throats to proclaim it–The chief business imposed upon me as a task at this season, was in my being set to work to scale the pastures and medows, that is spreading the Molehills over the surface of the ground–this & Gardning & such like jobs was very hungry work, and often made me think dinner time was long in coming, & when, at last, it was sent to me, be what it would I sat down on the *lown*[2] side of a hedge & eat it with a relish that neaded no Sauce.

–As soon as the Bushes & Trees began to put forth their buds & made the face of nature look gay–this was the signal for the Angler to prepare his fishing Tackle & in doing this, I was not behind hand, with any of them in making my own all ready–Fishing Rods –Set Gads[3] & night lines were all soon made fit for use & with them late & early I had a busy time of it during the long Summer Months & untill the frosts of Autumn, forbid me to proceed–The uneasiness, which my late evening wadings by the Water side, gave to my father & mother I have often since reflected upon with regret–they could not go to bed with the hopes of getting to sleep, while haunted with the apprehension of my being drowned, & well do I remember to this day, my father's well known Whistle which called me home–he went to a little distance from the House, where nothing obstructed the sound, & whistled so loud through his finger & thumb–that in the still hours of the Evening, it might be heard echoing up the Vale of the Tyne to a very great distance—This Whistle I learned to imitate & answered it as well as I could & then posted home.

From early in morning 'till Night I was scarcely ever out of an Action either good or bad–or when not kept close at School, or in doing jobs, such as those I have before described, I was almost constantly engaged in some mischievous prank or other, but with a detail of these it would be wearysome to load my narrative, they were occasioned by the overflowings of an active wild disposition–at one time, in imitation of the Savages described in "Robinson Crusoe" or some other Savages–I often, in a morning, set off *stark naked* across the Fell, where I was joined by some Associates, who in like manner run about like mad things–or like Bedlamites who had escaped—Climbing the tall Trees at Eltringham for Rooks nests at the hazard of breaking our Necks or our Bones, was another piece of business which engaged our attention–I also was engaged in another equally dangerous, & that, was by my having formed the resolution of *curing* a vicious *runaway* Horse belong[g] to my Father–which none durst mount–I however took the opportunity, when out of sight of any of the Family, to do so, & with my hand entwined in his Mane & bare-backed, I set him agoing & let him run over sykes[1] & burns up hill & down hill, untill he was quite spent–and in a short time I discovered that to make him run at all, he must be whipt to it–At other times I swam him in the River, till this & such like treatment made him look ill & quite tamed him—I have often since shuddered at the thoughts of doing these & such like desperate acts, and wonder how I escaped–but neither caution or fear, had at that time taken a place in the mind, on the contrary any uncommon or frightful exploit had charms in it that I could not resist.—One of these pranks however attracted the attention of the neighbourhood, brought me into a great dilemma & occasioned me a severe beating—Having engaged my constant associate, Jos[ph] Liddell, who was ever ready at my command to help me as soon as I communicated any design to him,–on this occasion I observed two Oxen in a little Savanna, or little bit of grazing ground, surrounded with hazel & other bushes, near the brink of the River,–thither we went in order to enjoy so tempting a sight as to see them plunge overhead into the Flood–When all was ready, we suddenly, with long branches in our hands, sprung upon them from the bushes, overhanging the Precipiece, the danger of which they did not see, & they were plunged with such a *delightfull dash*! overhead into the River–they however happened to be no worse for it, for they were driven down by the rapid current of the Flood, & landed safely at a distance below.

This exploit happening on a Sunday forenoon was an aggrevation of the Crime.—After this my Father mostly took me with him to Church–but while there, except shouting as loud as I could, while the Psalms were singing, there was little to engage my attention, I therefore employed myself in almost constantly drawing various Figures upon the soft-painted, Book Board with a pin –in doing this no one noticed me, especially as I held down my head, & having got the Church service off, I repeated it the same as the Congregation—This apparently regular behaviour was not, however, of long duration & was broken in upon at last–Sunday after Sunday a clownish fellow had obtruded himself into our Pew, I did not think this quite right & wished to put an end to it & this happened in a very rude way in the end.–A Dumb Man ("Dummy of Wylam") a "*constant regular*" *Churchman*, had a Seat in the Pew before ours–where regularly during the Service he fell fast asleep. In that state, & sitting right before our obtruder, I reached to aside & gave Dummy a smart blow on the head–and instantly as if I knew nothing of the matter, seemed quite grave & intent on looking on my Prayer Book, while the fellow was putting on a *broad grin*,–at this *poor Dummy* was so enraged, and with a distorted countenance he kept thumping the Man on the face & head, making at the same time a hideous Noise, which was heightened by the fellow's shouting & calling him a fool, at the same time assuring him that it was I that gave the blow & not him–to the deaf man this was a waste of words–it nead not be added that the whole congregation was greatly disturbed, while perhaps none knew or suspected the cause except my Father & my preceptor in the Pulpit.

Sometimes, the Lads in the same Class I belonged to, when we had been *doing amiss* were sent to cut birch rods to whip us with, at other times we were locked into the Belfry, where we often amused ourselves by drawing each other up, by the Bell ropes to the first Floor, but one of our Comrades who we were drawing up having by the Rope's slipping too violently through the hands of those who held it, he was precipitated to the ground, by which fall he was a good deal hurt, after this that mode of punishing us altogether was dropt—It sometimes happened to me to be confined there alone, but having got up to the top of the Steeple, and whether I had ventured a little down on the outside to look after Birds nests, I do not remember, but this was asserted by some of the Women in the Village, who, upon the occasion found a deal of fault with the Parson for putting me into a place where such risks were to be run–poor man, I think he had a troublesome time of it with one or another of us, and I remember well, once in particular of putting him into very great pain and distress of mind—After a great flood a large piece of Ice about the size of the Floor of a Room had been left in a place called "Ned's hole" by the side of the River, this I got upon & persuaded several others to do the same & then set to work, with a *Boat Stower*[1] to push it off shore and in this manner we got to some distance up the River, opposite to the Parsonage Garden, where our Master happened to be & saw us–I could see by his agitated Motions & his up lifted hands, that he was put into a state, much easier to be felt than described.—After having been guilty of misdemenours of this kind I did not go back to School that day, but waded or other wise crossed the River, & sat down or amused myself among the bushes on the Water Banks, untill the rest of the Scholars left school, when I joined them & went home–but as it would not have been safe for me to go to Bed (if consious [of] guilt, if otherwise betrayed) for fear of a visit from my father there, I always took up my abode for the Night in the Byer loft among the Hay or straw–knowing well that when his passion subsided I should escape a beating from his hands.

The first cause of my Preceptor's beginning a severe System of Flogging (besides the quantum of it I received for mischievous acts) was for not getting off my Latin Tasks,–when this was not done to his Mind, he by way of punishment, gave me another still worse to do & still longer, 'till at length I gave over even attempting to get through them at all, and begun to stand a flogging without being much put about by it–I think (at this day) my very worthy preceptor, in following this rather indiscriminate System of severe punishments, was wrong, for he very often beat his own Son* a youth of an uncommonly mild, kind & cheerfull disposition, whom I often felt more distressed, at seeing punished, than I felt for myself, for I mostly considered that I richly deserved the stripes inflicted upon me, and that he did not.—There was another misdemeanour (above all the rest) for which I was most severely punished, either at School or at home, than for any other fault & that was for fighting with other Boys–to put a stop to this practice was at the particular request of my Mother–to her it was odious in the extreme, her reasons for it I do not forget, & she quoted Scripture for what she advanced in favour of her arguments,–therein we were directed "if we were struck on one cheek to turn the other also"–(I forget the exact words) but it is a portion of scripture which I did not obey. She also maintained that the business of fighting was degrading to human nature & put a Man that did so, upon a level with Dogs.—I am conscious that I never sought a quarrel with any one, but when insulted I found it very bad to bear and mostly in the most secret or hidden manner contrived *to fight it out.*

—When the floggings inflicted upon me, had in a great measure begun to lose their effect, another mode was fallen upon & that was, after the School hours were over, to keep me behind & lock me into the Church, where I was kept 'till the dusk of the Evening–this solitary confinement was for sometime very irksome to me, for I had not at that time got over a belief in Ghosts & Boggles & for the sight of which, in this place I was constantly upon the look out –oppressed with fear, I peeped here & there into every corner in dread of seeing some terrible Spirit—in time however this dread abated, & I amused myself as well as I could in surveying the surrounding Objects, and having at last begun to climb up the Pillars, with the help of a rope or a Hankerchief as I used to do in climbing large Trees, it happened one Evening, when my Master, as usual, came to let me out, that I was sitting astride upon the Capital of one of the Pillars, where he could not, or did not see me, when he began to call on me & I made no answer–he then posted

* Christopher Gregson Esq[r] of Apothecaries Hall London–he died and was buried at Ovingham [1815]

off to see if the Door was fast & having ascertained this, he marched along the Aisles in great perturbation of mind, frequently exclaiming to himself, God bless me! &c—When he was gone I slipped down & found the Choir Door only bolted on the inside–so I waded the River & posted home & slept in my old Assylum the Hay loft–I have frequently bitterly repented of having given a Man who I afterwards so very highly respected through life, so much pain & trouble—

I have noticed before, the first time I felt compassion for any thing viz. my having caught the Hare in my Arms–The next occurence of this kind happened with a Bird–I had no doubt knocked many down with stones before, but they had escaped being taken–This time however, the little victim dropped from the tree and I picked it up,–struck with its beauty, I instantly ran into the House with it–it was alive & looked me so pitiously in the face, and as I thought (could it have spoken) it would have asked me, why I had taken away its life.—I felt greatly hurt, at what I had done & did not quit it all the afternoon–I turned it over & over, admiring its plumage–its feet its Bill & every part of it–It was a Bulfinch–I did not then know its Name but was told it was a "Little Mathew Martin"–this was the last Bird I killed, but many indeed have been killed since on my Account. I had before been at *Man fights*–Dog fights & Cock fights, without feeling much compassion–indeed with the last of these exhibitions, I was much more entertained at seeing the wry faces, the contortions & agitations of the Clowns who surrounded the Cock pit or circle, than I was at seeing the Cocks fight.—It was long before I felt disgusted at seeing Men fight, this however happened at last.—A Travelling Merchant, or respectable Pedlar, a slim made genteel looking Man, had perhaps forgot himself over a Glass and had *also* upon that occasion not minded what company he was in–he could not however, be long in such company without being insulted, but be that as it may, a fight ensued, in which the Stranger had been overmatched–I saw only the concluding part, and was extremely shocked at seeing it, for the Stranger was sitting propped up with his Arms, behind him, quite spent & speechless & looked like a Corpse–after sitting a short time in this helpless state, the sturdy barbarian, his opponent, walked coolly up to him, & with a blow on the Face or head, laid him flat on the ground–I thought he was killed, at which I became so frantic with rage & indignation, that I believe, at the moment, if I had had a Pistol at hand I would have shot him.–

In going along with my narratives I have noticed some of the first Impressions I felt, which produced a change & left a strong sensation in my mind, in some of these the change was quick & decisive, in others of a more tardy nature, & prejudices which were early routed were not easily removed, among the worst was that of a belief in Ghosts, Boggles, Apparitions &c. These wrought powerfully upon the fears, of the great bulk of the People at that time, & with many, these fears are not rooted out even at this day–The Stories so circumstantially told, respecting these Phantoms & supernatural things, I listened to with the dread they inspired and it took many an Effort, before they could be tapered off, and I suffered much before I could do so.–And what helped me very much to conquer fears of this kind was my knowing how much my Father constantly scouted & despised such idle or indeed such pernitious tales–he would not allow me to plead fear as any excuse, when he had to send me [on] any errand at Night, and perhaps my being frequently exposed to being alone in the dark might have the effect of enabling me greatly to rise superiour to this kind [of] Weakness—I have often had the opportunity of knowing Men, both old & young, who dared to encounter any danger, yet in this way were *affraid of their own Shadows* and I remember well of trying the experiment one Night, upon a Servt Man of my father's, who was a kind of Village Cæsar & fear'd not to stand the most desperate Battles with others of the same cast, upon every occasion –I begun by sneering at his courage, & then bet him a penny that I durst do what he dared not.–All I intended I set about doing rather deliberately, & then rose up to perform *this feat* & that was only to walk along the dark passage to the back Door & to repeat something (rather ominous indeed) about "*Silkey*[1] & *Hedley Kow*"[2] –after performing my Task I returned with apparent agitation & fear, and sat down in silence close beside him for sometime–& then asked him if he durst do the like–I however saw, by his hesitation that the performance by him was given up, and he only remarked that "one may soon get what they'l never cast".—At another time in fair day light, I took it into my head to make another tryal of this kind, upon my fathers Pitmen; for this purpose I detained our

Cur Dog, untill I buckld him up in a Pair of old Sods,[1] which quite covered him beyond both his Head & Tail & set him off to the Pit –knowing well that he would go straight there–for he was accustomed every day to leave the Pit Lodge & go home, where he waited untill he saw that dinner was ready, & then his reappearance at the pit was as good as telling my father & his Servants to come home–I durst not have thus amused myself if I had not known that my father was out of the way–but I set off on the inside of the Hedge, keeping pace with the Dog, all the way up to the Pit heap, near which I stopped & peeped, to see the effect that would be produced–and this was really curious–one of the Men, who first saw the odd appearance, of something alive, with a long body, without either legs, head, or tail, moveing straight forward towards him, he knew not what to make of it, and after rubbing his eyes, he ran off to his Companions–and when they had taken a peep, they all set off together with speed, on their way home.

–In a business of a similar kind, which happened not long after this, it was my lot to be the sufferer–A few companions used to come at nights to *our* house to play at Cards with me, and I in return visited them for the same purpose–we were however taken to task by a religious or biggoted old Woman, in the Neighbourhood, who called the Cards the "Devils Books", and she told me on the same Night, before my setting off on this errand–that if I looked under the Table I would see the Devil, and I recollect of my having several times, peeped under the Table that night to see if he were there. When we were done playing, two of the Gamesters, as was customary set me across part of the Fell towards home–I was however much surprized at their suddenly leaving me, without saying good Night, or making any reply to my shouting after them, and they were [soon] out of Sight. This was at a place called the "Sandholes" which I then left & was turning towards home when behold, to my utter amazement, I saw the Devil–it was a clear Moonlight Night–I could not be mistaken–his Horns–his great white goggle Eyes–and teeth & tail & his whole person, stood fairly before me–As I stood and gazed–I thought the Hair lifted the Hat on my head–he stood & I stood for sometime, and I believe if he had then come up to me I must have dropped down–certain it is however that desperation succeeded fear–I moved to aside & he did the same–the first thing I bethought of, or rather in an involuntary way, was getting out my *Jackleg Knife*[1] & if he had then approached or laid hold on me, he to a certainty would have got himself stabbed–I then slipped off my Clogs–made a run in a bending direction & then at full speed ran directly towards home. He pursued me nearly to the door, but I beat him in the race–I had always understood, that after any person had seen a Ghost or evil Spirit & as soon as he or she came into a house with a fire in it they would faint. I feared this, but I fainted none; and when my father asked me what was the matter, I told him I had seen the Devil, when he perhaps without thinking, gave me a slap [on] the head–It was not long, however, 'till this affair transpired–for the Man, who personated the Devil, when he met me, had been on his way to a *Kirn Supper*[2] & was going, in what was called a *guiseing*[3]–When my father heard the whole of this transaction he wrought himself up into a great rage, and very shortly after meeting with the Man (Tom: Usher) in the street at Corbridge, who had frightened me, he instantly paid him off by giving him a sound beating–When the people, who always considered my father as a remarkably peaceable man, saw him thus engaged, they expressed their surprize, but when they heard the reasons for what he had just done, they were in their turn also exasperated at him, and I was given to understand he was obliged to leave that Village.

–The first time that I took any notice of any of my female School-fellows, arose from a reproof I met with, and the manner it was given, from one of them–the amiable person alluded to was Miss Betty Gregson my preceptors Daughter* and somewhere about my own Age–She kept a Messet Dog,[4] and the sleek fat useless animal was much disliked by me, as well as by some of the other Boys; it having, as it sometimes did, made its appearance in the Churchyard–we set about freight'ning it–for this purpose, some of us met it at every Gate & outlet, & stopt its retreat, 'till it became quite distressed–this and such like was often Sport to us –The last time that this kind of sport was practised upon her little Dog, I happened to be the only actor,–having met with it at a little distance from its home, I stopped it from its entering the House & pursuing it about & about, or meeting it at the end of every Avenue–'till it was put into great *bodily fear*–This behaviour

* Betty Gregson Died 20 April 17[76] Aged [22] & was buried in [ ] of Ovingham Church

towards her little Favourite was very offensive to Miss Gregson. She could endure it no longer–and called me to an Account for it and I can never forget her looks upon the occasion–She no doubt intended to scold me but the natural sweetness of her disposition soon shewed itself in its true colours to me–and also that she did not know how to scold–for after some embarrassing attempts at it & some hesitations she put me in mind of my being related to her, & of her uniform kindness to me, and with irresistable arguments & persuasions made me see the impropriety of my conduct–With me this left its mark–for from that time forward I never plagued any of the Girls at School, nor did any thing that might give them offence–nor was this impression ever afterwards effaced from my mind but has been there fostered through life and settled into a fixed respect & tender regard for the whole sex—

Hitherto my whole time at School and at home, might be considered as a life of warfare, & punishments of various kinds had been inflicted upon me apparently to little effect. As a Cure for my misdeeds, my worthy master, however, at length found out a better and a more effectual way–he one day invited me to dine with him and after shewing me the greatest kindness, he followed this up in a friendly, plain and open way, of remonstrating with me, on the impropriety of my long past bad conduct,–& the evil tendancy of it together with the pain & trouble I had given him, urging me at the same time in such a persuasive tone instantly to desist from it, that I felt quite overpowered with this discourse & then fell into a flood of tears.–this however did my business, for I never durst encounter another of this kind of his friendly meetings–and while I remained at his School, he never more had occasion to find fault with me.

After this time, many of the transactions in which I became engaged, afforded me more pleasurable recollections than those I have before described, & as silent time stole away in the varied Seasons of the long-measured years, changes gradually took place in many of the erroneous notions I had formed of things–and as the mind became more expanded, curiosity led me to enquire into the nature of the objects which attracted my attentions–among the first, was that of the Birds, their nests, their eggs & their young & these to me were long a source of great delight–& many a Spring morning I watched & looked after them & many a Summer's

Evening, on my way home from School, I spent lost in wonder, in examining the works going forward among a Nation of pismires (Ants). The place they occupied, was on the top of the "Boat Hill" near Eltringham, & it was the largest I ever saw–from it their narrow Roads, through the grass radiated in various directions to a great distance–these were like as many turnpike roads, & as busily crouded as any among Men leading from or to a great Faire –As an experiment to see what effect might be produced I sometimes with a stick over-turned the accumulated gatherings of the stores of their Whole nation, on which ensued to them the greatest bustle & confusion and next morning, I beheld with surprize every thing apparently restored to the same order, as before I disturbed them*–I observed they had other enemies that broke in upon them & which perhaps injured them more than I had done–and these were the Turkeys from the Village, where great numbers were bred every year.–As soon as the young brood were able to walk abroad, the Mother led them every day to this great ant hill, where they no doubt made terrible havoc in destroying both their Works & the Inhabitants.

–Bees also attracted much of my attention; I could not see into the interior of their works, but made every enquiry of those who had long kept them, & gathered, in this way, as good a knowledge of their history & economy as I at that time could–and one of my morning jobs was to sit before the Hives with a stick like a Spatula, to kill the Wasps as they alighted to enter & rob them–I could see the Bees enter, loaded with what they had culled from every flower but never could see them attack or repel their enemies–

I also long amused myself in observing the constant *murders* of a large Spider, in his Web, placed in a corner of the little window at my bed head.–This I prevented the servant Girl from brushing away, being wishfull to see how he managed his Affairs, and these did not excite in me any favourable opinion of the successfull Murderer–having long seen him seize every innocent Fly that set foot on his Snares, I had a mind to try how he would conduct him-

* Ants The History & œconomy of these very curious Insects are (I think) not well known–they appear to manage all their Affairs, with as much forethought & greater industry than Mankind–but, to what degree their reasoning & instructive powers extend is yet a mistery–After they have spent a certain time toiling on earth, they then change this abode, get Wings, & soar aloft into the atmosphere–It is not well known what state they undergo, before they assume this new character, nor what becomes of them after

self towards a more powerfull opponent–for this purpose, I caught a Wasp which I held by its wings upon the Web untill its feet got entangled, when out came the hitherto unthwarted Tyrant, and after some apparent hesitation, he at length was tempted to pounce upon the obtruder–the struggle was however very short, for I soon saw the Wasp double itself up & dart its sting into the body of its enemy–who instantly retired–and I never afterwards saw the Spider make his appearance again.–this is only one experiment, & further trials of this kind might be made to come at truth.

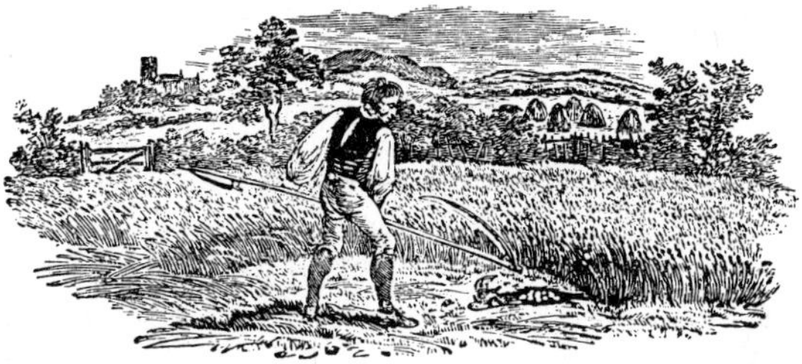

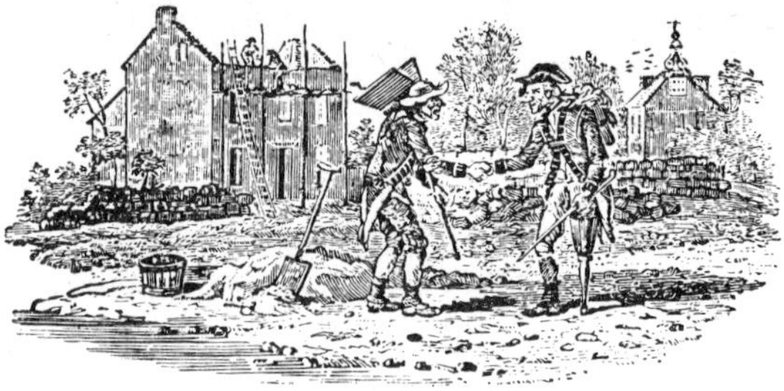

[3]

Cherry-bourne House the place of my nativity, and which for many years my Eyes beheld with cherished delight–is situated on the south bank of the Tyne, in the County of Northumberland, and about a quarter of a Mile from the River.–The House, Stables &c are situated on the west side of the little Dean & Burn* whose Bank was embellished with a number of Plumb trees & terminated with the Garden on the North of them–near the House were two large Ash trees, from one Root but the top of one of them was blown away in a high Wind, & another one, of the same kind, at a little distance from them–at the south end of the Premisses, was the spring Well, overhung by a large Hawthorn bush, behind which was a Holly Hedge, & bejond this again was a little boggy Dean with underwood & Trees of different kinds–Near the termination of this Dean, towards the River, was a good many remarkably tall small Ash trees and one of Oak, supposed to be one of the tallest & straightest in the Kingdom.–On the tops of these was a Rookery, the sable Inhabitants of which, by their consultations & cawings & the bustle they made when building their nests were among the first of the feathered race to proclaim the approaching Spring.–To the eastward were cornfields & pastures, mostly surrounded with very large Oaks & some Ash Trees–indeed at that time the country between Wylam & Bywell was beautified with a great deal of wood,

* This Bourne formerly was supplied by a copious spring of fine water but it found its way into some Pit workings & disappeared & is now only fed by day water from the fields.

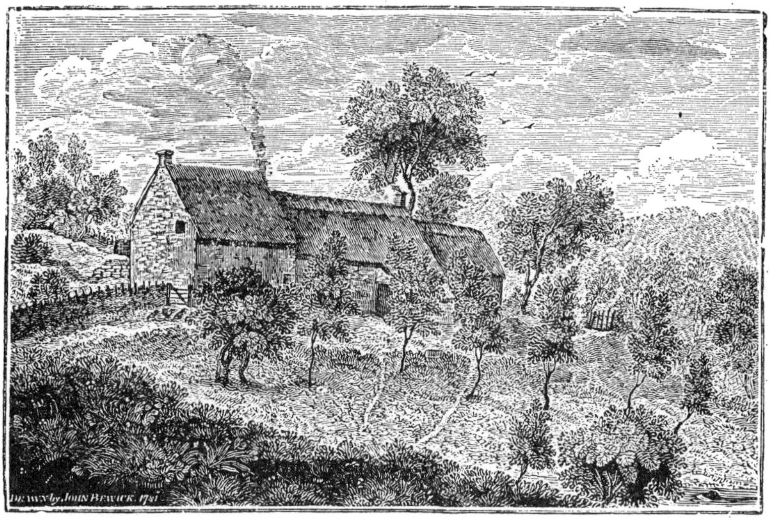

Cherryburn from the east. Engraved by John Bewick after his own water-colour drawing of 1781, and later finished by his brother

which presented the appearance of a continued forest–but these are long since stubbed up, needy gentry care little about the beauty of country & part of it now is comparatively as bare as a mole hill–

To the westward, adjoining the House, lay the Common or Fell, which extended some few Miles in length & of various breadths. It was mostly fine greensward or pastureage, broken or divided, indeed with clumps of *blossomed* Whins, Fox-Glove, Fern & some Junipers & to the westward with hether in profusion sufficient to scent the Whole Air–by the sides of the Burns, which *guttered* its sides or scouped out hollow *Gills*[1] were seen the remains of old Oaks, hollowed out by time–with Alders Willows & Birch which were often to be met with in the same state & these seemed to me to point out the length of time, that these domains had belonged to no one—On this Common, the Poor man's heritage for Ages past, where he kept a few Sheep or a Kylo[2] Cow & perhaps a flock of Geese & mostly a stock of Bee hives–It was with infinite pleasure that I long beheld the beautifull wild scenery which these exhibited, and it is with the opposite feelings of regret that I now find all these are swept away*–Here & there on this Common were to be seen the Cottage or rather Hovel of some labouring Man, built mostly at his own expense with his own hands, and to this he always added a Garth[1] & a Garden upon which great pains & labour were bestowed to make both productive & for this purpose not a bit of manure was suffered to be wasted away on the *Lonnings*[2] or publick roads–These various concerns excited the attention & the industry [of] these hardy occupants, which enabled them to prosper, & made them despise being ever numbered among the Parish poor—These men & their offspring might truely be called "a bold Pesantry, their Country's Pride"–their Children were neither pampered nor spoiled–& to this day (when grown up to manhood) I think I see their broad shoulders & their hardy sun burnt looks, which altogether bespoke the vigour of their Constitutions.—These cottagers (at least those of them I knew) were of an honest & independant character while, at the same time they held the neighbouring Gentry in the greatest estimation & respect, & these again in return did not overlook them but were interested in knowing that they were happy & well.–Most of these poor Men, from their having little intercourse with the World, were in all their actions & behaviour truly original–except reading the Bible, local Histories & old Ballads, their knowledge was generally limited–and yet one of these "Will Bewick", from being much struck with my performances which he called Pictures, became exceedingly kind to me, and was the first person from whom I gathered a kind of general knowledge of Astronomy & of the Magnitude of the universe–He had, the Year through noticed the appearances of the stars & the Planets & would discourse *largely* on the subject.

I think I see him yet, sitting on a mound or seat, by the Hedge of his Garden, regardless of the cold, and intent upon viewing the heavenly bodies, pointing to them with his large hands and eagerly imparting his knowledge to me, with a strong voice, such a one as one now seldom hears–I remember well with being much struck

* This Fell or common containing 1852 A[cres]–2 R[ods]–9 P[erches] was divided in 1812–By this division, the poor Man was rooted out and the various mechanics of the Villages, deprived of all benefit from it. The neighbouring Farmers who reared their young cattle & kept as many sheep upon it as they pleased–must now pay rent for the Allotments laid to their Farms–The wisdom which dictated this change is questionable, but the selfish greediness of it quite apparent.

with his appearance–his stern-looking brows–high cheek bones–quick eye and longish visage, and at his resolution (upon another occasion) when he determined upon risking his own life to save that of another man.–This Man, in the employ of my father, while at work as a Pitman, had lost his way, in the coal Workings and was a wanting, for perhaps a day or two (my father being from home) when our old neighbour, just described, who was also a Pitman & knew the workings equipt himself with every thing he thought necessary for so hazardous an undertaking, and when he was about to go down the Pit shaft, I felt much distressed at seeing my Mother trembling in great agitation of mind, for the safety of both him & his lost associate–After travelling & traversing through the old workings of the colliery, for a long time–so long that it was feared he had also lost himself–he however having found the Man alive at last–when with his well known thundering voice, from the bottom of the Shaft, he called "Alls Well"–to the inexpressible joy of all who now crouded the Pit *heap* or surrounded its mouth.

Another of our Fell-side neighbours, Ant^y Liddell, was a Man of a very singular character–he might truely be said to be like no one besides himself, and was noticed as such by the whole neighbourhood, but a full account of him would far exceed the bounds I wish to set to my narratives–He might indeed be called "the Village Hampden".–The whole cast of his character was formed by the Bible, which he had read with attention thro' & through–Acts of parliament which appeared to him to clash with the laws laid down in it, as the word of God, he treated with contempt–he maintained that the Fowls of the Air, and the Fish of the Sea were free for all Men–consequently Game Laws or Laws to protect the fisheries had no weight with him;–he would not indeed take a Salmon out of the Locks on any account–but whatever he could catch with his Click-hook[1] in the River he deemed his own. As to what he could do in Shooting Game, he was so inexpert that he afforded to sportsmen many a hearty laugh at his aukwardness, for he could shoot none 'till he fixed a hay Fork in the ground to rest his Piece upon,–in that way the very Birds themselves might, by a stretch of imagination, be supposed also to laugh at him–but his deficiencies did not deter him from traversing over the country-side, as eagerly as other sportsmen, notwithstanding his want of success–Whatever he did in this way, was always done in open day, for as he feared no man, he scorned to sculk or to do any thing by stealth–The Gaol had no terrors for him for he lived better there than he did at Home, and on one occasion of his being confined, when he returned home, he expressed his surprize to his neighbours, that all the time he was there "*he had not a single hands turn to do*" and exulted not a little that the opportunity was thus given him of again reading the Bible through and through.–He was a great reader of Histories, especially those parts where Wars & battles were described and in any Meetings with his Neighbours he took the lead in discourses founded on his knowledge of this kind.–Besides the Bible, "Josephus" was his next favourite author–next "the Holy Wars" & these & Bishop Taylors Sermons composed his whole Library, and his memory enabled him nearly to repeat whatever he had read.–His deportment & behaviour were generally the reverse of any thing like sauciness, but except in ability & acquirements which indeed commanded his respect, he treated all men as his equals–When dressed, he always wore a second hand black coat, in other respects he was like no other person–in what Kings reign his Hat had been made was only to be guessed at–but the flipes[1] of it were very large & his Wig was of the large curled kind, such as were worn about the time of the revolution,[2] with a waistcoat or doublet, made of the Skin of some animal, and buckskin Breeches turned black & glossy with long wear & of the same antiquated fashion as the rest of his apparel.–Thus equipt, & with his fierce look he made a curious figure before the Justices of the Peace & these together with his always (when summonzed before them) of undauntingly pleading his own causes, often afforded many of them so much amusement, that it was difficult for them to keep their gravity; others of them of a more grave deportment made use of threats to make him behave more respectfully–these he never failed to shew that he despised, & on one occasion of this kind, he told the Justice that "he was not a bit *flaid*[3] of him"–that there was "*nobbit yen* place that he was *flaid* of & that was Hell, and he could not send him there"–after this quarrell he was ordered out of court–he waited below in expectation of the Justice's following him to have the matter settled by a fight, & desired a Gentleman to tell the Justice that he waited for him for that purpose; when he was told he had behaved insolently to him

–oh Sir said he (spitting into his hands) tell him to come here–"he does not know what a fellow (aw is) I am".

Another of our Neighbours, Tom: Forster, was of a different character from the last, but singular enough in his way.–He was distinguished for his frugality & industry, and always shewed a wish to be looked upon in a respectfull light–he used to call at our house on a Sunday afternoon, for the purpose of having a bit of chat, or conversation with my father & mother–He took a liking to me & would observe that 'tho I was mischivous enough, yet he never heard, nor could see that I was "*parrentory*" that is impudent or saucy, with any one. Besides this part of the good opinion he had formed, he must have had a confidence, as to my keeping his secrets which he imparted to me–He kept a few Sheep, on the Fell & in pretence of looking after these, his secret & main business was looking after his Bees;–of these he had a great number of Hives, all placed in very hidden & very curious situations–the narrow entrances to all of these were at some distance from the Hives–some of these Apiaries were placed under the bounder hedge of the common, surrounded & hidden from sight by a great extent of old whin bushes, and besides, the Hives were sheltered under the branches of the old thorns and almost quite covered or over hung by Brambles, Woodbine & hip Bryars, which, when in blossom, looked beautifully picturesque, while at the same time they served to keep the eye from viewing the treasures thus concealed beneath.

Others of his Hives were placed in the midst of a "Whin rush" that is a great extent of old Whins, the stems of which were about the thickness of a Man's arm–his entrance to these was always by a *smout hole*[1] or small opening, through which we crept on hands & knees to the Hives, & which on our leaving them, the entrance was always stopped up by a bushy topped Whin–He also, by way of taking off the attention of the *over-inquisitive* as to his Stock of honey, kept hives in his Garden at home & sold the produce of them to his neighbours, while the greater quantity was all sold at distant parts of the Country–In this way & by his industry & good management in other ways, he got to be, what was accounted very rich, and as prosperity excites envy, people of that disposition, in a kind of derision (his Mother being a Midwife) always called him "Tom Howdey".

I might swell the list of such like characters among the unoticed poor, as those I have described, but I think it would perhaps be tedious, allthough I think it a pity that such were not better known to some of the unthinking *Great*, as it might take off some of that *hateur* which is too often shewn towards them–

Another of these uncultivated singular Characters, while it exhibits human nature left to the guidance of its uncontrolled will, may be found sometimes, from the force of innate natural pride, to soar above every meanness–this Man, 'tho clothed in rags, was noticed for his honour & integrity, and whose word was considered to be as good as a £1000 bond–he was one of my fathers workmen, either as a Pitman, a labourer or a Sinker,[1] and was of so hardy a constitution, that he thought it no hardship in a cold frosty morning, to be let down to the bottom of a sinking Pit, where he was to be up to the middle or perhaps to his breast, in Water, which he was to lave[2] all away into buckets, to be drawn up to the top–but in every job he undertook he endured its hardships without ever grumbling or thinking it so.– His living was of the poorest kind, bread, potatoes & oatmeal was the only provender he kept by him; with these & milk & water he finished his meals–When, by this mode of living, he had saved the overplus money of his wages, for a month or 6 Weeks–he then posted off to Newcastle to spend it in Beer, and this he called "*lowsening his skin*",–when this was done, he commonly borrowed two Shillings of me, to set him home again–and in this irrational way of life he continued for many years.–On one occasion, when changing his Beer house, and taking up his quarters in another, he had made no stipulations with his new landlord, as to the place where he was to sleep at night, and judging of him by his ragged appearance, he was thought not fit to be trusted as an inmate, without enquiring into his character–& for this purpose I was applied to by the Landlord, whom I satisfied by assuring him, that notwithstanding the outward appearance of his singular looking Guest, he might be trusted safely with any thing, even with untold Gold, and further that the Man who could sleep upon the fallen leaves in a Wood, wanted no bed in his house better than the wooden seats in his Boxes and that these would be as comfortable a Bed for him as he wished for–Matters being now perfectly understood & settled he was permitted on this, and on all future occasions, during his rambles, to make this house his home.–He had been but a short time in this happy assylum, untill he got a pretty numerous acquaintance, but particularly with the Tradesmen who frequented the House, to whom his singularity–his droll and witty stories, and his Songs often afforded most of them great entertainment.–Old age however, overtook him at last, and he was then obliged to seek parish or township relief–on this occasion a Neighbouring Laird persuaded him that his settlement was upon Eltringham, and got him to swear to it–When he called upon the Farmers there for his pittance they convinced him that he had sworn to what was false–he was much shocked at what he had done, and never having called upon them for his pay, they asked him why he had not done so–no said he I would sooner have this hand cut off, or be found dead on the highway through want, than claim, or receive from any one money to which he was not justly entitled–After this he wandered away from Eltringham and took up his abode in the Glasshouse at Bill Quay,[1] where he did any little jobs in his power, and at the same time made himself very agreable and often very entertaining to the Workmen, who long remembered Johnny Chapman–from this place he set off on a visit to a friend at some distance, when he was rather unwell & not very able to undertake such a journey–and was found dead on the road between Morpeth & Newcastle.

(Thus far was written at Tynemouth 10 Dec[r] 1822)

Before taking leave of these hardy inhabitants of the Fells & wastes, whose Hovels were surrounded with Whins & heather, I must observe that they always appeared to me, notwithstanding their apparent poverty, to enjoy health & happiness, in a degree surpassing that of most other Men–their dayly fare was commonly coarse bread, Potatoes, oatmeal porridge & milk, and was only varied by their boiling the pot, with animal food cabbage or other succulent Vegetables & broth, on the Sundays–When tired at night with labour, having few cares to perplex them, they lay down & slept soundly, and arose refreshed from their hard beds with vigour, early in the Morning–

After I left the country, I always felt much pleasure in revisiting them, and over a tankard of Ale to listen to their discourse –it was chiefly upon local biography, in which they sometimes traced the pedigree of their neighbours, along way back–and when good eating became the subject of their discourse & in telling what they liked best, one man would declare, that *ower all fruit that grew he liked potatoes & cabbage the best*, while another would press, upon the audience, the deliciousness of potatoes & onion sauce & in the warmth of his loyalty, wished that the King did but know how good a dish this was, he believed he would never want it for his supper.

With the aged men in the Neighbourhood, I felt very much amused at the avidity with which they gathered News–*they seemed to live upon it.*–Several of them met every day in the *Ludge* (or earth built Hovel)* close by my fathers Pit, for the purpose of being gratified in this way–the Carts & Wains came in all directions, & many of them from a great distance for coals, the drivers of which imparted to them all they knew of what was going on in their several neighbourhoods–in this kind of treat I often partook with them, when I was Gin driver,[1] by slipping in among them, between the drawing up of each Cart of coals to the *bank*–The information thus obtained by our neighbours, was then speedily given in detail at the Smith's Shop at Mickley, whence it was spread over the neighbouring country—One of these, a very old man, John Newton (the laird of the Neuk) almost every morning, while I was very young, met me & the rest of the scholars, going to Mickley school, at or near the *Hally Well* (holy Well) & he seldom passed me without clapping my head, accompanied with some good wishes–many years after this, while I lived at the Forth, in Newcastle, I met a little boy, one morning coming to school there, when I clapped his head, & hoped he was a good boy, –I had not long passed from him 'till I was rather struck with the coincident recollection of his Grandfather's Grandfather (above named) so long before having passed me in the same way.–

To these I must add another description of Men, scattered about the neighbourhood, with whose history & narratives, I at that time felt greatly interested–their minute account of the Battles they had been engaged in, with the hardships they endured & their hair breadth escapes–told with so much enthusiasm & exultation, emparted the same kind of feelings to me–This was long before I had reasoned myself into a detestation of War–its cruelty

* This Lodge having always a good fire kept on in it, with two beds of straw, on each Side bounded by two old trees to answer the double purpose of bed stocks & seats–often proved a comfortable Assylum to the benighted, weary, shivering traveller, wandering on the road–

its horrors & the superlative wickedness of the Authors of it–I had not pictured to my mind the thousands & tens of thousands of Men in their prime, being pitched against a like number of other young men, to whom they could have no enmity–to murder each other!! for what?–It is foreign to my purpose to enlarge upon this subject–I must leave that for others, of my mind, to do–and there is an abundant scope to dilate upon & to depicture its horrors in their true colours–The old soldiers, above alluded to were mostly the descendants of the borderers, whose propensity for War might perhaps be innate. I think, however, that the breed is thinned, from the numbers that have been killed off in our Wars–one of these, (a near relative) would describe his having had his Knapsack shot through & through as well as his coat laps & the cocks of his Hat, & yet escape unhurt–and others of them would give a similar descriptive account, and when a party of them met over their ale, it is not easy to depicture the warmth with which they greeted each other and prided themselves on the Battles they had won–One of these, during a walk, in which I fell in with him, from Newcastle to Ovingham, described the minute particulars of the battle of Minden & how, in the abscence of Lord Sackville, they shook hands, the whole length of the line & vowing to stand by each other without flinching–this tall stout Man, John Cowie, 'tho old appeared in all the vigour of youth–he lived at Ovington[1] but his associate Ben Garlick, of Prudhoe,[2] appeared as if his constitution had been broken down–they had served in a corps called Napier's Granadiers–Cowie appeared occasionally in his old Military Coat &c as long as he lived, & after he died this coat, which had been shot at both at Minden & else where, was, at last hung up–on a Stake on the corn Rigs as a scare Crow–This ferocious people formerly bore nearly the same names, on both sides of the Borders & their character seemed like a distinct people from both their English & Scottish neighbours & war & rapine had long been their almost constant employment–Many of these, the retainers, of the Chieftains of old, whose iron hands were grasped, & whose feet were swift to shed blood, were called by names, descriptive of their characters & persons–which nicknames were mostly continued by their offspring–and these consisted of a great variety, both of cunning & ferocious Birds and beasts, as well as some names, the meaning of which is now unknown–there were among them the Hawk, Glead,[1] Falcon, Fox, Wolf, Bloodhound, Greyhound–Raven, Crow, Gorfoot,[2] Crowfoot &c

The Farmers in the Neighbourhood, at the early period which I have been describing, always appeared to me, to be not of so intelligent a cast as the poor labouring man–their minds being more exclusively occupied with the management of their Farms & they read but little–They were mostly of a kind & hospitable disposition, & well intentioned plain plodding men, who went jogging on, in their several occupations, as their fathers had done before them.

The next advance in society bejond these were the Country Lairds, who lived upon their own lands.–I have always through life, been of opinion, that there was no business of any kind, nor any employment whatever, that could be compared with that of a Man's farming his own land–it appeared to me, that every earthly pleasure, with health & happiness, was more within his reach, than fell to the lot, of other men–but in these, my notions of their happiness, I have very often seen & felt, that I was grievously mistaken, for numbers of these men were grosly ignorant, & in exact proportion to that ignorance, they were sure to be offensively proud–this led them to attempt appearing above their station, which hastned them on to their ruin–but indeed, this disposition & this kind of conduct, leads to the same results, with all men of this stamp–There were many of these Lairds on Tyneside, as well as many who held their lands, on the tenure of "suit & service" & were nearly on the same level as the Lairds, some of the latter, lost their Lands (not fairly I think) in a way they could not help, while the former by their misdirected pride & folly were driven into Towns to slide away into nothingness & to sink into oblivion,–while their old *Haa Houses* (Halls) that ought to have remained in their Families from Generation to Generation for ever,–but these, with their forgotten ancient Owners, have also mouldered away–I have always felt extremely grieved to see the Ancient Mansions of too many of the Gentlemen of the country, from somewhat similar causes meet with a similar fate–

The Gentry of the country ought in an especial manner, to shew by their conduct that they are guarded against shewing any symptoms of foolish pride & at the same time that they soared above every meanness & that their conduct was guided by truth integrity & patriotism. If they wish the people to partake with them in these good qualities they must set them the example without which, no real respect can ever be paid to them by people in the lower stations of life–Gentlemen ought never to forget the respectable station they hold in society, & that they are the natural guardians of public morals & may with propriety be considered as the head & the heart of the country, while a bold peasantry, are in truth the Arms the sinews & the strength of the same, but when these are degraded they soon become dispirited & mean & often dishonest & useless.

I think the late Duke of Northumberland,[1] must have had an eye to raising the character of the peasantry, when he granted them small portions of land, at a reasonable rate–if so, in my way of judging, he was an honour to the pearage, & set an example worthy of himself, & worthy of imitation–by going a step further & planting healthy strong Men & Women on these spots his patriotism would have been *crowned with immortality*–for I cannot help thinking, that if the same pains were taken in breeding mankind, that Gentlemen have bestowed upon the breeding of their Dogs, Horses & game Cocks, that human nature might, as it were, be new modelled–hereditary diseases banished, & such a race of Mankind might people the country as we can form no true conception of, and instead of a nation of mongrels, there would, in time, appear a nation of "*Admirable Crichtons*".[2]—If the Lands commonly attached to townships, had been continued as such, or let in small portions, to mechanics & labourers, (as the late Duke had done) instead of dividing them by *Act of parliament*, among those who had already too much, the good effects to the community at large would have soon been felt–and in addition to this, if saving banks & benefit societies were encouraged by every possible means, there would be little occasion for poor Laws, except as a provision, for helpless children & the lame & the blind–By such means as these, perhaps this national evil might be done away–All men ought to provide for the necessities of old Age, & be made sensible of the manly pleasure of being independant.–It is degrading & in most cases disgracefull to those who look to parish assistance after a life spent in laziness & mismanagement–

I must not omit noticing a circumstance that happened to Eltringham while I was a boy–it was to have been called "little

Birmingham" but this was not accomplished–in 17–– a person of the name of Laidler, who was said to have amassed a large fortune in London, came to the North & established the Iron Works at "Busy Cottage" near Newcastle–and, on his taking a view of Tyne side, he fixed upon Eltringham, as a place at which he could carry on works to a much greater extent–This work he set about in great haste–all kinds of workmen were gathered together for the purpose of speedily accomplishing what he had in view, and while some of them were busy in making the Mills & Machinery, others were digging a Mill race of about a quarter of a mile in length–but lo! when this was done, it was found (not being permitted to encroach upon the bed of the river) they had not, it was said, much more than about a foot of waterfall, and as the sides of the Mill race was cut perpendicularly about two yards deep, through the dark fine soil–the first great flood of the Tyne, by the sides falling in, nearly levelled & filled it up–The Houses in & about the place, that had got licences to sell Ale &c, were obliged to shut them up & decline –and among the rest, my fathers house, & its sign of the seven Starrs, hung up between the two ash Trees, was taken down. The projector made our house his home while the works were going on & the Men were paid their wages there–all was as suddenly sold off, as it was begun, & my father came to some loss, after all the turmoil & trouble he had been put to.

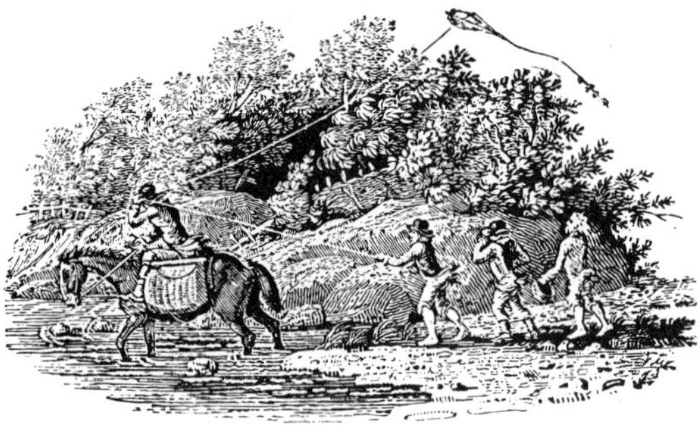

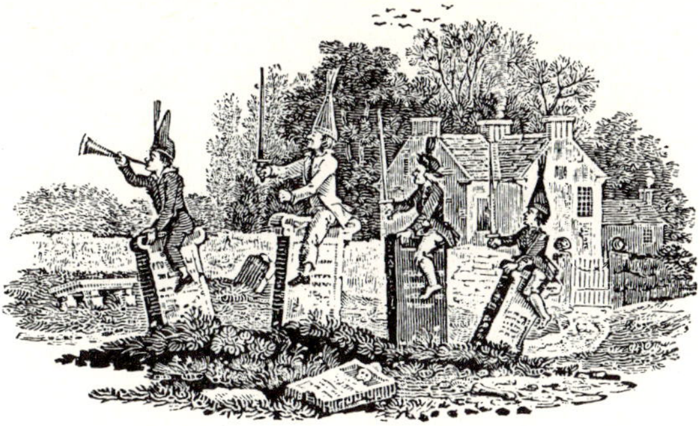

[4]

Being now nearly fourteen years of age & a stout boy, it was thought time to set me off, and my father & Mother had long been planning & consulting what business it would be best to put me to, in which they were greatly at a loss what to fix upon–Any place where I could see pictures, or where I thought I could have an opportunity of drawing them, was such only as I could think of–A Newcastle Bookseller whose windows were filled with prints, had applied to Mr Gregson for a boy & when I was asked if I would like to go there, I readily expressed my hearty consent, but upon my father's making every enquirey respecting this man, he was given to understand, that he bore a very bad character–so that business was soon at an end.

The same year 1767, during the summer, William Beilby & his brother Ralph, took a ride to see their intimate acquaintance, Mrs Simons at Bywell, who was my Godmother & the widow of the late Vicar there.* She gave them a most flattering account of me, so much so that they, along with her & her daughter (afterwards Mrs Hymers) all set off that afternoon to Cherry-burn to visit us & to drink tea.–When the Newcastle visitors, had given an account of their paintings, enamellings, drawings & Engravings &c with which Acct I felt much pleased–I was asked which of them I would like to be bound to and liking the look & deportment of

* Robert Simon

Ralph the best, I gave the preference to him–matters bearing upon this business being slightly talked over, & my Grandmother's having left me £20 for an apprentice fee it was not long before something of a good understanding between parties took place, and I soon afterwards went to R: Beilby upon trial—The first of October was the day fixed uppon, for the binding–the eventfull day arrived at last, and a most grievous day it was to me–I liked my master, I liked the business, but to part from the country & to leave all its beauties behind me, with which I had all my life been charmed in an extreme degree, & in a way I cannot describe–I can only say my heart was like to break, and as we passed away–I inwardly bid farewell, to the whinney wilds–to Mickley Bank, the Stob Cross hill, to the water banks, the woods, & to particular trees, and even to the large hollow old Elm which had lain (perhaps) for centuries past, on the haugh[1] near the ford we were about to pass & had sheltered the Salmon-fishers while at work there, from many a bitter blast–this old tree was swept away by the great flood of the 17 November 1771.[2]

We called upon my much esteemed Schoolfellow "Kit Gregson" at Ovingham, where he & his Father were waiting to accompany us to Newcastle, all on the same errand–we were both bound that day–While we were condoling–comforting each other–I know not what to call it–at the Parsonage Gates, many of the old neighbours were assembled at the churchyard Wall, to see us set off & to express their good wishes–and among the rest, to watch our departure, was a good sensible old woman of the village, named Betty Kell, for the purpose of giving both of us her blessing, and each a penny for good luck–this being done, our Horses were mounted & we commenced our Journey–The parties kept at a little distance from each other–I suppose our late preceptor was lecturing his son & my father was equally busied in the same way with me–He had always set me the example & taken every opportunity of shewing how much he detested meanness, and of drawing forth every particle of pride within me, for the purpose of directing it in this way–he began & continued a long while, on subjects of this kind, & on the importance & the inestimable value of honour & honesty–and urgently pressed upon me to do my duty to my master, in faithfully & obediently fulfilling all his commands–to be before-hand in meeting his wishes–and in particular to be always upon my guard in listening to the insinuations & the wicked advice of worthless persons, who I would find ever ready to poison my ear against him–He next turned his discourse on another topic, new to me from him, of great importance–Religion–& pressed this also upon me in a way I did not forget–he begged I would never omit, morning & Eveg addressing myself to my Maker & that, if I ceased to do so, then he believed & feared, every evil would follow it–I was greatly surprized to hear him dwell on this subject, for I think it was the first time–he used indeed to go to Church, but I do not recollect his ever commenting upon the Sermons he heard there, further than that the good man's discourse from the Pulpit seemed to him to be wasted upon the great majority of his audience and of his calling some of them "holy professors"–My Mother, who was of a religious turn, had, indeed, all her life endeavoured to make me so too–but as I did not clearly understand her well intended lectures, they made little impression –my father's pithy illustrations, as before hinted at, were much more forcably & clearly made out. I understood them well & their effect operated powerfully upon me*–I have often reflected since upon the very high importance & of the necessity of instilling this species of education into the minds of youth, for were pains taken to draw forth the pride, naturally implanted in their minds, for the wisest & best purposes, if properly directed, it would exalt human nature, and be of the utmost importance to individuals & to society –it is the want of this & the want of industry that occasions & spreads misery over the land–and how can I doubt it, if my father had been a thief, that I would not have been one also–& if a highwayman & robber, that I might not have been as expert a one as himself–

In my opinion there are two descriptions of person, who ought to forbear, or to be prevented from marrying–viz those of a base, wicked & dishonest Character, and those who have broken down their constitutions by diseases & debased both mind & body, by

* I recollect one instance where I felt the force of this species of education. I might enumerate some others, but this left its *mark upon me*–having fallen in with & joined two untutored lads, in Prudhoe lonning, they jumped over the hedge & filled their pockets with potatoes–The Farmer was watching, but they escaped–not having followed their example, I did not offer to fly, but he seized me & threatened what he would do; at this I was extremely distressed & had it not been that I consoled myself with the certainty that my father & mother would believe me on my asserting that I had not stolen any of his potatoes I believe I would have drowned myself.

their illicit & impure connections & dissipated lives–the latter entails misery upon their innocent tainted ofspring–and the former by the bad examples they shew to their children which grows upon them with their growth 'till they are perfected in their wickedness & they become a curse to the community in which they live–

—When we arrived at the Cock Inn, Newcastle, the documents were soon made ready to bind my companion & myself–he was bound to Messrs Doughty & Wiggins, Chemists & Druggists–but Mr Beilby (perhaps from his having heard of some unfavourable account of me) and my father not readily agreeing upon the exact terms of my servitude, some fears were entertained that the business between us might be broken off–on this occasion my preceptor interfered very ardently–spoke warmly in my praise, and dwelt forcibly in particular, (notwithstanding my boyish wild behaviour at school) upon my never being saucy or sulky, nor in the least indulging in any thing like revenge–in this business Mr Gregson was ably seconded by his relation & my kind friend Joseph Langstaffe of Newcastle, who was also accuainted with my new master & so the business of binding was settled at last.

—My new master, who I believe had laid down plans for the regulation of his own conduct through life, begun with me upon a system of riged discipline, from which he never varied nor relaxed, and it was not long before I gave occasion to his putting it in force –having walked out on a sunday afternoon, to see the environs of the town, the first place that attracted my attention & I visited was King Jimmy's Well–here I fell in with bad company consisting of three low blackguard 'prentice lads from the Close–Having no wish to have any thing to say to them, I endeavoured to shun their company–but they, seeing me in a strange & perhaps somewhat clownish dress, followed & insulted me & this they persisted in 'till I could bear it no longer, when turning upon one of the sauciest of them, I presently levelled him & was about serving the second in the same way–when they all three fell upon me & shewed no mercy, so that in the end I went home to my master's house with a scratched face & black eyes–This was an abominable sight to the Family which no excuse could palliate—After this I was obliged to attend my master to church twice a day (forenoon & afternoon) every Sunday, and at Night to read the Bible or some other good book, to old Mrs Beilby & her Daughter or others of the family–

and this continued during the time of the term I boarded in the House with them—The father of this family followed the business of a Goldsmith & Jeweller, in Durham, where he had been greatly respected–he had taken care to give all his family a good education –his eldest Son Richard had served his apprenticeship to a die sinker or seal Engraver in Birmingham–his second Son William had also learned enamelling & painting in the same place–the former of these had taught my master R: seal cutting & the latter taught their Brother Thomas & sister Mary, enamelling & painting –and in this way this most industrious & respectable family, lived together & maintained themselves–but prior to this state of things, while the family were more dependant upon the industry of their father he failed in business, left Durham & begun business in Gateshead where he, as well as his eldest son Richard died–

About this period, I was informed, that the family had to struggle with great difficulties & that by way of helping to get through them, their Mother taught a school in Gateshead–but this state of things could not last long, for the industry ingenuity & the united energies of the family, must soon have enabled them to soar above every obstacle.—My master had wrought as a jeweller, with his father before he went to his brother Richard to learn Seal cutting which was only for a very short time before his death–He also assisted his Brothers & Sister, in the constant employment of enamel painting upon Glass.[1]

–At this time a fortunate circumstance, for my future master, happened which made an opening for him to get forward in his business unopposed by any one in Newcastle–An Engraver of the name of Jameson, who had the whole stroke of the business in Newcastle to himself, having been detected in committing a Forgery upon the old Bank, was tried for the crime, but his life was saved by the perjury of a Mrs Gray, who was I believe transported for it, and Jameson left the town—For sometime after I entered to the business, I was employed in drawing Copelands Ornaments,[2] and this was the only kind of drawing upon which I ever had a lesson given to me from any one–I never was a pupil to any drawing Master & had not even a lesson from Wm Beilby[3] & his brother Thomas, who along with their other profession, were also drawing masters–and afterwards I never had any opportunity or time to spare for any such purpose, at which I felt much grieved

& disappointed, for my master kept me otherwise fully employed–The first jobs I was put to do was blocking out the Wood about the lines, on the Diagrams, which my master finished, for the Ladies Diaries,[1] on which he was employed by Charles Hutton* & etching Sword blades for William & Nich[s] Oley, sword manufacturers &c at Shotley-bridge–It was not long 'till the whole of the *Diagrams* were wholly put into my hands to finish–after these I was kept closely employed upon a variety of other jobs, for such was the industry of my master that he refused nothing, coarse or fine–he undertook every thing & did it in the best way he could–he fitted up & tempered his own tools, which he adapted to every purpose & learned me to do the same–this readiness to undertake, brought him in an overflow of work & our work place was filled, with the coarsest kinds of steel stamps – pipe Moulds – Bottle moulds – Brass Clock faces – Door plates – Coffin plates – Bookbinders Letters & stamps – Steel, Silver & gold Seals – Mourning Rings – Arms crests & cyphers on silver & every kind of job, from the Silver Smiths – writing engraving of Bills, bank notes, Bills of parcels, shop bills & cards – these last, with Gent[s] Arms for their Books, he executed as well as most of the Engravers of the time–but what he most excelled in was ornamental Silver engraving: in this, as far as I am able to judge he was one of the first in the Kingdom–& I think upon the whole, he might be called "an ingeneous self taught Artist"–The higher department of engraving such as Landscape or historical plates, I dare say, was hardly ever thought of by my master, at least not till I was nearly out of my Apprenticeship, when he took it into his head to leave me in charge of the business at home, & of going to London, for the purpose of taking lessons in etching & engraving & practising upon large copperplates–there was however little or no employment in this way in Newcastle,[2] & he had no opportunity of becoming clever at it, so he kept labouring on with such work, as before named, in which I aided him with all my might–I think he was the best master in the World, for learning Boys, for he obliged them to put their hands to every variety of Work–every job, coarse or fine, either in cutting or engraving I did as well as I could, cheerfully, but the wearisome business of polishing copper plates[3] & hardning & polishing steel seals, was always irksome to me—I had wrought

* Afterwards the great D[r] Hutton–he died 27 January 1823 in the 86 year of his Age

at such as this a long time, & at the coarser kind of engraving, (such as I have noticed before) 'till my hands became as hard & enlarged as those of a blacksmith–I however in due time, had a greater share of better & nicer work given me to execute[1]–such as the outside & inside mottos on Rings–& sometimes Arms, & crests on silver, and seals of various kinds, for which I made all the new steel punches & letters–we had a great deal of seal cutting, in which my master was accounted clever & in this I did my utmost to surpass him–While we were going on in this way we were occasionally applied to by printers, to execute Wood cuts for them, in this branch my master was very defective, what he did was wretched & he did not like it–on which acct such jobs were given to me & the opportunity this afforded me of drawing the designs on the Wood, was highly gratifying to me–it happened that one of these, a cut of the "George & Dragon", for a barr bill,[2] attracted so much notice & had so many praises bestowed upon it, that this kind of work greatly increased upon us, and were followed by cuts for children's Books, chiefly for Thomas Saint,[3] the printer, Newcastle, & successor of John White, who had rendered himself famous for his numerous publications of Histories & old Ballads–With the singing of the latter, the streets of Newcastle were long greatly enlivened, & many market day visitors, as well as the town's people, were often highly gratified–What a chearful lively time, this appeared to me & many others–this state of things however in time was changed, when public matters cast a surly gloom over the character of the whole country & these singing days, instead of being regulated by the Magistrates, were, in their wisdom, totally put an end to–

–My time now became greatly taken up with Wood cutting, a set of designs in that way, for "the Storey teller"[4]–"Gays Fables"[5] & "the Select Fables"[6] &c together with cuts of various & of similar kinds for other printers–Some of the Fables cuts were thought so well of by my Master, that he in my name sent impressions of a few of them to be laid before the Society for the encouragement of Arts &c and I obtained a premium–this I received shortly after I was out of my apprenticeship & it was left to my choice whether I would have it in a Gold medal or in Money–£7.7s.–I preferred the latter, and I never in my life felt greater pleasure than in that of presenting it to my Mother–On this occasion among the several congratulations of kind neighbours–those from Mr Gregson, my old School Master stood preeminent–he flew from Ovingham, where the news first arrived[1]–over to Eltringham to congratulate my father & mother, upon the occasion & the feelings & overflowings of his heart–can be better imagined than described.

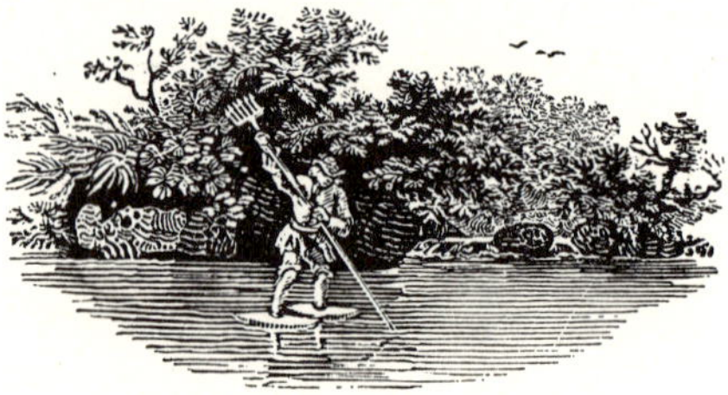

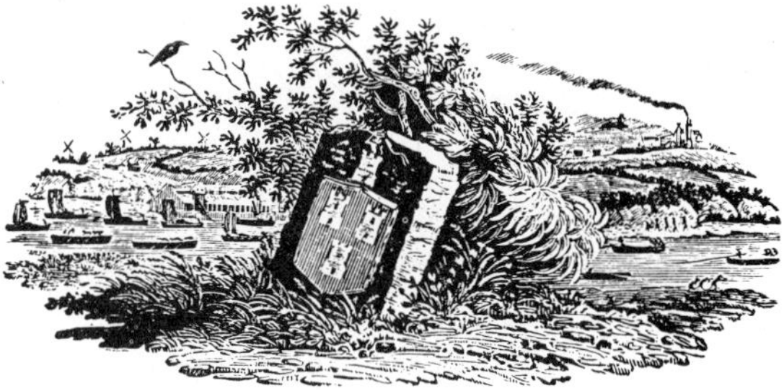

[5]

During the time I was an inmate in my Masters house along with his Mother, Brothers & Sister–I attended his brothers Horse & made myself as useful to the family as I could–At that time I had no acquaintances, at least none to be very intimate with,–I neaded none–I wandered in the fields & on the town Moor alone and amused myself with my own thoughts–When the time arrived that I was to cater for myself, upon 4/6^{d} & afterwards upon 5^{s} ꝑ Week–I went to lodge with my Aunt Blackett[1] in the Pudding Chare[2] & she being a freemans Widow* kept Cows upon the Moor & I was abundantly supplied with milk, which was the chief thing I lived upon.–

At this place I first got acquainted with Gilbert Gray the Bookbinder & this remarkable, singular & worthy man, was the most Valuable (perhaps the most invaluable) acquaintance & friend I ever met with–His moral lectures & advise to me, was a most important succedanium to those imparted by my parents–his wise remarks–his detestation of vice–his industry & his temperance, crowned with a most lively & cheerfull disposition–altogether ever through life made him appear to me as one of the best characters of the age–In his work.shop I often spent my winter's evenings & this was also the case with a number of other young men, who might be considered as his pupils–many of whom (I have no doubt)

* of Thomas Blackett, Silversmith. This man, who was one of my Godfathers, had been foreman to the late John Langlands where he was much noticed as a man of a most intrepid spirit & rendered remarkable for his honour, honesty & punctuality.

he directed into the paths of truth & integrity & who *revered* his memory thro' life—He rose early to work, he lay down when he felt weary, & rose again to it, when refreshed–His diet was of the most simple kind, and of this he eat when hungry & drank when dry without paying regard to meal times–By steadily pursuing this mode of life he was enabled to accumulate sums of money from ten to thirty pounds, this enabled him to get Books of an entertaining & of a moral tendancy, printed & circulated at a cheap rate[1]–his great object was, by every possible means, to promote honourable feelings in the minds of youth & to prepare them for becoming good members of society–I have often discovered that he did not overlook ingenious Mechanics, whose misfortunes, perhaps mismanagement, had led them to a lodging in Newgate–to these he directed his compassionate eye, & to the deserving (in his estimation) he paid the debt & set them at liberty–he felt hurt at seeing the hands of an ingenious man tied up in a prison, where they were of no use, either to themselves or to the community. This Worthy man had been educated for a priest but he would say to me "of a trouth, Thomas, I did not like their ways", so he gave up the thoughts of being a Priest, & bent his way from Aberdeen to Edinburgh, where he engaged himself to Allen Ramsay the poet, then a Bookseller, in the latter place, & in whose service he was both a shopman & Bookbinder–from Edinburgh he came to Newcastle & engaged himself I believe to Mr Slack as a Bookbinder and as a faithfull & carefull inspector of the Books printed in that Office–Mrs Slack, who was a woman of uncommon abilities & great goodness of heart, did not overlook Gilbert & he was her *right hand man* as long as she lived,–he was afterwards employed in the same way to the end of his life, under Solomon Hodgson, the successor to Thomas Slack—

—Gilbert had had a liberal education bestowed upon him–had read a great deal, & reflected upon what he had read, this with his retentive memory enabled him to be a pleasant & communicative man–but something of a prejudice against priests stuck by him as long as he lived–I lived in habits of intimacy with him to the end of his life, & when he died, I with others of his friends attended his remains to the grave–at the Ballast Hills[2]–he died on the 12 Feby 1794–in the 86th year of his age–I think his age was not known–some people said he was 84 while others called him 90.[3]

In my attendance at the workshop of Gilbert, I got acquainted with several young men who like myself admired him–but one of the most singular of these, was Anthony Taylor, a Glass maker–he was a keen admirer of drawings & paintings, but had no opportunity of shewing his talents in the Arts, otherwise, than in his paintings & his enamelling upon Glass, in which way, considering his situation, he was a proficient and in other respects he was a man of genious & observation–but the first interview I had with him was singular enough & was owing to his having been told, that I was the best whistler in England–he himself being remarkable in this way–we soon tried our respective powers & had many a meeting afterwards for that purpose–he expressed himself highly pleased with the loud & powerfull way in which I performed my double whistle, and I was equally so at hearing his inimitable shakes & quavers with which his small shrill *pipe* was graced–I came nearly up to the loud shrill tones of the fife & the deeper ones of the Flute & improved greatly in imitating him, but he could make no alteration or amendment in his manner of performing & with all his attempts could never whistle louder or deeper than before–We sometimes amused ourselves, turn & turn about, in this way & both agreed that it was a great pity that Whistling was not more countenanced & encouraged than it was–We kept up an agreeable intimacy for some years untill he went to the Glass Works at Leith–where he ended his days.—While I remained at my Aunt Blackett's, she never would allow me to whistle in her house or to try to perform upon any musical instrument–& I could not afterwards find either time or opportunity to gratify my propensity in this way, so I was obliged to make whistling serve for all–I often think it was scarcely possible for any one to have a better ear for music than I had, for what ever tunes I heard at Fairs or Hoppings[1] &c I could next morning whistle them correctly & not only the tune but the manner of the various performers. I have ever since that time been more & more, confirmed in this opinion, and think it is not at all known to what pitch of perfection, this most agreable species of music might attain to, were it encouraged.–It would, I have no doubt, be found to surpass, in natural sweetness, any Wind Instrument whatever–To set it agoing would only require the Aid of a few Amateurs, who by forming themselves into something like a managing Committee, in every Village where Fairs or Hoppings are held–and by collecting a small subscription from the performers–and from others a more liberal sum; & the money to be thus raised, to be awarded to those who excelled in this way & who surpassed their competitors –There can be little doubt, that contests of this agreable kind, would be found to throng the place & give a new character of cheerfulness to these meetings–

I think, were whistling encouraged at the Theatre, from its novelty, it would draw together fuller meetings, than is too often met with there, and empty seats would not be quite so common.

How long I lodged with my aunt, I have now forgot–After I left her house I went to lodge with Ned Hatfield, whose wife, was an excellent Cook & Market woman & had long lived in the family of "Willy Scott", the father of the present Lord Chancellor of England –She was now chiefly employed in keeping the dancing School of Neil Stewart, clean & in good order, & sold Oranges & fruit &c to his pupils–above the School she had the Rooms taken to live in & to let out to Lodgers & it happened that the young man, John McDonald, Mr Stewarts Fidler, was lodged with her along with me –he was accounted an excellent performer on the Violin* & to his performances (the scottish tunes particularly) I listned with great delight. When Neil Stewart declined, or perhaps died, he was succeeded in this school by Ivey Gregg & his Fidler John Frazier, lodged in the same house with me and with his music I was also pleased as I had been before–

After this my landlord, got into a very unfortunate way of doing business, for being a Heckler (flax dresser), his brethren prevailed upon him & his Wife to permit the tramps or *scamps*, in that line, to take up their lodgings with them–here I was introduced, or at least had an opportunity of becoming acquainted with them–*and a pretty Set* they were–their conduct, was wicked in the extreme–it had however the proper effect upon me, for I looked upon their behaviour with the utmost disgust–After poor Ned had for sometime been cheated & defrauded, by this set, he at length got done with them & boarded & lodged others of a better *cast of character*–Long before the death of my friend Gilbert I had not the same opportunities of getting or of reading his Books & what I could save out of my wages, could only afford me a scanty supply

* He afterwards was a dancing master of eminence at Perth in Scotland, where he died.

in this way. I had however an opportunity ꝑ favor of my masters servant girl, who admitted me early in the Morning into his parlour, of reading through with great attention, the new publication of Smollets History of England–for a long time afterwards I clearly remembered every thing of note, it contained–with some of the characters which he depictured I was greatly pleased, but with others for the most part, I was shocked & disgusted for they appeared to me like fiends obtruded upon society–as a curse & a scourge to Mankind–& yet how surprizing it is that some of these can be spoken of, by Authors, with complacency—Another source of my getting a supply of information presently fell in my way, through the kindness of William Gray,* the son of Gilbert whose work shop now became a place of resort to me & to others–he was a Bookbinder of repute & this led him into employment of a superior cast to that of his father and his workshop was often filled with the Works of the best Authors, to bind for Gentlemen–To these, while binding, I had ready access–for which purpose I rose early in the morning–and to him, my well known whistling in the street, was the signal for his quickly preparing to get to his Work & there I remained with him 'till my work hour came.

I feel it a misfortune that a bias somehow or other, took place in my mind at this time–and led me deeply into the chaos of what is called Religious Works, & for the purpose of getting into a thorough knowledge—of all matters of this important kind, I spent much time and took great pains & labour to obtain information but instead of which I got myself into a labyrinth, bewildered

* William Gray was a most active & industrious Man; of an ardent but changeable temper. He began business in Newcastle & prospered–he went to London & did the same[1]–he returned to Newcastle & to the binding business he added that of Bookseller–on this occasion Jonathan Kidd & myself became bound for him for £60–for the payment of which, his goods & books were left to us to sell–in this *freak* for he had no occasion to fail, he wrote to me begging I would send him the Books & goods & knowing his integrity, I got my fellow bondman (with a good deal of trouble) to assent to this proposal & the Books were sent off to him–he commenced auctioneer & soon paid us every penny of the money–he afterwards begun business in Nottingham as Booktrader printer and Stationer & there he failed–he continued his Auctioneer[g] from place to place for some time–and at length became a Soldier–in this, his energy & activity became so conspicuous that he was employd as an inspector (I believe) of some of the Military hospitals in Ireland–& had a pension settled upon him–he afterwards commenced the Business of Bookseller, Bookbinder &c at Stonehouse, Plymouth–and at the same time followed that of Auctioneering–at length however he took entirely to auctioneering & that of the Shop was turned over to his Son, who knew better than his Father had done to conduct himself steadily.

with dogmas, creeds and opinions–mostly the finatical reveries of bigotted, or the inventions of interested or designing Men that seemed to me to be without end, and after all my pains I left off in a more unsettled state of mind than when I begun–I may be mistaken but I think many a well meaning man has spun out his life & spent his time on subjects of this kind, in vain, and waggon loads of sermons have been published & have disappeared–some of them perhaps good–while others have been labouring to prove matters (in my opinion) of no kind of use or importance either to religion or morality–If it be true that every thing in perfection is simple, so it will be with religion, as well as with other things–In this case there may be many moral & Religious duties for Man to fulfill in his passage through life, but the rules for doing so are so plain & easily understood that commonsense only is necessary for all that is required of us–The beauty & simplicity of the doctrines laid down by the inspired and benevolent Author of the Christian Religion, however they may have been distorted & disfigured, are yet in themselves perfect–they may indeed be compared to a mathematical point–a point of perfection–for all Men to aim at, but which they cannot fully attain–The inspired writings of the prophets of old, are also full of simplicity as well as of indescribeable beauty & may be read & considered without the fear of being tired of them–The inspired writers, poets & moralists, of more modern times have also laboured & most clearly so, to point out the paths which lead to virtue, to religion & to happiness.–After all this, as far as I am able to judge of these matters, all we can do is to commune with & to reverence & adore the Creator, to yeild with humility & resignation to his Will–With the most serious intention of forming a right judgement on this business all the conclusion I can come to is, that there is only one God & one religion, & I know of no way, so well of what is called serving God, as that of being good to his creatures–& of fulfill[g] the moral duties, as that of being good Sons, Brothers, Husbands, Fathers, Neighbours & members of society.

About this time I had few, that I could call intimate acquaintances, my almost only ones were Books, over which I spent my time, mornings & evenings, late & early. This too intense application to Books together with my sedentary employment, & being placed at a very low work bench took away my healthy appearance, & I put on a more delicate look–after being some time in this way, I became poorly in health, and when my Master saw this, he sent for medical Aid & Nathanial Bailes,* Surgeon was consulted–but before he uttered a word as to my ailment he took me to his own House & there he stripped & examined me, & then, looking me in the face, told me I was as "strong as a Horse"–he then made up some slight medicine to cause me to spit up some phleghm which was gathering in the glands of the gullet or throat–this was all soon done, but not so with the lectures he gave my master, whom he addressed in terms which I thought both long & rude–What! said he, & have you no more sense than to set a growing country lad to work, doubled up at a low bench, which would inevitably destroy him & in his passion, cursed poor Beilby for his ignorance –or for something worse.

From this time the Doctor took a liking to me & often criticised the work which I had executed–he also took great pains to direct me how to live & manage myself, under so sedentary an employment, & an intimacy took place between us, which lasted as long as he lived.—He urged upon me the necessity of temperance & exercise–I then begun to act upon this advise–& to live as he directed, both as to diet & exercise—I had read Lewis Cornaro[1] & other Books which treated of temperance & I greatly valued the advise in the Spectator, which strongly recommended all people

* He was commonly called Dr Bailes. He was a Newcastle worthy and accounted a man of great skill in his profession, he was also eminent for his learning & other attainments–he was also called "the eloquent Sword Bearer"–He headed the committee of the Burgesses in 17[73] who tried & beat the Magistrates respecting their exclusive claim to the Town Moor & was active in every thing relative to the good of the town–he was of an ingenious & enterprizing mind, –a tolerably good Engraver & a good mechanic–he invented a Harpoon for killing whales, for which he got a patent–this was the most dreadfull instrument I ever saw, it was of a triangular shape & looked like 3 Razors, back to back & brought to a sharp point & strongly barbed at their termination towards the socket. If this instrument was thrown so as to fall flat upon the back of a whale–the two undermost barbs were sure to lay hold of the skin & enter deeper & deeper–but if the animal was struck with the point of the Instrument, it was sure to bury itself, shaft & all, overhead in the whale & could not be pulled out, without making a large hole, even into the crang or fleshy part–& thus wounded, the Whale soon died & the usual lines & cords were nearly all saved–his charge for the harpoons was 3 guineas each–this price was deemed too high & was the cause of a confedracy of harpoon makers, sea captains & others, who knew not how to appreciate their value, to set their faces against using them–The '"Doctor", who did not like to be kept debating with ignorance & prejudice, & not being actuated by pecuniary motives suffered the business to go to neglect. He died after being cut for the stone by Dr Ingham, 16 July 1791 Aged 74 & was buried in St Ns Church.

to have their days of abstinence, in this thro' life, I have experienced the uncommon benefits derived from occasionally pursuing that plan–for this always kept the stomach in a proper tone–I regularly pursued my walks & while thus exercising, my mind was commonly engaged in considering upon plans about how I should

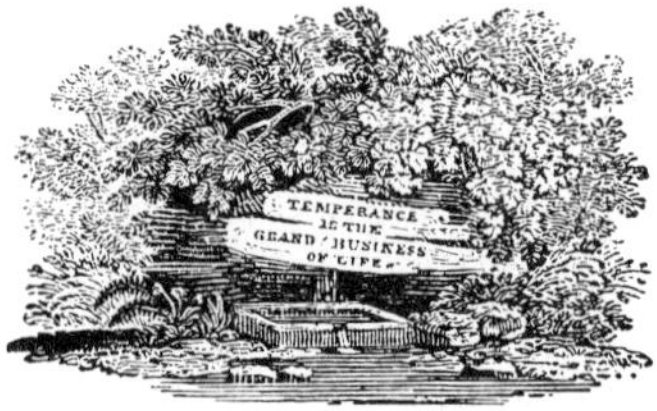

conduct myself in life & of forming resolutions on such as I approved of & of strictly acting up to them—For a long time, in both summer & winter, I mostly went to Elswick,[1] three times a day, at the expence of a penny each time, for bread & milk[2]–I had an hour allowed for my dinner time, & as to my mornings & Evenings, I could take a much longer time–a very small matter of animal food, when I missed going to Elswick, was amply sufficient for me, for I think my constitution was of that kind, which did not require to be stimulated—By persevering in this system of temperance & exercise I was astonished to find how much I improved in health strength & agility–I thought nothing of leaving Newcastle (occasionally) after I had done work (7 oClock) in a winters night & of setg off to walk to Cherryburn–in this I was stimulated by an ardent desire to visit my parents as often as possible, & this desire continued to act upon me as long as they lived—In my solitary walks (as before noticed) the first resolution I recollect of having made, was that of living within my income & another, of similar import, was that of never getting any thing upon trust—my limited income indeed led me carefully to observe these rules, but I never afterwards forgot them–the train of reflections they brought along with them, have also dwelt upon my mind.–I could not help observing the inevitable ill consequences, which a contrary course, at first perhaps unthinkingly, led thousands into, and the misery which it entailed–The more I have thought upon this subject through life, the more clearly do I see the importance of it –for getting into debt, is followed by leading on people to live bejond their income–& this makes all who do so, soon become demoralised & dishonest & when the mind has been thus blunted and degraded, anxiety & trouble must be its attendants, 'till vice & misery close the scene. Among the acquaintances I made at the Work shop of Gilbert & William Gray, was William Bulmer, afterwards rendered famous as the proprietor of the Shakspere printing offices in Cleveland Row & who was the first, that set the example & soon led the way to fine printing in England–he used, while he was an Apprentice, to prove the cuts, I had executed–in this he was countenanced by his Master, John Thompson Esqr who was himself extremely curious & eager to see this succeed, but at that time, the printing of wood cuts properly, was very imperfectly known—About the same time, I commenced a most intimate Acquaintance & friendship with Robert Pollard, afterwards an Engraver & printseller of eminence in London–he was bound

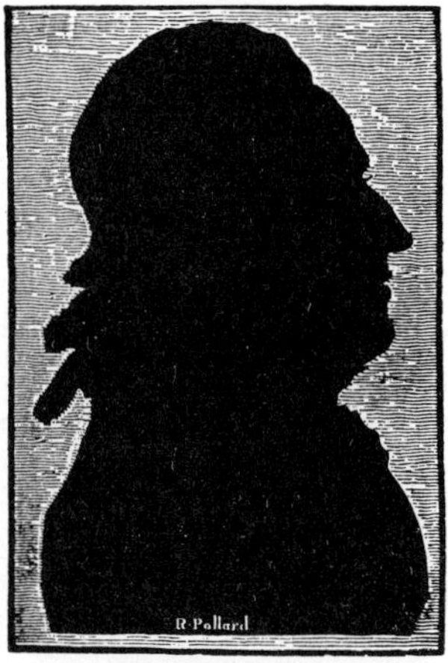

Robert Pollard

Apprentice to John Kirkup, a Silversmith, in Newcastle, and from his being frequently sent to our work place with Crests, Cyphers &c to engrave, he took a great liking to engraving & was indefatigable in his endeavours to become master of it–in furtherance of this, we spent many of our Evenings together in his fathers House, which to me was a kind of home–on his master Kirkup's declining business, my young friend was engaged for a term of years, to learn Engraving with Isaac Taylor of Holborn, London.

–In my frequent visits to the work shops of Gilbert Gray or to his son William's I first fell in with Thomas Spence*, & afterwards became very intimate with him. He was one of the warmest Philanthropists in the world–the happiness of Mankind, seemed with him, to absorb every other consideration; he was of a most cheerfull disposition, warm in his attachments to his friends & in his patriotism to his country–but was violent against people, who he considered to be of an opposite character–with such he kept no bounds. For the purpose, chiefly I believe, of making converts to his way of thinking, about "property in land being every ones right"–he got a number of young men gathered together & formed into a debating society, which was held in the evenings, at his first School Room, in the Broad-garth, Newcastle–One night, when his favourite question was to be debated–he reckoned upon me as one of his *backers*–in this however he was mistaken for notwithstanding my tacitly assenting, in a certain degree to his plan, viz. as to the probable eligeability of its succeeding in some uninhabited country or Island, yet I could not at all agree with him in thinking it right to upset the present state of society, by taking from people what was their own & then to launch out upon his speculations–for I considered that property ought to be held sacred, and besides I considered the honestly obtaining [of] it, was the great stimulant to industry, which keeps all things in order, & society in full health & vigour. The question being given against him, without my

* Rendered, afterwards, famous in London as being at the head of the *Spenceans*, & sent to Dorchester Gaol for (I believe) some of his publications, for promulgating his doctrines in that way–He taught a School in the broad garth, Newcastle–afterwards taught writing & arithmetic &c in the great school at Haydon Bridge & lastly he was master of S[t] Ann's public School in Sandgate–At this time his Wife kept a shop at the black Gate, & by her mismanagement–Spence (who was a carefull sober man) failed & was led into great difficulties–on which account he gave up S[t] Anns School, & went to London–Sometime before this, he was a member of a most respectable literary & philosophical society in Newcastle–one of their Rules required that each member should read in turn a written lecture on any subject he pleased–Spence's was of course on that of "property in land" &c. These Lectures of the Members, was by them prohibitted from publication–This Rule Spence broke through by publishing his lecture, on which account he was expelled.

having said a word in its defence, he became swollen with indignation which, after all the Company were gone, he vented upon me, to reason with him was useless–he began by calling me (from my silence) a Sir Walter Blackett,[1] and adding "if I had been as stout as you are I would have thrashed you"–indeed! said I "it is a great pity you are not"–but said he, "there is another way in which I can do the business", and have at you!–he then produced a pair of cudgels–& to work we fell–he did not know that I was a proficient in this art–& I soon saw he was very defective–after I had black'ned the insides of his thighs & Arms, he became quite outrageous, & behaved very unfairly, which obliged me to give him a severe beating—This however did not make a breach between us, for I believe the respect & kindness for each other was mutual—I cut the steel Punches, for his new Types & my Master struck them into the Matrixes, for casting his newly invented letters of the Alphabet, for his spelling & pronouncing Dictionary—He published many curious books,[2] in the same way of spelling, in London, & I believe all or most of them, on this favourite subject of his, about "Property in land being every ones right"—However mistaken he might be in his notions on this subject, yet I am clear in opinion his intentions were both sincere & honest.[3]

The next most singular, or excentric, and at the same time one of the most worthy characters, I early got acquainted with was George Gray, the son of Gilbert, & half brother to William Gray, —he was bound apprentice to a Man of the Name of Jones, a fruit painter; this man who I believe was accounted eminent in his profession–lived bejond his income & departed from Newcastle–George being thus left to himself, commenced in the same way of business–greatly succeeded in it–and then also became eminent as a fruit painter–this he pursued many years–but from his versatility of disposition, he dipped into almost every art & science & became of first rate estimation in many of them–he was accounted one of the best of botanists & chemists in this country–he was also a Geologist, and was fixed upon as a leader or director to a party, employed by Prince Poniatowsky, to take a survey of the various strata of Poland–but George, from the slovenly appearance of his dress, in which he was very negligent,–felt himself slighted & left those who put on a more respectable appearance, to profit by his superiour knowledge to do the best they could & he returned home.—Whether it was before or after this time, I have forgot, but he paid a visit to North America & travelled in quest of knowledge pretty far back into the interiour of that country—He returned home to his old employment & there in a Room, never cleaned nor swept out he pursued his business—surrounded with models, Crucibles, gallow pots,[1] brushes & paints—Pallets—bottles, Jars, Retorts & Distills, in such a chaos of confusion as no words can describe—from this Sanctum Sanctorum, he corresponded with Gentlemen of science in London & other parts—few men were better liked by several private friends of this character—as well for his knowledge as for his honesty & the genuine simplicity of his manners—he died on the 9th of December 1819 Aged 61 years, & was buried in St John's Church yard.

In addition to the various jobs already noticed, as keeping my master and myself, so fully employed—I had others which fell exclusively to my lot to execute, & these were the Mathematical Figures for Charles Hutton.[2] This frequently drew him into the Room, in which I worked, to inspect what I was doing—he was always very civil but seemed to me to be of a very grave or shy deportment—he lived in habits of intimacy with my Master, & at that time used occasionally to write pieces for him to engrave from, but particularly for the Heads of Invoices or Bills of parcels—& I remember well his writing them with an Ink or preparation which was easily transferred to the Copper—this was before his appointment in the Royal Military Academy of Woolwich in 1773 & long before he had the well merited title of LLD added to his respected Name.—Dr Hutton was that kind of man who never forgot his old friends and some years after this, when I was in partnership with my old Master, he recommended us to the notice of Dr Horsley,* who was commencing his publication of the whole of Sir Isaac Newton's Works—Materials were furnished us, on which to give an estimate of the expense of the whole. For this purpose, my partner first took this business into consideration, & when done, it next became my turn to estimate & when we were both done, these were compared & the difference being trifling—a line was drawn between them & sent to Dr Hutton & our charge was quite agreed to—when without delay, the figures were begun upon & being now quite expert at this kind of Work, the execution

* Afterward Bishop of St Asaph

of the whole devolved upon me—This transaction took place in the [year] 1778.

But before this period, I still continued to take up my abode with N[d] Hatfield & the spirits being bouyant every thing pleased me. I cannot help noticing the happy time I spent with him–I was also entertained with the curious characters who resorted to his house–these were mostly Bird catchers & Bird dealers, with whose narratives respecting their pursuits, I listened to with some interest while they were enjoying themselves over a Tankard of Beer.–Ned was almost constantly busied in rearing a very numerous brood of Canaries, which he sold to a bird Merchant, who travelled with them at set times to Edinburgh, Glasgow &c for sale—I also at various periods of the time I remained under his Roof, got fully into a knowledge of the misguided ways, which too many young fellows pursued–and I watched, & saw the wretched consequences of the kind of life they led–The first of these was a young man from the country of a hale healthy look & also of a good disposition, whose friends had it in their power & intended to enable him to prosper in the world, but he was chopped down in his *youthfull prime* solely by his connecting himself with the bad Women of the Town & becoming perfectly tainted by his intercourse with them–two others, his companions, the same as to health, vigour & prospects in life as himself, fell sacrifices in the same way.–I felt grieved for them and did all in my power to dissuade them from pursuing such a wretched course of life–for this advice they laughed at me & called me "the old man"–it was not very long, however, after this 'till two of them sent for me to come & see them–*on their death beds*–the die was then cast–and I cannot forget their thanks to me & the bitterness with which they reproached themselves for not listening to what I had so sincerely recommended–Doctors may palliate this odious disease, thus contracted–and some may think in certain stages of it that it can be routed out of the habit–but this I think is doubtfull–and under this impression I think that men so patched up, ought never to be allowed to marry, for [fear of] a tainted innocent offspring, and an endless train of diseases, which must continue to puzzel Medical Men, & mostly appear in one shape or other to hang upon them for life–Another young fellow (& I am done with them) whose prospects in life was as fair as those I have described, but whose character was of the basest kind, had led a similar course of life, & had got the disease patched up & shocking to relate he married –yes he married–as healthy, beautiful & innocent young woman as could be seen–with a fortune too–Well in due time there appeared a prospect of his becoming a father–the time came–but it is too shocking & disgusting to relate further particulars–Shortly after this, he married another young woman of a similar description as the last, and a similar wretched fate attended her–for a great length of time after this I lost sight of him, but by chance fell in with him again, when he accosted me with all the familiarity of an old acquaintance & fellow lodger–I was so overpowered with disgust that a civil return was out of my power to give him.–So said I and is it you, I suppose you think, by your having turned Methodist you will rub off your enormous crimes–no no you may think that preaching & praying will wipe off the stain–but I think not, and in the heat of my indignation, forgot myself & said if I were God I never would forgive you–What God may do in his infinite mercy I know not–He died in his prime a short time after this. Such conduct as I have been attempting to describe appears to me to be of the very blackest die, it is amongst the most cruel & the most shocking of murders–It is to be regretted that the seducer & the seduced, cannot, by any known law, be obliged to live together for life, & while they lived–to be allowed to herd only with such as themselves, for they ought to be banished from the society of the modest & virtuous part of the community–I think it a great omission in parents & teachers, not to make unguarded youth fully apprized of the risques they run, in Towns, of getting acquainted with the lost & polluted women of this stamp –nothing can be so sure a guard against this vice, as that of making young men see it in its true light to be disgusted at it—Magistrates, no doubt, have it in their power, in some degree to lessen this great evil, by preventing bad women from appearing in the Streets of a Town & perhaps in Brothells–but I have often felt for Magistrates on account of the great & gratuitous trouble they take & the difficulties they must have to encounter in their endeavours to keep the Wicked within due bounds.

My last fellow lodgers & associates at Ned Hatfield's, before I was done with my Apprenticeship, was John Hymers (or Hindmarsh) who had been a Sergeant in the Life Guards & had retired upon his Pension–and Whitaker Shadforth, Clock & watch maker & also a Musician*. The latter was of a quite different character from those before noticed, but was wild enthusiastic & romantic–When he first came to lodge with us, he had a pale pasty & unhealthy look, with his stomach quite out of order–for the amendment of which, I began to prescribe for him & for this purpose I ordered him to prepare a quantity of warm camomile tea & then to set himself to work in smoking several pipes of tobacco–the effect produced by these kept him up all night, but gave him a most thorough clensing, and in a little time he appeared with a ruddy complexion & in good health–I next put him upon the same way of living as that I practised myself & in this he persevered untill he became strong and active–Among the many whims & fancies, which we indulged in, one of them was to learn the manual exercise–the Sergeant who had often laughed at our frolics very readily agreed to undertake this task, provided we would stricktly obey the rules he prescribed to us–this we agreed to–he begun a kind of Lecture upon the necessity of Soldiers being obedient to their officers & to stand like a brick wall without flinching, adding that he would not use his cane upon our backs but only to put us in mind that we should be very attentive–this being settled, we were in the mornings to appear before him in *bare buff*, that is without our shirts & upper clothing–this discipline we pursued steadily for sometime, notwithstanding the switches he gave us on our bare backs with his rod or cane–which we both bore with the utmost *sang froid*–I think the serjeant, notwithstanding the entertainment we thus afforded him, begun to tire first, for he at last lay in bed while he was giving us our lessons, & at length gave the business up–

From the length of time I had known & noticed Miss Beilby, I had formed a strong attachment to her, but could not make this known either to her or to any one else–I would have married her before I was done with my apprenticeship without any fears on my part–but I felt for her & pined & fretted at so many barrs being in the way against any union of this kind–one of the greatest was the supposed contempt, in which I was held by the rest of the family, who I thought treated me with great hateur, 'tho I had

* he left England & went to America before the War broke out between the two Countries & when this happened, he was obliged to serve in the American Army.

done every thing in my power to oblige them–I had like a stable boy waited upon their Horse & had cheerfully done every thing they wanted at my hands–'till one of the Brothers grossly affronted me in the business of the stable–this I instantly resented & refused attendance there any more–before I was out of my time Miss Beilby had a paralitic or palsy stroke, which very greatly altered her look & rendered her for sometime unhappy–she long after this[1] went with her eldest brother into Fifeshire where she died.

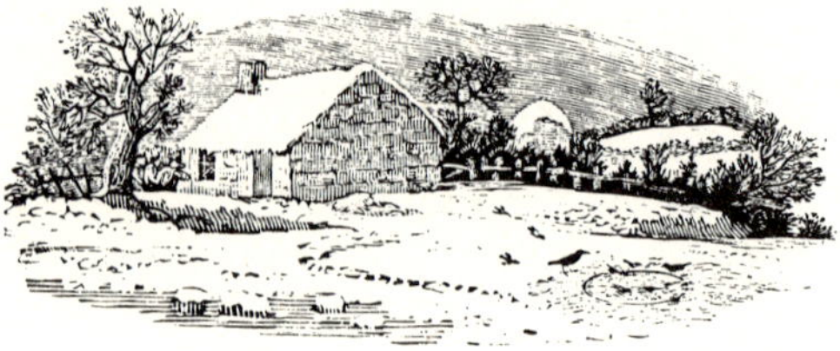

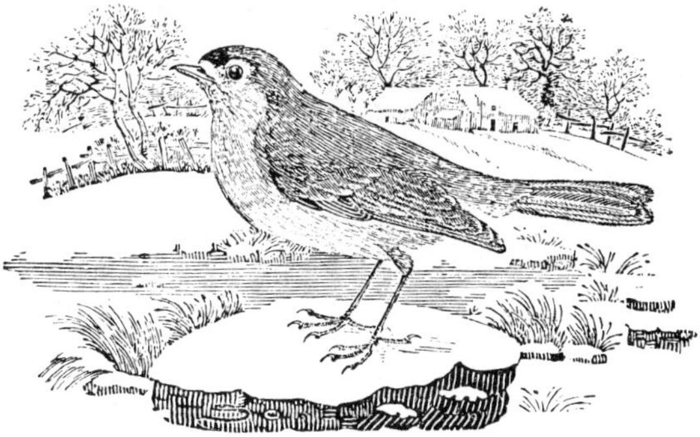

[6]

–The first of October 1774 arrived at last & for the first time in my life I felt myself at liberty–I wrought a few weeks with my old master & then set off to spend the winter at Cherryburn–there I had plenty of work to do, chiefly from my friend Thomas Angus, the printer in Newcastle–I continued there, employed by him & others and when wanted, by my old Master, 'till the summer of 1776. This was a time of great enjoyment, for the charms of the country was highly relished by me, and after so long an almost abscence from it, gave even that relish a zest, which I have not words to express–I continued to follow wood cutting & other jobs, but often rambled about among old neighbours & became more & more attached to them as well as to my country. In the storms of winter (as before noticed) I joined the Nimrods of old,–in spring & summer my favourite sport of angling, was pretty closely followed up–About Christmas, (as I had done before when a boy) I went with my father to a distance to collect the money due to him for his Coals–In these rounds I had the opportunity of *seeing* the kindness & hospitality of the People–the countenances of all, both high & low, beamed with cheerfulness, and this was heightened every where, by the music of old Tunes from the well known exhilerating wild notes of the Northumberland pipes,[1] amidst the buz occasioned by various *foulploughs* (morrice or sword dancers) from various parts of the Country–These altogether left an impression on my mind, *which the cares of the World* have never effaced from it–The Gentry, the Farmers & even the working people of that day had their Christmas home brewed Ale, made only from malt & hops before the pernicious use of chemical or druggists' compounds were known, or Agricultural improvements had quickened the Eyes of Landlords–banished many small farmers–soured their countenances, and altered the characters for the worse of the larger ones that remained.

Having all my life, at home, at school & during my apprenticeship lived under perpetual restraints–when I thus felt myself at liberty, I became as I suppose, like a bird which had escaped from its Cage–even angling of which I was so fond, and of which I thought I never could tire, became rather dull, when I found I might take as much of it as I pleased–While I was pursuing this sport, on a hot day in June–I gave it up & laying down my rod awhile–I then tied it up & walked home–having resolved to see more of the country. I requested my mother to put me up some Shirts &c & I told her I was going to see my uncle (her Brother) in Cumberland–this was soon done amidst her expressions of fears for my safety, and shewing the natural feelings of a good mother–after sewing three Guineas in my Breeches waistband–I set off that afternoon & walked to Haydon-bridge–here I visited my old crony Thomas Spence, (then a teacher in Haydon-bridge School) with whom I was a welcome guest, and with whom I stopped two days & leave of abscence from school being given, I rambled with him over the neighbourhood & visited every thing worth notice–When I departed he accompanied me on the Road nearly to Haltwhistle –After this I met with little to attract notice except Naworth Castle, & when I left it and in proceeding across the country I lost my way by following paths which led only to holes, which had been made by digging peats & turf, and did not reach my uncles house at Ainstable, till late in the Evening—I remained at Ainstable about a week in which time I rambled about the neighbourhood–visited my friends at Kirkoswald & elsewhere & spent what time I could spare in fishing for trout in the Croglin–& after I had seen Armthwaite & Penrith, I began to think of moving farther abroad –and my cousin having occasion to go to Carlisle I went with him there–where we parted–I wandered about the old City & in the afternoon looked into the shop of Lowrey the Watchmaker, to whom I was only known, so far as having been employed by my master engraved many Clock faces for him during my Apprenticeship–While I was in his shop in came a Man a *kind of scamp* of the Name of Graham, who asked me what road I was going–to Scotland I replied–so am I said he, and added if you can keep foot with me I will be glad of your company–We had no sooner set off 'till I found he was one of those vapouring fops who was very proud of his great prowess as a pedestrian–I could soon see that he wanted to walk me *off my foot*, but having been long trained or practised in this way he felt himself mistaken & long before we reached Longtown he called in at several public houses for a refreshment & invited me to do the same–I however was not thirsty & not being used to drink, I sat on the seats at the doors untill he came out–he kept on in this way 'till we reached Langholm, when he surveyed me with an attentive eye but said nothing –At Langholm, the landlord, who was a Cumberland man & knew my relatives there, was very kind to me, and among many other matters concerning them–he told me, my cousin who accompanied me to Carlisle had won nine Belts in his wrestling matches, in that county–From Langholm I set off to Hawick & Selkirk & from that place, next morning by Dalkeith to Edinburgh–I had been, in this short tramp, particularly charmed with the Border scenery, the roads, in places twined about the bottoms of the hills, which looked beautifully green like velvet, spotted over with the white sheep which grazed on their sides–watched by the peacefull shepherd & his dog–I could not help depicturing in my mind–the change of scenery which had taken place in these times, & comparing them with the times of old that had passed away, & in inwardly rejoicing at the happy reverse.—It is horrid to contemplate upon the ferocious battles of that day between Men discended from the same stock & bearing the same names, on both sides of the border, only divided from each other by a River, a Rivulet, a Burn or a stripe of ground–[that they] should be called out to the wild Foray, by the Slogan horn, or at the nod of their chieftains be gathered together, by the shrill notes of the Bugle & led on to meet & slaughter each other–to manure the ground with their blood, amidst the clash of Arms–& the thrilling music of their pipes which helped to exert them on to close their eyes in death–These transactions, which is handed down to their descendants of the present generation, in traditionary tales, & kept in remembrance by the songs & tunes of old times, serve only now as food for reflection or amusement–

On entering Edinburgh, having been recommended by Mr Robertson, Silversmith,[1] to the Landlord of the George Inn, Bristoe Port, I halted there, but being quite unacquainted with the customs of living in such places–I knew not what to do, or how to conduct myself–I however called for a Pint of Beer, & I think it was the first I ever called for in my life, when lo! a good looking Girl, bare footed & bare legged entered with a pewter pot almost the size of a half leg of a Boot–this I thought I could not empty in a week–As I found I could not remain in this place, I sought about for another, & luckily fell in with an old Newcastle acquaintance Mrs Hales the wife (or widow) of – Hales, the coachman to Lord chief Baron Ord–to her I stated my case–went with her & felt quite at home in her House–After I had seen as much of *Auld Reeky* as I could, lost in admiration at the grandeur of its situation, and also the grandeur of its internal old buildings–I then next day called upon Hector Gavin, an Engraver in Parliament Close–this kind man, a stranger to me,–when after having had a bit of chat with him about the Arts &c he threw by his tools and was quite at my service–The warmth of his kindness I never can forget–he took me all over Edinburgh & gave me a history & explanation of every thing he thought worthy of notice–Having parted with him with his best & warmest wishes–I rose early on the next morning & walked to Glasgow & after leaving my Bundle at the Inn there to which Mr Robertson, had also recommended me, I took a ramble through Glasgow–here I fell in (by chance) with an old acquaintance Alexr Steedman a clever Cutler, who had lodged with me, at Ned Hatfields, and who I supposed was dead long ago–he was not like me, for he could drink plenty–so that I was at no loss what to do at the Inn, as I had been in Edinburgh–he called upon me the next morning, along with a curious & well informed man, when they shewed me every thing they thought worth notice in Glasgow,–I could see that Glasgow was a large City with many handsome buildings in it, but I was not so charmed with it as I had been with Edinburgh–

From Glasgow I set off to Dumbarton & on my way took as

good a survey of the country and whatever was new to me or curious, as I could–My Landlord at Dumbarton had seen a deal of the World, either as a soldier or as a Gentleman's Servant, was very kind & communicative to me & I think I spent the next day with him in walking about & viewing every thing that he could think of that might please or entertain me–After leaving him, I wished much to see the cotton works & the printing of it, at the printfields,[1] as they were called, on the River Leven near Dumbarton. To these however I could not get admission–so I kept passing onward up the Leven, 'till Smolletts monument, near the side of it arrested my attention. Here I stopped, for I had read Smolletts Works and almost adored him as an Author–On the Pedestal of the Monument was a long latin inscription,[2] which I was endeavouring to translate into English, but in this I was puzzled to make it out, having never looked into a latin Book since I left school & this was the first time I felt mortified at having done so[3]–while I was thus employed, up came a *leish*[4] clever young man a Highlander, smartly dressed in the garb of his country–he jumped down beside me & begun his translation, which we together made out–When this was done, on learning from me that my sole object was to see Scotland, he pressed me to accompany him, to some place or other, the name [of] which I do not now remember–we however walked on the western side of Loch Lomond, along way together, but I know I did not visit Inverary the Seat of Argyle–but stopt with him at a Graziers or Farmers house perhaps not a long way from it—Having made up my mind not to visit any City or Town, nor to put up at any Inn–I commenced my *Wild Goose chase* & bent my way in many a zig zag direction through the interiour of part of the Highlands–by the sides of its Lakes & its mountains–the beauty & serenity of the former & the grandeur or terrific aspect of the latter I gazed upon with wonder & with both, was charmed to extacy–In moving forward I was often accompanied or directed to some Farmers or Graziers House, by the herds or drovers which I fell in with, & in some of these Houses I took up my abode and often by the pressing solicitation of my host or hostess was prevailed upon to remain with them for a day or two—These kind, these hospitable people I never forgot–often, the Mistress of the House, in these remote places, never having seen any person from England, examined my dress from head to foot & in English which it was easy to discover, had been imperfectly taught her, made many enquiries respecting the country from whence I came, while the Herds with their bare knees sat listning around, very seldom knowing what we were talking about–These herds or some of the family generally set or directed me to the house of some other distant Grazier, where I met with the same kind & warm reception, throughout my wanderings as I had experienced at first–It sometimes happened that by my having stopped too long on my way in admiration of the varied prospects I met with, that I was benighted and was obliged to take shelter under some rockey projection, or to lay myself down among the heather 'till day light–In my traversings & wanderings, I called in at all the Houses on my way, whether situated in the beautifull little vallies, watered by a brook, a burn or rivulet–or those in Glens, or on the sides [of the] heathery hills–In these places, it was common to see three houses, one added to the end [of] another–the first containing the young healthy looking children, of the last married couple--in the next or middle one was the father & mother & perhaps the brothers & sisters of this couple, and farther in, at the end, was the habitation of the old people, the Grandfather & Grandmother of the whole–these places had alway Garths or Gardens adjoining–with peat stacks & other fuel at hand, for the winter & the whole enlivened with numbers of Duck, Chickens &c–On my getting some refreshment of Whey or Milk &c, in such like places as these, I always found it difficult to get payment made for any thing–as it seemed to give offence–and when I could get any money slipped into the hands of the Children, I was sure to be pursued & obliged to accept of a pocket full of Bannocks & Scones–On one occasion, having been detained all day & all night at a house of this kind, in listning to the tunes of a young man of the family, who played well upon the scottish pipes & my having in turn whistled several Tyneside tunes to him, we could hardly get seperated–Before my departure, next day, I contrived, by stealth to put some money into the hands of the children –I had not got far from the House 'till I was pursued by a beautifull young woman, who accosted me in *baddish* english, which she must have got off by *heart* just before she left the house, the purport of which was to urge my acceptance of the usual present. This I wished to refuse, but she pressed it upon me, with such sweetness & with a face & neck blushed with scarlet, while I thought, at the same time she invited me to return–on which (I could not help it) I seized her & smacked her lips–she then sprung away from me, with her bare leggs, like a Deer, & left me fixed to the spot, not knowing what to do–I was particularly struck with her whole handsome appearance, it was a compound of loveliness, health & agility–her hair I think had been flaxen or light, but was tanned to a pale sandy brown, by being exposed to the Sun–this was tied behind with a ribbon & dangled down her back, and as she bounded along it flowed in the air–I had not seen her while I was in the House, & felt grieved because I did not hope ever to see her more—After having wandered about in this way for sometime longer, in which I uniformly met with the same kind treatment, among these unpoluted, unspoiled, honourable & kind people, I began to think of the long way I had to get over on my return towards home, for although my money was not greatly diminished among the Highlanders yet I knew not how much I might want in or near towns, in more *civilized* districts–so I turned back in a south easterly direction through the country where I met, in my various windings, among the same kind of people, the same warm & friendly reception—from that time to this I have ever felt pleased at the name of Highlander–Were not these people proof against the bribe, of thirty thousand pounds, held out to them to betray the unfortunate prince Charles Stewart?–have not *agricultural improvements* taught the Landlords or chieftains, to whose forefathers they owed so much, to turn numerous farms into one? & by that means banished thousands of these hardy descendants of the Ancient Britons–these brave race of men, to seek an Assylum in foreign climes, and in exchange for whom, they have peopled the country with sheep. Property in every country ought to be held sacred, but it ought also to have its bounds, & (in my opinion) to be in a certain degree held in trust jointly for the benefit of its owners & the good of society of which they form a part–bejond this is despotism, the offspring of misplaced aristocratic pride—I have not noticed that I was sometimes, in passing along detained at fairs or Trysts–these with their merry makings, were something like the hoppings[1] & feasts on Tyne side & the Girls had the same ruddy look as the farmers servants who were put to do field work in Northumberland & Durham–with the

Scotch music & dancing I was very much pleased–they were certainly good dancers & seemed quite wild or exhilerated to excess–

LINES

Written in a Steam Boat, on leaving Scotland, by S. W. Riley, author of the "Itinerant," &c. July, 1819.

Farewell ye sweet, health-breathing, untainted gales—
Farewell mighty mountains—farewell lovely vales—
Farewell classic country, thou high-favour'd ground,
Where the great names of Burns and of Scott may be found—
Farewell Bannock-burn, and those plains of renown
Famed for unequal contests 'twixt people and crown;
Where numbers and skill were deprived of their use,
By the personal courage of Wallace and Bruce;
Tho' oppos'd ten to one, yet their cause was so pure,
That the yell of the pibrach made victory sure;
Success smil'd on freedom, sweet, fair-featur'd omen,
Like the silver complexion of lovely Loch Lomon—
Farewell to all these, and ten thousand times more—
Farewell rural country, that none can explore
Without feeling a pleasure ne'er tasted before!
That land surly Johnson once left in a pet,
I entered with pleasure, and leave with regret.
Thus I thought—thus I mused--and became heavy-hearted—
Said once more *farewell*—heaved a sigh--and departed.

[*Mitchell, Printer, Newcastle.*]

I left this country with regret–and the last days journey from it was a very long one, & a very hungry one, after which, I was obliged to enter Stirling in the night–I told the Landlord of the public house, that I was almost famished not having stopt at any house on my very long journey to that place–and begged of him to hasten to get me something to eat–he told me, he had nothing left but Eggs, for his company, that day had eaten every thing that had been in [the] house quite up–I did not get my Eggs 'till midnight, for a quarrel or an affray happened in the House at the time I ought to have had them–they were brought in to me at last & were boiled as hard as Eggs could be–with them in my eagerness to eat I was nearly choaked–At Stirling I remained about two or 3 days, chiefly on acc[t] of my face having been so blistered by the heat of the Sun, that I thought it best to halt 'till the effects of it could be removed–my landlord was very kind & was also one of those who had seen the world–when he found that I was an

Engraver, he expressed his surprize that I had not carried my tools with me, for if I had done so, he said he had no manner of doubt, with my knowledge of heraldry &c that I could have found plenty of employment among the gentry, & the Lairds in engraving their arms, crests & other devices–& have earned easily far more than double the money of our Newcastle charges, besides being handed from chief to chieftain, & seeing the whole country in a very different way from that which I had, through wildernesses so wildly pursued–On my way to Edinburgh by Falkirk, I visited Carron Works[1] & passed under the Canal, where for the first time I saw Vessels passing over my head–I was also shewn the ground where the Battle of Bannockburn was fought–As soon as I could, I made my way by Linlithgow to Edinburgh, & took up my abode again with Mrs Hales–and having engaged a passage by sea, in a ship belonging to Whitby which had to *touch* at Shields I attended upon this Vessel every tide late & early for several days–and at last I missed my time & was left behind–In this emergency I got on board a Leith Sloop, bound for Newcastle, commanded by Capt Kay, then moving from the Pier–We no sooner got down the Firth of Forth to the open sea than we met a very heavy swell, & presently was suddenly attacked by a violent gale which soon tore our *sails to shivers* & drove us far out of sight of land. This put our small crew in a great bustle & dilemma–In this small vessel the whole people & crew amounted to 26, for these there was no accomodation–the Boat upon deck was full of the sick, covered by an old sail, & the rest were obliged to sit or to *lie* down in any corner where they could find a bit of room–the first night was a sickly suffocating one & for three more, & three days (the length of our voyage to Shields) there was little or no amendment of our situation–on board this sloop there were only two beds, that were not stowed with goods, and from my wanting rest, so long before I left Edinburgh, I crept into one of them as soon as I could, but found it so low, that I could not lie on my side, nor easily turn over, so I could get no sleep & to mend the matter I had not been long in this wretched bed 'till a sucking infant was put in beside me, its mother being dismally sick in the boat upon deck–& the child fell exclusively into my charge. I nursed it as well as I could during the whole voyage & I think had I not done so it must have died–After resting a day or two at S^o^ Shields I set off to Newcastle, where I arrived (in the Assize Week) I think on the 12 Augt 1776–after all my long abscence, I found I had a few shillings left–On this occasion my old friends in Newcastle quizzed me not a little, for having as they termed it, begged my way through Scotland–[1]

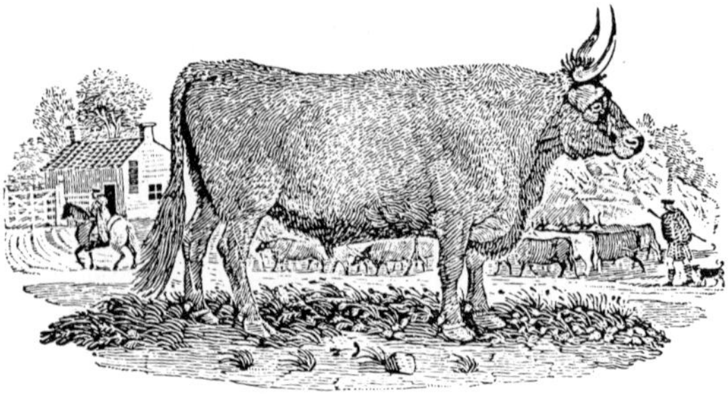

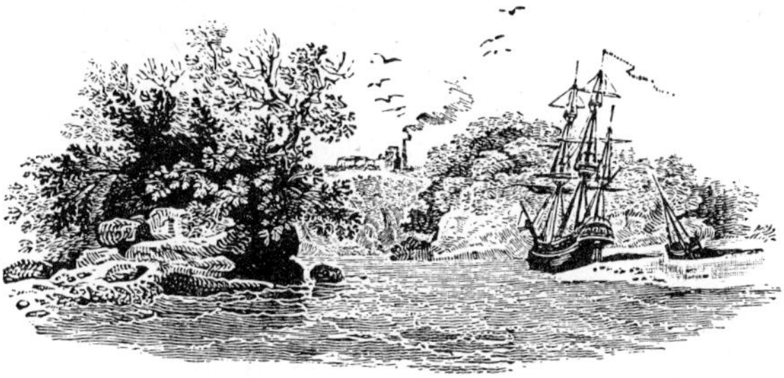

[7]

I remained no longer in Newcastle than untill I earned as much money as would pay my way to London, & I then took my passage on board a Collier bound to the Great City–and after beating about in good weather & bad weather for about three weeks, we arrived in London on the 1st of October 1776.–The first Cockney I met with was the scullar man, who was engaged to land me & my baggage at Carnegie's the hair dresser near Temple Barr–I was amused with his slang & his chatter all the way to London Bridge–and on his approaching it, he asked me if I was *affeared*, but not knowing what I was to be affraid of, I asked him the same question at which he looked *quere*–and in this way we passed the gulph, about which he wanted to talk, & I then asked him if he had been *affeard.*—It was not long before I found out my old school-fellows Chrisr & Philip Gregson, & my old companion Willm Gray, now a Bookbinder in Chancery lane, and my old friend Robert Pollard–the first had provided me with a Lodging, & the last, through the kindness & the influence of his Master, Isaac Taylor, with plenty of Work–Before I sat down to work, I thought it best to take a ramble through every part of both the City & its environs –The first day I went alone & saw nobody I knew–on the second day I fell in, by chance with Serjeant Hymers, in the Strand–who on seeing me, seemed quite surprized–he held up both his hands–he looked–he laughed–shook me by the hand over & over again & seemed not to know how to be kind enough–he then took me back with him, 'till he got himself dressed, & when this was done, he made a very handsome appearance indeed–The rest of this day he wholly devoted to my service–He first took me to the blackguard places in London–I supposed this was with a view to corroborate the truth of the stories he had before told me in Newcastle–After I had seen enough of these places, he then took me to others of a more respectable character better worth notice –After rambling about afterwards with my warm friend the Serjeant, 'till I had seen a good deal of the interiour & the exteriour of London–of which it would be surpluflous to give an Account–I then sat down closely to work, untill I got through the Wood Cuts, which through Isaac Taylor's kindness had been provided for me–I then called upon Thomas Hodgson, printer in Georges Court Clerkenwell who had also provided Work for me, to meet my arrival in London & who had waited impatiently for my Assistance.*

Having served my time, as a kind of "Jack of all trades"–I felt desirous to Work among the Cockneys, to see if I could find any thing new among them, but in this I was disappointed–for I never could be permitted to see any of them at work–they indeed seemed desirous of seeing what I was doing, & occasionally peeped in upon me for that purpose–and I thought such of them as did so were a most saucy ignorant & impudent set. Where ever I went the ignorant part of the Cockneys, called me "Scotchman". At this I was not offended, but when they added other impudent remarks, I could not stand them, & this often led me into quarrels such as I wished to avoid & had not been used to engage in–It is not worth while noticing these, but only as they served to help out my dislike to London–but this was only trivial compared with other matters–The first of these that struck me & what constantly hurt my feelings, was the seeing of such a number of fine looking women engaged in the wretched business of *Street Walking*. Of these, I often enquired as to the cause of their becoming so lost to themselves & to the world–their account of this in their common replies was that they had been seduced & then basely betrayed.

* Thomas Hodgson[1] had served his Apprenticeship as a printer to John White of Newcastle (before named) and having taken a liking to wood ingraving, he employed most of his time in embellishing the endless number printed at that office of the old Ballads & Histories, with rude devices as head-pieces to them–He was a most assiduous, carefull & recluse Man–What he published in London, I cannot enumerate the number of–but I understood he employed some Germans as well as myself, to cut blocks for him, he also employed me to make designs, for many of these Cuts.–When he died he left me a legacy of five Pounds–& this was the first money I ever rec[d] that I had not wrought for.

This I believed & I was grieved to think that they were thus prevented from becoming, perhaps the best of mothers to an offspring of lovely & healthy children–this I often told them & this ended in their tears,–& if they were in poverty I contributed my mite to relieve them.

What a pity this wretchedness is not prevented–base men treat women as if they were inferiour beings made only to be used like brutes & tiranized over as their slaves–I have always beheld such conduct towards women with abhorrence for my conceptions of this wretched state of things are of the most soul harrowing description–It would be extreme weakness to maintain an opinion that all women were good & that the faults here noticed were always ascribeable to the men only–this is not the case, for I must be obliged to admit that there are good & bad of each sex–I have often attempted to make an estimate of their comparative numbers. in which I have felt some difficulties–sometimes my Barometer of estimation has arisen to the height of ten to one in favour of the fair sex–at other times it has fluctuated & fallen down some degrees lower in the scale, but (with me), it is now settled & I cannot go lower, than four good women to one good man.—I have often wondered how any man could look healthy beautifull, sensible & virtuous women in [the] face, without considering them as the link between Men & angels, for my part I often felt my self so overpowered with reverence in their prescence that I have been almost unable to speak & they must often have noticed my embarresment–I could mention the names of many but it might offend their delicacy–Where a *good* man can get such a help-mate for life–his happiness must be secured for such a one is of inestimable value–"her price is far above Rubies". On seeing such, & indeed others of the fair sex, I always inwardly thought, or muttered out–I cannot bless them,–I would if I could–but may God bless them.

In London one man does one branch of business & another another of the same kind of work & it is by this division of labour they thus accomplish so much & so well–I however soon tired of thus working alone, and as I had plenty of work to do on my own account, from my former friends, to which were added Mr Carnan & Mr Newbury of St Pauls church yard–I turnd my back upon the Masters who took in all kinds of work–& stuck to working for myself–[1]

–Having now been weaned from taking bread & Milk–I had learned by degrees to call for a pint of Porter, & often spent the evenings in the George, in Brook street, kept by a person of the name of Darby–whose wife, a very good looking woman, from Cumberland, claimed a distant relationship to me–At this House I often spent my Evenings among some very respectable & pleasant tradesmen–While I was there one Evening, a stranger to me joined with us, I think he was a traveller, he had however been in Scotland & had a mighty itch to speak very disrespectfully of that country & was vociforous in attempting to entertain the company with his account of the filth & dirt he had met with in it–this I could not bear–their kindness was fresh in my memory & I felt resentment rising in me. I however quashed that feeling–and only told him, that I believed I had travelled on foot, perhaps about 300 miles, through Scotland & had met with no such people there, nor such dirtiness as he described, there might indeed be some such in every country, for ought I knew–but that I was confident such might be found without going much bejond the street we were in & who in addition to their filthiness, were also the most wretched & abandoned of the human race–some of them indeed appeared to me to be scarcly human–I concluded by observing that I was affraid he had been keeping very bad company in Scotland–a laugh by this, was raised against him & he felt himself quashed by his own folly—I very frequently visited Westminster Abby, on some part of the Sunday, and on the fore-noons of that day I mostly went with my friend Pollard to hear the Rev^d–Harrison at St Andrews Church Holborn–I sometimes also went to hear eminent preachers at other places–I was once invited by my friend Willm Watson of the treasury (who had married the eldest Miss Beilby) to go with him to hear Dr Dodd preach, at the Magdalen Chappel, but whether this was at the time he was arrested for forgery or not, I am not certain, but I know I never saw him nor heard him preach–I also went with Mr Watson to a place of this kind to hear the Rev^d–Maxwell another eminent divine, but indeed I believe I did not miss hearing any of the popular preachers in London–For many years after I left London I still kept on in the same way & went occasionally to hear the preachers of various persuasions, and attempted to find out the general Character of their several Congregations–Having been brought up under the Creeds & doctrines of the Church of England, I *may* perhaps have some partialities about me respecting it, but I have ever considered that its Clergy were the most learned of any & that (excepting some of the higher orders of them) they were, as well as their hearers the most tolerant—But I have ever felt greived that such a great number of them should consist of very learned & good men, with Curacies or poor livings, that did not afford them a much better income than the wages of common Mechanics, & that however great their abilities might be, it was only by patronage, that they could be advanced, while enormous stipends were lavished upon others, very often for the most useless, or perhaps the most corrupt purposes–I think it would be much better if their incomes could be equallized–but so long as matters are managed otherwise so long will it be considered a system of revenue, of which Religion is only the pretext—The Roman Catholic mode of faith is the oldest & they seem the most of any sect attached to it & its old customs & its old creeds, which they seem obstinately to value & persist in–and this most likely will continue, so long as they give up their own reason & implicitly obey that dictated to them by their Priests–they are the strictist of all disiplinarians in their Worship–and are also generally good members of society—The next, & most numerous sect, are the Methodists, and I fear if they had the upper hand they would soon shew a persecuting spirit but which I hope will never more be suffered to rear its head–this Sect took their rise under the able auspices of John Wesley & at that time he did a great deal of good –in this neighbourhood, it was soon made to appear for he greatly civilized a numerous host of demi barbarians, the Pitmen & others employed in the coal works,–these seemed like tribes of Cherokees & Mohawks, but they were more wicked–What I have ever been able to discover of the general character of this Sect is that a great number of them are ignorant bigotted Fanatics–before I left off going to hear them, it appeared clear to me, that their discourses, from the Pulpit, were mostly unintelligible & the more so this appeared to be, the more numerously were the congregations crouded together to hear such preachers & their jargon. There is another sect growing into great importance as a religious society & that is the Quakers–The "Friends" as they properly denominate themselves–they have many excellent rules laid down by which to regulate their conduct in life, & with all their peculiarities–their simplicity of manners command the respect of the thinking part of mankind–They have, it is true, been characterized as "English Jews" by some, and others have said of them, that they are not now a religious Society, like the Methodists–"they are an aristocratical civil community; a trading company, and a set of respectable, industrious economical, money getting disciplinarians; who possess no more practical religion than the members of the church of England". This may no doubt be the opinion of some, but I could never form such a one, of at least, the great majority of them for they appear to me to deserve a better character–I wish, indeed, to see them leave off a part of their Puritanical appearance & some other stiffnesses in their deportment–Were all men Quakers, I think the world would have a very sombre appearance–but this is balanced by their keeping their word,–by their detestation of war & by their constant endeavours to live in peace with all men–I have often wondered at their rejecting Music–Music is an emanation from heaven–it is perfectly natural to man, to drive away gloom & to solace & to chear him–The beautifull choristers of the Woods & the Fields lead the way & set us the example–

The Unitarians are generally a well informed & respectable description of Men–they think for themselves, and are not bewildered with dogmas and Creeds. But to swell these opinions of mine with a further acc[t] of the peculiarities of each sect–or attempt to go through the numerous descriptions of religionists would be an endless & a dreary task–they ought each of them [to] be made wellcome to follow their own opinions & I can only observe that if they are founded in truth, there can be no fear that they can be injured by unreserved discussion & whatever their creeds may be, there can be no objections to the religion of a virtuous man–It is hoped that this opinion will universally prevail, & that the distinctions & bickerings among different denominations of christians will cease, & the causes of them be thought of no more importance, than whether a man uses his quid of tobacco in the right cheek or in the left.

After this long digression I must now turn my attention again to London. My friend M[r] Watson was very desirous to get me to work with M[r] Pingo in the mint, & from his being so well known & respected, by the Gentlemen in most of the Government offices, he thought this might be easily accomplished–my mind was however bent quite another way, & no more was done for me in this business –The constant attention & kindness of my London friends, whose company I enjoyed was unabated. They walked with me every where & the House of William Gray was a home to me–I met other Newcastle friends every monday night at the Hole in the Wall,[1] Fleet street where I went to see the Newcastle papers. Some of these indeed occasionally wanted assistance & got my last six-pence–At this time I earned a deal of money, & from my habits of temperance I spent little for my own living & thus for the first time, discovered what a small sum was sufficient to make me independant & I never lost sight of the inestimable value of being so–I however, never had a surplus of cash long in my possession, for one or another had occasion for it–and I could not bear to see distress without relieving it—Notwithstanding my being so situated among my friends, & of being so much gratified in seeing such a variety of excellent performances in every Art & science–Painting, statuary, Engraving carving &c were to be seen every day, yet I did not like London–it appeared to me to be a World of itself where every thing in the extreme, might at once be seen–extreme riches–extreme poverty–extreme Grandeur & extreme wretchedness–all of which were such as I had not contemplated upon before. Perhaps I might indeed take too full a view of London on its gloomy side–I could not help it–I tired of it & determined to return home[2]–The Country of my old friends–the manners of the people of that day–the scenery of Tyne side, seemed altogether to form a paradise for me & I longed to see it again—While I was thus turning these matters over in my mind my warm friend & patron Isaac Taylor waited upon me, and upon my telling him I was going to Newcastle, he enquired how long it would be before I returned–never–was my reply, at which he seemed both surprized & displeased–he then warmly remonstrated with me upon this impropriety of my conduct–told me of the prospects before me, and among many other matters, that of his having engaged me to draw in the Duke of Richmonds gallery[3] & urged me strenuously to change my mind–I told him that no temptation of gain, of honour, or of any thing else, however great could ever have any weight with me & that I would even enlist for a Soldier–or go & herd sheep at five shillings ℔ week as long as I lived, rather than be tied to live in London[1]–I told him how sensible I was of his uncommon kindness to me & thanked him for it–My kind friend left me in the Pet, & I never saw him more–he afterwards, when an old man, visited Newcastle, but left it again without my knowing it 'till after he was gone–at this I felt much grieved & disappointed–he did not live long after this–I do not remember how long–but a memoir of him was published in the Annalitical Magazine at the time,[2] together with a letter I had written to him sometime before his death, which he never answered,[3]–he was in his day accounted the best Engraver of embellishments for Books, most of which he designed himself–The Frontispiece to the first Edition of Cunningham's* Poems,[4] was one of his early productions, and at that time my friend Pollard & myself thought it the best thing that ever was done.

–The same kind of persuasions were urged upon me by Mr Hodgson, to remain in London, as had been used by Mr Taylor–which ended in a similar way, he however went further & told me, if I was determined upon leaving London, & would continue to work for him, in Newcastle, he would furnish me with plenty of it, & that he would begin by giving me as much as would keep me employed for two years–this was particularly pleasing to me because I could not bear the thoughts of beginning business in Newcastle in opposition to my old master, for whom I had the greatest respect–this to me appeared like "bring up chickens to peck out your Eyes"–

Having spent the Evening 'till a late hour with my friends at the George in Brook street–& in the morning taken leave of my Landlord & Landlady (Mr & Mrs Kendal) & family, in Whartons Court Holborn–I then posted off to the Pool & got on board of a Collier, & after a very short passage, arrived in sight of St Nicholas Church steeple about the 22 June 1777.

* John Cunningham, the pastoral Poet died Sepr [18] 1773 Æ 43 years & was buried in St John's Church-yard Newcastle.

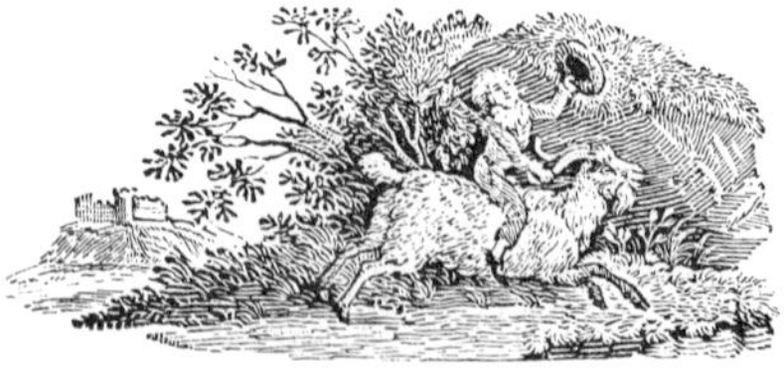

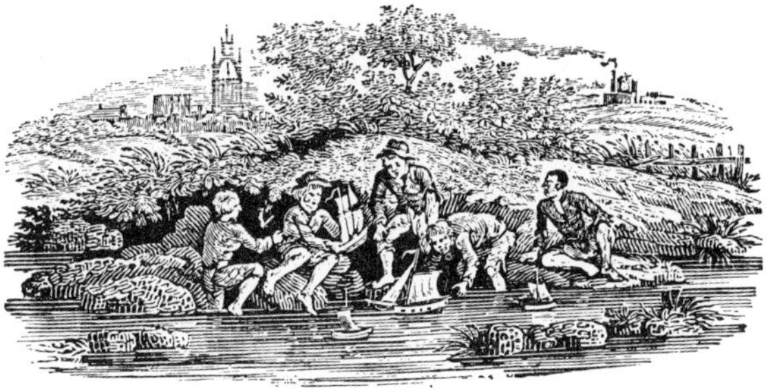

[8]

The first thing, after my arrival in Newcastle was to see my old master & the next to engage my old Lodgings at Ned: Hatfields & to fit up a work bench in it & then to set to work upon my wood Cuts–this was however interrupted by other jobs, & the first of the kind was that of Engraving a Copper plate of the figure of the "Theban Harp"[1] for the Revd James Murray* for some of his publications of which he was the Author of several—some of the Silversmiths also began to press their jobs upon me—I had not, however been long at work for myself, 'till proposals were made to me to join in partnership with my late Master, and this was brought about by our mutual (friend?) John Robertson the silver-smith–This proposal which was to set me down at once in a well established business, I did not relish so warmly, as our mutual friend expected—I had formed a plan of working alone without any assistance from Apprentices, or of being interrupted by any one–and I am not certain at this day whether I would not have been happier in doing so than in the way I was led to pursue–I had often, in my lonely walks, debated this business over in my mind, but whether it would have been for the better or the worse, I can now only conjecture–I tried the one plan & not the other–perhaps

* The Revd James Murray, a Church of Scotland Minister, with whom I had been long acquainted–he was accounted one of the best Hebrew scholars of his day, his "Sermons to Asses" attracted much notice, & so did many of his other works. He was a keen satirical writer in some of his controversies–among his friends he was of a lively, witty & pleasant temper–& greatly valued by a numerous acquaintance, who admired him for his humanity & good sense & much courted his company–He died in 28 Jany 1782–aged 50 years–and was buried in St Andrew's Ch yard.

each way might have had advantages & disadvantages–I would not have experienced the envy and ingratitude of some of my pupils, neither should I, on the contrary, have felt the pride & the pleasure I derived from so many of them having received medals or premiums from the society for the Encouragement of Arts–& also of their taking the lead, as Engravers on Wood in the Metropolis.

Notwithstanding this pride & this pleasure, I am inclined to think I should have had (ballancing the good against the bad) more pleasure in working alone for myself, than with such help, as apprentices afforded, for with some of them I had a deal of turmoil & trouble–and others who shewed capacity & Genious, & perhaps served out their time without an interchange of a cross word between us, yet these, from coming under the guidance of people of an envious & malignant disposition perhaps in unison with their own, were, after every pains & every kindness had been shewn to them, when done, ready to strangle me–I have much reason to remember, on an occasion of my partner & myself, being obliged to take one of the most impudent–malignant & worst apprentices, we ever had,[1] before the Magistrates, one of them (John Erasmus Blackett Esq[r]) calling me to aside, to enquire if I knew his associates, I told him I did, & he sent for some of them & in the mean time told me, he never knew of any *bad* Apprentices being brought before them, who had not been spoiled by the wicked advice of some worthless person or other—It is painful to me to dwell on a subject of this kind, which indeed I might spin out to a great length with much additional matter, but it may be sufficient to observe that I have taken a Boy & behaved to him uniformly with the kindness of a Father or a Brother & have watched with every pains in my power to instruct him–been liberal to him in pecuniary matters–employed the best physician to attend him when he was unwell–let him want for nothing–paid him his wages besides, whether at work or not at work, & in this my partner contributed his share,–and along with myself used every endeavour in our power to advance him in the world, & when all this was done, he shewed not a particle of gratitude, but observed that any "cart-man would take care of his Horse", & then put himself under the guidance & directions of a Company or confedracy of ill disposed envious & malignant persons, who after having laboured to poison the ears of the public & of the Jury–to bring us to trial, for the pay for work done without the leave of his masters, while he was our apprentice! & the business was so managed that a verdict was given against us–I did not fail to attack this Jury individually & to send the confiderates a message, that there was not a man among them who was not a coward & a scoundrel.[1]

During my abscence in London, Mr Beilby had taken an Apprentice,[2] with a premium, and to make us equal, I took my brother John as mine–with my brother, I was extremely happy–we Lodged together, he arose early in the Morning, lighted our fire–blacked our shoes, dusted the Room, made every thing clean for breakfast, as well as any servant Girl could have done & he sewed & mended his own clothes &c and to crown all he was constantly cheerfull, lively & very active, & my friends were his friends–Mr Beilby was also as pleased with him as I could possibly be, for besides his affable temper, he took every kind of work in hand so pleasantly & so very soon learned to execute it well that it could not miss giving satisfaction & this he continued to do as long as he was with us–but other parts of his conduct, when he arrived at Manhood was not so well and gave me great uneasiness, for he got acquainted with company which I thought badly of, & my remonstrances to him respecting them proved in vain, he would not (as he called it) be dictated to by me, but this I persisted in 'till it made us often quarrel–this was distressing to me for my regard for him was too deeply routed, ever to think of suffering him to tread in the paths which led to ruin, without endeavouring to prevent it –to the latest day of his life he repented of his turning a deaf ear to my advise, & as bitterly & sincerely did he acknowledge the slightest obligations he owed me–he *rued*, & that is as painful a word as any in the English language–

As soon as I thought he might be able to work his way in the world, he having been (I think) about five years with me, I gave him his liberty, and he set off for London, where, from his reformed conduct, & where, from every information I could learn, he was much liked & respected–He was as industrious in London as he had been with us & had plenty of work to do–he was almost entirely employed by the Publishers & Booksellers in London, in designing and cutting an endless variety of blocks for them & as he was extremely quick at his work he did it slightly & at a very low rate for them[1]—his too close confinement, however, impared his health & he revisited Cherry-burn, where he did not remain long 'till he thought himself quite recovered & then he returned again to London where he continued a few years longer, & where the same kind of confinement, brought him down as before–a similar visit to his native Air was found necessary, & where his health was again restored to him & he again returned to London–he however found that he could not pursue the same kind of close confinement –on which acct he engaged himself to teach the boys drawing at the Hornsey Academy, then kept by Mr Nathaniel Norton, which obliged him to keep a Pony, on which he rode backwards & forward, & thus dividing his time between his work office in London & the school, for some few years; when his health began again to decline & he finally left London early in the summer of 1795 and returned once more to the banks of the Tyne, where he intended to follow the Wood engraving for his London friends & particularly from William Bulmer, for whom he was engaged to execute a number of Blocks for "Fabliaux or Tales by Le Grand"[2] & for Somervilles Chace–many of the former he (I believe) ⟨with assistants⟩ had finished in London & had sketched others on the blocks which he finished at Cherryburn–he had also sketched the designs on the blocks for the chase[3] & these I put the finishing hand to, after his decease[4]–which happened on the 5 December 1795–Aged 35 years —The last thing I could do for him was putting up a stone to his memory in Ovingham Church yard–where I hope, when my *Glass* is run out to be laid down beside him.

While my Brother was my Apprentice, he frequently accompanied me on my Weekly visits to Cherryburn, he was then a clever springy youth & our bounding along together was often compared to the scamperings of a pair of wild colts. These journeys commenced while I was an Apprentice. I then went & returned on the same day but when I became my own master, I seldom missed a week for years, and for many years throughout, "in Summers heat & winters freezing cold", I did not miss a single one week–When I was an apprentice I had a few days *holly days* at Easter & Whitsuntide allowed me, according to promise, & these were wholly employed in Angling–but after the time came when I might do as I pleased I mostly stopped, when the weather suited in spring and summer, & spent the Mondays in various streams, at this my favourite & indeed only diversion–In this I was accompanied with my cheerfull assosiate Jack Roe with his flies & his tackle & when we had got a number sufficient, I returned that night or the next morning with my Creel filled with fish, which I divided among friends in Newcastle–With an account of these hungry stream wading ramblings & the days spent in Angling, & with a description of the beautiful scenery of water sides & the renovating charms which these together inspired, a Volume might be filled, in imitation of the Patriarch of Anglers, Izaak Walton, as might also one of a descriptive or sentimental Journal of these my weekly visits to my parents–these visits continued regularly from 1777 till 1785, in which year my mother, my eldest sister & my father all died— It will readily be believed that if I had not felt uncommon pleasure in these journeys I would not have persisted in them, nor in facing then the snow storms, the floods & the dark nights of so many Winters–this to some appeared like insanity, but my stimulant as well as my reward was in seeing my father & my mother in their happy home, which I always reflected would have an end, & that the time would come when I would have no feelings of warm regard called up on their account—Besides these gratifications I felt others in observing the weekly changes of the long lengthened & varied year, which by being so measured out, appeared like living double ones time–The "Seasons" by the inimitable Thomson had charmed me much, but viewing them experimentally, much more so–To be placed in the midst of a Wood in the night, in whirlwinds of snow, while the tempest howled above my head, was sublimity itself & drew forth aspirations to Omnipotence such as had not warmed my imagination so highly before–but indeed without being supported by extacies of this kind, the spirits, so beset, would have flagged & I should have sunk down–As soon as the days began to lengthen & the sprouting herbage had covered the ground, I often stopped with delight by the sides of Woods, to admire the dangling Woodbine & Roses & the grasses, powdered, or spangled with pearly drops of dew–& also week after week the continued succession of plants & wild flowers–the Primrose, the wild Hyacinths the Hare bell, the daisey, the cowslip & these altogether I thought no painter ever could imitate–I had not at that time ever heard of the name of the great & good Linnaeus & knew only plants by their common English Names–While admiring these beautifully enamelled spots on my way, I was also charmed with the equally beautifull little songsters which were constantly pouring out their various notes to proclaim the Spring–While this exhilerating Season glided on by imperceptable degrees unfolding its blossoms 'till they faded into summer & as the days lengthened, my hours of rising became more & more early–I have often thought that not one half of mankind knew any thing of the beauty, the serenity & the stillness of the summer mornings, in the country, nor ever witnessed the rising Sun's shining forth upon the new day–I had often listned with great pleasure and attention to my fathers description of the morning–with his remarks upon the various wild quadrupeds & the strange birds he had seen or heard in these still hours throughout the year, for he left his bed very early in summer & seldom later than 4 or 5 oclock in the Winter—The Autumn I viewed as the most interesting season & in its appearance the most beautiful of the varied year–it is then that the yellow harvest of the fields & the produce of the orchards are gathered in as the rewards of the labours of the Year—While the picturesque beauties & varying foliage of the fading woods–with their falling leaves & the assembling, in flocks, of the small Birds put me in mind of the gloomy months with which the year is closed.–

This is the short account of many years of great & uninterrupted health, bouyant spirits & of great happiness to me–I had begun betimes & by degrees, to habituate myself to temperance & exercise, which hardened the constitution to such a pitch that no wet, nor cold had any bad effect upon me–on setting out upon my weekly pedestrian *flights* up the Tyne, I never looked out to see whether it was a good day or a bad one–the worst that ever fell from the skies never deterred me from undertaking my journey–on setting out I always waded through the first pool I met with & had sometimes the River to wade at the far end–I never changed my cloaths, however they might be soaked with wet & though they might be stiffened by the Frost, on my returning home at night 'till I went to bed–I had inured myself to this hardihood, by always sleeping with my windows open, where a thorough air, as well as the snow blew through my room–in this I lay down, stripped into *bare buff* except being rolled in a blanket, upon a mattrass as hard as I could make it—Notwithstanding this mode of treating myself, I never had any ailment, even in the shape of a cold, while I continued to live in this way, nor did I experience any difference, untill, when married I was obliged to alter my plan & to live & behave like other Folks—To persons brought up in & habituated to the tender indulgencies, common in the World–the mode of life I have been describing, would (perhaps) not be believed–& if any such, who, were not brought up to bear it by degrees in the same way, were unprepared to try the experiment–it *would be at their peril*—My travelling expences for the day was commonly only a penny or two pence for crossing the water–On the hottest day I was never made violently to perspire & commonly only felt a dampness on my brow–I carried no useless weight of fat about me & the muscular parts were as hard as it was possible to be on any human being—On being asked by a Gentleman, an acquaintance, who I met with in Ovingham, what I got to drink on such hot days on my road–my reply was nothing, he had not been used to such doings himself, & was surprized, and could hardly believe me–he then earnestly persuaded me to try the experiment of the amazing good, a Glass of Brandy & water wou'd do me in hot weather, this I took no notice of for some time–at length, however, on a thundery hot day, on my being scorched with heat, & threatned with being struck with the lightning, which darted from a Sky almost as black as Ink–I stepped into a Public House in Crawcrook, & for the first time in my life, called for a Glass of Brandy & water. I was then about 28 years old–and surely I thought this Brandy & water was the most delicious beverage in the World–this would not be worth noticing, but only on account of its being a beginning to me, and which I did not, when occasion pressed me, leave off for some years afterwards–I often called in, almost every Sunday Morning, for my Glass while my Rout lay on that side of the River, and untill being *quized* for visiting "Maggy Hay's bonney lassess"–I then left off & walked up the north side of the Tyne & crossed at Wylam, Ovingham or Eltringham Boat & now only sometimes at Scotchwood when I had occasion to visit my friends at Hedley–but indeed I varied my roundabout ways in these Journeys, pursuing the one I had haunted myself to, for perhaps a quarter of a year to an end, before I left it off, and thus became known to most of the Villages on both banks of the Tyne–and as nothing can pass, unnoticed in Villages–so they noticed me & set it down for granted that I was sweethearting some pretty female on my way–This life of raptureous enjoyment has its acids and at length comes to an end, & so did my Walks & my reflections or contemplations, which passed through the mind, while engaged in them–these at the time were mostly communicated to a moralizing & sensibly religious friend, Joseph Hubbuck, who waited my return on the Sunday evenings, when over our supper of a pint of Ale & a cake, for each–he in return detailed to me the import of the Sermons he had heard through the day–

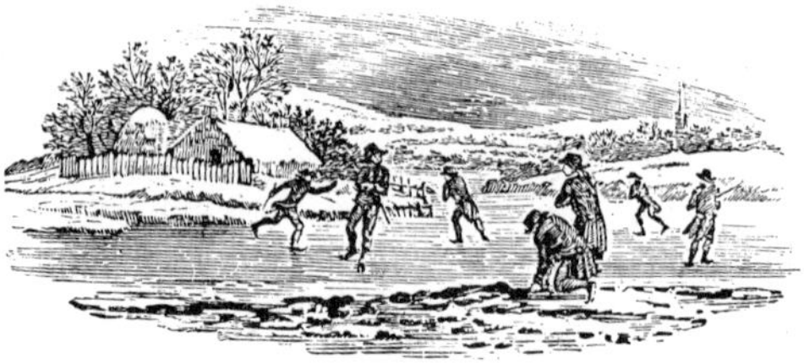

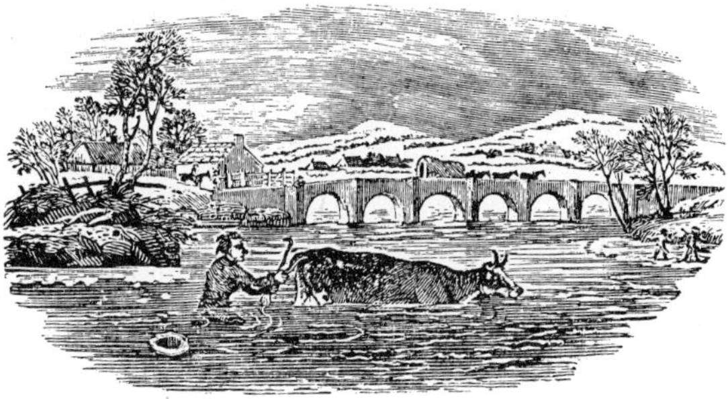

[9]

In Christmas Week 1784, while I was on some errand to Ovingham, amusing myself with sliding on the Ice, as smooth almost as a Seeing Glass, between Eltringham & that place–I know not what came over my mind, but something ominous haunted it, of a gloomy change, in the family taking place–At this I was surprized, for I had never before felt any such sensation & presently scouted it as some whim of the imagination–It was to be a day of cheerfulness, for Mr & Mrs Storey distant relations of my father, & for whom my parents had the greatest regard, had been, with other friends invited to dine with us at Cherryburn that day—At dinner all was kindness & Cheerfulness and my father was, as usual full of his jokes & telling some of his fecetious stories & anecdotes—For two or perhaps three Sundays after this I was prevented from getting over the water by the Ice & other floods & returned from Ovingham, without seeing or hearing how all were at home–The Sunday after upon making my constant call at John Gilchrists, the Gardner in Ovingham, where, when at School, we always left our dinner poke & dined,–he informed me with looks of grief, that my mother was very unwell–I posted off in haste, along with him, & across the river to see her–upon my asking her earnestly how she was, she took me apart by myself, & told me it was nearly all over with her & described to me how she had, "got her death"–she had been called up, in a severe frosty night to see a young woman, in the Hamlet below, who was taken ill, & thinking the Bog she had to pass through at the nearest, might be frozen hard enough to bear her, she slumped deep into it & before she waded through it she got very wet & a perishment of cold, & in that state she went to give her advice about what was best to be done with her patient—I employed my friend Dr Bailes to visit her & I ran up from Newcastle two or three times a week with his medicines for her–but all would not do—She died on the 20 February 1785 aged 58 years–She was possessed of great innate powers of mind, which had been cultivated by her own endeavours as well as by a good education, for these & for her benevolent humane disposition & good sense she was greatly respected & indeed revered by the whole neighbourhood–My eldest Sister, Hannah Chambers, who was down from London, on a visit to her home, at the time of my mothers illness & death, had by her over exertions & anxiety, brought on a miscarriage & became very ill, and for the convenience of Medical Aid & better nursing I brought her to my hitherto, little happy Cot at the Forth,[1] where she died on the 24th of June 1785 aged 30 years—These were gloomy days to me–Some short time before my sister died, upon her requesting me & my promising her that I would see her buried at Ovingham, she proposed to sing me a song –I thought this very singular, and at it, felt both sorrow & surprize–but she smiled at me & began her song of "all things have but a time"–I had heard the old Song before, & thought pretty well of it, but hers was a later & a very much better version of it —during this time I observed a great change in the looks & deportment of my father, he had what is called "never held up his head" since the death of my Mother & upon my anxiously pressing him to tell me what ailed him, he said he had felt, as if he were shot through from the breast to the shoulders, with a great pain that hindered him from breathing freely & upon my mentioning medical assistance, he rejected it & told me if I sent him any druggs, I might depend up[on] it he would throw them all behind the fire–he wanderd about all Summer alone with a kind of serious look & took no pleasure in any thing, 'till near the 15 of november, which I understand was his birth day & on which he completed his 70th year, & on that day he died & was buried beside my mother & sister at Ovingham–after this I left off my walks to Cherrybourn–the main attractions to it were gone & it became a place, the thoughts of which now raked up sorrowfull reflections in my mind

–Having left out some particulars respecting my father & illustrative ⟨to some peculiarities⟩ of his character, which may perhaps not be thought uninteresting–I shall give a few of such as I recollect —In his person he was a stout square made, strong & active man & through life was a pattern of health–I was told by some of my Aunts, who were older than him, that he never was ill from a disease, in his life–I have heard him say "*he wondered how folks were, when they we*[*re*] *bad*"–he was of a very cheerful temper, & possessed an uncommon vein of humour & a fund of anecdote–and was, by the Gentlemen & others of the Neighbourhood, much noticed for these as well as for his integrity–he had however, some traits that might be deemed singular & not in order–he never would prosecute any one for thefts, he hated going to Law, but he took it at his own hand, & now & then gave thieves a severe beating & sometimes otherwise punishd them in a singular & whimsical way–I have known him, on a winters Night, rise suddenly up from his Seat, & with a stick in his hand, set off to the coal pit in order to catch the depredators who he might detect, stealing his coals,–I remember one instance of his thus catching a young fellow a farmer, with his loaded fother[1] & of his giving him a severe beating, or what was called a "hideing" & of making him leave his booty, & go home empty–the thieves themselves were sure to keep the business secret & he himself never spoke of it bejond his own fire side–in these robberies, which he saw with his own eyes, he conceived he did not need the help of either witnesses, judge or jury, nor the occasion to employ any attorney to empty his pockets—I have sometimes heard him make remarks upon people, who he knew to be hypocrites, and on their loud praying & holding up their hands in the Church–After noticing one of these at church one Sunday acting thus, in this way & of his remaining to take the sacrament–some person called in on the afternoon with the news, of this very man's having, on his way home caught poor Tommy Cook, the shoemaker's Galloway,[2] which had gone in through a gap in the hedge, into one of his fields & that he had driven it before him into the pinfold[3]–This was sufficient–this was the spark, which kindled up & increased to a blaze, which my father could not muster temper enough [to] keep down–& next morning he set off to the Smiths shop & sent for this choleric purse proud man, to whom in rude terms he opened out upon, about his finished hypocracy–and at length insisted upon & obliged him immediately to release the Galloway from its hungry imprisonment & further that he should instantly go & make his peace with this poor but honest & much respected man–he further strongly recommended to him to go no more to church to shout & pray, nor to take the sacrament 'till a change of conduct took place in his mind–& that he ought, that very night, before he slept, to sit down on his bare knees, & implore forgivness of the God of truth justice & mercy for his past crimes—The last transaction on this subject I shall mention & which bore a more serious complexion than the foregoing, happened while I was an Apprentice–a Pitman of the name of George Parkin, who had long wrought in the Colliery & who was highly valued by my Father for his industry sobriety & honesty–he would not do any thing unfairly in working the coal in the boards himself, nor suffer others to do so–for this conduct he became deservedly a great favourite –so much so that one of the old Lodges had been comfortably fitted up for him & his family to live in, without rent & a garth besides was taken in off the common for his use. With these he often expressed himself so highly pleased, that he used to say he was happier than a prince–My father for many years–ever, indeed, since the Gin[1] once ran amain, & in his attempting to stop it, he got his scull fractured, had made it a point, if possible, to let the men down to their work himself, so that he saw that all was safe with his own eyes–all passed on pleasantly in this way for a long while–'till one morning–when he was thus to be employed, & in letting down the men, George was always the first Man to his work, & who having fixed himself in the chain, with his Son on his arm to be both let down together, & he had given the signal "wiseaway" & at the same time holding up his "low rope" he observed the pit rope which was to bear their Weight had been cut near the chain–on this he shouted "stop"! & started back upon the "*seddle boards*"[2] just in time to prevent their being precipitated to the bottom of the Pit–he was like to be over powered with the shock when my father, keeping the dreg[3] upon the "Start" caught hold of him & the Boy & conducted them both into the Lodge–he then examined the rope & found it had been cut through to the last strand & he then stopt the working of the Pit for that day—Poor Geordy, in great distress of mind, set off to Newcastle to inform me of what had happened–I was grieved to hear his tale & this was heightened by his declaring that all his pleasures were at an end, for he could never go back to his work, nor to his happy home again—for sometime my father seemed lost in pondering over this misterious affair in his mind–he however at length began to be fixed in his suspicions & as was usual on such occasions, his indignation step by step rose to the greatest height–In this state of mind he set off unusually soon to let the men down to their work, knowing that the subject of his suspicion, a wicked ignorant young fellow, would, that morning be the first & alone–he began by accusing him of the horrid deed & then instantly to give him a severe beating & overpowered him & then made him believe he would drag him to the pit & throw him down the shaft if he did not confess–the threat succeeded–he was affraid for his life, & he confessed, & my father then instantly dismissed him from his employment–when the rest of the Men came, they saw, by the blood & the retaliating blows on his face that something had been the matter–he then told them the particulars, at which they felt eased in their own minds & greatly rejoiced–In this state of things, the accusing *culprit*, while he bore the marks of violence upon him, set crippling off to lodge his complaint to the justices–and my father was summonzed to appear before them–When met together the Justices, Captains Smith & Bainbridge*, of the Riding, heard the charge for the Assault, which from the first appearance of the complainant before them they had no reason to doubt about it–They then both expressed their surprize, to find my father, with whom they had been in habits [of] neighbourly intimacy, & who was the last man on earth they could suspect as capable of committing such an outrage & after laying down the law, in such cases–they wished to hear what he had to say for himself–he readily acknowledged what he had done & his reasons for doing so–they then seemed much shocked at the horrid narrative, & after confering together in private a short time the business was resumed –and pray said one of them–were not you the very man, who

* Now Major Bainbridge–who has been many years in the commission of the peace, in which he has been much respected both as a Magistrate & a Man–without knowing any thing about what side he took in politics–I have always considered him as a local patriot–keen in promoting every thing for the benefit of Tyne side–while I am writing this (23 June 1823) he is now living & in his 87 year–Cap[t] Smith I did not know. Major Bainbridge died 6 Dec[r] 1826 in his 91 year.

robbed Bywell Lock? & then looking him sternly in the face–and was not this master of yours the very friend, by whose unceasing endeavours & influence you were saved from transportation?–Begon! leave the country & let us never see you more–he left the country for many years & on his return I was both pleased and surprized to find he was a very reformed man–(In addition to this long account, I must add that my father could not be troubled to harbour ill will in his mind & that if he was passionate he was equally compassionate.)

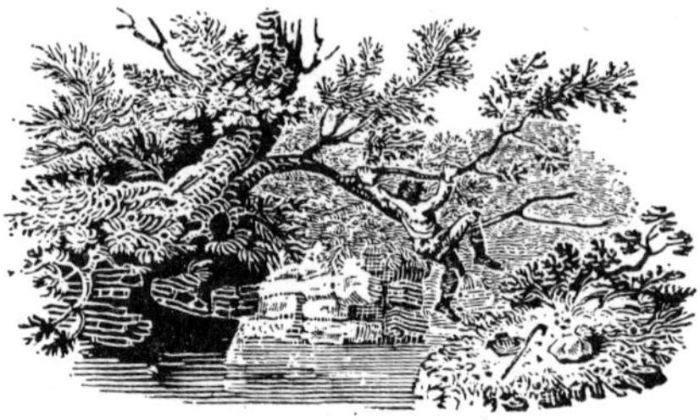

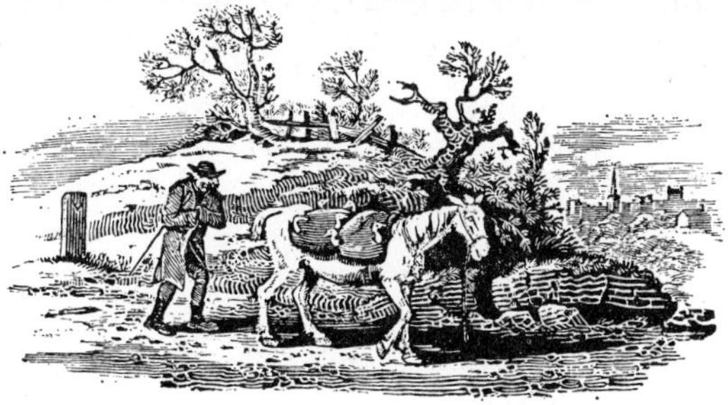

[10]

For many years past, including a part of those of my apprenticeship, we were fully employed upon such work as I have named before, from Silversmiths, Hardwaremen & Watchmakers–but a new customer (Isaac Hymen a Jew) came early into notice, with his seal cutting orders, which amounted to more in that way than all the rest put together–This man besides his Box of watches, trinkits &c had got gathered together a great collection of Impressions of well cut Seals, & being a Man of good address & a good Singer, he introduced himself into Coffee Rooms frequented by Gentlemen & respectable tradesmen & there he exhibitted his Impressions as the work of his own hands, & by his own good management (for he knew nothing whatever of engraving of any kind) he got his orders–and somehow or other it was well propagated through the Town that his Seals surpassed, by far any thing we ever did or could do, & though we had done the whole of his orders, yet this was believed & there seemed [to be] only one opinion as to his very superiour excellence–I remember of once rising early in the morning & working 'till late at night & in that day of cutting five steel Seals, with Cyphers, or initials–for which our common charge, retail[1] was 3/6 and to our own customers, five shillings. For these he charged 12^s or $12^s/6^d$ each to his friends–he observed to me, upon my telling him of his extravagant charges, that it was "foolish in us to do as we did"–but for himself he said "you know I must live"–my wages for the short time I worked for my late master after I was out of my apprenticeship, was a guinea ℔ week–but Isaac offered me two, if I would travel with him–the travelling part, I liked well enough, but not that of travelling with a Jew–he went on in this way with his orders, till we had no other customer & my master, then as well as when I became his partner often expressed himself highly chagrined, that even some of his old private friends went past him & even joined others in lessening our Work–Our *friend Isaac* continued long uninterruptedly thus *to carry all before him*, 'till some of our old customers became irritated at him & particularly John Harrison the Watch maker, who seemed to do nothing besides that of going about to open out & expose the business–Isaac then left Newcastle & common report said he was found dead on the road between Sunderland & Durham —I have often seen in London, & perhaps the same may be seen in every large town, "the pale Artist ply his sickly trade" to keep in affluence such managing, money making, pretended artists, something like Isaac Hymen–and this must continue to be the case so long as Gentlemen will not be at the pains to encourage merit & to go themselves to the *fountain head* for their nice jobs.—Our main supporters in the Silver Engraving were John Langlands & his partner John Robertson.[1] Before they entered into partnership Mr Robertson was well known & much respected in almost every principal Town in Britain & (I believe) in Ireland, as a travelling Silversmith & Jeweller & by his superiour knowledge of business he greatly augmented that of their joint concern–Mr Langlands* was of a cheerfull, hospitable & charitable disposition, & full of stories & anecdotes & that kind of man who greatly esteemed men of ability, integrity & industry–these he never forgot when age or infirmities brought them down–he then shook hands with them as he had done before, but now his own mostly concealed his token of respect–a half guinea. Mr Robertson was also, in many respects, of a similar disposition as his partner.[2] I spent many a cheerfull evening in Mr Langland's House with these kind friends, in company with others who also partook of his hospitable board–but the most remarkable of these was Matthew Prior, who had the character of being one of the best mechanics in the kingdom–he was Assay Master–musical instrument maker & a turner, in which last he particularly excelled, many remarkable pieces of dextrous workmanship he had done in that way, which drew him into the notice of many Gentlemen in the two northern counties, with whom

* John Langlands died 10 April 1783 aged 78 & was buried in St Nicholas Church.

also as an Angler, a sportsman & a jovial companion he was their welcome Guest–It happened on some pretence or other, that an attempt was made to take away the Assay business from Newcastle, which occasioned Prior's being sent for to be examined by (I believe) a committee of the House of commons, as to his ability &c of conducting that business–the ease, the clearness, as well as the streight forward way in which he answered all questions, excited some surprize as well as approbation–he at last when he was questioned as to the accuracy of his scale beam–told them that a hair clipped from the back of his hand, would cast his scales either way, and this was actually true.–For a Wager he turned two Billiard balls of such equal weights that the difference was as nothing–he was of a most independent cast of character & open & frank in his conversation–upon one occasion it had been reported that Prior, should have said of a proud high minded Gentleman, that he "durst do what neither the Gentleman nor any of his family durst do". Prior had never said any such thing, but this Gentleman took him to task about it with great indignation & accused him of saying so–at this Prior in his turn felt offended & told him 'tho he had never said so, he would say so to his face now –this produced a wager between them & Matthew told him he would double the bet if he pleased–now said the Gentleman in high ill humour & what is it you dare do!–do said Prior–I dare spend the last sixpence I have in the world.*–

During [a] great part of the time & the transactions I have been noticing, the American War was going on–The Press broke out just after I landed in London, & to escape the gang, one of our crew came & took refuge with me–this poor fellow, a decent man, had in his youth been on board of a Ship of War & as far as concerned himself he said he did not mind going again, but the thoughts of being digged from his family threw him into very great distress–Political writings & debatings sometimes ran very high between those who were advocates for a system of corruption & profitted by the Taxes–and those who were advocates for the liberties of mankind–but it always appeared to me that a very great majority of the people were decidedly against the War.–These writings & debatings which the War occasioned certainly served greatly to alter the notions & the opinions of the people

* Matt[w] Prior died 15 June 1800 Æt[t] 65 & was buried in St Nicholas Church.

respecting the purity of the British government & its representative system and this attempt at doing it away altogether in America seemed a prelude or forerunner to the same system of misrule when by slower degrees a future opportunity offered of doing it away at home.–In this state of political debatings, the question was often asked "whether the Government was made for the people or the people for the Government?" & this seemed very feebly to be answered–but great numbers, who hoped for the best, still clung to the Government under which they had been brought up & had been taught to revere as excellency itself–While others were contending whether a kingly Government or a Republic were best it was admitted that a deal might be said pro & con for many examples might be produced of maladministration under both forms; then some of these disputants would repeat what Pope had said, "for modes of faith let graceless Zelots fight–"his can't be wrong whose life is right–"For forms of Government, it is confessed–"That which is best administered, is best"—In England the people may boast that their forefathers had a King, in "Alfred the Great" the wisest the bravest & the best, the World ever knew, & by whose whole excellent conduct was laid the foundation of the liberties of his country from the influence of which, there can be no doubt that the English language will be spoken over almost the whole Globe–Were kings to endeavour to follow his example & ever keep in mind, that they & their ministers ought to consider themselves as a Royal society for the promotion of Arts and sciences & of every thing that can enlighten the minds and ameliorate the condition of their Subjects they would then do right–Were this the case Kings would reign in the hearts of the great over whelming mass of the people, which no confedracy or conspiracy of Nobles or others could ever upset–but while they continue to suffer themselves to be surrounded by flatterers, sycophants & selfish knaves, no good nead be expected, for they are thus brought up like petted children & have not the same chance left them of becoming wise like other men–thus situated they are to be pittied–one would think that the respectable part of the old nobility or other opulent Men of great abilities might be found with patriotism enough to do the offices of the Ministry gratis, scouting high saleries & only looking to honourable distinction–this would of itself put an end to corruption–Justices of the peace take the very great trouble of acting their parts gratuitously–Church Wardens & overseers do the same & why [do] not the great & rich men of the land follow the praiseworthy example.

In reverting back to take another look at this War, one may reckon to a certainty of its having been made the subject of debatings & of furnishing matter for the thinking part of mankind, over the whole of the civilized World–George the third & his advisers did not perhaps think of this nor its consequences neither did they ever contemplate upon the mighty events they were bringing about in thus rearing & establishing the wisest & greatest Republic & nation the World ever saw–which, when its immense territory is filled with an enlightened population & its government like a Rock founded on the Liberties & the Rights of man, it is bejond human comprehension to foresee the strides they will make towards perfection & it is likely they will cast a compassionate eye on the rest of the World grovelling under arbitrary power, banish it from the face of the earth, & kill despots with a frown.*

To prevent this, one would fain hope that Kings & their advisers would coolly reflect upon the improving intellect of man kind, and take measures to govern them accordingly & in a way more befitting the state of the people over whom they are called upon to rule–

During the long continuance of this War & the debatings, as before noticed, I got acquainted with a number of genteel young men,† of a literary turn, who kept a library of Books & held their meetings in a Room at Sam: Alcocks, at the Sign of the Cannon, at the foot of the old Flesh market–& I used to frequent this house in the Evenings, to get my pint of ale & a cake & to hear the News & to have a bit of chat or conversation with some of them, when they adjourned from their Book society–I did not join them in this society, but I sometimes dined with them at their annual cheerfull Dinner–I was never fond of Dinners or dining parties, and I think I would not have partaken with them, had I not been tempted to do so, by way of hearing their Songs, with which I felt much charmed, but particularly with the Scotch Songs with which one of their Members, Walter Cannaway the Carver &

* Thus far, from page 35 [p. 29 of this book] was written, while confined by a fit of the Gout, at home, from 29 May till 24 June 1823.

† Joseph Hubbuck, Woollen draper,–Moses Marshall, Cashier & at the Bank, John Gale, Sword Bearer,–Gilfrid Ward (of facetious memory) Woollen Draper & many others of an intelligent chearfull & pleasant character.

Gilder, used so highly to delight the Company, on these occasions –he, according to my notions of singing was the best I ever heard –I had always been more charmed with the human voice, when well attuned, than with any instrumental music whatever, & Cannaway's voice was extremely good–he could in a natural tone go to the highest & the lowest pitch, with his pauses–his shakes or quavers–all in time–with many others, perhaps, who might have as good a voice and as correct an Ear for music, as him & would have been equally as charming, had they not been spoiled by the fashion they had got into, to please the surfeited tastes of coxcomical Connoiseurs & a vitiated aping public–I have ever been much disgusted to hear & see one of these spoiled performers, quavering & spinning out his or her assumed unnatural falsetto voice untill he or she was almost spent. It shewed well how long winded, these kind of performers were, but I never could sit to hear any of them–as it appeared to me to be any thing but music–or music run mad.

On my first coming to business, I had an opportunity of sometimes hearing Musical Concerts. My Master belonged to a Musical Society held at Moore's in the Close & when I had any message to take, or other errand to him, I was commonly invited to remain–The two Sons (Edwd & Charles) of Charles Avison, the great musical composer, belonged to this Society & Mr Beilby & family were on terms of intimacy with them–I also occasionly heard the Band at the Theatre, but I cannot say I felt much pleasure in listning to them–And I well remember, on one occasion of setting them aside–the late Mr Dibden, who often called upon me, had some performance to exhibit at our Theatre, & had quarrelled with the Theatrical Band, on acc^t of their exorbitant demands & in this delemma he expressed himself to me how much he felt disappointed & knew not what to do–I told him, I thought, if he would leave the matter to me, I could set all right, & instantly applied to old William Lamshaw, the Duke of Northumberland's Piper to ask him if he thought he could engage to play at the Theatre that night; being well acquainted with the old man he readily assented–I then told my friend Dibden of what I had done, & satisfied him, as to the preference the Audience would give to the Piper–in this I was not mistaken, for all went well off & every one expressed both pleasure & surprize at the change.

For sometime before the American War broke out, there had

been a lack of musical performers in our Streets & in this kind of interval, I used to contrive to get into the company, or to engage John Peacock, our inimitable performer to play on the Northumberland or small pipes, and with his old tunes, his lilts, his pauses & his variations, I was always excessively pleased. At one time I was affraid, that these old Tunes and this Ancient Instrument, might from neglect of encouragement get out of use, and I did every thing in my power to prevent this, and to revive it again by urging Peacock to teach pupils to become masters of this kind of music–and I am vain enough to believe that my efforts were not lost.[1] I was suspicious that the Northumberland Family were beginning to feel indifferent or to overlook & slight these their ancient Minstrels, who had for ages past been much esteemed by their forefathers & kept in attendance upon them.

It was however, with great pleasure I found that they had appointed William Cant, (a pupil of old William Lamshaw) to be piper to the Northumberland Regiment of Militia & he kept up with great spirit & effect this department of their music, while he remained in the Regiment.*–And it seems that the other departments of their music were not behind Cant in this respect, for it was allowed by judges that their Fifers & Drummers were inferiour to none in the Kingdom–one man in particular, John Bowman, it was asserted was the best performer on the Fife that was "known in the world"–certain it is, however, that he chalenged the Fifers, of every Regiment who were stationed in Newcastle, to a trial of skill on that Instrument, every year for twenty two years–but none of them could compete with him,–he could draw out tones from it the most soft & graceful, as well as the most stunning & loud, such as the Ear could not endure in a Room, & which was only fit to be heard in the open Air.

* July 15 1821–Died Mr William Cant, master of Blue Bell, head of the Side Newcastle, Aged 70 years, formerly piper to the Northumberland Militia.—He was an excellent performer on the violin and the Northumberland pipes; and like his great predecessors, on the latter instrument, Turnbull, Gilley, old Lamshaw & Peacock, he kept up the ancient tunes, with all their charming lilts and pauses, unspoiled by the *modern improvers* of music, with their "Idiot Notes impertinently long". He played "his native Wood Notes wild", such as pleased the Ears of the yeomanry of old, at Otterburn, Hedgley Moor, and Flodden field. For

"Whene'er his pipe did silence break
You'd thought the Instrument would speak"

When Cant died, I sent the above to Mr Walker's paper, but am not certain whether I sent the distich at the end or not. T. Bewick.

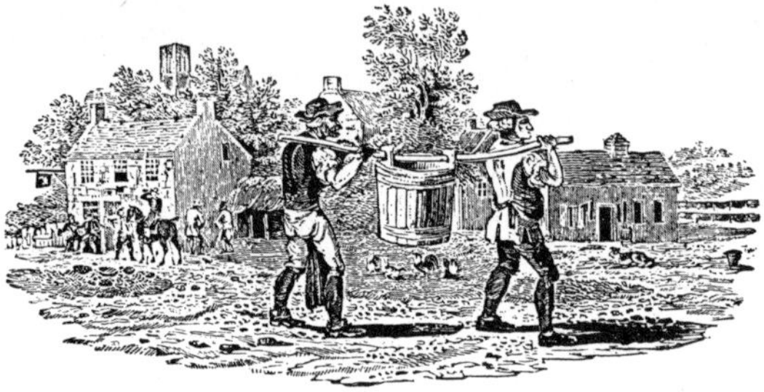

[11]

I have hitherto noticed several of my friends & acquaintances, whose characters stood high in my estimation–I have now another to introduce, the play fellow of my youth, Thomas Lawson, as remarkable as any of them. He left Tyne side, his & my home & came to Newcastle about the year 1777 or 1778 to launch out into the World of exertion & turmoil & who from his abilities & great integrity seem[d] well befitted to make a great figure in it, & who, had he been spared, would, in my opinion have shone out like another Benjamin Franklin. He was for a short time one of my schoolfellows, at Ovingham, but from his Father's having been beggar'd by the faileur of a great Coal Owner, for whom he had been employed for many years, while his Mother brought up a large Family with the small profits of a public House, the Sign of the White Horse, in Ovingham. The House was his fathers, but the Brewer got it for what was owing to him for Ale–This Brewer however, being a generous Man, still did not take the House as his own, but permitted the Family to keep it, for the support of themselves & some of the younger children—My young friend was obliged to leave school & to seek out some employment for himself,–in the interem he took up his abode in my fathers house as a home–his Mother having been much respected by my Mother & between whom a close intimacy had long subsisted. The first employment that my companion got, was that of a Plough driver –then a Farmer's Servant–then a manager of a farm, and the last he held in the country, was of a two fold nature in which he had to look after the concern of a Farm & a Brewery. In all these departments, he was greatly distinguished, for his industry, his good sense, good management & great integrity–It however happened, he being handsome in his person & manly in his looks & deportment, his employer began to suspect that the young lady of the House was shewing a marked partiality towards him, and this having occasioned some frowns & some hints, which his spirit could not brook, he gave up the place,–and having seen an Advertisement, from a Gentleman going on his travels, who wanted a young man as a Servant and a manager of his affairs–Poor Lawson was struck with this as a thing worth looking after & he immediately set off to Newcastle, to make the proper enquiries, and for that purpose, waited upon Mr Slack, Bookseller & Editor of the Newcastle Chronicle–as soon as he entered the shop or office Mrs Slack* eyed him from head to foot, and after a short pause, she broke silence & began by telling him she thought it a great pity, that such a young man, as he appeared to be, should not do better than putting himself to be a Gentleman's Servant, and asked him if would not like better to be [put to] some trade or business–this he readily admitted, but at the same time observed that he had not the means of doing so–to this, being a very sensible, cleaver woman, she told him she would endeavour to help him to accomplish this, and after some bargain making, it was agreed, that he was, for a few years to be bound to Mr Slack as a Pressman, for which he was to be paid eight shillings ℘r Week. At that time, and with this wage, he contrived to maintain himself, and also to pay out of it for a Night school education, under the Revd John Bailie,† & his progress in this way was truely astonishing, both in the Languages & in figures, the use of the Globes &c. But his memory was such that he retained what ever he learned, and could repeat the longest harangue (as far as I am able to judge) verbatim from end to end. I once had an opportunity of witnessing this, in his repeating the whole of a Charity Sermon, preached by the eloquent, the Revd Dr Scott of Simonburn. While he was employed in the drudgery of the Printing Press, he, at the same time made himself master of the business of Compositor, and presently became a secondary Foreman or manager under Robert

* She selected and published "the pleasing Instructor"–was the Author of "Fishers Grammer &c" and was quite a literary character.

† Revd John Bailie, author of ["Lectures on the Revelations," "Impartial History of Newcastle," 1801, etc.] died [in Gateshead 12 December 1806] aged [66].

Carr* who had long conducted the business in that Office—I do not recollect how long Lawson remained in Mr Slack's employment, but shortly after he left him, he married a young woman, of respectable parents, who had long been in love with him. It happened that the printing of a Bible in Numbers[1] had been established, but the Editor, either from his mismanagement or something amiss, was on the verge of a faileur–in this state of things, Lawson turned his attention to this business, & applied to his Wife's friends for assistance, but they could at that time only spare him about thirty Pounds, with this sum in hand, he made his proposals for purchasing the Types & every thing belonging to the printing office. It is singular enough that, at this time this Printer (having left Newcastle) lived in & had his Printing Office in the Governor's House at Tynemouth, & I went down with my friend to this House, when the bargain was closed between them—He now commenced printer on his own account, but how long he had to strugle through great difficulties before he got the business well established, I have forgot–but it is remarkable that he met with unsolicited aid from many friends, for every one who knew him became interested in his welfare. He lived untill he surmounted every obstacle to his prosperity, but in doing this, his too great application & exertions ruined his health–he pined away & died (in a house close by mine at the Forth) on the 7th of March 1783 aged thirty one years–I, with many other of his friends accompanied his remains to Ovingham, where he was buried–This was the first time in my life that I felt poignant grief.

My old schoolfellow & friend, Philip Gregson of the Custom House, London, being on a visit to his relatives & friends in the North in 1780 & I being always fond of rambling, proposed setting him, on his return home, as far as York, if he would walk with me to that City, to which he agreed–we set off, and after spending a day or two with him there, we parted–I then took the road by Borough-Bridge to Ripon, where I stayed a short time 'till I had viewed the country around it & particularly Studley Park & its beautiful scenery–I then returned to Darlington, & changed my rout to the westward by Barnard Castle, Bowes, over Stainmore

* Mr Carr was a man of ⟨great literary⟩ attainments & was considered as respectable for his talents as a Poet–he was the friend and Associate of Cunningham. [He died 4 June 1783, aged 45].

to Brough, Appleby & Penrith–and from thence to my Uncle's at Ainstable–on leaving him & his Family, I walked home that day to Cherrybourn & so on the next to Newcastle. As I have not interlarded this journey with any of my remarks on the road–the grandeur of York Minster–the large upright Stones (called I believe the Devils Arrows) near Boroughbridge–the extensive prospects from Cross Fell &c and therefore my dear Jane must regard the whole of this merely as one of my *Tramps*,[1] and a description of these places by others, may be referred to.

In another of my projected perambulations, I prevailed on my acquaintance Walter Cannaway to accompany me–We set off on an Easter Sunday morning, in 1784 by the Sea side to Berwick and did not halt untill we arrived at Chevington, bejond Widdrington –I had not broke my fast & was quite ready to make a hearty meal upon some dry, barley cake & cheese, while my thirsty companion was with equal pleasure enjoying himself with hearty draughts of Ale.–We reached Lesbury in the afternoon, & when my fellow traveller sat down, he observed that I might go on, if I pleased but that he would not move a foot further that night—next day, after sauntering a little about in the Villages on our road, we reached Elwick, the hospitable Mansion of my friend Thomas Younghusband Esqr, where we stopped that night–Mr Younghusband happening to have a few of his friends to spend the Evening with him they got on to make all merry & to singing songs and when it came to Cannaways turn, they begged he wou'd favour them in this way, he readily did so with his usual ease & ability–at his performance they were both so agreably surprized & pleased, that the company from his so entertaining them did not seperate 'till the morning.–& that day we set off for Berwick, where after getting some refreshment & viewing the Town &c we returned again to Elwick by Holy Island. In the performance of this days journey we had to encounter some difficulties which might have been attended with fatal consequences–We had been cautioned, after a certain hour, against attempting to undertake walking across the extensive flat, left bare by the ebb tide, and in doing this we were bejond the time named, and had to run the greatest part of the way & it was well we did so, for before we reached the Island we found the tide was rapidly advancing between us & the Shore, & we had to wade deeply before we reached it–on looking back, over the flat space we had just left, we were surprized to view it as a Sea–my companion, being rather corpulent was in a sad state of perspiration with over exertion, and I think I was not much better from the anxiety I felt for him, while I was constantly urging him to mend his speed–We now hastened, dripping with wet, to a public house, where, he eagerly took a few glasses of Gin & prevailed upon me to take one, along with him & this was the first glass of that liquor I recollect of ever having taken before—Our next business was to get a Boat to set us across the arm of the Sea between the Island & the nearest Shore towards Elwick, it was then nearly dark, & before the Boatmen got us rowed across it was quite so–where they landed us we knew not, but we had to wade to the dry beach. In shaping our course to Elwick we lost ourselves in the fields & it was late before we arrived there,–we were in as dirty a state as wet and mire could make us–M[rs] Younghusband however lost no time in fitting us up with dry clothes & making us as comfortable as she could. After remaining a day or two at Elwick & making some visits along with M[r] Younghusband in the neighbourhood–my fellow traveller had somewhat similar visits to pay, in collecting some debts due to him, which when done he met me at Alnwick–where M[r] Younghusband, having to attend a meeting of the Freeholders on some Election business, at the Town Hall, I accompanied him thither,–Never having heard any speaches made before, I was much entertained in hearing those now made upon this occasion–This being about the time that M[r] Pit came into the Administration, & being the Son of the great Chatham, most people hoped & expected he would follow the bright, the patriotic example, that had been set him–but one Gentleman appearing to differ in opinion from the majority of the audience, and in what I conceived, an eloquent speech, foretold that he would turn out in character to be a quite different kind of Man.

Sometime about the year [1790] I used occasionly to attend the social meetings held in the evening & which for many years afterwards was held at the "Black boy" & then called Swarleys Club and in a short time I became a more regular member of it. This was the most rational Society or meeting I ever knew–The few Rules were only verbal, which bound us together, & the first one was this, that it was expected every member should behave with decorum & like a Gentleman–If any one transgressed in this point, he was immediately fined–if he did not comply with this, he was sent to Coventry, or perhaps dismissed–on entering the room, every Member paid down fourpence, which was to be spent in Beer only & any Member might introduce his friend, at the same expense –there was no fines for non attendance & no regular debatings allowed on any subject–nor any other debatings but such as might occasionaly arise out of the passing conversation, and the club was ended, at ten oClock–George Carlton, was perpetual President, & in that Office always conducted himself in a pleasant & Gentlemanly manner–William Preston the printer was secretary & treasurer and always acquitted himself in the same agreable way as the President had done–Conversations among the friends, thus associated, consisting of Merchants or respectable Tradesmen, was carried on without restraint–and only interrupted for the moment while the President claimed their attention to listen to any particular news of the day that might be worth notice. Such a place of meeting proved greatly convenient & pleasant to many a stranger, who visited the Town and the expense was as nothing to them–It may seem strange, that out of a fourpenny club, like this, there was commonly an overplus left, to give away at Xmas & Easter, to some charitable purpose–I went to this Club, when I had time to spare, in an Evening, & seldom missed a week to an end–This happy society was however, at length broken up, at the time when the War on behalf [of] despotism was raging & the Spy system was set afloat–some Spies, & others of the same stamp contrived to get themselves introduced & to broach political questions, for the purpose of exciting debates & feeling the pulse of the company, which before this had very seldom touched upon debates of this kind.

Besides being kept busy with the routine of the business of our work office, I was often engaged in executing Wood Cuts for Publishers & Printers, the dates of which, at this moment, I do not recollect, but they were done at various times from about the year 1788–to 1790–but the first, of any importance, was the Wood Cuts of Roman Alters &c & the Arms of the Bishops of Durham, for "Hutchinson's History of Durham",[1] in which my friend the late George Allen Esq[r] of the Grange, Darlington took a conspicuous part—A set of cuts were done for Goldsmiths deserted Village,[2] for M[r] Walker, printer of Hereford–M[r] Nicholson, printer of Ludlow & Poughnill, the publisher of elegant selections from various Authors, employed me to embellish some of these with Wood cuts but I at this time have quite forgot what I did for him[1] –My old friend Mr Bulmer, of the "Shakspere printing office" London, also employed me to execute the Cuts for Parnels Hermit[2] & Goldsmiths deserted Village–many other cuts were done from time to time for printers in various parts of the Kingdom, these formed an almost endless variety, but at this day I have forgot both who they were for & what they were for.—I engraved a series of Copper plates at a low rate, for Sir Harry Liddell's & Captain Conset's tour to Lapland[3] in 1786—My partner & self were busily engaged about the year 1796 in engraving the plan of the projected Canal from Newcastle to Carlisle for Ra. Dodd the Engineer–& plans of the Estates & views of the Mansion Houses of a few Gentlemen, who opposed the line of [the] Canal on the north side of the Tyne, as projected by Mr Chapman the Engineer–After a great deal of scheming & maneuvering under the management of Ralph Heron, an Attorney of great abilities, the whole *scheme* of this great, *this important national as well as local undertaking*, was baffled & set aside–and most men of disurnment were of opinion that the coal owners *below Bridge* were the cause of it–The canal, as projected by Mr Dodd, in 1795 would have certainly opened out a *territory* of coal, that might have affected their interest & it would appear, at least, that they dreaded it & in this case as in almost every other case, private interest is & was found to over power public good.

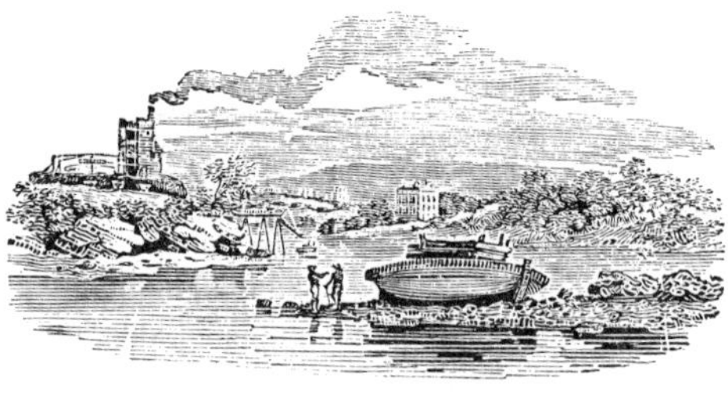

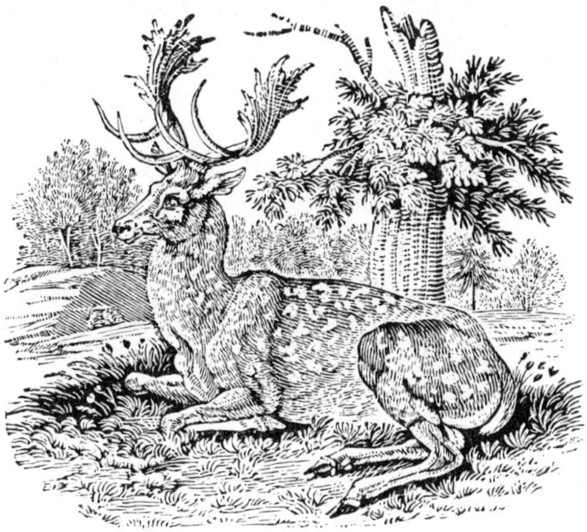

[12]

Having from the time that I was a school Boy, been displeased with most of the cuts in children's books, & particularly with those of the "Three hundred Animals"[1] the figures of which, even at that time, I thought I could depicture much better than those in that Book; and having afterwards, very often turned the matter over in my mind, of making improvements in that publication–I at last came to the determination of commencing the attempt. The extreme interest I had always felt in the hope of administering to the pleasures & amusement of youth & judging from the feelings I had experienced myself that they would be affected in the same way as I had been, this whetted me up & stimulated me to proceed–in this, my only reward besides, was the great pleasure I felt in imitating nature–That I would ever do any thing to attract the notice of the world, in the manner that has been done, was the farthest thing in my thoughts, & so far as I was concerned myself, at that time, I minded little about any self interested considerations. These intentions, I communicated to my partner, & 'tho he did not doubt of my being able to succeed, from what he had seen of my work, yet being a prudent cautious & thinking man, he wished to be more satisfied, as to the probability of such a publication paying us for our labours—on this occasion, being little acquainted with the nature of such like undertakings, we consulted ⟨our friend⟩ Solomon Hodgson (Bookseller & Editor of the Newcastle Chronicle) as to the probability of its success &c when he most warmly encouraged us to proceed–Such Animals as I knew, I drew from memory upon the Wood–others, which I did not know were copied from Dr Smellie's abridgement of Buffon & from other naturalists, & also from the Animals which were, from time to time, exhibited in Shows. I made sketches, first from memory, & then corrected & finished the drawings upon the Wood, from a second examination of the different subjects–I begun this business, of cutting the blocks, with the figure of the Dromidary on the 15 of November 1785* (the day on which my father died). I then proceeded in copying such figures (as above named) as I did not hope to see alive—The figures which were done from nature, or from memory so much attracted the notice of our friend, that he most ardently insisted upon our making our work assume a superiour character to that of the "Shabby Book" we had been only thinking of surpassing–and from the opinion, we had formed of his being better acquainted with business than we were†, we offered him a third share free from any expense for the Cuts–a proper agreement was made on the [ ] of April & he became our partner in the "History of Quadrupeds"–

While I was busied in drawing & cutting the Figures of the Animals & also in designing & engraving the Vignettes,—Mr Beilby, being of a bookish, or reading turn, proposed, in his evenings at home, to write or compile the descriptions, but not knowing much about natural history, we got Books on that subject to enable him to form a better notion of these matters; with this, I had little more to do, than in furnishing him, in many conversations & written memorandums, of what I knew of Animals, and of blotting out, in his manuscript what was not truth—In this way we proceeded untill the Book was published in 1790.–It is worthy of remark, that while the title page was in hands, Mr Beilby wished to be made the Author of it and wrote his name as such, "by R Beilby"–on Mr Hodgson seeing this, without saying a word he stroked the name out with a pen, while Mr Beilby was

* Novr 1785 29 Begun the Natural History wth the Fig of the Dromedary Decr 2^d The Camel 10th Elephant 12th Mufflon–Zebu 27 Eve^g The Zebra *

† In this we were greatly mistaken, for Solomon's dissipated life prevented him attending to it.

looking on–I knew nothing about this transaction for sometime afterwards, and it might have passed so, for any thing I cared about the Authorship, or whose name was put to it as such.–It was sufficient for me that I had the opportunity of giving vent to my feelings and gratifying my desires in doing my part of the work –The greater part of these Wood cuts were drawn & engraved at nights, after the days work of the shop was over.[1] In these Evenings I frequently had the company of my friend & companion the Rev[d] Richard Oliphant*[2] who took great pleasure in seeing me work, while, at the same time he read to me, the Sermons he composed for the next Sunday, where he at that time might happen to officiate–I was also often attended, from a similar curiosity, by my friend, the Rev[d] Thomas Hornby†, Lecturer of S[t] John's–he would not, like my friend Oliphant adjourn to a public house & join in a Tankard of Ale but he had it sent for to us at my workplace,–we frequently disagreed in our opinions, as to religious matters–he being, as I thought an intolerant high Churchman–but notwithstanding this, he was a warm well wisher & kind friend to me–and was besides of so charitable a disposition in other respects that his purse was ever open to relieve distress and with an occasional Guinea, he would commission me, anonimously, to dispose off to persons, in want & to sundry other charitable purposes.–

As soon as the "History of Quadrupeds" appeared in the World, I was surprized to find how rapidly the Book was sold, as well as several successive Editions & this was followed by a glut of praises bestowed upon it–The first time I was obliged to hear personal praises, in this account, was from D[r] David Ure LLD of Glasgow, who called to see me, & not being used to such Compliments I blushed over the Ears & left him talking to M[r] Beilby— These & such like praises, however, excited envy, & was visibly followed by the balance of an opposite feeling, from many people at home, for they raked together & blew up the embers of envy into a transient blaze–but the motives by which I was actuated stood out of the reach of its sparks, & they returned into the heap whence they came & fell into dust–I was much more affraid to

* afterwards Curate of Longhorsley.

† The Rev[d] Thomas Hornby (Son of Alderman Hornby) Died, in the prime of life, on the 28 of August 1798 and was buried at Gosforth.

meet the praises which was gathering around, than I was of the sneers which they excited, and as soon as the annexed poetry appeared in the paper, I felt obliged on its account, for sometime to shun Swarley's club, of which Geo. Byles* was a member, to avoid the warm & sincere compliments that awaited me there.

For the NEWCASTLE ADVERTISER.

To Mr T. BEWICK,

On his excellent Engravings on Wood, in the HISTORY *of* QUADRUPEDS, *publiſhed at Newcaſtle.*

GO on great Artiſt in thy pleaſing way,
And learn us Nature as the riſing day:
Thy juſt Creator's wond'rous beings ſhow,
And teach us from thy art—his boundleſs pow'r to know:
Thy charming pencil claims our warm applauſe,
And leads us on to ſtudy Nature's laws.

Though diſtant climes produce a ſavage race,
And Britain's realms preſent their beaſts of chace,
At home we ſit—peruſe thy well-form'd plan,
And vindicate the ways of God to man!
Charm'd with the ſubject, we the theme purſue,
Nor yet forget our thanks are due to you.

Oh! at ſome future period may thy breaſt,
With other pleaſing ſubjects be impreſt:
Pourtray the warbling ſongſters of the woods,
The ſcaly tribe that range the briny floods;
Depict the reptile, and the inſect race,
In well-wrought lines, drawn with thy uſual grace;
So ſhall we in this field of wonder find,
An art diſcover'd, and an end deſign'd.

GEO. BYLES.

—I had long made up my mind, not to marry, while my Father & Mother lived, in order that my undivided attention might be bestowed upon them–My Mother, had indeed, sometime before recommended a young Woman in the Neighbourhood to me as a wife–she did not know the young lady intimately,–but she knew she was modest in her deportment, beautiful & handsome in her person & had a good fortune–and in compliance with this recommendation, I soon got acquainted & became intimate with her, but was carefull not to proceed further, and soon discovered that

* George Byles came from some of the southern Counties & commenced schoolmaster or Teacher, in Newcastle–he had lost a leg, which probably had obliged him to take to this kind of employment, he was Gentlemanly in his manners & conversation, and of a most lively & animated cast of character.

'tho her character was innocence itself she was mentally one of the weakest of her Sex. The smirking lasses of Tyne side had long thrown out their *jibes* against me as being a Woman hater, but in this they were greatly mistaken–I had indeed been very guarded in my conduct towards them, as I held it extremely wrong & cruel to sport with the feelings of any one of them in making them believe that I was in love with any of them, without really being so, in this (which was one of my resolves) sincerity & truth were my guides—As I ever considered a matrimonial connection as a business of the utmost importance, and which was to last 'till death made the seperation. While, looking about for a partner for life, my utmost attention and anxiety was directed to this important change —I had long considered it to be the duty of every man (in health) on changing his life, to get a healthy woman for his Wife for the sake of his children, and a sensible one, as a companion for his own happiness & comfort–that love is the natural guide in this business, and much misery is attendant upon it, when this is awanting. This being the fixed state of my mind, I permitted no mercinary considerations to interfere. Impressed with these sentiments, I had long, my dear Jane, looked upon your Mother as the most suitable Inmate for me–I had seen her in prosperity and in adversity, and in the latter state she appeared to me to the greatest advantage–in this she soared above her Sex, and my determination was fixed–In due time we were married and from that day to this, no cloud so far as concerned ourselves has passed over us to obscure a life time of uninterrupted happiness.

> My dear "Bell" died, after a long &
> Painfull illness, on the 1st Feby 1826 Æ 72
> (the best of wives & very best of Mothers)

During the time I was busied with the Figures for the History of Quadrupeds many jobs, which I have forgot, interfered to cause delay–one of which (I ought to have remembered) was the Wood Cut of the Chillingham Wild Bull, for the late Marmaduke Tunstal Esqr of Wycliffe, this very worthy Gentleman & great Naturalist, honoured me with his approbation of what I had done & was one of our Correspondents–He, or my friend George Allen Esqr employed me to undertake this Job–and on Easter Sunday 1789, I set off on foot to Chillingham accompanied by my acquaintance William Preston, the Printer, on this business–After tarrying a little with friends at Morpeth and Alnwick we took Huln Abbey in our way across the Country to the place of our destination–besides seeing the various kinds of Pheasants &c at the last-named place, little occurred to attract attention except our being surrounded or beset (on passing a moor) amidst the fire of burning heather & afterwards passing over the surface of immense old, winter wreaths of frozen Snow–We took up our abode with my old kind friend John Bailey[1] & spent a cheerfull Evening with him after our fatigues, and next day he accompanied us to the park for the purpose of seeing the Wild Cattle. This however, did not answer my purpose, for I could make no drawing of the Bull, while he, along with the rest of the herd were wheeling about & then fronting us, in the manner as described in the history of Quadrupeds—I was therefore obliged to endeavour to see one which had been conquered by his Rival & driven to seek shelter alone in the Quarry holes & in the Woods,–and in order to get a good look at one of this description, I was under the necessity of creeping on my hands & knees, to leward & out of his sight–and I thus got my sketch or memorandum, from which I made my drawing on the Wood[2]–I was sorry my figure was made from one, before he got furnished out with his curled or shaggy neck & mane. On our return home, we took up our abode for two days & nights at Eslington, in the appartments of our kind & hearty friend John Bell, then a steward & Agent to Sir Harry Liddell Bart. & afterwards a Merchant at Alemouth–having made a drawing from the large Newfoundland Dog, kept there[3]–and rambling about & visiting some of Mr Bell's friends we then bent our way homewards, highly satisfied with our journey, crowned as it was with hospitality & kindness which could not be surpassed.

In the year 1790 I was employed, much in the same way as I had been in other years about that period, as before noticed, but this was besides, marked with an event which enwarped & dwelt on my mind–no doubt, all thinking men in their passage through this life, must have experienced Epochs of a similar kind–my old & revered preceptor, the Revd Christopher Gregson, died this year –No sooner did the news of his extreme illness reach my ears, than

I set off, in my usual way & with all speed to Ovingham–I instantly bounced into his room, & there I found his Neice, Miss Dinah Bell (afterwards Mrs Johnson) in close attendance upon him –With her, being intimately acquainted, I used no ceremony, but pulled the curtain aside & then beheld my friend in his last moments–he gave me his last look but could not speak–multitudinous reflections of things that were passed away hurried on my mind, & these overpowered me–I knew not what to say–except–farewell for ever–farewell!—His Sons were written to, to leave London with all speed, ⟨I think I must have done this myself, for I cannot recollect of any person's being there at the time of their father's death (which happened that night or morning) who could undertake that office on the spurr of the moment, besides myself⟩

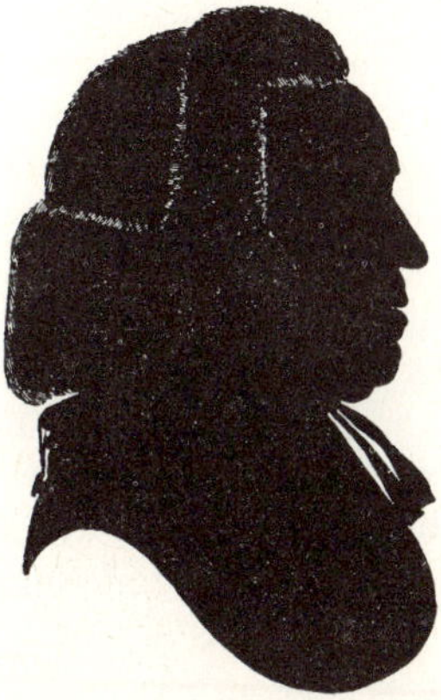

Revd. Christopher Gregson

Few men have passed away their time on Tyne side, so much respected as Mr Gregson; when he was appointed to the curacy of Ovingham, I understand his income was not more than about, thirty pounds ℔ Annum–thus set down, he begun by taking a few pupils to board & educate chiefly as Latin Scholars, and Mrs Gregson (late Miss Langstaff) after my mother left him, did every thing in her power to make the Seminary respectable–he however commenced Teacher on a more extended scale by taking in scholars of all kinds from their A B C's to the Latin classes–In this, his task must have been of the most arduous & laborious description, all of which he got through without any Usher or Assistant–his assiduity & industry must have attracted the notice of the late Thomas Charles Bigge Esqre of Benton, the lay Rector, for he added some land to the Glebe, by way of bettering his condition. Little as this farm was, as to its magnitude, it enabled him, by his good management & unceasing industry to shew himself a good Farmer, and he was not a little vain on being complimented on this score–As a Clergyman he was not one of the fittest for that very important Office, but this was chiefly owing to his defective voice, which was so low & raucous that his hearers could not profit by his sensible discourses–In another way, I mean as a *Village Lawyer*, he stood preeminent–his pen was ever ready at the service of his Parishoners & whatever dispute arose amongst them, there never was any objection to leave the matter to the descicion of Mr Gregson, and I have often heard it asserted, that there was not one lawsuit in the Parish, while he was Minister there–He set out in life, on this poor Curacy, upon a system of great economy & perhaps, like other frugal people, it grew upon him 'till he was accused of nearness–but be this as it may, he accumulated a sum (as I have heard) at the time of his death, after a life of great good management, to the amount of about nine hundred Pounds–if his pen was ever ready to serve his Parishioners, so on certain Occasions *was his purse*, for he eyed with great attention the situation, of such of his Neighbours as were industrious, & when he found these were struggling under untoward circumstances or unforeseen losses, he without being solicited, lent them money to ward off the evil & to serve their nead.

The Publication of the Quadrupeds led me into a close intimacy with Solomon Hodgson* & others of his friends–and also with other Men of distinguished abilities–with Andrew Young MD†, Samuel Burton Pearson MD‡ & Nathan Surgeon, Surgeon§–these Men were eminent in their professions and were besides of charitable humane & noble dispositions & it is equally true & distressing

* Solomon Hodgson, the bold & independant Editor of the Newcastle Chronicle died 4 Aprill 1800 Æ^t 39 and was Buried at St Johns

† Andrew Young Died on the [–March 1806] and was on the 23 March 1806 Buried at St Andrews

‡ Dr Pearson, who had left Newcastle & resided near Penrith, died there

§ Nathan Surgeon Died 10 November 1817 Æ – Buried at St Johns

to think, that 'tho nature had done every thing, they, as it were, threw her favors in her face & all fell victims to *the Bottle*–with this company & their conversations, I often felt much pleased, but it sometimes led me to join with them in their excesses. There were also others with whom I occasionally spent my Evenings, over a cheerfull Glass in their agreable company viz–The Revd John Hogarth (afterwards Rector of Kirknewton), my friend the Revd Richard Oliphant–John Stokoe Architect & John Howard the Author of a Work on Spherical Geometry*—To ennumerate one half of the people with whom I was acquainted, would swell the list to an extent that might be wearysome to read over–but I may venture to name a few with whom I was in habits of intimacy & who also stood preeminent on account of their great worth & the estimation in which they were held by the public–Among the first was William Charnley† Bookseller–this intelligent & honest Man I account as one of the Newcastle Worthies–The Revd William Turner Secretary to the Literary & Philosophical Society in Newcastle and Minister of the Unitarian Chapel–he was in my way of judging a Master of Arts, his talents were great in various departments of science and lecturer on such subjects and I know not how I can say more or less of him than that his character was composed of every thing, great, good, amiable and praise worthy–his friend and Associate Robt Doubleday‡, vice President of the Literary & Philosophical Society, also partook very greatly of the same good qualities & attainments as Mr Turner. There were others, set after Set, with whom I lived in habits of intimacy, and some of these may be dated a long way back–Gilfred Ward, Woollen Draper (of facetious memory) he died 25th of Jany 1798 Aged 52 years & was buried at St Johns–Joseph Bell, Painter, he also displayed considerable abilities as a painter, poet, & a Man of talents in other respects–but with keeping much company he became also much dissipated–he died 26 April 1806 Æt 60 & was buried in St Andrews–I was also long acquainted with Wm Bell, Portrait painter &c he was, as a painter, accounted eminent in that profession, and was awarded a gold Medal, from the Society of Arts for the best Historical painting in the year—He died in

* John Howard died 26 March 1799 Æt [46] and was buried at St Johns

† William Charnley died 10 August 1803 Aged 76 & was buried at St Johns

‡ Robt Doubleday died 27 January 1823 Aged 70

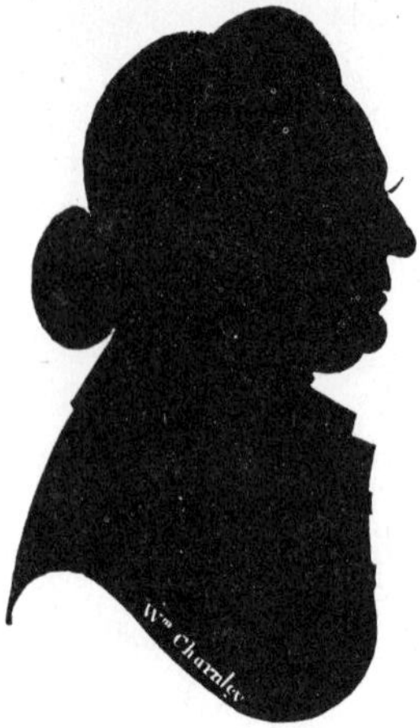

William Charnley

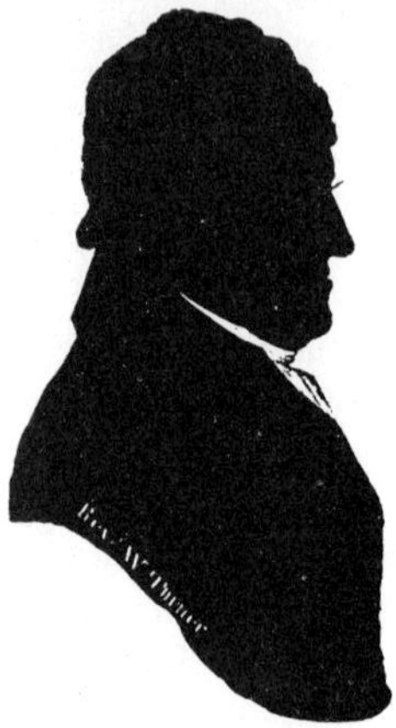

Revd. William Turner

Newcastle Infirmary in the year 1800 Æt 60. I was also, long afterwards on the most friendly terms, with James Ramsey, the very eminent portrait painter. Another *worthy* with whom I spent many a pleasant Evening was William Gill*–he had long been Colliery Agent to Lord Windsor (one of the partners of the Grand Allies) in which Office he was much esteemed–He was a man of great reading & had reflected upon what he read–he was also, like all men of sense & spirit, of a patriotic turn, and foretold the consequences of the late war of Kings, which he considered as an attempt to destroy the civil liberties of Mankind; and I have often, since, wondered to find his predictions, unfold themselves so truely, as they have done,–in this he was simple plain and argumentative & they were dictated only by truth & sincerity–He was of a social turn of mind, and for an old man was wonderfully clear, sensible & chearfull & this prompted him to select such as he thought were of the same stamp & these he often invited to spend the Evenings with him—He also, besides these pleasing qualities, was an attentively judicious & charitable man, and in this way did not do that business by halves, for wherever he found an honest man industrious, with a family struggling to get forward, he never lost sight of him, untill he placed him in a fair way to prosperity–he

* William Gill died 20 Feby 1802 Æt 83 and was buried at Whickham

however outlived his faculties and left all his property past his poor relations, particularly a Brother who was a poor Schoolmaster, but who, I believe, he was persuaded was dead, as well as others of his near relations, whom he once intended to provide for.

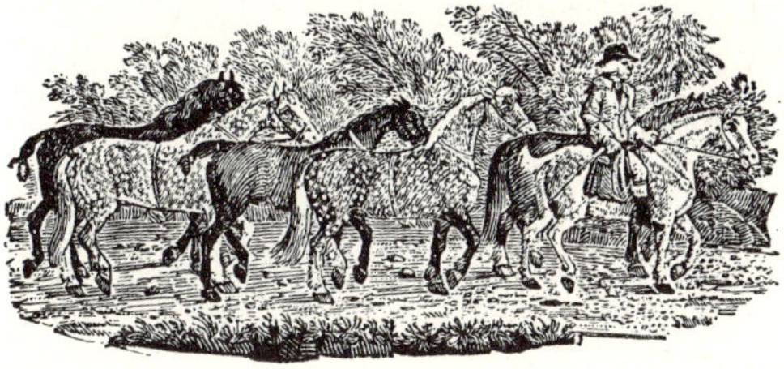

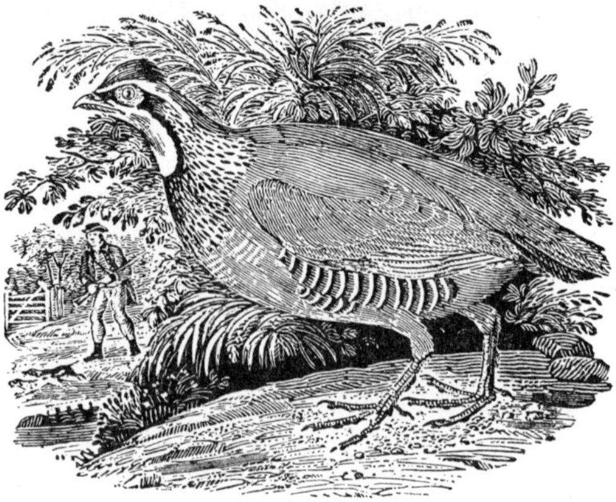

[13]

–While the sale of the Quadrupeds was going on, Edition after Edition with great success–I turned my thoughts to the History of British Birds. With these, I had long felt *greatly* charmed, paid great attention to, and busied myself very much in reading various descriptions or accounts of them–the first, (as far as I can now recollect) was Brookes and Miller's "Natural History"[1] & Dr Smellies abridgment of Buffon[2]–these, which were now thrown, as it were, in the background, was succeeded by Pennants Works[3] –first & last, I might name many others, which I had perused–chiefly lent to me by [my] kind friend George Allen Esqr–those consisted of Albins "History of Birds"[4]–Belon's very old Book,[5] & "Willughby & Ray"[6] &c and Mr John Rotheram* gave me Gesner's Natural History.[7] With some of these I was in raptures–Willughby & Ray struck me as having led the way to truth and to British Ornithology–The late Michael Brian Esqr† of London (formerly of Newcastle) lent me the splendid Volume (planches enluminees) of Buffon–& George Silvertop Esqr of Minsteracres,

* Mr John Rotheram Son of the late Dr Rotheram of Newcastle and a pupil of the good & great Linnaeus–died at [St Andrews] in the year [1804] Æ [?54]

† Michael Brian Esqr Picture dealer, London, died there on the 28 March 1821 aged 64 years

Edwards "Natural History"[1]–I was much pleased with "Whites History of Selburn"[2]– Pennants, however opened out the largest field of information, and on his works I bestowed the most attention. Latham[3] seems to have wound up the whole, and I have often lamented, that it was not, by being embellished with correct figures, made a great National Work like the Count de Buffon's— The last of our Ornithologists, and one of the most indefatigable, was the late Colonel George Montagu* Author of the Ornithological Dictionary[4]—As soon as it was spread abroad, that we were engaged with the History of Birds & their Figures, I was, in consequence, led into a seemingly endless correspondence with friends & amateurs in this way, so much so, that I often felt myself unable, duly to acknowledge the obligations I owed them– and many a letter I have written, after being so wearied out with the labours of the day, that I often forgot how to spell the very commonest words–& I fear the rest of many of my letters would be of a piece with this, and not clear nor very intelligible.–At the beginning of this undertaking, I made up my mind to copy nothing from the Works of others but to stick to nature as closely as I could–And for this purpose, I being invited by Mr Constable, the then Owner of Wycliffe, to visit the extensive Museum there,[5] collected by the late Marmaduke Tunstal Esqre, and to make drawings of the Birds[6]–I set off from Newcastle on the 16 of July 1791 (the day on which my friend Dr Bailes died) & remained there, drawing from the stuffed Specimens, nearly two months–at this beautiful place I lodged in the House of John Goundry, the person who preserved the Birds for Mr Tunstal, and I boarded at his Father's, George Goundry, the old Miller there–While I remained at Wycliffe, I frequently dined with the Revd Thomas Zouch, the Rector of the Parish†–he watched my going out of the Church, on the Sunday, where I often attended, accompanied by old Goundry, to invite me to dinner. On these occasions, he frequently made the characters of his late neighbour Mr Tunstal, and George Goundry, the subject of his conversation, and dwelt with great pleasure on the excellent characters of both–Mr Tunstal

* George Montague Esqr died in July 1815–I have heard that he was killed by the overturning of a carriage in which he was travelling–the Horses having taken fright & run away with it

† The Revd Thomas Zouch DD FLS Died at Sandal 17 Decr 1813 Æt 76–He had been offered the Bishopric of Carlisle, but refused it

was a Roman Catholic and kept a chapel in his own house–Mr Zouch a Church of England Minister–and George Goundry was a deist, and yet these three uncommonly good men, as neighbours lived in constant charity and good will towards each other–Mr Zouch would sometimes say, to me, "do you know this old man can beat me in argument"–and would then regret that he was not orthodox in his religious opinions–but setting that aside, as to his moral conduct, he was one of the best christians he knew–poor Goundry was equally warm in his praises of these two good men, his Neighbours, and with the tear on his cheek would enumerate the charities & liberality of the late Mr Tunstal, and as a proof of the latter he instanced his being at great expense in privately contributing *very greatly* towards the pewing of Wycliffe Church–One might dwell long with pleasure on such singularly good Characters–I wish the world were better stocked with them—I have often reflected with pain, on the asperity with which one description of christians have commonly treated others who differed from them in opinion, on religious matters, or rather as to their different modes of faith–and have thought that the time would come, when that cruel bloody and disgusting portion of History, would not be believed, which has recorded the facts, that one denomination of Christians actually burned others alive, who differed from them in opinion, in matters which ought to have been considered as beneath contempt—but, judging from the past, it is certain that when men give up their reason, and substitute faith, or any thing else in lieu thereof, there is nothing, however absurd, that has not been believed, and no punishments, however cruel that have not been resorted to, to enforce that belief–Men thus degraded may fairly be called *Man tigers* being fitted for any wicked purpose, and under equally wicked Governments, they have been guided & commanded to deluge the Earth with blood. —It is strange to think that this should have been the case, when it is considered that the whole of the authorities are derived from one & the same pure source, bewildered indeed by the twisted imaginations of ignorance bigotry & superstition–The inspired and benevolent Author of christianity taught neither intolerance nor persecution–The doctrines he laid down, are plain pure & simple. They teach mercy to the contrite, aid to the humble and eternal happiness to the good–For my own part, it is long since I left off bewildering myself with dogmas & creeds & have felt pity for those that did so–but am quite clear *& willing to believe & to allow*, that whatever modes of faith, honest & well meaning people, have thought best to adopt, they might, in sincerity of heart, & to the best of their judgment be doing, what is called serving God–but they surely ought not to interfere with the creeds of others who are equally as sincere, as themselves, in the means they pursue for the same ends–but however various these modes of faith may be, there is one rule that ought to guide the whole, & it appears to me simple & easy to comprehend–and that one is that all men to the utmost of their power, should endeavour through life to stear clear of every thing that may degrade their own minds & souls, that the misterious incorporated compound may not, when summonzed to leave this world, have to appear before their maker polluted & debased–The man who attends to this will fear nothing but that of erring & doing wrong–he will fear the face of no man–the little strutting authorities of despotism he will despise & the virtuous Magistrate will ever be his friend–he will break no good laws that have been made for the guidance of man in society, & as to his religion, that is an affair between himself & his maker only–with the author of his being, he will with unentangled mind commune freely at all times, when his spirit moves him to do so–and no man ever did, or ever will feel himself happy, that does not pursue this course through life.

Ever since I habituated myself to think, I have always seen, as clearly as I could see any thing that it is the intention of the Deity that Mankind should live in a state of civilized Society & that no period of human existance can be comfortable without the pleasures & endearments of social intercourse. Every object in nature that can be contemplated upon shews this, and the full and exact fitness of all its component parts clearly prove that man from his social nature is destined to live in this state–He has been endowed with reason, as his guide for the purpose of regulating and conducting the whole, but when that guide is neglected & he suffers his selfish propensities and bad passions to mislead him from the path of rectitude, from that moment every thing, so far as this reaches, goes wrong–for reasons of this kind, it is necessary that equitable & just Laws should be made and inforced to restrain vice from breaking down the barriers that are erected to protect virtue and patriotism–and to break through these laws is Sin—But in the present wretched state of society, it may be difficult to bring about such a reformation of manners, as would ensure the accomplishment of so desirable an end, for it appears to me that the character of mankind ought to be new modelled before this can be effectually done.

Having long busied myself in wading through Systems on natural history, its orders, Genera, Species & varieties, the whim has often struck me to lay down an imaginary one, of classing mankind–The Genus Homo may be made to consist of three species & their varieties–the first (including in one the wise & good) is honest men, the second is Knaves and the third Fools–these and their gradations & varieties gliding into each other, form the present jumbled mass of society–the community of which we all form a part–as any of these may happen to predominate in the government of society, so in exact proportion will the good, bad & indifferent effects of their management be felt by the whole people–I think it will be admitted that out of the first species ought to be chosen every man, according to his mental powers & the education he may have received to call forth these powers, to enable him to fill every public office from the constable up to the king–out of the two latter Species, when conjoined are formed, the great Mass of the wicked gross vulgar herd (high & low) of mankind. Among these, Knaves of great abilities ought to be particularly guarded against. They are a kind of splendid Devils, who have from time immemorial spread abroad much misery in the world–but notwithstanding their abilities they would not have got forward in their public wickedness, nor have formed their majorities without enlisting, as tools, their ready made auxiliaries the fools–And if we take only a slight glance at individual misery it will be seen that most of it is inflicted by one man upon another: "mans inhumanity to man makes countless thousands mourn"–could this be remedied, what a beautifull World would this appear to thousands, instead of being obliged thus to view it through the medium of an almost perpetual cheerless gloom.

I have often amused myself in considering the character of the Canine Species, and of comparing it and its varieties, with those of the untutored part of mankind & it is curious & amusing to see the similarity between them–To his master the Dog is an uncommonly submissive, obedient & faithfull servant, & seems to look upon him as if he were an angel–his sagacity & his courage are equally conspicuous, and in the defence of his master he will suffer death. But to his own Species he is ill behaved, selfish, cruel & unjust, he only associates with his fellows for the purpose of packing together to destroy other Animals, which cannot be effected otherwise. They will sometimes indeed let a supplicating Dog, into which they have inspired terror, sneak off, & I have often watched to see the wary circumspect plan that a strange Dog adopts, on his being obliged to pass through a village, or through among those of their equally ill behaved brethren, the Butchers Dogs, in a town–it is curious to see the stranger, upon these occasions view his danger and then to affect lameness and go hirpling[1] through amongst them unmolested. I knew their instinct was surprizing, but to know some of their reasoning powers I had not tried, and for this purpose, when a Boy, I cut two thin slices of meat and plastered the insides with mustard, and then threw it to one of my fathers dogs. This, he being very very apt at kepping, caught in his mouth, and as quickly as he could, got quit of it again, but from that time, he would rather run the risk of losing it, than kep any more. And to prove how far selfishness and malignity would operate upon him,–I have placed two Basons filled with very hot fat broth, at a distance from each other,–he ran from one to the other, to prevent a beautiful spaniel bitch, from partaking of either of them–his attention was taken up with thus watching & preventing her, 'till at length his patience was exhausted by going so often from one Bason to the other, and then, with the utmost vengeance he seized her & tore away his mouthfull of skin from her side.

On my return from Wycliffe, being thoroughly drenched with an incessant rain, I called upon my old & much valued schoolfellow, John Forster, at Bishop Auckland & spent a day or two with him in busy converse about our former transactions at School &c–perhaps few have passed through life without experiencing the pleasure that a retrospect of the times passed thus afford to old cronies, in talking over the recollections of youthfull frolics & even the disipline which followd in consequence of them.—As soon as I arrived in Newcastle, I immediately began to engrave from the drawings of the Birds I had made at Wycliffe, but I had not been long thus engaged 'till I found the very great difference between preserved Specimens & those from nature, no regard having been paid at that time to place the former in their proper attitudes, nor to place the different series of the feathers, so as to fall properly upon each other. This has always given me a great deal of trouble to get at the markings of the dishevelled plumage & when done with every pains, I never felt satisfied with them. I was on this account driven to wait for Birds newly shot, or brought to me alive, and in the intervals employed my time in designing & engraving tail pieces or Vignettes. My sporting friends however supplied me with Birds as fast as they could, but none more so than my kind friend Lieut Henry Forster Gibson* of the fourth Dragoons, Lieut Col! Dalton, Major Shore, Capt Dalbiac (now General Dalbiac) and other Officers of the same Regt also shewed great attention to our growing Work. George Strickland Esqr of Ripon also interested himself in his contributions for the same end – besides these many Birds were sent to me from various parts of the Kingdom but the obligations I owed to these are mostly acknowledged in their proper place in the work. After working many a late hour upon the Cuts, the first Volume of the Book was, at length, finished at press in September 1797—Our friend Solomon Hodgson, had no share with us in this Work – Mr Beilby undertook the writing or compilation of this (the first) Volume, in which I assisted him a great deal more than I had done with the Quadrupeds – I was however surprized to find, that in an Introduction written by him in which he took occasion to bestow the most unqualified praises upon me, for the Assistance I had given him, by which I found he was this time determined upon being an Author – I only observed that I thought, the Quadrupeds, with the title of "Beilby & Bewick" as the Editors[1] had done very well and I could see no reason for making any change – I found Mr Beilby had imparted his intentions of becoming Author to the Revd Thomas Hornby,[2] while the latter was at Supper with him, as indeed he often was, when Mr Hornby took occasion to express his opinion of the business and to advise him not to think upon doing any such thing, observing that he could have written a History of birds for me, and that some of the Doctors I was so intimate with, would with pleasure have done the same, perhaps

* Major Henry Forster Gibson died of a fever.

better than he could have done it, but that in neither case could they have hoped to sell a single Edition without my Cuts.–After Mr Hornby had slept & turned the business over in his mind, he called upon me and with a kind of indignant feeling advised me not to permit any such thing–other friends also did the same & used the same kind of reasoning—In this unsettled state of our affairs, Mr & Mrs Beilby set off in the pet, upon a visit to Mr Wilkinson's at Sleekburn, where they remained about a fortnight —On Mr Beilby's return, I asked him if he still persisted in being named as the Author of the Book to which he replied in the affermative–Then Sir said I, if you can point out any single sentance, from one end of this Volume of the History of Birds to the other, of original matter as your own, I shall be glad to see it–at this he hesitated–I then proposed to him to leave the discussion, as to the Authorship, to our mutual friends, who knew every thing relative to the matter in dispute between us, adding that if they agreed in thinking that he ought to be "the author" it should be so, & that I never would say a word more about it–to this he agreed, and as the Work was at a stand, no time was to be lost–after naming our referees–Mr Charnley, the Revd Wm Turner, Mr Sol. Hodgson & Mr Robert Doubleday–were instantly for that purpose summonzed to meet that afternoon–We both guessed, without saying a word to each other, that Mr Charnley would be fixed upon as President, and he being very deaf, we each of us, without mentioning our intentions, stated our seperate cases in writing directed to him[1]–as soon as he & his collegues had read Mr Beilby's he handed it to me & I read it–mine was next given to Mr C who in like manner shewed it to the others & then gave it to Mr Beilby, but he declined looking at it and it was given to me again–after this we were desired to retire, when they committed what they had agreed upon to writing, the whole of which was printed in the concluding part of the preface to the first volume of the Birds. And so the matter was left, without naming either him or myself as Authors of the Work, otherwise than as before, & of the Wood Cuts being acknowledged as my own. After this Mr Beilby gave up the Engraving business & dedicated his whole time to the Watch cristal & Clock manufactory, in which he had been long engaged before our seperation.

–The printing of other Editions of the first Volume of the Birds still met with a ready sale–but some disputes happening between us & Mrs Hodgson the Widow of our much esteemed friend, respecting the printing of the Quadrupeds–Mr Beilby who now sought repose, & could not be turmoiled with disputes of any kind, sold me his third share of that publication. Sometime before the second Volume of the Birds was put to press, he also sold me his half share of this first Volume. For his third share of the Quadrupeds I paid him one hundred pounds, and for his half share of the first Volume of the Birds, I paid him *three hundred pounds*–I had no sooner agreed to give this latter sum, than many recollections of the past crouded upon my mind, and looking at the unfavourable side, I could not help thinking of the extra labour & time I had spent in the completion of these works, wherein he bore comparatively a small part, nor even an equivelent as to his time and labour in the other department of our business, & in this instance I could not help thinking that he had forgot himself & had suffered greadiness to take possession of his mind–but having promised to pay this Sum I made no further observations, about it, to any one–On the other side of this account, I called to my remembrance the many obligations I owed him for the wise admonitions he had given & the example he had set me, while I was only a wild & giddy youth–these I never could forget & they implanted so routed a respect for him that I had grudged nothing I could do to promote his happiness–I noticed, for sometime past, that he had been led, under a guidance & influence, that made an alteration in his conduct & character for the worse and he appeared to me not to be the *Ralph Beilby** he had been, for before this he deservedly bore the character of being a sensible, judicious, Fair dealing & industrious man & a good member of society–I used always to think him carefull & sometimes near & this disposition might indeed have crept & increased upon him–but whatever natural failings might be in his composition, these had hithertofore been checked & regulated by the rules of morality & religion.—It seemed to me that it must have been a maxim with him to do justice to all, but not to confer favors upon any one–and yet he often joined me in conferring such in various ways, upon our Apprentices & other of our work people, for which we commonly

* Ralph Beilby, Engraver Newcastle Died 4 of January 1817 Æt 74 and was buried at St Andrews.

had dirt thrown in our faces–It does not require any great stretch of observation, to discover that gratitude is a rare virtue and that whatever favors are poured upon an ungratefull man, he will conclude that these favors would not have been bestowed upon him had he not deserved them–In these our Gifts to 'prentices & others of that stamp, I was to blame, in thus conferring our favors that it would have been as well to let alone–In other charities he was not backward in contributing his mite, but in these matters he was led by Wisdom–in the former case–mine, by giving vent to my feelings, was led by folly–but indeed these follies were trivial compared with others relative to money matters, in which I had also given vent to my feelings, in lending Money to some & in being bound for the payment of it, for others,–in which, if I had been more of his disposition would not have happened, and I now clearly see & feel had it not been for these imprudencies, I should at this day, have found myself in better & very different circumstances from those I am in–my partner indeed often watched & sometimes prevented me from engaging in such ruinous concerns[1] –& would remark to me that it was impossible to serve, any man who would not serve himself.

After Mr Beilby was done with any concern, in the Publications, I found I could not go on pleasantly with Mrs Hodgson in the Printing of the Quadrupeds,[2] & I therefore offered, either to buy her share or sell her mine, but this she declined doing and sometime after this, she sold hers to Messrs Longman & Co London–& since that time, the publication, shared in this way, has gone on between us–

As soon as Mr Beilby left me, I was obliged from necessity–not choice, to commence Author–As soon as each Bird was finished on the Wood, I set about describing it from my Specimen–and at the same time consulted every Authority I could meet with to know what had been said, & this together with what I knew from my own knowledge, were then compared, and in this way, I finished, as truely as I could, the second Volume[3] of the History of British Birds–I also examined the first Volume with a view to correct its errors, and also to add many new figures & descriptions of them to it.–Although all this of thus taking the whole upon me, could not be done, but by close & indeed severe confinement & application, yet I was supported under these by the extreme pleasure I felt in depicturing & describing these beautifull & very interesting aireal wanderers of the British Isles–I also hoped that my labours might perhaps have the effect of inveigling my youthfull Countrymen, as far as I could, to be smitten with the charms which this branch–& indeed every other department of natural History imparts, and these endless pleasures they afford to all who wish to trace nature up to Nature's God.

While I was thus proceeding, I was countenanced, encouraged and flattered by Amateurs who took a deep interest in my growing Work & seemed to partake of the ardour in which I had long indulged myself–from them Birds were sent to me both far and near–but to give a list of the names of those friends, & to detail the kindness I experienced first & last,–might indeed be giving vent to my feelings of gratitude but it would far exceed the bounds prescribed to this memoir–

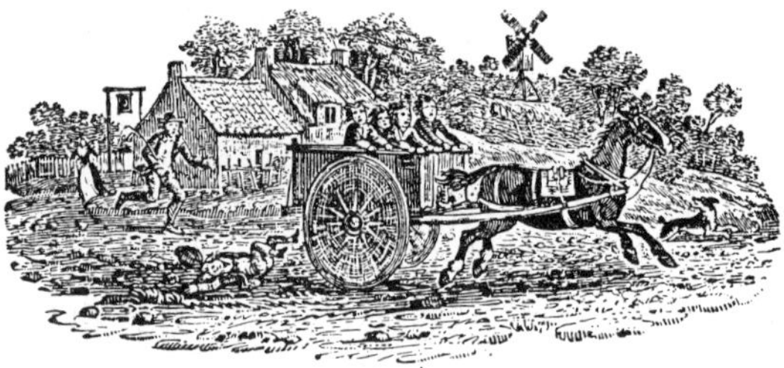

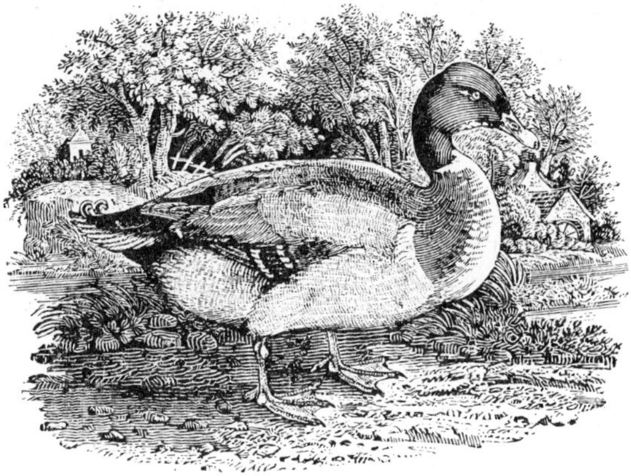

[14]

While I was engaged with the Figures of the Water Birds & the Vignettes, and writing the History, this business was greatly retarded by my being obliged often to lay that work aside & to do various other jobs in the Wood Engraving, and also the work of the Shop for my customers in the Town, but particularly, writing Engraving,[1] which I may say I was obliged to learn & to pursue after Mr Beilby left me, and the most interesting part of this kind of work, was plates for Bank notes, checks &c–but as one of the most important of these was a 5£ Note for the Carlisle Bank, which attracted much notice, it may be right to give some account of it –It happened one Eveg while I was in company with Geo: Losh Esqr who was some way connected with that Bank, he asked me if I could engrave a Note that could not easily be forged,–in reply I told him I thought I could–then said he do it immediately & I lost no time in beginning upon it–I had at that time never seen a ruling Machine,[2] nor the beautifull Engine turning[3] lately brought into use by Perkins, Fareman & Heath, which was at that time (I believe) utterly unknown–I however proceeded with my plate & my object was to make the device look like a Wood cut, and in this ('tho a first attempt) I succeeded & the Number of Impressions wanted were sent to Carlisle—Not long after this, I was told by Sir T[homas] F[rankland] Bart, that his Brother, who held some

Office under Government, and who was in the habit of being much with the late King Geo III, whose curiosity was insatiable, as to every thing relative to the Arts, had got one of these Bank Notes and greatly admired and approved of it—About two years after this (in the year [1801] Samuel Thornton Esqr of the Bank of England, wrote to me respecting this Note, and wished to know how it was done & whether it was executed on Wood or on Copper &c. I was strongly advised by a friend not to give the Gentlemen of that Bank, any information whatever about my plate, for, said he, as soon as they know the nature of what they are enquiring after, you will hear no more from them–I did not take his advice, and after a deal of trouble in writing to them & stating, among many other matters, that 'tho my plate would do well for country Banks–it would not do for the great Number, wanted for the Bank of England–so the business ended in nothing, and I heard no more from them—It may perhaps be well, while I am on the subject of Bank Notes to pass over a number of years, and come down to the year [1818] when a Commission was appointed to investigate the business of forgeries & to endeavour to prevent them in future.—But sometime previous to this, I was employed by my friend John Bailey Esqr of Chillingham to engrave plates to prevent the *pen & Ink* forgeries[1] which had been committed upon the Berwick Bank, which it was found had been better imitations than could be made from copper plates–in this I succeeded–and also (by a simple process) on the plates for the Northumberland Bank.

Immediately on the heel of this & as soon as the Commissioners, above mentioned commenced their enquiries, it seemed as if the services & abilities of all the Artists in the Kingdom were held in requisition, to give in their Specimens & their schemes for this purpose—and willing to contribute all in my power to accomplish so desirable an end–I among many others gave in my plan–and the leading objects with me were perminancy, or in other words to aim at executing a device that would *never* nead either alteration or repairs–and the other part of my plan, was that the Device should be of such a nature that all men of common discernment could easily recognise the note as a legitimate one–I did not mention, in my letters, to Sir Joseph Banks, any thing about using Types or how highly I approved of their use, because I believed that others had done so before, & to point out in which way I conceive they would have been of great importance, would now be useless–since the Commissioners or the Bank, have rejected every scheme (so far as I know) that had been laid before them.—This to me always appeared strange, since, in my opinion there has been several specimens laid before them perfectly efficient for the purpose of preventing Forgeries, or perhaps totally setting that nefarious work at rest–The beautifull specimens first produced by Fairman, Perkins and Heath from their steel plates or blocks, were in my opinion inimitable and quite sufficient to answer the end intended, and those afterwards brought forward under the auspices of Sir William Congreve are nearly of the same character and import–and if an Engine turner cannot set his Lathe, so as to trace or copy the same delicate & truely exact curves & lines &c which are shewn in both, it is not likely that any forgery will ever be attempted upon either of them–if they had been left complex, I would have liked them better–but as they are, the best Engravers on either Copper, Steel or wood, will not attempt an imitation–they may indeed gaze at them–*but that is all*—It was always surprizing to me, that none of the ingenious schemes, so long under the consideration of the Commissioners were not adopted–But when I read, in a Newspaper, that Mr Pierce had stood up in the House of commons, and in answer to some questions put to him there, said in reply, "that the Commissioners were of opinion *that nothing better than the old Bank note could be devised to prevent forgery*!!! then indeed, on reading this, I could scarcely believe my own Eyes–my astonishment was complete–and my opinion of the whole business of this Mountain in labour was fixed.

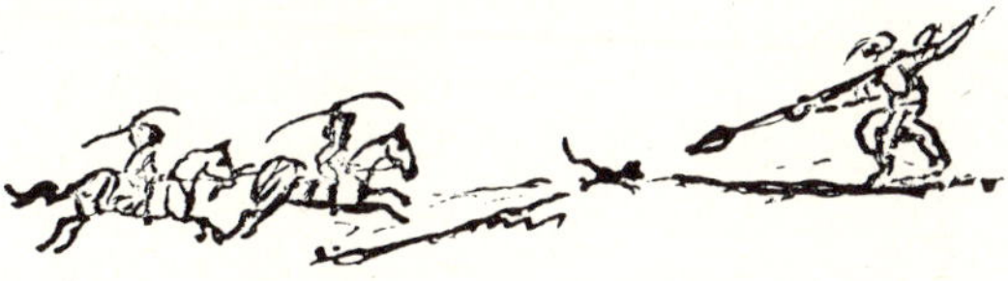

During the time that the business of the Commissioners seemed to me, to be hanging in suspense, I wrote a letter to Sir Joseph Banks, in which I endeavoured to press upon the attention of him and the rest of his collegues, the necessity of having the blank paper of country Bank Notes, printed with whatever new device they might have approved of, to prevent forgery, instead of the little duty stamp, used by Government, which had only the duty in view—Sometime after this, a long account of the invention of Sir William Congreve Bart, was published in the "Repository of Arts" in March 1822 setting forth how much Country Bankers and the whole country was obliged to him, as the inventor of, or the person who first suggested this scheme so essentially important to them, as that of preventing forgeries upon their Banks—As soon as I had read this, I answered it in the Monthly Magazine of May 1822 in which I quoted my letters to the Commissioners, with the dates, bearing upon this very Subject, and claiming the priority of my suggestions to them, at the same time I only requested Sir Wm Congreve, would on the word of a Gentleman, say whether or not this suggestion was his or mine—of this neither Sir William nor any of the Commissioners took any notice–excepting indeed, something *purporting to be an Answer* to what I had said, by a person, in the employ of Sir William as an Artist–which 'tho it begun very impudently, did not answer my letter at all–this, I could not help treating with contempt, & to enter into something like a paper War with such a person I thought would be great folly. Sir William appears to be going on prosperously by furnishing Bankers, with his stamped Notepapers & printing them in the Way above described,—Sir William, as a Commissioner had the opportunity and advantage of seeing the various devices and knowing the opinions of the various Artists, upon these devices which enabled him to cull & select such, as appeared to him best calculated to prevent forgery, and, I think, as he was no Artist himself, he should not have taken any of the credit to himself, either as the inventor or executor of any of these specimens–nor have turned the profit arising from them to his own private account.[1]

Long before the Commissioners were appointed to investigate the business of forgeries–I got engaged in another work, on my own Account.

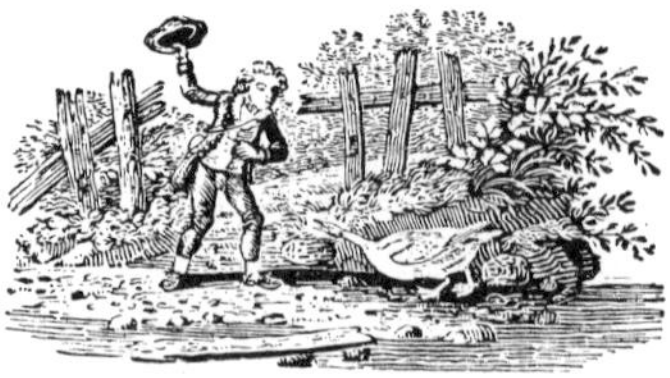

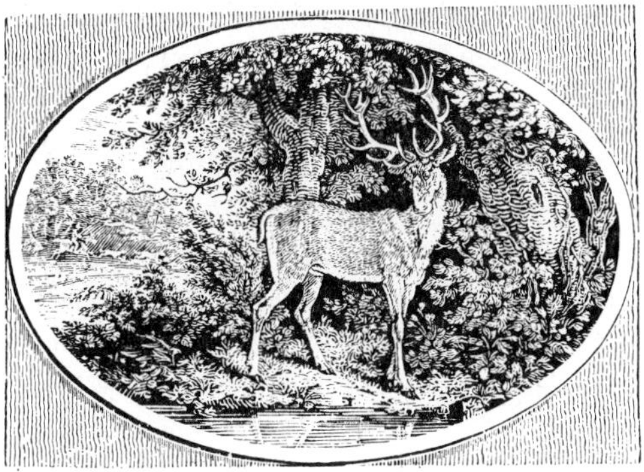

[15]

During a severe illness, with which I was visited in April 1812, brought on by a violent perspiration suddenly checked,–the particulars of which I nead not detail to my dear Jane–as the part you & your Mother & Sisters took to nurse me night & day, for so long a time, must be fresh in all your memories & I only here mention the circumstance on acc^{t} of its having given rise to a determination, if I did recover, to go on with a publication of Esops Fables—While I lay, helpless from weakness & pined to a Skeleton, without any hopes of a recovery being entertained either by myself, or any one else–I became, as it were, all mind and memory,–I readily had presented to my recollection almost every thing that had passed, through life, both of what I had done and what I had left undone–and at last, when after much debating in my own mind where I should be buried–I fixed upon Ovingham–and when this was settled, I became quite resigned to the will of omnipotence and felt happy–I could not however help regretting that I had not published a Book, similar to "Croxalls Esops Fables",[1] as I had always intended to do–I was always extremely fond of that Book, & as it had afforded me much pleasure, I thought with better executed designs, it would impart the same kind of delight to others, that I had experienced from attentively reading it–I was also of opinion, that it had in the same way, while admiring the cuts, led hundreds of young men into the paths of wisdom & rectitude, & perhaps in that way had done more good than the pulpit—As soon as I was so far recovered as to be able to sit at the window at home, I immediately begun to draw designs upon the Wood, of the Fables & vignettes, and to me this was a most delightfull task–In impatiently pushing forward to get to press with the publication, I availed myself of the help of my pupils, (my son, Wm. Harvey & Wm. Temple)[1] who were also eager to do their utmost to forward me in the engraving business & in my struggles to get the Book ushered into the world—Notwithstanding the pleasurable business of bringing out this publication, I felt it also an arduous undertaking–The execution of the fine work of the Cuts, during the day light, was very trying to the Eyes, & the compiling or writing the Book by candle light in my Evenings at home, together injured the Optic nerve & that put the rest of the nerves *out of tune*, so that I was obliged, for a short time to leave off this intense application, untill I somewhat recovered the proper tone of memory & sight again–and I found in this Book more difficulties to conquer than I had experienced with either the Quadrupeds or the Birds–The Book was finished at press on the 1st October 1818 and was not so well printed as I expected & wished. The Ink for such fine work being much too strong, black & thick[2]–I am pleased to find the second Edition Decr 1823 better printed & otherwise managed in other respects.

Thus far from page 101 [p. 95 of this book] was written, during my stay in Tynemouth which I left on the 22 December 1823.

During the eventful period of the French Revolution, & the wide spreading War, which followed in consequence of it, and in which our Government became deeply engaged & commenced its war operations in 1793 & continued 'till the peace of 1814–A life time of Blood & slaughter–I frequently, by way of unbending the mind after the labours of the day, spent my Evenings (chiefly at the Blue Bell) in Company with a set of staunch advocates for the liberties of Mankind, who discussed the passing events mostly with the cool sensible & deliberate attention, which the importance of the subject drew forth–I have already before, named some of these acquaintances, to which I may now add some others, forming altogether a missellaneous group, but over whom some Men of sense & consequence in Newcastle, who were commonly of the party, & from their superiour attainments seemed to preside to set the example of propriety of conduct to those of a more violent turn of mind, but indeed the political enormities of the times excited the indignation of many & which it was not easy to keep within due bounds—The parties which frequented the Blue Bell, & the News Room there, consisted of Tradesmen, Bankers Clerks, Artizans & Agents of various kinds–But those with whom I particularly associated there were Ralph Crawford, Shoe Maker, Joseph Bulmer, builder*–Phineas Crowther, Founder, Michael Charlton White Smith[1], John Mitchell Editor of the "Tyne Mercury", Count Raymond, French teacher & fencing Master & my more constant companion David Sivright Gent^{n}–he was a Man of extraordinary Abilities & Attainments–he belonged to an opulent family near Edinburgh, had been brought up to business in a Bank there–and was afterwards a Wine Merchant in London, where he had associated with the highest ranks of Society–I believe he failed, or at least did not prosper in business–He had been in the West Indies, and returned home in a Merchant Ship, in company with Rodney's fleet & the French Ships of War, his prizes, of which so remarkable a destruction took place in the great storm they had to encounter on their Voyage to England—Whether he had been a disappointed Man in the World, I know not, but to me he appeared so–he had a routed bad opinion of most of the people in very high life–with respect to whom he might be called a Misanthropist–but to others he was affable & kind, and felt most poignantly for the distress of the unfortunate & was ever ready to relieve them–against the former description he appeared to me to be too violent–to the latter I think he shewed something of a sickly sensibility–he could make himself extremely pleasant in company he liked, but to such as he thought badly of either as fools or knaves (& in this he was whimsical) with them he became quite outrageous. I think I was the last person he associated with & even with me he often shewed petulant & as often apologized for it–he had long been used to wander about alone & took to drinking to excess–he left Newcastle & went to Blyth where he died on the [ ] of [ ] Aged 68.

* Joseph Bulmer was a man of talent, he died 23 November 1817 aged 69.

—I sometimes dropped in upon other parties of friends of various political opinions & attainments, at M[rs] Jane Elliots,* at the Sign of the Unicorn,–these were mostly tradesmen of the genteel sort–and besides them, this House had been a kind of rendezvous, or house of resort to the Comedians of our Theatre during the season, for many years back–from the time of Heaton & Austin's Company, down to those conducted by Charles Whitlock, Joseph Munden, Stephen Kemble &c & still later–comprizing a period of the times of Massey & Jeffries, Plat, Emery, Cook, Liston & many others who made a figure in their day–With Jo: Munden, I often associated & still oftener & to a later period with my friend Stephen Kemble† & his friends. In her House & indeed in every house, Politics formed the topic of conversation & less or more, for years back seemed the order of the day.

In my partaking in these debatings, I now find I spent rather too much time–I fear it was useless–for it requires little descernment to see that where a man's interest is at stake he is very unwilling to hear any argument that militates against it and people who were well paid, were always very loyal–to argue on any subject, unless a principle, or what Mathemeticians would call a datum, is first laid down, to go upon, the conversation is only gabble–it begins & must end in nonsense–And I suspect that many of the long wearisome speeches & debatings, for such a number of years, in the House of Lords & Commons–as well as many of the innumerable weekly or dayly essays & some of the pamphlets, which the Revolution & the War gave rise to, were very often carried on without laying down a right principle–a principle of rectitude, to guide them—But the causes of this horrid Revolution & the equally horrible war which ended it, will form a most interesting subject for the head & the pen of some future Historian, of a bold & an enlightened mind, truely to depicture it, in all its bearings–long after the animosity of party feelings & the parties themselves have died away.

From the best consideration I have been able to give the

* Jane Elliot, as a landlady, conducted herself with great propriety. She was sensible, spirited, clever & obliging & from these qualifications & from her handsome & majestic appearance, was called the Queen of Landladies–She died 12 Octr 1822 Æ 74 and was buried at St Johns & on the same day, with her friend Mrs Sarah Hodgson the widow of Solomon Hodgson.

† Stephen Kemble died 5 June 1822 Aged 65 and was buried in Durham Cathedral.

question on this momentous dispute, I cannot help viewing it otherwise than in this way–In the Year 1789 the French Revolution broke out first of all from the income of the Government not being sufficient to defray its expenditures, or in other words, from its finances having became deranged for want of money–& which the people, having been taxed to the utmost & brought down to poverty could no longer supply. The Aristocracy & the priesthood (the priviledged orders as they were called) contributed little or nothing, to support the state, & they quite forgot, that instead of their being the natural guardians, or depositories of the honour & virtue to the nation–they were chiefly known only as its oppressors, & their exactions & their cruelties & tyrany by which the people had long been born down, to the lowest pitch of degradation and were long considered, not as rational human beings, equal in mind & intellect to themselves, but as beings made for the purpose only of continually labouring, to support them in all their real and imaginary wants, & then to be treated worse than beasts of burthen, and this is nearly the case in all countries where such numbers of the Aristocracy are kept up, blinded by misplaced pride & guided by ignorance–and these again have what may be called their Satellites–a kind of bastard breed, who in aping the worst part of the character, of those exalted above them, shewed themselves off as the opulent, aspiring, purse proud Gentry of a country

"If aught on earth the immortal powers deride,
"'Tis surely this,–the littleness of pride."

This kind of treatment, so long shewn to the people of France could be endured no longer–they indeed seemed heartily disposed & would have settled a rational & just representative Government, quietly enough themselves–but this did not suit the views of the surrounding Despots, to whom the very word Liberty, was offensive to their Ears–it was terrible, & not to be listned to for a moment–and it was determined at once, that this attempt of that People to resume their Rights, should instantly be overwhelmed & crushed at once, & for this purpose, their immense Armed well deciplin'd Mercinaries, were gathered together & almost surrounded the country. Thus situated, and remembering the traditionnary tales handed down to them, of the cruelties and oppressions, under which their forefathers had groaned, the french people could not bear the thoughts of it any longer–they were driven to madness, and instantly retaliated those long matured enormities, upon those, who they conceived meant, in like manner, that they and their children's children should continue to be doomed to bear the same for ages to come. In this state of the public mind, the French people rose simultaneously, as one man, and with unconquerable energy & bravery, like a whirlwind, swept off the advocates & the armies of despotism in heaps, or one after another, from the face of the earth.—Thus roused, this confedracy of Legitimates, finding or fearing that they might be baffled in their attempts, it would appear, looked to England for support–and grieved indeed were the advocates for rational liberty & well wishers to their country, to find that the enemies of freedom had not looked in vain–for the Government, the Government of this free country! & free people!–long veering indeed from the right line of rectitude *& freedom* had readily found pretexts for bending it to aside, that it might be the more easily broken when the fit opportunity presented itself–and pretexts & pretences, were also as readily found for entering into this War of despotism & war was begun in the year 1793 against the then Republican Government of France—It had long been the settled opinion of many profound politicians, that corruption had spread & was spreading its baneful influence among the Members of the Government of this Kingdom, & that the majority of them, cared nothing about maintaining the constitution in its purity, & which to them was become like an old Song—In this state of things & ready primed, with M[r] Pit at their head & the resources of the British Isles in his hands, it was calculated upon as a certainty that this weight added to the already powerfull confedracy, would soon put a stop to the march of intellect, & if found necessary, put an extinguisher upon the rights of man–it is horrible to contemplate the immense destruction of human beings & the waste of treasure which supported & followed this superlatively wicked War—Under the mask of patriotism M[r] Pit had begun his career, but he soon changed sides & (blinded perhaps by ambition) became the powerfull advocate of an opposite & perverted order of things—Thus situated, nothing could to a certainty serve his purpose so well, as corruption & the

House of commons had long been growing into a state befitting them for this purpose, for they had, in a great degree ceased to be the representatives of the people–and he had now only to begin an invigorated new, or more extended system of place & patronage, to have the majority of the House at his nod, & in aid of this to add an extension of the Peerage–and this Demi Oligarchy, cemented together by the same fellow feeling of rapacious interests thus set agoing–this British government, in his hands, was at once the best organised system of extorting money ever acted upon to fleece their subjects that had appeared in the world—they then met together to tax, tax–tax & under various pretexts to rob the people "according to law" & to divide the spoil among themselves & their friends.–They passed arbitrary laws–gaging bills[1] were passed & a system of espionage spread over the whole kingdom, to keep the people down, many of whom seemed to have forgotten the exertions of their forefathers whose blood had been spilt to purchase a better order of things—I felt particularly hurt at the apathy of country Gentlemen, in these (politically considered) worst of times,–their faculties seemed benumbed–but indeed most of them fell into the vortex of corruption themselves–they appeared to me to have lost their former independant character–& to be now looking out to that evil source as a provision for the younger branches of their own families, unmindfull of all other ill consequences which this selfishness blindly supported and maintained–The Minions of power & spies were countenanced & protected, by which they became insolent & impudent & walked in stately array hand in hand in safety—Altho the friends of liberty & the Constitution in its purity, were both numerous & intrepid, yet for want of, what they termed respectable heads, they were widely spread and divided & their efforts proved in vain.–There was also an intermediate or kind of nutral race, of those who had not laid down any principle in Politics to guide them–they were mostly such as advocated the cause of corruption, and in listning to them, I was often disgusted at their senseless arguments, they were proof against reasoning & thoroughly convinced me, that a wise man changes his opinion, but a fool never does–they however kept on the safe side–they *were loyal*, and the jist of their arguments, with which they ended all their disputes, were summed up in this–"if you do not *like your Country* leave it–What do you want ?are not *we* very well off?"—their reflecting powers reached no further, and they could not see the slow degrees, by which the Arm of despotism had so often circumspectly stretched its iron hand over the liberties of the people & then crushed them—While bickerings & debatings were going on among politicians at home, the continent was deluged with the blood of many destructive battles–the Sea was also stained with it in the same way–and it was on this element that the Tide of affairs was first turned in favour of Britain, who now by the valour of her seamen reigned complete "Mistress of the deep" and the commerce of the World seemed to be poured into her lap–Estates rose in value to an extraordinary height & the price of grain &c still more so in proportion–the shipping interest wallowed in riches–the Gentry whirled about in aristocratic pomposity, they forgot what their demeanour & good, kind, behaviour, used to be, to those of inferiour stations in life & seemed now, far too often, to look upon them like dirt.–The character of the farmers, were also *totally* altered, from what it used to be, and they now acted the Gentleman very awkwardly–they could not, in these times, drink any thing but wine, & even that was called "humble Port" & they were to have such kinds as bore a higher price–when they left the market, they were fitted to ride over all they met, or overtook, on the way. –but this was as nothing compared to the pride & folly, which took possession of their empty, or fume charged heads, when they got dressed in scarlet–they were then fitted for any purpose & were called "*Yeomanry Cavelry*"[1]–pride & folly in them then became personified—When peace came, it brought with it, a sudden fall of the prices of corn–but the taxes continuing the same to them, & rents still keeping high, they (with few exceptions) suddenly experienced a woefull change–I cannot say, after seeing so much of their folly, that I was sorry for them, for they mostly deserved this reverse of fortune—Not so with the industrious labourer, his privations were great & he was undeservedly doomed to suffer, for want of employment & often to waste away & die of hunger & want.

–During the War the Landholders may be said to have paid little or nothing to support it, for their extra rents paid almost all their Taxes–at length the evils brought on, by so long a war, fell also heavily upon numbers of them who, on account of Tythes &

Taxes, with which the land was loaded, they could hardly get any Rent at all—It will seem a wonder to future Ages, how the British People could so long support the squandered expenditure of the Government–but they are still not like the long-worn-down Subjects of continental Despots,–for what they can get from their Subjects is like clipping the fleece from the back & sides of swine–while the ingenuity–the industry & the energy of the British People furnish the well grown fleeces of Sheep–and it is a great pity they should have been so often wickedly fleeced to the bare skin. This state of temporary internal prosperity first excited to agricultural improvements, and Societies for the promotion & premiums for the encouragement of its various desiderata blazed forth over [a] great part of the Kingdom–Cattle, Sheep, Horses & swine–all of which was called "live stock", occupied *a great deal* of their attention & in the improvement of the various breeds they surely succeeded to [a] certain extent–& in some cases, perhaps to a great extent, and yet I cannot help thinking that they often suffered their whimsies to overshoot the mark & in many instances, to lead them on to the *rediculous*.–But after all these enquiries evil it seems, must be mixed with good in this life, for the eyes of the Landlords were so opened to their own interest, in what was made apparent, that the man of industry, the plain plodding Farmer, did & will have to pay for these improvements.

My kind–my intimate–my old friend John Bailey Esq[re]* of Chillingham in conjunction with another friend of mine, George Cully Esq[r] of Fowberry were the active judicious & sensible Authors of many of the Agricultural reports[1] in which they did not lose sight of the Farmer & they wished to inculcate the principle "to live & let live", between the Landlord & his Tenant.

It will readily be supposed, that where such exertions were used, and pains taken to breed the best kinds of all the domestic Animals, that jealousy & envy would be excited & contentions arise, as to which were the best–but for me to dilate upon this, would only lead me out of my way.—I shall however notice an instance, as it happened to be between my two friends M[r] Smith, of Woodhall & M[r] Bailey–the latter, in his report of the Cheviot Sheep, had given a bad figure of a Ram, of that breed,–this was construed into a design to lessen the character of M[r] Smith's

* John Bailey Esq[re] died 3 June 1819 aged 68 & was buried at Chillingham.

Cheviot Sheep, on which occasion, in April 1798 Mr Smith sent for me to make a drawing of one of his Rams, to be engraved–partly by way of contrasting it, with the figure Mr Bailey had done in the same way for his Report–The colour Mr Smith gave to the business was not to find fault with Mr Bailey's figure–but to shew how much Mr Smith had improved the breed since Mr Bailey had written his report, & given his figure along with it.—While I was at Woodhall I was struck with the sagacity of one of Mr Smith's shepherd's dogs–that part of their character was well known–but this was exemplified *before my own eyes*–Mr Smith wished to have a particular Ram brought out from among the flock, for the purpose of my seeing it–before we set out, he observed to the Shepherds, that the old Dog, (he was grey headed & almost deaf & blind), he thought, would do well enough for what he wanted with him–Before we reached the down where the flock was feeding, I observed Mr S was talking to the Dog, before he ordered him off on this errand, and while we were talking on some indifferent subject, the dog brought a Ram before us, upon which Mr S. found a deal of fault with the Dog–"did I not order you so & so"? & scolded him as if he had been a Man, for bringing a wrong one–and then set him off again to bring the Ram he wished to see–this was then soon done, & the other animal was suffered again to join the Flock–after fresh directions had been given, we then returned home & shortly after our arrival there, the Dog brought the very Ram wanted, along with a few of the Sheep, into the fold, where I took the drawing of him.

Shortly after my return home from Woodhall, I was sent for to go to Darlington & thence to Barmpton, to make drawings of Cattle & sheep to be engraved for a Durham Report.–After I had made my drawings, I soon saw, that such as I had made from the fat Sheep, were not such as were wanted, but these were to be made like the *such & such* paintings as were shewn to me–I observed that these paintings were nothing like the animals whose Figures I had made my drawings from & that I would not alter mine to suit the paintings that were shewn to me nor put my name to such–but if it were wished that I should make engravings from these paintings, I had not the slightest objection to do so, & that I would also endeavour to make fac similies of them—but this proposal would not do–and my journey, as far as concerned these fat Cattle makers, ended in nothing–I would not put lumps of fat here & there to please them where I could not see it–at least in so exagerated a way as on the painting before me–so I got my "labour for my trouble"–many of the Animals were, during *this rage* for fat Cattle, surely fed up to as great a weight & bulk, as it was possible for feeding to make them but this was not enough, they were to be figured monstrously fat before the owners of them could be pleased—some painters were found who were quite subservient to their guidance & complied with their wishes, but nothing less would please.—Many of these paintings will mark the times & by the exagerated productions of the Artists, serve to be laughed at, when the folly & the Self interested motives which gave birth to them, are done away.

Sometime after the death of Mr Gill, he was succeeded by another hospitable friend, Thomas Maddison Esqre* of Birtley, at whose Town's house I spent many a social Evening–he, like the former delighted in gathering together a few friends to talk away the Winter evenings, on various subjects, but never to a late hour.—his most constant visitors were–John Anderson, Surgeon–old John Walker†–patent Sadler, with his friend & assistant in that business, John Hall–Captn John Reay, of the light House–low lights, No Shields–and Charles Whitlock comedian & other occasional visitors–he also frequently had some of us in parties, along with him to Birtley–where he also constantly invited the Roman Catholic Priest of the place & other Neighbours to partake with us, of his good cheer.–

* Thomas Maddison died 12 October 1811 Aged 73 & was buried in Chester le Street church–he was of an independant character.–he was one of the committee (the youngest) who tried the Magistrates of NC respecting the Town Moor, in 1774

† John Walker died in Paris, in 182[ ] at about 100 years old

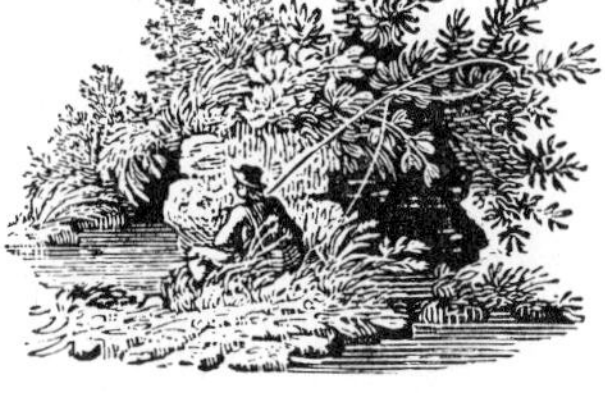

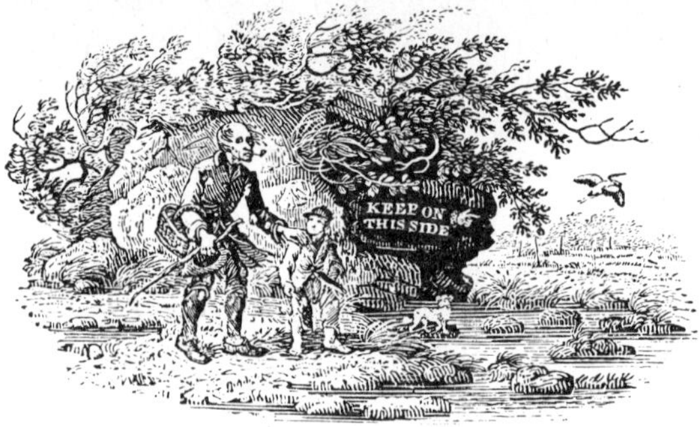

[16]

From this time 'till the peace was concluded, the same kind of political debatings, continued & were almost the constant subject, in all companies, and I have often sat & listned with wonder, at the jargon of the protected fools & the impudent faces put on by those who lived upon the taxes, to hear them argue, if so it may be called, in defense of all the measures, now pursued–a great portion of these seemed to me to be smitten with blindness & knaves & their abettors appeared to predominate or over rule the country & this they carried to such a length, that I think if Mr Pit had proposed to make a law to transport all men who had Pug noses, & to hang all men above 60 years of age, these animals (those excepted who came within the meaning of the act) would have advocated it as a brilliant thought & a wise measure. If we examine these times and look back at such like, of old, we may indeed wonder at both–the inroads of ignorance have been the same–The time was (see "Englands Grievance"[1] &c by Ralph Gardner of Chirton in the year 1655) when the Magistrates of Newcastle sent to Scotland for a Man, who was reputed as being very clever in discovering Witches–he came & easily convicted many a fine Woman as well as those who were wrinkled with age & wisdom, & they were by his means tried & put to death,–he returned home very rich, and as soon as General (Leslie? Hobson?)[2] knew all the circumstances from his friends in Newcastle, he sent for this wretch to Berwick, where he then commanded his Army, and hanged him at once without either judge or Jury–did he do wrong?*—I think, if there be a plurality of Devils, Ignorance must be their King—The wretchedness which Ignorance has, from time to time spread over the World, is truely appalling–*This is a King that should be deposed, without loss of time*–and that portion of mankind, who are under the guidance of his Imps, should have nothing to do with the affairs of Society & should be carefully looked to & kept out of every kind of command, & even the poor innocent unreasoning Animals should, in mercy, not be allowed to be goaded & to suffer under their folly & cruelty.

To attempt giving any thing like a detail of the history of this eventfull war, would in this place be useless–that must be left to the Historian—It appears to me that M[r] Pit was urged into it, chiefly by ambition & that his disappointments broke his heart—General Bonaparte, from his unparalelled victories, became in his turn blinded by ambition, which ended in his being conquered, & banished to S[t] Helena for life—He had divided & conquered, in victory after victory, almost all his continental enemies, one after another, & then, mostly generously returned them their dominions back again, but this would not all do–despotism, urged on & supported by this country, was rooted too deeply in their Governments, for them to think of making any change to better the condition of their people. It would appear, it is a business they cannot think of, and the old maxim with them, that the many, were made only to support the few, seems continually uppermost, in their resolves.—If Bonaparte had been as good a Man, as he was a great one, he had it in his power to settle all this, & to have established the happiness of both the Governments & the people, over all the civilised World, for ages to come–but although he had the example of the incomparable Washington before him, he did not copy him. He ceased to be the first consul of France & then managed to get himself made Emperour,–married the princess of Austria, and became one of the legitimates & this, added to the stock of his Ambition, and from that time he began to decline–Fortune at length seemed to frown upon him & the frost & Snow of Russia, cut off & destroyed his immensely large & well appointed

* This part is traditionary–Gardner says–he was for such like "villanie" hanged in Scotland–"and upon the Gallows, he confessed he had been the death of two hundred & twenty women in England & Scotland, for the gain of twenty Shilings apiece, and beseached forgiveness, & was executed".

Army & quickly afterwards, baffled his future strenuous efforts to repair his loss & paved the way for his defeat at Waterloo, which sealed his ruin.–

One would think that the gaining of Worlds, would not compensate the misery & the horrid waste of human life, which are the certain attendants of War, and one would wonder, what kind of materials men are made of or what kind of *minds & souls* direct the actions of the Authors of it—were they to reflect, it may fairly be concluded, they could not bear their own thoughts & that they would after taking a cool survey of the wretchedness they have occasion'd, go immediately & hang themselves—But it would appear, that the lives of human beings weigh little in the scale of great Man-killers–they are perhaps not fitted for reflection, or perhaps only that kind of it, which can look at nothing but their own misguided ambition, or private gain.—It would be well for the abettors and advocates of war, to try to weigh the good & bad (setting aside the inhumanity) attendant upon such a wicked & disgracefull course of things–This we should begin at home–and instead of celebrating the birth day of the "Heaven born Minister" –ask his admirers how he is entitled to this–to shew the birth of *this babe of grace*, & then to compare his actions with the title his friends have thus bestowed upon him–Might not the lives of say a Million of Men have been saved? and better employed than cruelly wasted in this way? could he have done it? with his consumate abilities I humbly think he could–Would not these men if so directed, have been sufficient in number, to colonise or otherwise people & civilise immense unoccupied territories, & the money wasted would have done almost any thing–Would not the men & the money have canalled Britain & Ireland from end to end, and intersected them from side to side? and also have made Piers (if wanted) at the Mouths of every River in the two Islands & besides have converted both into Gardens–but to point out more improvements would be a waste of words, with such means in hand, they might have been almost endless–Then ꝑ contra what has been done with the Millions of lives and Millions of money thus spent?–they have restored Legitimacy! they have restored Louis "the desired" & Ferdinand "the beloved"! & the Inquisition! & they are still to be called "Gods Viceregents here on earth"!–When by their actions they shew themselves deserving of such like titles–

mankind will not disturb them in these their dreams–but 'till then they will continue to smile at the conceit, as well as the *glitter* they keep up to dazzel the sight only of their purblind *loving Subjects.* All wars, except defensive ones are detestable and if Governments admitted morality into their institutions and were guided by its precepts, all wars, would in all probability grow into disuse & cease–but hitherto that treasure of inestimable value I think has been discarded from their councils–And I cannot discover much difference between them & the lesser Banditti of old–for in the former as well as the latter they were guided by the strong disposition to rob as soon as they thought themselves able, successfully to do so & to shew that they thought "*might was right*".—From the Feuds of the Nobility down to Rob-in-hood, Will Scarlet & Little John, and from the ferocious combats of the Percy & Douglas on the Borders–of Johnny Armstrong & his "eight score of Men", down to Adam "(Yeddy) Bell", Clem o the cleugh & "William of Cloudsly" & the Mosstroopers, the same wicked principle guided them & their ferocious retainers to murder each other & soak the earth with their blood.

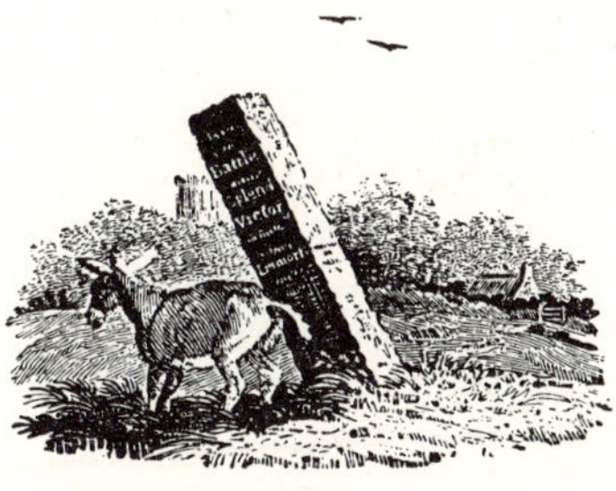

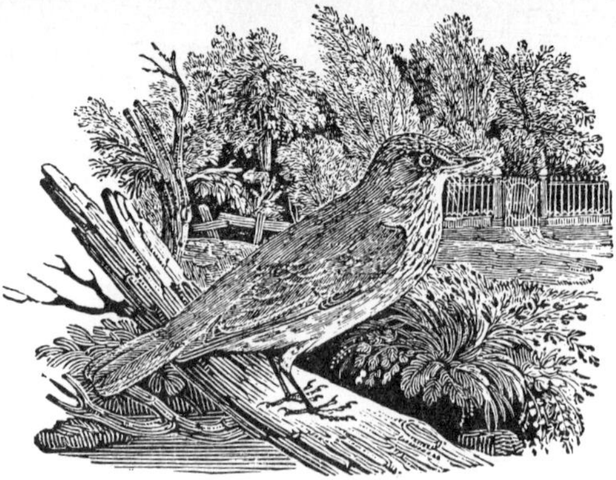

[17]

Without presuming to scan the intentions of omnipotence, in his gifts to the human race, or to probe into the nature & cause of his endless Works of Wisdom–or to grope into matters, intended to be out of our reach and bejond our comprehension–yet the reasoning power he has given us we cannot doubt was to guide us in our researches, to the extent, for which it is capacitated, and to which its uses are fitted to be applied. In venturing thus, as far as our limited understanding can go, we may, with diffidence attempt to trace the designs of the creator perhaps to the verge, of some of his wonderful Works, and without bewildering the mind with Metaphysical reveries–enter at once upon the extended or endless plain, to view indeed with dazzeled vision, what objects our conceptions present to us, respecting the life the mind or the Soul of Man–And without being better able to account for these mysterious matters one may be allowed to say, it appears to us, that as soon as the child is born–with the first breath it inhales, is imparted the etherial spark of animation, which then becomes a living soul–and which is to make its way into its earthly habitation of nerves & brain &c befitting its reception & then kept up in perpetual motion by the air inhaled & again pumped out again & also to receive the gift of a greater or lesser degree of its innate powers, which Omnipotince willed it shall be possessed of, to serve its purposes in this World where it must remain for a time, progressively to improve, while it is thus connected with this its earthly Tenemant–and this is the allotted time for the fulfilling of its relative moral & religious duties, 'till this habitation falls into decay & whether the atoms of which it was composed, will, by the same power be again altered & united, is at the will of the creator.—Then commences a new era when the imperishable spirit the emanation from omnipotence takes flight to regions unknown–our reasoning powers of prying further stop here, & their place is supplied with instinctive knowledge, a gift equally powerfull to guide us to the *unknowable* God–in whose presence this animated spark, this enlightened mind & soul must appear, to be prepared for some other change for which it may be better fitted, to soar thro' endless Worlds & more towards perfection to all eternity—To doubt this, is like doubting the wisdom & goodness of omnipotince–for, if otherwise, we are left in the dark & led to wonder, what for, & why we have with a mind & soul been placed here, for a limited time, to view this beautifull World & the immensity of the universe & then to be all together anihilated—we may stop here & with surprize ask ourselves, what it is all about? and are driven to the conclusion that this is all labour in vain.—In returning back, from these reveries, to view man, as connected with this world & with his station in society, I think it will appear clearly, that the various gradations & degrees of his intellectual & reasoning powers are the gift of providence, & however high this boon may be, the possessor of it, ought to be thankfull but never vain. It is this innate power, drawn forth and acted upon by observation and industry, that enables the Poet, the philosopher, the painter & the Musician, *easily* to arrive at excellence–and the same is more or less applicable to all Men, bent upon any other pursuit in the whole round of the Arts and sciences, to enable them to attain to the summit of their wishes, but without using the means to cultivate this power, it will remain inert and be of no use, either to the individual or to society–and men with these qualifications, and men without them are brought down to a level of uselessness–and it is greatly owing to such like causes that we mostly see the origin of the inequallities of rank & fortune of which the community is composed.—The intelligent & industrious man, guided by honour & honesty, will ever be aiming to rise in the scale of eminence–while, on the contrary, the lazy the ignorant or the wicked Man, commonly led by his misdirected pride, dissipation & negligence is whirled into the vortex of disgrace, attended by poverty, & perhaps misery, & if he cannot redeem his character, but becomes abandoned, he is then in his last stage.—his days will be full of sorrow, and if it be true that "none are *wretched* but the *wicked*" he will have his fill of it.—But to remedy these evils, attendant upon ignorance, as far as possible, and to give every Man, a fair chance, his reasoning powers ought to be drawn forth by a *rational & virtuous education*, and it is a first & imperative duty upon the community invariably, either to provide for, or to see that it is done to every one, as far as his capacity will enable him to go–for to the neglect or omission of this kind of instruction, may be, traced almost all the wickedness and misrule which disfigure the social compact and spread misery over the world–to check the reasoning power, thus bestowed, is a public crime, which, like individual crimes, follow the perpetrators of them like a shadow–To argue against this gift is attempting to thwart the intentions of Omnipotence–it is blasphemy–it never will pollute the tongues of good & wise men, and could only, like dregs, be reserved to defile those of tyrants & fools–To men who are not actuated by the principle of "doing as they would be done by" this order of things do not relish, and from a mistaken notion, or twisted imagination they would have their fellow men kept in ignorance, like Machines, or to pass away their lives like unreasoning Animals, lest as they suppose they might not have sufficient homage paid to themselves, or that they would forget their duty as Servants & cease to work for or wait upon their employers—a sensible servant will never omit doing his duty but an ignorant one will, and the reciprocal duties between Master and servant ought to be clearly defined when they will [*illeg.*] there is no difficulty in the way and a first step to go upon, is that the former ought not to act the tyrant & the latter who should be obedient, but not be treated like a slave & equal & just laws ought to guide and govern them and the whole community—All men of sound understanding and who are capable of reflection will clearly see, that there is not, and cannot be any such thing as equallity in a state of society–there must, and ever will be, high & low, rich & poor, and this inequallity of rank & fortune, which in well civilised states, is necessary for the comfort & happiness of all, & a Cement is thus formed which binds together in union the strength, the beauty and symetry of the whole–In the freest state, man must not expect to have the unrestrained liberty of the Savage but must give up a part of his own freedom for the good of the whole, for liberty consists in this, that every man may do whatever he pleases, provided in doing so, he does nothing to injure his neighbour–nor to the community, of which he is a member and his morality ought to be guided by the "golden rule" of "doing unto all men, as he would they should do unto him"–Were men made sensible of the rectitude of this order of things, and that in whatever station in society fortune may have placed them, and their abilities enabled them well to fulfill, they ought to consider it as the will of providence that it should be so–and this would greatly contribute to their peace of mind & contentment–for no man should think himself degraded by following any honest calling & remember that

> Honour & shame from no condition rise
> Act well your part–there all the Honour lies

Patriotism ought to direct every man to do honour to himself and to his country–for great energy in individuals, produces also a union of individual energy & it is in this, that national power principally consists–it is also from the good conduct & consequent character of the great mass of the people, that a nation is exalted–these give the pleasure, the true satisfaction, which renown conveys–the Crown, the richest diamond of our life is the love of our country, & the man who does not do so and reverence & adore his Maker is good for nothing.–The country, surrounded by the briny deep, where all our ancestors lie buried–in which, from youth upwards we have felt the benefit of equal Laws, first acted upon and handed down to us by the Great Alfred & maintained from time to time amidst all the attempts of despotism to overturn them, by Men famed for matchless wisdom & virtue—"A Country so renowned as England" so famous for all that most strongly attracts the Admiration of men–a Country whose genious & power, have for ages, been such as to make her views & intentions an object of solicitude with every nation & with every enlightened individual in the World–a country famed for her laws, famed in arts & arms, famed for the struggles which age after age, her Sons have held with tyranny in every form it has assumed, & bejond all these famed for having given birth to, & reared to Manhood, those men of matchless wisdom & virtue, whose memories will be held up to admiration & whose example will be followed in ages to come, they have rendered the very name of Englishman respected in every civilized country in the World. (may this be eternal!)—Should this country ever sink into despotism, its reputation will sink also & with it, the high name of its once enlightened Sons–but this renown & this exalted station cannot be stable unless a pure representation of the people can be kept up, for without that, corruption will creep in, justice will be perverted & in time will overturn the best & wisest laid plans–Governments will become the owners of their Subjects property or have a hand in all their great concerns, instead of being the umpires between the general owners, & standing by, like a strong man to see that justice is done —Lord Bacon says "The ultimate object which Legislators ought to have in view & to which all their enactments & sanctions ought to be subservient is–*that the citizens may live happy*–For this purpose, it is necessary that they should receive a religious & pious education; that they should be trained to good morals; that they should be secured from foreign enemies by proper military arrangements; that they should be guarded by an effectual police against seditions and private injuries; that they should be loyal to Government, and obedient to Magistrates; and finally that they should abound in wealth, and other national resources". Well constituted Governments if occasionally revised, and as often as necessary scrupulously amended, may be rendered as permanent as time. If wisely & virtuously administered, they would be indestructible & incalculably contribute, by their vigour & uninterrupted duration, to the mental & moral aggrandiscment of Man—It is a truth, confirmed by Universal history, that the happiness or misery of a people almost entirely depends upon the principles of their Governments & the conduct of their Rulers. Where just & honourable intentions exist, there is nothing to dread, but where only the semblance of these are put on to cloak wicked & sinister ends, delusion & artifice of every kind must be resorted to for their accomplishment–Thence follows the degredation of Man & the consequent decay of states & Nations. But it is not for want of knowing better, that Governments get out of the path of rectitude –it is by the individuals who compose its parts becoming dishonest.

—To the sage advice of such men as Bacon or Lock, or any other philosopher or Politician of more modern times, they turn a deaf ear–they are lost in considerations about their own private selfish concerns, or are led on, blinded perhaps by a false ambition, regardless about promoting the public good, or the happiness of mankind; and untill they are checked in this their career, by an enlightned people, it is in vain to look for any amendment in them–but the great bulk of the people must be first enlightned & amended, before liberty peace & happiness can be spread over a civilized World—The first step preparatory to this desireable order of things, must be that mankind should learn to respect themselves as reasoning beings, which is the noblest priviledge bestowed upon them by the creator–to slight this Gift is to act ungratefully to the donor–for it is only by the free exercise of their understandings that men can see the face of truth or can have the full use of all the means of advancing in knowledge or are capable of Science, religion, virtue & rational happiness or can be enabled to look backward with comfort or forward with hope—It is a sure sign that all is not right, or as it should be in Governments, when they fear even the fullest investigation of any & of every subject—truth & honesty fear no discussions & good Governments will freely encourage instead of checking them–can any Man say in the face of the World, that truth ought not to prevail. There ought to be no libels but falshoods (these ought indeed to be tenderly dealt with) and folly ought to be answered by redicule—It is owing to inquisitorial checks & restraints, that two of the most important concerns to mankind–Religion & Politics–and on which their happiness & every thing of infinite importance to them, so much depends, should by the community taken as a whole be so imperfectly understood, & so blindly acted upon, at this day.—It is only by seeing public matters, as they have been lately conducted, by Public Men, in a clear light, that a just judgement can be formed of them & their measures, and of their fitness or unfitness to conduct the important concerns intrusted to their control—they indeed may fear, if tried *in the balance*, that they will be found very light–and that wise & honest councils must be resorted to & adopted, before Morality, Religion & politics, Arts & sciences, and a better knowledge of this World of wonders, and the intentions of the all-wise and omnipotent Creator can be developed &

apreciated. Till then, no amendment need be expected—Religion will not be freed from ignorance superstition & bigotry—nor Political institutions purged from venality & corruption and conducted by honesty & good sense.—Those who have fixed themselves like a disease upon the body politic, should have warning to depart, but to let them & their illgotten sinecures & enormous wages cease only with their lives. In glancing back upon the transactions of the world, as they have recently passed in review before us, how can it afford any matter for wonder, that the advocates of liberty should entertain fears for its safety, and wish, as a check, the reestablishment of the British constitution in its purity—there was indeed little hopes of this being acted upon, when foreign despots were leagued to enslave their own people & our own Government, supported by a demi Oligarchy, was so deeply connected with them—& by whose excessive expenditure in loans after loans, of money, wrung from the people under various pretexts, but in reality to support despotism under the disguse of legitimacy—an honest house of commons, might indeed have supported legitimacy but they would have put in their word and openly expressed their disapprobation about the lost liberties of nations of enslaved people—Enquiries of this kind however did not fit with the notions of the representatives of Boroughmongers who composed the majority of the "*hon*[ble] *House*" & had long been used to treat the people & their petitions with unblushing neglect or contempt—In this state of things, politics ran high,—an unpleasant ferment soured the minds of a great majority of the people and it cannot be wondered at that they were with difficulty kept within bounds:—Those who had been used to batten on the wages of corruption became excessively alarmed, & under the pretence of preserving the constitution, resorted to a system of espionage & Goals & Bastiles and left no stone unturned to throw odium upon their opponents—the advocates of liberty, who were branded with the nicknames of Jacobins levellers, radicals &c. The pen of literature was prostituted to overshade the actions of good men & to gloss over the enormities of the base—The energies of many members of both houses of parliament were unavailing against this compact confedracy of undiserving placemen & pentioners who were bound together by fellow feelings of self interest, in which all ideas of public trust were lost in private considerations—they had sinned themselves out of all shame–this Phalanx kept their ground, & it will do so, 'till, it is to be feared, violence, from an inraged people will break them up, or, perhaps, 'till their growing opinions against this crooked order of conducting the affairs of this great nation, becomes quite apparent to an immense majority, whose frowns may have the power of bringing the Agents of Government to consider the brink of the precipiece, on which they stand & to provide in time by wise & honest measures to avert the coming Storm; it is appalling to think of matters of this import being brought to extremeties, especially when the whole might so easily be settled without any convulsion at all—A word from the King (whose interests are the same as the peoples) if freed from the advice of evil counsellors & the unfitting trammels by which they have him bound–might insist upon having the constitution restored to its purity & this would at once do the business & make him adored by his whole people, as well as his name being revered, by the enlightened in every civilised country, to the latest posterity.

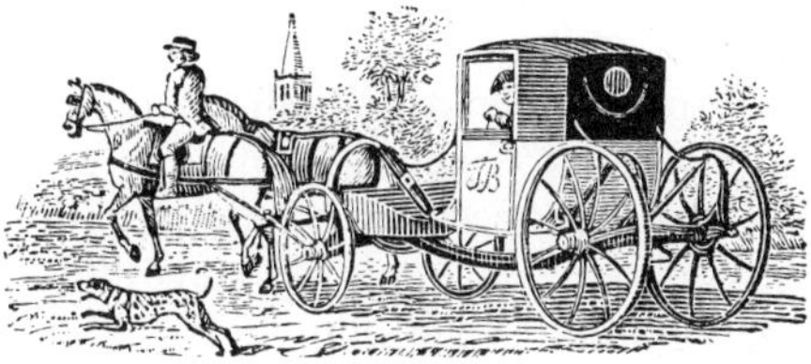

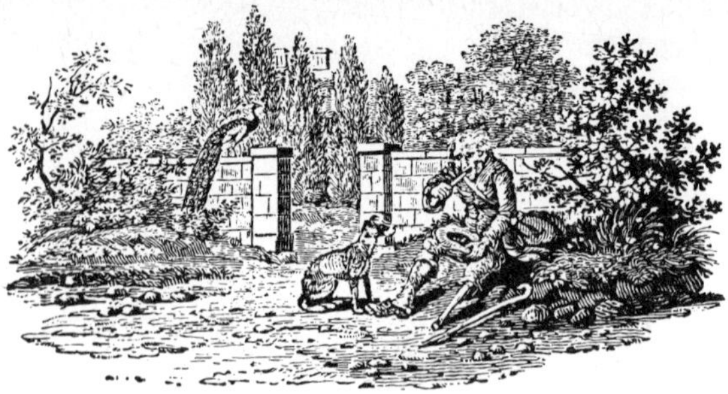

[18]

I never could agree in opinion with the philanthropic, well intentioned & honest Major Cartwright* in his unqualified scheme of universal suffrage–because I conceive that the ignorant & wicked ought to be debarred from voting for any thing–they should be honourd with no privilidges nor be employed in any office of public trust and a virtual representation is allsufficient for them–and could matters be so managed, that none but sensible honest men, should be allowed to vote either for members of parliament or for any other public functionaries, matters would, in a short time, put on a very improved appearance–It is quite natural to suppose that were elections entrusted to this description of men, they would elect none but men of similar characters to their own–but should it be found impracticable thus to order public matters–then the next respectable plan & which might easily be accomplished, would be to confer the additional elective franchise upon Householders, of probity & honour, for it must be admitted that information & impartiallity are not confined to any class, & the poor are frequently as wise as the rich, and as remarkable for integrity—If an overwhelming mass of selfism did not paralise every improvement how easily & how soon all this might be done & make elections simple, without putting the candidates to the expense of a canvass –and prevent the drunken base, wicked effects consequently attendant upon it–this business might, through the whole king-

* Major John Cartwright died 23 September 1824 Æt 84–an honour to himself–his country & to human nature–an upright, unvarying, inflexible Patriot.

dom be done in a few days–by Summoning the Electors (as soon as the candidates were nominated) to attend the Vestrys of their several Sects & to begin with the names, alphabetticaly arranged in a book–either to vote by ballot, or otherwise as might be determined upon. No canvassing ought to be allowed and the public addressed only through the medium of news papers.–What a real honour would this be, to be thus elected!–What a saving of expense!–What can any Gentleman, after spending thousands in the present mode, say for himself? does he mean to say, "that he expects to be repaid, (somehow or other) by the Nation or has he lavished away such sums, "*for the honour of the thing*" & thus *robbed* his own family, by such wastefull expenditure?—While sentiments of patriotism similar to the foregoing were greatly entertained in our country–clouded indeed with the fears of an opposite tendancy, as noticed before, the attentions of all were drawn to aside to view the confedracy of despots actually entered upon, and wholly directed to stop the march of intellect & shackle the understandings of mankind, with the view of keeping them in a state of ignorance, befitting them for slavery & degradation–would any man, in his senses, in the present enlightened state of the civilised world have thought this possible–and as a finish to this *thing*, they have *piously* called it "*the holy Alliance*"—this uncommon dose of inequity–this Royal patent Quack medicine, composed of a jumbled compound of political poisons–will no doubt *be puffed off & praised throughout the civilized World*, long after the devouring Beetles & worms, have crept in at their mouths & noses & out at their ears–in short, this their mark, left behind them, will immortalize their names and entitle them to be held in detested remembrance, by the sons of liberty & an enlightened world, as long as God is pleased to bestow intellect upon Mankind–my most fervent prayer, is that no King of the British Isles, will ever keep such company or call them his cousins & that he will ever stand firm, uncontaminated by them or the infectious effluvia of arbitrary power, upon this proud ground–this soil, fitly tilled, but only wanting some weeding, to render it perfectly ready to produce a rich crop of liberty–

Most men were beginning to hope, that Emperors & Kings, would have, by this time begun to discover that despotism is not a good way of governing their subjects, and, that though long in making the discovery, they had at last found out, that if the people were not enlightened, it was high time for them to use their kingly influence & utmost exertions to make them so–and that it was safer & better, as well as more wise & honourable to preside over & govern a sensible people, than over men brought down to the leval of unreasoning brutes—

The wretchedly ignorant, biggotted & consequently oppressed people of Spain, will no doubt see things in their true light at some future day–& rear the *appropriate Statue* to the *beloved* Ferdinand–after his holy priests have canonized him & made him a Saint–his effigies will be set up, as an object of *worship on all the hill tops, throughout their fine country*–And have we lived to see such times as those, in which Gallileo lived! still continue? and the same kind of despotism & superstition, ready as ever, to burn such men alive, and others who might oppose their wickedness,–& then strew their ashes in the Wind–The affairs of mankind, managed in this way, will most likely, at no distant period put such Kings and their priests out of fashion–But superstition allways makes despots & tyrants of all the Sovereigns whom it influences–they become the confirmed enemies of all knowledge–the die is then cast & superstition never did, nor ever will listen to reason, for credulity is the offspring of ignorance, & superstition is the child of credulity, & this breed is nursed & kept up by despotism as its mainstay and darling–The Sun of reason may indeed be clouded for a time and as long as falsehood in the garb of truth continues to lead the great mass of Mankind, so long will they struggle in vain to attain the paths which lead to perfection & happiness—"We should always repute it as our business in the world–the end & purpose of our being–our duty to our kind–the natural use of the powers we enjoy–and the suitable testimony of our gratitude to our maker to contribute something to the general good–to the common fund of happiness to our species"*–benevolent & patriotic sentiments of this kind ought indeed to be kept up, and the Mite of the humblest individual to that end ought to be received & attended to–but, in that case, the reveries of such, ought not to pass, without being coolly examined by men of wisdom & experience—I well remember my name having once been set down, as one who would, without hesitation become a member of a society in Newcastle "for the

* Dr F. Hutchinson.

suppression of vice"–this I decidedly at once rejected, for I considered such a society as worse than useless, and told my well meaning, but mistaken neighbour* who named the business to me–that I thought the magistrates were quite sufficient to keep this business in their own hands, but that I could have no kind of objection, to join their society, if they would change their plan and make it a society for the promoting and rewarding of virtue—I have often thought, since that time, if such a Society as the latter, *to be called the society of honour* was established in every parish, it might do great good, if it could be put under the guidance of proper Men selected for the purpose–and that they were annually to elect others of the same character, by an unanimous ballot into this honourable society—they ought to be bound, by their own rules, not to annoy any one in a troublesome way, by being over officious–nor to meddle otherwise than by *quietly* & yet publicly rewarding or expressing the good opinion they entertained of the conduct of the person so elected.—Another society of a very different character, to this last named, is at this time winked at, *in this land of liberty*–I mean the present great & mighty inquisition, held under the denomination of the "Constitutional Association". These Men, the secret admirers of the "holy Alliance" may more properly be called the supressors & dreaders of truth–acting indeed under the mask of advocating the cause of religion & liberty but in reality in lurking enmity to the latter & to all free enquirey & investigation, & at the same time impudently arrogating to themselves the power of punishing any man, for his unbiassed thoughts even on any subject which does not militate against good morals & consequently against the Happiness of society, while they are thus taking the power out of the hands of the national authorities, as if they were unfit & insufficient to do their duty–a House of commons *ought to see this* with indignation–and invite this self erected inquisition to answer truths with truths, as well as they can, & let the world judge of the question & how it stands between them & the parties they ruin by their persecutions—

Many matters, perhaps of minor consideration, might be of benefit to society–I have often thought, were all Children, when

* Benjamin Brunton died on the [ ]. Mr Benjamin Brunton–he was quite a popular man & was often chairman at charitable & patriotic meetings & had been one of the committee who tried the Magistrates on [the] Town Moor business.

christened, to have the maiden name of their mother added to whatever other name, it might be thought well of to give them–it would greatly serve more fully to identify & distinguish them in after life, than a single name would do, and might on some occasions be of great import–and as a further improvement to this plan–when youth arrived at the age of puberty, these names might be *tatooed* upon their Arm or Arms, to fix & confirm this identity. And in carrying this tatooing scheme still further it might be a great stimulent to virtuous conduct, if upon Men's being admitted as associates or members of the society of honour, before named, if they would consent to have hieroglyphic marks added, expressive & descriptive of their belonging to that society, or of having been approved of by it–I have also often thought that tatooing for a very different & opposite purpose, might in some cases, be restored to, to mark villany in all its different shades & degrees upon the backs of convicted criminals, & hieroglyphics might be invented, which could not fail of doing this with certainty & *effect* and have a mighty effect in checking every vice—but this mode of punishment ought to be very coolly and very deliberately weighed, by the wisdom of the legislature before it is put in force–for, with some few, who have the power of reflection & might repent it could bear heavily upon & be like carrying a curse upon their backs for life, which would be worse than death.—When men break through the *good* laws made with care (& made public) for the *good* government of the community, they ought, as at present, to forfeit their liberty–& in some cases, their lives, murderers ought all to be given to the Surgeons, & perhaps some other criminals also–but those I think, who have betrayed the innocent & robbed the fatherless children & widow, are no longer fit to live in civilised society–they ought to be sent to live with savages, in the back settlements & to have their backs ornamented with tatooed hieroglyphics expressive of their crimes—It has often been wondered at, in the circle of my friends, that criminals were not transported to the west Indies, and there to undergo a purgation 'till they had redeemed their characters and in that case be allowed to return home–It has also appeared to us, that the law is defective, in not, somehow or other, protecting men, who could not be convicted of the crimes laid to their charge & yet, then being turned adrift without further ceremony–it matters not howsoever fervently a man might wish to redeem his character–it is by this process, gone, in so much as no body will employ him & he is thereby often driven to the necessity of flying to any villainous scheme to enable him to live–some association ought to be formed –some friends to him & to humanity ought to be invited forth to pass their word, for a time, for his good behaviour, to prevent his being thus turned adrift friendless, upon an unforgiving and censorious World. It is painfull to speak about new punishments, to be inflicted upon ones unfortunate fellow men–it is also equally so to contemplate upon their self degradation–but when it is considered what a voluminous mass of criminal laws, neither understood by them nor explained to them & which also hang over the heads of all one cannot wonder at their being broken–indeed, as the Laws at present stand, to be understood seems almost impossible, they are so multifarious & complex–that, as to the illiterate description of persons, they are meant to keep in order, they are almost useless–but indeed the same may be said of the whole laws of England–an abridgement of them, would perhaps fill Fifty Folio Volumes—These Laws in the times they were made might be good & proper–but most of them are surely, now, inapplicable & obsolete–to amend them seems impossible & an Act to amend and explain an Act, by adding confusion to confusion seems truely farciccal–it is a pity, the whole of them cannot be abolished at once, by having short clear new ones ready prepaired beforehand in their stead–as they stand at present few men can understand them, & to men of plain good sense or of ordinary capacities they appear altogether a great mass of unintelligible matter or a complete "*Riddle-ma-ree*"—This may indeed be intended or winked at–for it gives employment to a great number of *Men of the Law* of all kinds of characters, from the basest up to others who are ornaments to their country–indeed were it not for the latter description of them, the rest would not be endureable–they are more to be dreaded than highwaymen & house breakers and as such, are viewed by the thinking part of the community–but the former find employment from clients of their own character, who trust to them for their ability in twisting, evading & explaining the law away. I have had the honour of being acquainted with some of the respectables of this learned profession–but to enumerate all of those I knew intimately would swell out an unnecessary list of names–I therefore think it sufficient first to notice such only as were held in great public estimation–of these, in this neighbourhood, as councellors, stood Robert Hopper Williamson Esq[r], Recorder of this Town–a *Newcastle Worthy* & James Losh Esq[r] worthy of the like designation–among the latter, as men of the Law whom I greatly respected & with whom I associated on terms of closer & in more social intercourse were John Davidson Esq[r], Clerk of the Peace for Northumberland* & his Brother Thomas,† who succeeded him in that office–the character which both these affable & kind Gentlemen bore thro' life was, that they were never known to undertake any dirty job in hands to steer a villanous Client through his crooked wicked ways–What business I had to do in law matters was transacted by my two intimates Thomas Carr & Armorer Donkin both Gentlemen of such abilities as placed them at the head of their profession–there were several others for whom I entertained a high regard, both for their share of talents as well as for their social & friendly dispositions–of these I felt particularly a warm attachment to my Neighbour Joe:Willis Esq[r] & Richard Scruton Esq[r] of Durham—In passing through life it has fortunately been my lot to have the pleasure to be intimate with both military & Naval Gentlemen, as well as those of the learned professions–tho several of each class stood high in the estimation of the world for their Gentlemanly Manners & unsullied worth, to which I may be allowed to add my testimony, as well as to acknowledge the debt of gratitude I owe some of them for their kindness & attention–yet on taking a comparative survey of the whole I cannot help giving a preference to medical Gentlemen for besides their learning & attainments in common with the other professions–they appear to me generally to be further removed from prejudices–more enlightned & more liberal in their sentiments than the other labourers in the vinyards of science & literature—Some of the latter description of gentlemen I had occasion to mention in the earlier part of this memoir–since that time, a succession of them have risen up, to claim my thanks for their kind attentions–of this kind is John Ramsay MD Esqre who watched at my bed side, when, from my too close application to business and over exertions, I neaded his advice & medical aid–

* John Davidson died at Tynemouth 21 June 1818 Æ 66 & was buried at All Saints.
† Thomas Davidson died at Lemington near Alnwick 29 July 1823 Æ 69 D°. D°.

as well as his being the humane & feeling attendant upon my family—I might swell out a list of the names of medical friends were it of any use to them and thus give vent to my feelings. I cannot however omit acknowledging the civilities of Dr Headlam Dr Mc Whirter and Dr Thomas Trotter Esqr well known over all England as Physician to the Fleet—my thanks are also due to Mr Henry Edmondston, for his good wishes to see the "History of British Birds" appear among the first Publications of the kind–for this end both he & his Brother Mr Lawrence Edmondston exhausted the ornithological stores of Zetland, and our other Northern Isles which have enabled me to add some new matter to this work–to these ornithological friends I must add G.T.Fox Esqre of Westoe, both as a contributor in rummaging the stores of the Metropolis, for specimens, and also as being equally desirous to see the Books appear in perfection—My thanks are also due to several Gentlemen Amateurs, in distant parts–but as friends–the warmest of the warm & as standing prominently conspicuous is J.F M Dovaston Esqr[1] of Westfelton in Shropshire,* for his ardent desire to afford his aid to the "History of British Birds" & his

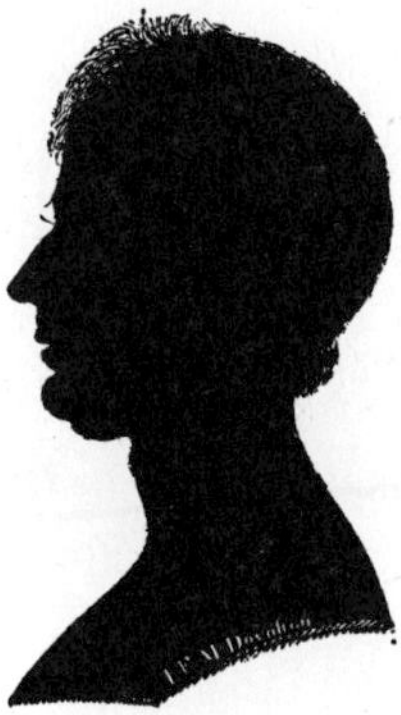

J. F. M. Dovaston

having been in some instances enabled to do so from his close observations (by means of his ornithoscope)[2] of the habits of several of them–in this pursuit, he was cordially joined by his two

* I was visited by this Gentleman (in Octr 1823). Mr Bowman [accompanied him.]

friends, John Clavering Wood Esq of Marsh Hall Salop & by [John Eddowes] Bowman Esq[r] of Wrexham both equally enthusiastic in their admiration of the Works of nature–

To these friends & contributors, I must add a nearer neighbour M[r] Rich[d] Routledge Wingate, whose unceasing attentions I have reason to value for his having in several cases greatly assisted me, in the last Edition, to discriminate, by a comparative view, the difference between the doubtfull Genera, species & varieties of Birds:–this he was enabled to do, from the long experience he attained in his pursuits of collecting their Eggs & their nests–and also from his having, in every doubtfull case, dissected his subjects, before he gave them the appearance of the living birds to their preserved skins—Among all these contributors & well wishers to the Histories of the Quadrupeds & Birds and the Fables, I have to acknowledge the obligations I owe to my friend M[r] Edward Walker, in Edition after Edition, the printer of the whole, for his uncommon attention & assiduity in correcting the press–surveying the literary complexion of the text, and watching his compositors, lest a single word might escape their notice & be wrong.

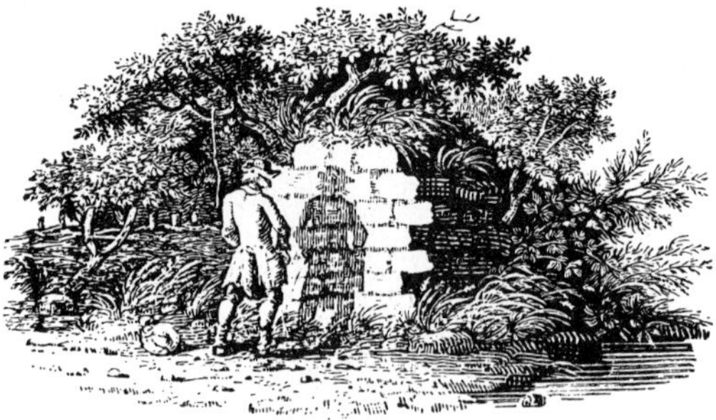

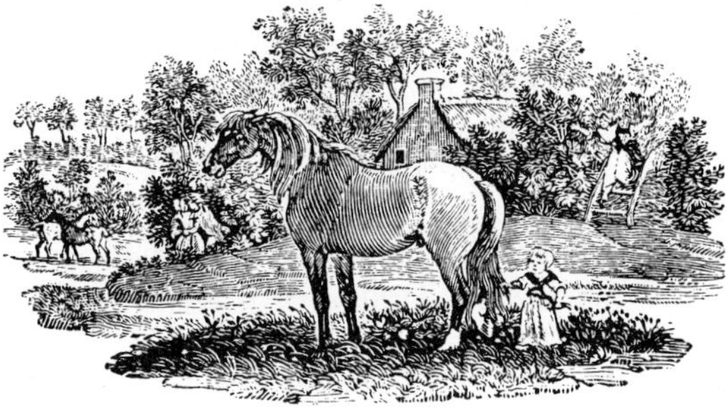

[19]

It is of the utmost importance to individuals & to society, that care and attention should be watchfully bestowed upon children, both with respect to their health & morals–their future happiness in life depends upon these & in this important charge the lot falls greatly upon the Mother to take the guidance of her offspring–& her first lessons (their talents being only imitation) to learn a child before it is enabled to reason, should be those of obedience (mildly enforced) for reason, being the faculty of comparing ideas already presented to the mind, cannot exist in a child to whom few or no ideas have been presented–Then follow lessons of truth, sincerity, industry, honesty. It ought to be impressed upon their minds that, though they are young, yet the longest life is only like a dream; and, short as it is, it is rendered shorter by all the time lost in wickedness, contention, and strife. They ought to be taught that all they can do, while they sojourn in this world, is to live honourably, and to take every care that the soul shall return to the Being who gave it as pure, unpolluted, and spotless as possible; and that there can be no happiness in this life unless they hold converse with God. With respect to their healths, I fear the present management is not right–the mistaken indulgencies of parents in pampering & spoiling appetites of children, lays the foundation of a permanent train of diseases–which an endless supply of medicines & nostrums & trash will never restore to its prestine vigour–skillfull medical aid, may indeed sometimes be of use–but nothing is so sure, as a recurrence to a plain diet & temperance & exercise, which only can effectually cure this distressing evil—The next obstacles to remedy, I fear, will not be easily removed, for they are built upon the prejudices of Mothers themselves–dictated by notions of fashion & gentility, which have taken too deep a root–for when folly has given the fashion she is a persevering dame–and "folly ever dotes upon her darling"—Instead of impressing upon their minds the importance of knowing household affairs & other usefull knowledge–& of instilling good sense, cheerfullness & affability along with the inestimable value of the courteseys of life & making these her primary objects–her lovely offspring must, as if it were the only business of their lives, treat some of these as of *no importance*–they must undergo a training befitting them for appearing in frivolous company & to insure this the Mother, or some Boarding school Misstress, will insist upon it, that these delicate young creatures must be tightned up, in a shape destroying dress, & sit & move in *gracefull* stiffness; they must not spring about, nor make use of their limbs untill they know not what agility & exercise mean for fear this might be called "*romping*" & be compared to the wild Roe on the mountain, and besides it might give them so *vulgar, so robust & so red cheeked a look*, that they would not appear *like Ladies*—The consequence of all this is that they become like hothouse plants, the Air must not blow upon them, & in this state they must attend Routs & Balls and *midnight* or *morning* Assemblies,* which send numbers of them to an untimely grave–If they survive these trials, still they leave behind them a want of health & vigour which hangs upon them through life, & they then become the *nerveless* outcasts of nature–they are then unfit to become the Mothers of Englishmen–they twine out a life of ennui & their generation dies out—I have all my life, been grieved to find, this & similar descriptions too often realized–this is paying too dear for such like Female accomplishments & makes it desireable that a change should take place, by which fashionable follies might be narrowed in their boundaries and a better line drawn out, prescribed by propriety, affability, modesty & good sense, on which the courtesies of life and the invaluable embellishments of civilization upon which every thing gracefull & charming in society is founded—I wish the Ladies of the British Isles, may set the

* If these Assemblies are & *must* be kept up (to the Gentry who can afford it) they ought to be held in the day time, that they may get their natural rest at night.

example & take the lead in this–and be crowned with this brilliant diadem of civilization, studded with Gems, so as to attract the attention of the rest of the World, & illumine the paths which would lead them to pursue the same object, and of banishing ignorant rudeness & vulgarity from the face of the earth—If I could have any influence with the fair sex, there is one thing more to which I wish to draw their attention and that is Horticulture, and connected with this, I could recommend to all of them, as far as convenient, to become florists, as this delightfull & healthy employment (which has been long enough in the rude hands of men) would entice them out into the open air–stimulate to exertion and draw them away from their sedentary mode of life stewed up in their close rooms, where they are confined like Nuns–this would contribute greatly to their amusements & enliven or exhilerate their spirits. To see this ought to be the wish of every sensible man–for what would this world be without their help to alleviate its burdens–it would appear a barren waste–it could no longer be a wide spread garden of Eden nor an earthly paradise within the reach of our enjoyments–may the fruits & flowers of it, reared & presented by their fair hands ever operate as a charm in insuring the attentions & unabating regards of all Men & of *all good Men* it would—In thus dictating and prating to them–it is behind their backs,–no embarrassments can follow & if they ever know of the liberty I thus have taken–it will probably be when all embarrasments are at an end; & I can now only, further leave behind me a wish, that health may eternally blush their cheeks & virtue their Minds.–

Next in consideration to the Ladies, who they must, in courtesy follow, are the Freeholders of this favoured land–such of these, as by their attainments arrive at the degree of Gentlemen are, or ought to be the pride & glory of every civilized country in the world–placed in opulence & independancy, with a liberal education, they are & must be looked up to as patronizers of every virtue in the people–who, in their station of life, may nead such help to encourage them—may they never lose sight of this important charge, and ever be able to stem the torrent of gambling & dissipation, that their ancient mansions may remain in their name *for ever*, as ornaments to the country and as pledges of their worth–Without their countenance arts sciences & Artisans would languish–industry would be paralized & barbarism again rear its benumbed hands & stupid head—May the business of their wine vaults, their Horses & their Dogs cease to be the main business of their lives and only be looked to as matters of amusement to unbend their minds—and as no man can, while he is in possession of his faculties–rest in happiness unless he is exercising them, & some Hobby Horse must ingage his attention, it therefore becomes a question for their consideration, in what way they can best employ themselves–they may indeed have much to do–but were I allowed to dictate or persuade Gentlemen as to what is best to be done–I would first advise them that they should endeavour to improve their lands and lay the foundation of fertilizing them, and instead [of] spending, perhaps squandering their money, in follies abroad, they ought, as far as possible to spend it at home–The late good and wise, first Lord Ravensworth used to say, there was nothing gratefull but the Earth, you cannot, says he do too much for it–it will continue to pay for *ten* fold the pains & labour bestowed upon it–their Estates would then exhibit the appearance of a clean weeded Nursery—And as an Act of justice due to the industrious farmer, he ought, on entering upon his lease, have his valued, and when that lease is out, valued again, and whatever improvements he may have made in that time ought to be paid to him, on his leaving it–I am well aware that this may not be relished by those whose pride, dictated by the wish to domineer, will not give into this fair proposal, for fear of the independant spirit it might rear–but it must be allowed that the landlord could come to no loss by it, and that the community would be greatly benefitted by the adoption of such a plan—Those Gentlemen who have moor lands, however exposed and bleak they may be, may yet do something to make them, in a greater or *lesser* degree, more productive–by inclosing them within dry stone dykes[1] beset & bound with Ivey & intersected with Whin hedges*[2] and thus sheltered, would be a *beild*[3] for sheep or cattle, and besides would produce grass both in quantity & quality such as never grew there before.

The chief offices which Gentlemen & freeholders are called upon to fulfill are members of Parliament–the Magistracy and juries—

* the very clippings of which (as noticed before) would be healthfull fodder for both Sheep & Cattle.

The first is the most important but indeed, in that, as well as the others, the requisite ingredients for forming the characters of each are honesty & intelligence–if we look at the wretched tools which Boroughmongers obtrude upon the nation, we may anxiously look to the importance of having Gentlemen who will unceasingly & boldly oppose such ever being allowed to sit as representatives—but these have already gone far on the road towards paralizing the British constitution and establishing on its ruins an Oligarchy, which is the worst & most odious of all governments even scarcly excepting a mob government—In the troublesome & gratuitous office of Magistrate, great sagacity & penetration are requisite, to enable them in their political capacity to discriminate between stretching too far, the perhaps ill defined & often arbitrary laws, bejond the due bounds prescribed by justice & mercy–they ought to detest being made the tools of despotic Acts of corruption, and being, like Turkish Bashaws, spread over the provinces—In their civil capacity, matters come more nearly home to them, and in this, they have also much nead of cool deliberation, as well as extreme vigilence, for without these there would be no such thing as living in peace, while such numbers of the dregs of the people remain in ignorance & depravity–they do not know the meaning of either religion or morality, and it is only the strong arm of the law that can keep, people of this description in order–their evidence ought always to be suspected–oaths have little weight with them–they are so used to them–one of our Poets says "of all the nausious complicated crimes–which both infect & stigmatize the times–theres none which can with impious oaths compare–where vice & folly have an equal share" . . but bad as the reprobate oaths are, there are others which I think are still worse, and these are the numerous ones used, and indeed imposed, on so many, and, on such improper occasions, where Omnipotence is so impiously appealed to in all the little dirty transactions between Man & Man—it ought to be remembered that "An honest mans word is as good as his oath & so is a rogues too"—'tis a pity some better way cannot be hit upon to remedy these evils–perhaps a tatooing upon the shaved head, might have some effect, in checking these swearing vices especially in perjury–bearing false witness–and when a man is proved to have broken his Word & his honour—There is another vice of an odious complexion, advancing with rapid strides to enormity which cries aloud to be checked, and that is the doubly degrading intercourse of illicit love and the effrontery with which base men become hardened and only laugh at their breaking down every barrier to modesty & virtue & thus disrobe[g] innocence deform that which ought to have been the brightest feature of civilization—this crime neads only to be examined to be convinced of its cruelty to the fair Sex, and its extensively demoralizing influence on society–let any man ask himself how he would like his daughter or his sister to be betrayed–or to become a concubine to any man—this question ought to be asked, and fairly canvassed–is it for the benefit of society, or even of individuals that such a vice should be allowed?–altho it will be allowed that men devoid of modesty & of honour, who have let loose their unbridled bad passions, will not be readily stopped in their career–for to them "love is as strong as death, jealousy is cruel as the grave" but notwithstanding this, it may be, by "the strong Arm of the Law" greatly banished from the land & innate modesty planted in its stead—All men and women, in health & of good characters ought to be countenanced in marrying, and it is for them to consider whether they can properly rear & educate, their family, and if an over abundant population should ever happen, then colonization at the public expense ought to be resorted to, and this Globe will be found large enough to hold additional millions upon millions of people—There are few contracts between human beings, which should be more delicate than that of marriage–it is an engagement of the utmost importance to individuals and to society, & which of all others ought to be the most unbiassed for it can not be attended with honour nor blessed with happiness if it has not its origin in mutual affection–but the rules to be observed in thus selecting & fixing the choice, are few, simple & easily understood—both male & Females, if of unsound constitutions ought to forbear matrimony–It is the duty of every man, in commencing this change of life–to get a healthy woman for his wife for the sake of his children –and an amiable one for his own domestic comfort–the fair sex should observe the like rules, in their choice–for if she marries a man, who has broken down his constitution by his own dissipation –or has imbibed a tainted one from his parents–she must not be surprized at becoming a nurse, to him and his *nerveless* puny offspring—one cannot help wondering at the uncommon pains a

Gentleman will take in buying a Horse, to see that the Animal is perfectly sound & without blemish in every part–and that he should not take the same pains in choosing a Wife which is of infinitely more importance to him–he, perhaps, to repair his shattered fortune will marry any woman, if she has plenty of money–she may, indeed be the innocent heir to the full-charged hereditary diseases of a pair of voluptuous citizens–just as that may happen to be.–No Gentleman nead to look far from his home, to be enabled to meet with a *help mate* possessing every requisite to make him happy–but if he cannot meet with such a one or cannot please himself in his own neighbourhood–he had better travel in search of one even from lands end to John o groats house, than not get a proper inmate for the mother of his progeny.—I have often thought that the children of Gentlemen (boys particularly) are too soon put to school, under improper restraints, and harrassed with education before their minds are fit for it—Were they sent to the edge of some Moor, to scamper about among Whins & heather, under the care of some good old man–some "Mentor" who would learn them a little every day without embarrassing them–they would there lay in a foundation of health (as well as education in this kind of preparatory school) which a temperate or milk diet, would ensure, if they were thus allowed to run wild, by the sides of burns–to fish–to wade & splash in–they would soon find their minds intently employed in sports & pleasing amusements of their own chusing. It would be found, that youth, so brought up, besides thus working out any little hereditary ailments, would never forget the charms of the country–which would impart to them a flow of spirits through life, such as very few or none brought up in a town ever knows–and besides laying in a strong frame work on which to build a nervous constitution, befitting the habitation of an energetic mind & a great Soul. Let any man look at the contrast between men thus brought up and the generallity of cockneys or other early matured Lilliputian plants, and he will soon see (with very few exceptions) the difference both in body & mind between them.–

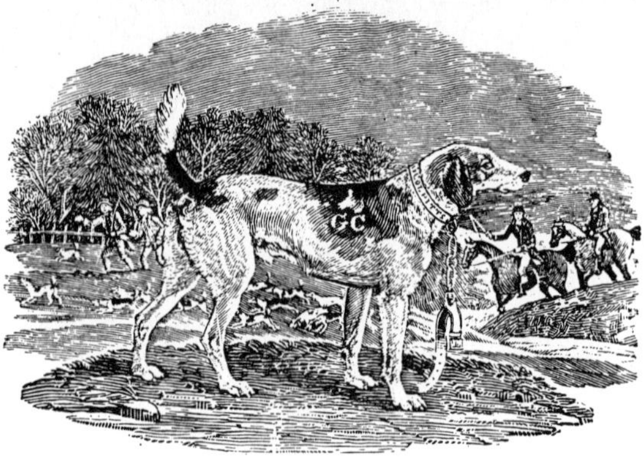

[20]

The game laws have for ages past been a miserable source of contention between those rendered unqualified by severe & even cruel game laws, enacted by those who had the influence to get such laws made for their exclusive priviledge of *killing the game as their own*–To convince the intelligent poor man, that the fowls of the air were created only for the rich, is impossible & will for ever remain so–if it be pleaded that the game are fed on the lands of the latter & thus become theirs–this may indeed, be carrying the notions of the sacredness of property too far, for even this ought to have its bounds–but were this conceeded, as property is at present enjoyed, by a rental, & as the farmers feed the game, they would appear to belong more properly to them than to any one else–In thus viewing this business, it would only appear to be an act of justice to make an express Law to secure the Game to the farmers as their exclusive property & putting it out of the power of the Landowners of rendering such a law (by their influence) of non effect, as well as to prevent the nightly or the day-light poacher from his intrusions & his trespasses. In thus attempting to point out what may be justice & what injustice, respecting the game laws–I own I feel great repugnance in saying any thing that might have a tendancy to curtail the genteel & healthy enjoyments of the country Gentleman in his field sports, which his fortune & his leisure enables him so appropriately to pursue—While, at the same time, it is greatly to be regretted that any thing,-any overstretched distinctions, should ever happen to make a breach between the poor & the rich, or to make the former feel himself like an outlaw, for it ought ever to be considered, that they both are members of the same community, and that equal & just Laws should guide & govern men in every station of life—It is, however, a pity that the *unqualified* man cannot find his attentions engaged & his mind sufficiently excited in some other way, or by his business, than that of becoming a poacher—but the strange propensity (however unaccountable) in almost all men to kill, and the pleasureable excitement to do so, is equally strong in the Gentleman sportsman, as it is in the Poacher-This excitement, or an extreme desire to exhilerate the spirits and to give them energy as well as pleasure, pervades more or less the minds of all mankind and shews itself in every species of gambling, from cock fighting, Dog & man fighting-hunting-Horse racing and even up to the acme of excitement or excitement run mad, that of horrid War—It seems to be no matter what it is, that affords this kind of pleasure—I wish it could be contrived to find out something of a more rational & better sort—but be this as it may, certain it is that the heart that never tastes pleasure, shuts up, grows stiff & incapable of enjoyment, and the minds of all men ought to be unbent, at certain times-therefore, it would appear there ought to be something or other fallen upon to whet the mind to rouse its energies in all men (especially in some constitutions) to prevent their becoming *nerveless* & hipocondriac-the worst of all diseases-in which the mind sees every thing, with an obliquity of intellect, & creates numberless, cruel & imaginary evils, to continually surround & embarras itself—only make a man, who cannot employ his mind with some hobby horse or other, sit down, to know that he is provided for & has nothing to do, and it will soon be seen how ennui with benumbing steps is thrust into his mind & what a stupid and unhappy being he is-If I have reasoned correctly in the forgoing observations, it is then desirable that sports and pastimes should be invented that might (in many cases) turn out to public good & for this purpose, I have often thought (as one of these schemes) that very small sums might be subscribed *& collected* & to make a great amount to be given as a prize to the best shot, at a mark—

the utility and national purpose of this, may at sometime or other be felt–for so long as surrounding despots can gather together immense mercinary Armies they ought to be *effectually* guarded against–& they certainly might be as effectually checked by hundreds of thousands of rifle men, including in them the militia, thus trained, for this kind of self defence of this kingdom at a comparatively small expense—they might have their bullets made of baked clay, & that would probably be found as efficient as those made of lead & cost almost nothing.

The last subject I shall notice, as being kept up, by unjust or unequal Laws, is the fisheries throughout the Kingdom—The laws respecting them originated in the times of Feudal Tyranny–when "*might was right*" & every thing was carried with a high hand in its own way–It was easy then for an overbearing Aristocracy to get grants & charters-made by their influence entirely in behalf of themselves–The rights of the community was set at nought–the rights of mankind, as members of the same community, was treated with contempt, & never entered into their deliberations. These were absorbed in feelings of self interest which was their only guide —but these days are passed away, the march of intellect is spreading over the World, and all public matters are now viewed with feelings of a very different kind, than they were, when such laws were made & which ought to have become obsolete or repealed long since–but they are still kept in force, & will continue so, as long as the potent feelings of the same overstretched self interest is made the guide of those who have the power to keep the grasp of this their antiquated hold—for such can hear no reason, against their private interest, however unanswerable it may be—No reasonable plea can ever be set up, to shew that the fish of rivers ought to be the private property of any one–can it be pretended that because a river or a rivulet passes through an estate, whether the owner of it will or not, that the fish which breed in it, or which live in it, ought to be theirs?–They are not, like the game, which are all fed by the Farmer, for Fish cost nobody any thing, and ought only to [be] preserved so far as they may be for the public good–therefore they, in common justice ought to belong to the public in every county, through which the Rivers pass, and let at a rental from the clerk of the peace & the money arising therefrom applyed to making Bridges & roads, or for other county rates. Stewards ought to be appointed to receive the rents, and a committee of Auditors, elected annually by ballot, as a check upon the management of the whole—If the fisheries were not thus rented, the public would derive little benefit from such an immense supply of food, for without they were thus disposed of, the county would soon be overrun with such numbers of poaching vagabonds, as would become intolerable—All this however ought to be considered again, for notwithstanding the selfish principle which dictated the original grants of the fisheries long since obtained the present possessor is not to blame–and suddenly to deprive any Man of what he has been accustomed to receive, may be deemed a harsh measure & in some cases a cruel one–therefore some equitable sum ought to be paid to him at once, as a remuneration, for his being entirely done with all future claims, and they ought not to be considered as an inheretance to descend to the heirs of any one—From about the year 1760 to 67 when a boy, I was frequently sent by my parents, to purchase a Salmon from the Fishers of the *Strike*[1] at Eltringham Ford–at that time I never paid more, and often less than three half pence ℔ pound (mostly a heavy guessed weight) about which they were not *nice*[2]—Before, or perhaps about this time there had always been an article inserted in every Indenture in Newcastle that the apprentice was not to be obliged to eat Salmon above twice a Week, & the like bargain was made, upon hiring ordinary Servants–it nead not be added, that the Salmo tribe then teemed in abundance in the Tyne[3]–and there can be little doubt, the same immense numbers would return to it again–were proper measures pursued to facilitate their passing up it from the Sea, to breed–All Animals excepting Fish only increase but they *multiply*, and *that* in so extraordinary a degree–that, for their numbers, set all calculation at defiance—It is well known, that they asscend up every River Rivulet & burn in search of proper places to deposit their spawn–& this is the case with both those kinds which quit the sea & those which never leave the fresh water—in their thus instinctively searching for proper spawning places they make their way up to such shallows, as would make one think it impossible for any animal wanting legs & feet, could ever crawl up to–therefore every *improper* weir & dam that obstructs their free passage ought to be thrown down, as they are almost the only cause of the

Salmon's quitting their proper spawning places in the River to return to spawn in the sea as well as they can, where it is fair to conclude their Fry or their Roe are swallowed up by other fish as soon as they or it are spread abroad along the shores[1]—it will readily be perceived that the fishers weirs are made, chiefly with a view of preventing their neighbour fishers from coming in for their due share, but were the fisheries let as before named, the different fishing places, would be planned out by the stewards, as well as remedying other faults, with an impartial hand–there are besides weirs and dams, other causes which occasion the falling off of the breed of the Salmon by greatly preventing them from entering & making their way up rivers, for the purpose before named—they have a great aversion to passing through impure Water & even snow water stops them, for they will lye still & wait untill it run off–The filth from Manufactories, as well as many tons in a year, washed off the uncleaned streets of large towns *only* by heavey showers of rain,–judging from those of Newcastle & Gateshead I think my estimate of the quantity, may be within bounds—were this filth in all cases led away & laid on the land it would be of great value to farmers & some persons should be appointed to do so not in a slovenly & lazy manner, but with punctuallity & dispatch–in this, the health & comfort of the inhabitants ought to be considered as of great importance to them, as well as that of keeping the river as pure as possible, on account of the fish—should the business of rectifying weirs & dams & the other evils attendant upon them & the other matters be settled, then the next necessary step to be taken should be the appointment of river conservators & vigilant Guards to protect the kipper, or spawning Fish from being killed while they are in this sickly & imbecile state–for notwithstanding their being very unwholesome food, they are so easily caught, that very great numbers are taken, in the night & eaten by poor people who do not know how pernitious they are–but should all this be found not to answer public expectation, the time now allowed, to continue the fishing, might be shortened & in some years, if ever found necessary, the fishing might be laid in for a season—The next matter, of great importance, to be taken into consideration, is respecting what can be done to prevent the destruction of Salmon (on their first entering a River & while they are in full perfection), by their most powerful & most conspicuously destructive enemy, the Porpoise*–can they not, by giving premiums for catching them, be greatly thinned of their numbers? can their tough skins not be tanned, or otherwise dressed, so as to be applied to some use? can oil not be obtained from them, partly to pay for the trouble of taking these kind of Fish? and lastly can they not be used as an article of food? They were eaten formerly, even by the Gentry, and why not make the attempt to do so again?–perhaps by pickling or drying them, and by other aids of cookery, they might be good & wholesome, for every animal in season is wholesome, & which when out of season, is quite otherwise–no doubt the old adage "that one mans meat, is another mans poison" may be partly true—and what people have not been used to eat, they seldom like or wish for–but being, at length accustomed to the taste, it is well known that food, to which they once had an aversion, after a few times using it, it became very agreable. If the parent fishes of the Salmo tribe were protected, the fry would soon be seen to swarm in an incredible number–and perhaps a pair of them would spawn more, than all the Anglers from the source to the mouth of any River could fairly catch in one season–

Having, from a boy, been an Angler, it is with feelings painfully rankling in my mind, that I live in dread (from hints already given) of this kind of recreation being checked or abridged—Angling has from time immemorial been followed and ought to be indulged in unchecked by arbitrary laws, as the birthright of every one (but particularly of the sedentary & studious) for ever–It is cruel to think of debarring the fair Angler by any checks whatever—The Salmon fishers may, indeed, begrudge to see such, fill his creel with a few scores of the Fry, and say to themselves–"he is taking away what might have returned to us full grown Salmon in a short time" (for all fish, as well as birds return to the same places at which they were bred)–but for reasons, before named, their selfishness should not be attended to, for a moment, and they ought to take the fisheries, subject to this kind of toll or imaginary

* I have seen a shoal of porpoises, off Tynemouth, swimming abreast of each other & thus occupying a space of more than a hundred yards from the shore & crossing the mouth of the River, so that no Salmon coud enter it–they went backwards & forward, for more than a mile, along shore & with such surprizing rapidity, that in their course, they caused a foam to arise like the breakers of the Sea, in a storm. Might not a couple of steam packets, with strong nets sweep on shore hundreds at a time?

greivance–I have always felt extremely disgusted, at what is called proscribed Waters (except fish ponds) that is, that the fish, in these waters, are claimed exclusively as all their own–the disposition which sets up claims of this kind, is the same which wou'd if it could, sell the Sea, & the use of the Sun & the rain—Here the angler is debarred, by the surly selfish owner of the adjoining land, the pleasure of enjoying the most healthfull and comparatively the most innocent of all diversions–it unbends the minds of the sedentary & the studious–whether it may be those employed at their desks–or the "pale Artist plying his sickly trade" and enables such to return to their avocations or their studies, with renovated energy to labour for their own, or for the public good—But as any thing, however good in itself may be made a bad use of, *therefore* some regulations should be laid down as a guide to the fair Anglers, in this *their legitimate right*, and some check imposed upon the poacher, who might be inclined to stop at nothing, however unfair—I think Waltonian societies would be all-suciffient to do this, if composed of men of good character & good sense–there ought to be one of these Societies established in the principle Town, in each district and have its honorary members branched out over the more distant parts–perhaps a fine imposed or even the frowns of the society might be sufficient to deter Poachers. Their object ought to be to regulate the times for Angling–and to frown out of countenance, or send to *Coventry* such as spend the whole of their time almost continually in "*beating the streams*"—they ought also to keep a watchfull eye over such as care not how, or in what manner, they take fish, so as that they may only get plenty of them–therefore the "Honourable Society of Waltonians" ought to use every means in their power, to protect their "glittering inhabitants of the Waters" from being unfairly taken or destroyed—*Pought* Nets[1] ought to be prohibited–all catching of the salmon Fry, in Mill races, by pulling thorn bushes into them, to stop their passing through, and then letting off the water–in this way a Cart load of these have often been known, to be taken at once; & another method, still more destructive than this, is far too often put in practice & that is what is called liming the burns–this ought to be utterly put a stop to by severe punishments–A Clown, perhaps from ignorance, but perhaps from something worse, thinks nothing of putting a few clots of unslaked or quick lime into a pool or hole, in a burn, for the sake of killing a few trouts that he sees in it–& thus poisons the water running down to the Rivulet or the River, destroying every living creature, to such a distance as might seem incredible—The attentive angler, must sometimes have observed the almost invisible–insipient but living spawn in thousands appearing only like floating mud, sunning themselves on a shallow sand bank, which as soon as the water, thus poisoned, reaches them, they drop down, like mud indeed, and are no more seen—How vividly do recollections, of the enjoyments angling has afforded me, return to the mind, now when those days have passed away, never more to return–like the Patriarch of Anglers–Izzak Walton in his pleasing Volume, volumes might yet be written on the same subject to point out, and depicture the beautifull scenery of woods & water sides, in the midst of which, the pleasures attendant upon this exhilerating & health restoring, hungry excercise, is pursued–how many narratives of the exploits of the days thus spent, might be raked up to dwell upon when they are all over, like a pleasing dream.

–From mounting the last stile, which gave the first peep of the curling or the rapid stream over the little intervening dewy enambled daisey covered holme, boundered by the early sloe & the hawthorn blossomed hedge–and in succession hung with festoons of the wild rose, the tangling woodbine & the bramble, with their bewitching foliage & the fairey ground–& the enchantment of the music of the lark, the blackbird, the Throstle & the Blackcap & rendered soothing & plaintive by the cooings of the Ringdove which altogether charmed, but *perhaps retarded* the march to the brink of the scene of action, with its willows its Alders or its Saughs,[1] where early commenced the day's patient *campaigne*—The pleasing excitements of the Angler still follow him, whether he is engaged in his pursuits, amidst scenery like such as I have attempted to describe–or on the heathery Moor by burns guttered out by mountain torrents and boundered by Rocks or grey moss covered stones, which form the rapids & the pools in which is concealed his beautifull yellow & spotted prey–here when tired and alone, I used to open my Wallet–or pocket & *dine on* fat meat and coarse rye bread, with an appetite that made me smile at the trouble people put themselves to, in prepareing the sumptuous feast–the only music in attendance, was perhaps the murmuring burn, the whistling cry of the Curlew–the solitary water ouzel or the whirring wing of the moor game—I woud however recommend to Anglers not to go thus alone–a trio of them is better, & mutual assistance is often necessary—It is foreign to my purpose to give any history in this place, of the various kinds of fishes which Anglers pursue & of this there is no nead, for I think more treatises on this subject than on any other (except sermons) have been printed to direct the angler to perfection in his Art–but I cannot help noticing it as a pity that more pains have not been taken to *multiply* Fish–& to increase the breed of Eels, than has been done, as every permanent pool, might so easily be fully stocked with them–and they are, when properly cooked the most delicious of all fish kind–Walton has been particular in describing his mode of cooking them–but unless he killed them before hand–his method is a very cruel one, and is, besides of not much consequence–After being killed they then only nead to be gutted & cooked unskinned in an unabating heat, 'till they are done enough, for if they are cooked on a slow fire, they are apt to turn oiley & often disagree, with some stomachs–

In thus dwelling on Subjects which stimulate Man, eagerly to pursue the work of destruction and to extend his power over these animals of which he considers himself as the lord & master, and that they are destined to contribute to his pleasures or to his support–yet he ought not totally [to] forget that what is sport to him is death to them*–and the less of cruelty that can be avoided the better.

I think had I not begun so early to be an Angler, and before feelings of tenderness had ever entered the mind, my eagerness for Angling might have been on this score somewhat abated–but I argued myself into a belief that fish had little sense & scarcely any feeling–and they certainly have very much less of either, than any of the land Animals–but we see, through all nature, that one kind of animals seem destined to live upon others–and fishes are the most voracious of all—

Before concluding this Memoir, it would be ungratefull in me, not to acknowledge my obligations to my well-wishers, who have through life been steady in their friendships, and also in conferring

* one of our humane Poets says Take not away the life you cannot give, all creatures have an equal right to live.

their favors in the way of business—but a long list of names might seem tedious–and many of them are long ago numbered with the dead—for several years I had the favors of all the Banks in Newcastle, as well as those of most of the fitters,[1] but a steady underhand dark influence detatched several of both of these different employments from me—The first of friends to whom my thanks are due, is the Corporation of Newcastle for their long and unabating favors, as a body, and from time to time all its members individually–the most particular one of these was Alderman Arch^{d} Reed Esqre—among many of such friends, as I had reason

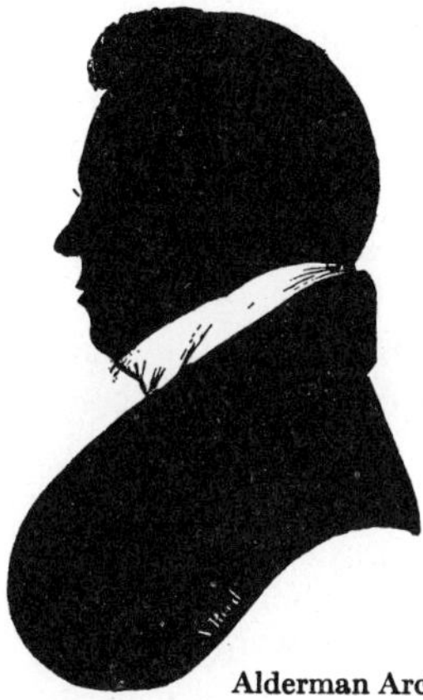

Alderman Archibald Reed

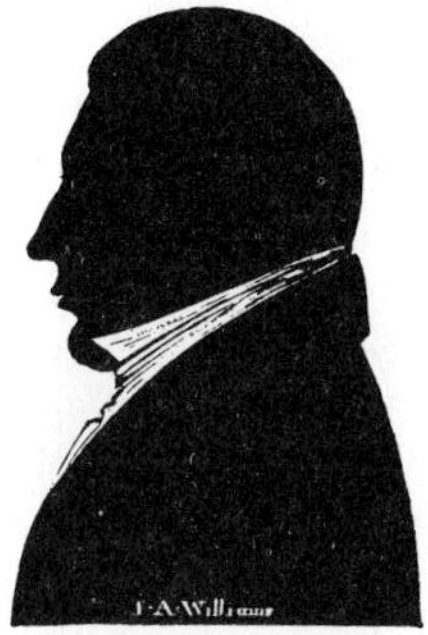

John Ambrose Williams

to respect, both privately & publickly, one of the oldest in intimacy affability & kindness was Anth^{y} Easterby Esqre now of Coxlodge—Another whose eye of kindness watched my struggles to prosperity, was Mr Edmund Robson, patent Sadler & Hardwareman, who upon his suspecting, that, in my Publications, I might be labouring under difficulties–he called me out of Swarley's club Room, to say that he had two hundred pounds at my service whenever I pleased–this I considered as an uncommon thing in the World–but I startled at the idea of getting into any kind of debt–so I thanked him sincerely & declined his kind offer—Two other friends of whom I had a high opinion, for their truth & integrity–were William Leadbitter, sadler & Hardwareman, and

Francis Coates Bookseller–the former died 3d Augt 1801 Aged 38 and the latter on the 24 Feby 1803–An intimacy of long standing had subsisted between the Crawhall family & mine & I had a particular regard for two of the Brothers–Thomas & Joseph, the latter was particularly an Amateur of the Arts & excelled as a painter, for which nature had furnished him with the requisite innate powers–but in this he was taken off by his business of a Rope maker—I might name others of the like character but they also have departed this world long ago—A few of such only being left, both as friends and social companions–and thus noticing them puts me in mind of its being like creeping out of the World as at least out of this kind of society–for excepting that of my own happy fire side–I think I shall bid all adieu—My warm friend Mr Wm Maving, Brush Manufacturer–his Brother Robert, builder–Mr Alexr Reed–china dealer, Mr Adam Hutton Hardwareman, Mr Wm Wilson Solicitor–Mr Robt Gruisburn Stationer (& occasionally some others) were the last with whom I spent my social Evenings–*the full Moon* was generally the signal for our assembling–when we gave full vent to whatever was uppermost in our minds–this was called "getting the froth off our stomachs"–under the exhilerating excitement of ‹*illeg.*›

–At other times, some of my Evenings were spent much in the same way in company with John Marshall, printer, and others, along with John Ambrose Williams the Editor of the Durham Chronicle–in which paper, he had spoken freely of the Durham Clergy, respecting their conduct towards the Queen–little suspecting that they had 'till this day, kept ready by them as much of the sour liven of old as was sufficient to puff up or foment the lump of their clerical pride & dignity to an overflowing height—in short with their prosecutions & persecutions & law suits, they ruined this clever *advocate for liberty* & *patriotic Man*. It might be tedious to swell out a list of names or dwell upon the occasional visits of Men of sense & ability who from time to time spent their evenings with me—Mr Anthony Scott of Southwick pottery was one of these, & when he was in Newcastle he seldom missed this kind of social exchange of our sentiments—on these occasions my ingenious self taught friend Mr Robert Wilson, Engineer & Engine Maker always made one of our party–in their Company the longest Evening seemed very short. I was also often visited by *poor old*

Mr John Rastrick of Morpeth[1] who, in his day, was by many men of judgment, accounted one of the most able & ingenious Engineers in the Kingdom–he died . . . June 1826 Æt 88—I also spent much time (while he remained in Newcastle) with my gallant friend Col! Wemys, of Wemys hall in Fife Shire formerly of the 11th Regt of foot & afterwards Col! of the Fife Shire Militia—he was ardent in his pursuit after mechanical knowledge & greatly valued ingenious work men in that way–& begged I would introduce him to such–he said "he cared not what kind of coat they wore" & I was not long in introducing him to such, in whose company he gained the desired information he wanted, & seemed highly gratified.

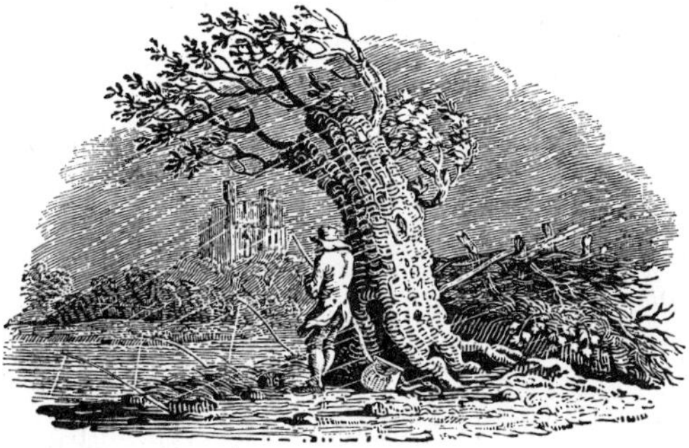

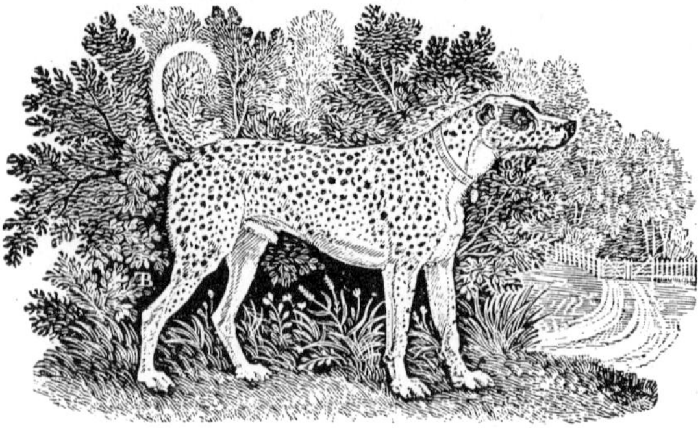

[21]

Not having seen Edinburgh since August 1776–I longed to see it again & accompanied with my Jane & Isabella, we set off on this Journey on the 11th of Augt 1823 & went through, by Coach, on that day—I always thought highly of Edinburgh & its bold & commanding situation–but the new Town (or City of palaces, as it is now sometimes called) had been added to it since that time, but all these splendid buildings, are of trivial import, compared with the Mass of intellect & science, which had taken root & been nurtured & grown up to such a height as to rival & perhaps outstrip every other city in the World. Our stay in it was only a fortnight and this was a busy time with us, both as to its being taken up with the kindness & hospitality, we met with every where, as well as in visiting its various scientific & other establishments—It being at a vacation season, when most of the learned professors were out of town–we saw only professors Jameson & Wallace & the kindness of these Gentlemen I never can forget–We were often at the Table of the former, surrounded by Men of learning & science who visited him, on which occasions, the amiable manners & affability of his sisters, the Misses Jameson, made every place appear like a home—The civility of Professor Wallace was also of the most friendly complexion. He shewed me the use of the Eidograph, an Instrument which he invented,[1] for the purpose of either reducing or enlarging any drawing or design, accurately, to any size that might be wished for–We also visited Mr Patrick Neil, along with the Misses Jameson, & were besides greatly pleased with seeing his tamed birds & other curiosities, which embellished his little paradise–his uncommon kindness will ever remain impressed upon our memories—we also often called upon my friend Mr Archd Constable–accounted the first Bookseller in Scotland, ('tho ill at the time) & partook of his kind attentions–Mr Robt Miller, Bookseller also did every thing in his power which affability & kindness could dictate to make us altogether pleased with Edinburgh–our friend Mr William Reid, Bookseller, Leith did the same, only with this difference, that his attentions were unceasing, & Mrs Reid & his hospitality made their house, a kind of home to us–almost constantly accompanied by Mr Reid, as our guide, we visited *every place*–and he besides introduced me to such Artists, as I did not know. In this way he took us to Mr William Allen, the Historical Painter–to the Rooms of the splendid exhibition of the paintings of the late Sir Henry Reaburn Bart–to Mr [James] Stewart the Engraver–to Mr – Howe the Portrait and Animal painter & to the painting Rooms of others, who were absent—To some other Artists, who were known to me, I spent some time in several calls–these consisted of my old friend, Mr [Alexander] Nasmyth the excellent Landskip painter–my townsmen Mr William Nicholson & Mr [John] Ewbank both of whom were eminent painters & Mr Thos Coulson distinguished in his line as an Ornamental & house painter—I also made some calls upon Mr James Kirkwood, now up in years & past his work, but who had in his prime led the way to excellence, particularly in writing engraving in which he was succeeded by his son & Grandson—I also paid my respects to the son & successor of my kind friend of former days, the late Mr Hector Gavin, and the same to the Sons & successors of the late Mr D. Lizars, all these in my estimation were doing credit to their instructors as engravers–and all these Artists, as well as the painters, had attained to their various ways to that degree of excellence which did honour to Edinburgh, now the seat of learning, and rendered brilliant by the Gems both of Arts & sciences with which it is adorned—We left Edinburgh on the 23d of Augt 1823 & I think I shall see Scotland no more–I think so well of these, our northern countrymen, both English & Celtic, that in most things they may serve as a pattern of both good sense

& good conduct worthy of imitation by the other less civilized nations of the World—I have almost forgot to name my being introduced to Mess[rs] Ballentine & Robertson, the Lithographic Printers–while I was in their Office, the latter pressed me to make a sketch on the stone for him.–We were then preparing to leave Edinburgh, and the only time left me, was so short that I was obliged to do this sketch before breakfast, the next morning, and they got proofs from it the same day–In doing this, 'tho very slight, I could see what that manner of making prints was capable of performing.[1]

After my journeys (long ago) to Cherry-burn were ended–I used as formerly, seldom to miss going in the mornings to Elswick Lane to drink whey or Butter milk–in this I commonly fell in with a party who went there, for the same purpose, and this kind of social intercourse continued for many years.

I also, at that time, on the Sunday afternoon, frequently went to visit & contemplate in the Church yards & there give vent to my mind in feelings of regret, & in repeating to myself a kind of soliloquy over the graves of those with whom I had been intimate

> "And then, I loved to haunt lone burial places
> Pacing the Church-yard earth with noisless tread
> To pore in new-made graves for gastly traces
> Brown crumbling bones of the forgotten dead."

–but as this at length, appeared to be unavailing sorrow, I left it off–recounting in my memory the numbers of my friends thus put by, to be forgotten among the millions of others, who had been, at longer & shorter periods also, in this World passed away into oblivion.–Some men from the first, as soon as they die, are quite unnoticed–some are remembered only for a day & some a little while longer and even the "frail memorials", erected to *perpetuate the memory* of those who had been esteemed by some seemed to me to be of as little avail, and their mementos as well as those decked out with ornamented flatteries in time would all go to decay & be remembered no longer than untill all who once knew them were also dead–And the numbers of both the one & the other appeared to me so immense, that to estimate them, seemed impossible & like attempting to count the grains of sand on the sea beach, which had been tossed to & fro & then left by the Waves–it is thus that the grave swallows all up without distinction–the true estimate of their various characters & merits can only be known to the Creator of all, who, according to the reasoning & instinctive powers, given by him, in a greater or lesser degree, to all mankind–but called forth only by those whose souls habitually adore & commune with God, while they remain in this stage of probation–to these it appears clear that he will, in his infinite goodness, wisdom, truth, justice & mercy, on quitting this mortal abode, place every one in the unknowable worlds appointed for & befitting their reception—but notwithstanding the temporary mementos, dedicated to private worth, thus described–to others of a different or public character they may have their use–and as no man ever lived that was not better pleased with being praised than blamed the minds of such may be soothed by the good opinion of their fellow men–therefore Monuments erected to those who have by their virtues & patriotism promoted the happiness of mankind–ought to have every respect paid to their memories–it is a debt of gratitude–due from the public to the Author of our being for the loan of departed worth, & may stimulate others to "do so likewise" 'tho the posthumous praise or blame of the world, is to them of no avail–they are done with all things on this side of time and are out of the reach of both the one & the other—While I was pursuing my wild (Goose chase) ramblings in the Highlands & beheld with admiration the great projecting Rocks, so often to be seen, holding up their bare useless heads to the winds–it struck me that it was a great pity they could not be converted to a better use, and that, as the best I could think of, was, that the names of their illustrious worthies Wallace & Bruce, as well as their other worthies was not inscribed upon them–to hold up their heads with these names to the Sun *for ever*—I have often since that time thought that the bare rocks in other parts of our Islands might with good effect be filled up in the same way–and the first name to be fixed upon, ought to be Alfred the Great–followed by many others–Statesmen–patriots–philosophers–poets &c–who have shone out like polished diamonds & who have embellished & illumined this country & civilized the world–their venerated names with their maxims, or quotations from their works would fill up many of these Rocks (which are waiting for them) & might make all who beheld them be inclined to profit by or to imitate their virtues–How many incomparably good, wise, & *beautifull* texts from the Bible, might also with great propriety be added to fill up every vacant spot[1]–I often lamented that I had not the means to enable me to be at the expense of getting inscriptions & such like quotations inscribed in this way–Often, while I was angling by the watersides, in a hot sunny day, which slackened my sport, I have sat down and thought over some of the beautifull lines of our Poets fit to be applied in this way–and remember well my having first thought of, those from Cunninghams poems–which I would, if I could have afforded it, have *committed to the care of a Rock*–he says

"How smooth that silent River glides
  Progressive to the deep
the poppies pendant o'er its sides
  have soothed the waves to sleep.
Pleasures intoxicated Sons!
Ye indolent! ye gay! reflect!
for as the river runs, time wings
  his trackless way"

} This is from memory

How easy would it be for Gentlemen to get the Names of the illustrious dead thus inscribed upon rocks–or where that could not be done to erect pillars–or small obelisks over copious springs (like the holy wells of old) to contain such inscriptions, as those I have hinted at & thus leave this their marks behind them–and which would long continue to put the passing stranger in mind, of some religious Moral or patriotic sentiment, & while he was refreshing himself by quenching his thirst he might be put in mind that

"Man wants but little here below
Nor wants that little long"

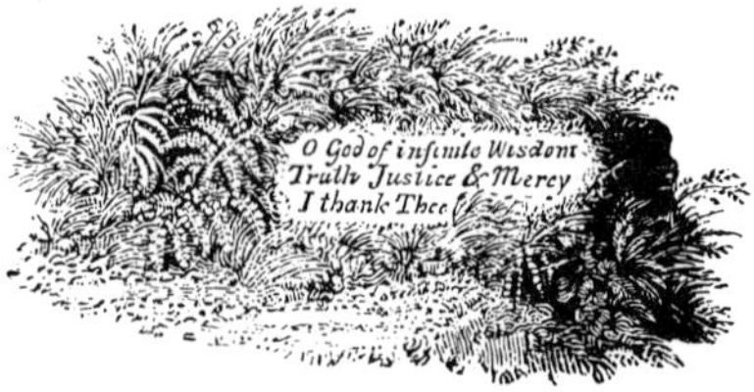

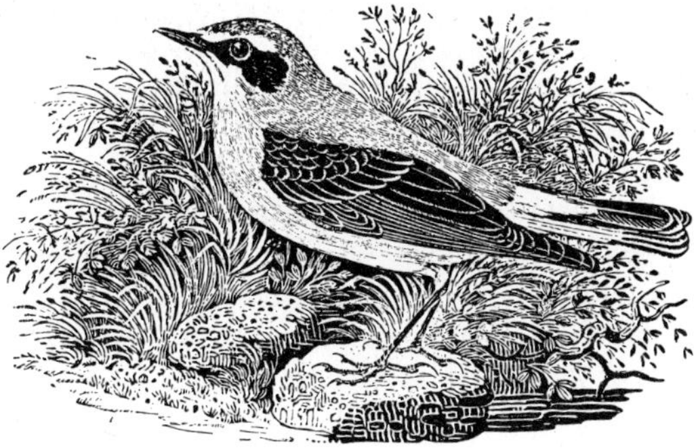

22

Having already noticed my beginnings, or first efforts in engraving on Wood and as at that time, this branch of the Arts, was at the very lowest ebb, in this country, and I believe also, in every other country, in Europe–it may perhaps be of some use, or at least may excite some curiosity to know the part I took in renewing or bringing into use (this to me) new art, as far as I was able, with the slender means in my hands, and the many difficulties to contend with and surmount, before any thing like an approach towards perfection could be arrived at–I ought first distinctly to state, that it never entered into my head, that it was a branch of Art that would stand preeminent for utility, or that it could ever in the least compete with engraving on Copper. I ought also to observe, that no vain notions, of my ever arriving at any eminence ever passed thro' my mind, and that the sole stimulant with me was the pleasure I derived from imitating natural objects (& I had no other patterns to go by) & the opportunity it afforded me of making & drawing my designs on the Wood, as the only way I had in my power of giving vent to a strong propensity to gratify my feelings in this way—In process of time however, as I began to improve, and then seeing the practical use printers were making of Wood Cuts, that the utility & importance of them began to be unfolded to my view–and the more I have since thought upon the subject, the more I am confirmed in the opinions I have entertained, that the use of wood cuts would know no end–or so long as the great importance of printing was duly apreciated & the liberty of the press held sacred.—The first difficulty, I felt, as I proceeded, was in getting the cuts I had done, printed so as to look any thing like my drawings, on the blocks of wood, nor in corresponding to the labour, I had bestowed upon the cutting of the designs.–At that time pressmen were utterly ignorant as to any proper effect that was to be produced–or even if one of them possessed any notions of excellence bejond the common run of Workmen his materials for working were so defective that he could not execute even what he himself wished to accomplish–the common Pelt balls then in use, so daubed the cut & blurred & overlapped its edges, that the impression looked disgusting–to remedy this defect, I was obliged carefully to shave down the edges round about, and this answered the end I had in view–The next difficulty was worse to surmount, and required a long time to get over it, and that was to lower down the surface, on all the parts I wished to appear pale, so as to give the appearance of the required distance–and this process will always continue to call forth & to exercise the judgement of every wood engraver, even after he knows what effect, his *carefull pressman* may be enabled to produce, from his manner of cutting–on this all Artists must form their own ideas–I think no exact description can be laid down by him, as a rule for others to go by–they will, by practice, have to find out this themselves—[1] While I was patiently labouring & contending with difficulties, which I could not over come, I was shown some impressions from Wood Cuts done long ago, with cross hatching, such as I thought I should never be able to execute–these were wood Cuts by Albert Durer & perhaps some others of his day, in the collection of the Revd John Brand (the Newcastle Historian) & from these I concluded that Albert Durer, must have had some very easy way of loading his blocks with such an useless profusion of cross hatching, or he would not have done them so, without he had found out some easy means of etching the Wood (or perhaps metal plates), quite unknown to me, but if otherwise, I then, in changing my opinion, could think of no other way than that he must have cut his blocks on the plank side of the Wood, on which it would be more easy to pick out the interstices between the squares or the lozened shaped lines, than as I (at that time) thought it possible to do on the end way of the Wood–One of these plank blocks, said to have been drawn by Albert Durer, was shewn to me, by my kind friend Geo. Allan Esq[r] of the Grange, Darlington–the drawing, which was done with great accuracy, seemed to me to have been done by a crow quill with a kind of varnish ink, the strokes of which from their regularity looked as if they had been printed from a well executed copper plate, & transferred to the block–After labouring for some time, in endeavouring to produce the like effect, on my blocks, on the end way of the Wood, not indeed to my satisfaction, I felt mortified, in not succeeding to my wish and I then begun to think the impressions must have been printed from two blocks,–this indeed I soon found to be quite easy to do, as well as being beautifully correct–and any Artist, may see this, in a few minuts, by cutting parallel lines on a piece of Wood, & from it, taking, by his hand, an impression on a piece of paper, & then again inking the same cut, & printing it in the same way, either directly in a cross, or in an oblique direction, upon the first impression–this can also be easily done, from two cuts, at a printing press & is much easier to do & better than the labour necessarily bestowed upon one cross hatched block—When I had accomplished this, and satisfied myself, that that the process was both simple & perfect, as to obtaining the object I so much wanted, my curiosity on this score ceased, and I then begun to conclude, that in this way the cross hatching, might be set aside as a thing of no use at all–The Artists, indeed, of the present day have brought it to such a pitch of perfection, that I do not know that it can be carried any further; and in this they have also been so marvellously aided by the improved methods now used in printing their cuts, that one would be led to conclude this department has also attained to perfection, & had not this been the case, the masterly execution of wood cuts either by crossed lines, or otherwise, would have continued to be beheld with disgust or contempt. I have long been of opinion, that the cross hatching of wood cuts, for Book work, was a waste of time, as every desired effect can be much easier obtained by plain parallel lines, & that the other way was not the legitimate object of wood engraving, and that, instead of their drawing & imitating the manner of copper etchings, with great labour & time on the Wood, such drawings might have been as soon etched on the copper at once; and where a large impression, of any publication was not wanted, the copper plate would have cost less, and lasted long enough for the purpose intended. I never could discover any additional beauty or colour that the crossed strokes gave to the impression, bejond the effect produced by plain paralel lines, and this is very apparent when to a certainty the plain surface of the Wood, will print as black as ink & balls[1] can make it, without any further labour at all–and it may easily be seen, that the thinest strokes cut upon the plain surface, will throw *some light* on the subject or design–and if these strokes are made wider & deeper, it will receive more light & if these strokes again are made, still wider, or of equal thickness to the black lines, the colour these produce, will be a grey–& the more the white strokes are thick'ned, the nearer will they, in their varied shadings approach to white–and if quite taken away, then a perfect white is obtained.—The methods I have pursued, appear to me to be the simple & easy perfection of wood engraving, for Book printing–and, no doubt will appear, better & worse according to the abilities of the Artists who execute them–The first time I ever heard any thing about colour being produced by plain engraving, was in the compliments bestow'd upon me by Dr Thomas Stout for my engraving on a large Silver Box for him,–the device or design, I have now forgot, but never what he said upon the occasion and from that time I attempted *colour* upon the Wood, & though I felt much difficulty, in my attempts at producing it, yet the principle is there & will shine out under the skill & management of any eminent engraver on wood who is gifted with a painters eye, & his work will be complete if seconded by a pressman of ability, who may happen to have a talent & fellow feeling for the Art. I have before noticed my lowering down the surface of the Wood, in order to produce the effect of distance & the same thing holds good with every figure, where different shades of colour is desired–leaving the surface of the block without being pared down at all, & relying only on the lines being left thicker or smaller for producing the requisite depth of shade, and this surface thus left, acts as a support, to the more delicate lines, which have been engraved upon the lowered part of the cut–After all the parts are thus lowered, a further paring down of the edges, of the various figures, which the cut contains, may be necessary, to prevent their appearing as if surrounded by a white line–The delicate lines thus lowered so as

[to] print pale, or distant parts, & thus protected by the stronger lines left on the surface, a Wood cut (with care) will print an incredible number–how many, it may be difficult exactly to say, but it once happened that I had the opportunity given me of guessing pretty nearly at this, & it was from the calculations of the late Mr Sol: Hodgson, who, when he once called upon me along with a Gentleman (a stranger to me) who seemed extremely curious to know every thing about engraving on Wood–and one of his queries was with a view to enable him exactly to know how many impressions a wood cut could print, before it was worn out–not having any thing in mind at the moment to enable me to satisfy him I begun to consider & then it struck me that a little delicate cut, a view of Newcastle, was done for Mr Hodgson, many years before as a fac[1] for his newspaper–I then got out my Ledger to shew him the date when it was done–he at first startled & said "it must have printed a million"!–he however sat down & calculated exactly, and found it had printed above 900,000–this cut was continued in the paper several years afterwards, untill the columns of it were altered.–This cut, was protected in the manner before noticed by a strong black line, or border, surrounding it, within which the surface was lowered, previous to cutting the view–This cut is still kept, and except being somewhat damaged by being tossed about in a drawer among other cast away cuts, it might (by being a little repaired) yet print many thousands—this is mentioned with a view to show the great length of time that cuts, done in this way, will last, if they are carefully adjusted to the height of the type, & kept out of the hands of ignorant rude pressmen—I am of opinion that cuts done in the manner called "surface cutting" cannot stand any thing like so large an impression, as when they thus are lowered, for the delicate lines, when left on the surface must soon break down, from the heavy pressure to which they are exposed—[2]

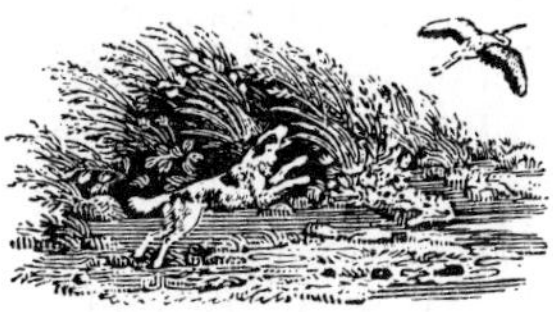

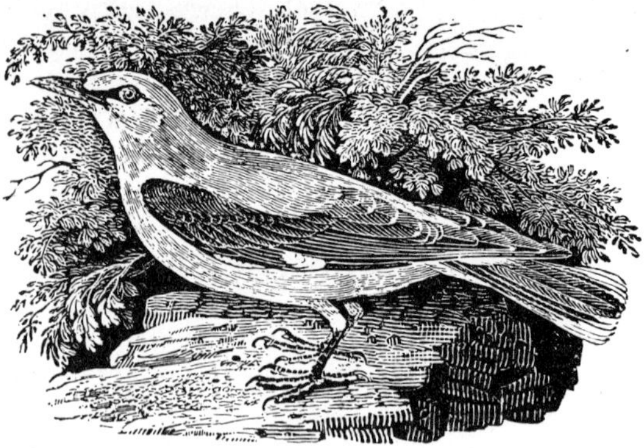

[23]

It is foreign to my present purpose to criticise the works of brother artists of the present day–I behold their excellent productions with pleasure–in them there is no falling off, they surpass those of the artists of the *olden times*—

–I cannot, however, help lamenting that in all the vicissitudes which this art has undergone, some species of it, is lost & done away–I mean the large blocks, with the prints from them, so common to be seen, when I was a boy, in every Cottage & farm house throughout the whole country–these blocks, I suppose must, from their size, have been cut the plank way[1] on beech or some other kind of close grained wood, & must also, from the immense number of impressions from them, so cheaply & extensively spread, over the whole country, must have given employment to a great number of Artists in this inferiour department of Wood cutting, and must also have formed to them an important article of traffick —these prints, which were sold at a very low price, were commonly illustrative of some memorable exploits–or perhaps the portraits of emminent Men who had distinguished themselves in the service of their country, or in their patriotic exertions to serve mankind–besides these, there were a great variety of other designs, often with songs added to them, of a moral, a patriotic or a rural tendancy which served to enliven the circle in which they were admired–To enumerate the great variety of these *pictures* would be a task–A constant one in every house, was "king Charles's twelve good rules"[1]–representations of remarkable victories at Sea, and battles on land, often accompanied with portraits of those who commanded & others who had born a conspicuous part in those contests with the enemy.—The House in Ovingham, where our dinner poke was taken care of, when at school, was hung round with views or representations of the battles of Zondorf & several others–the portraits of Tom Brown the valiant Granadier[2] –Admiral Haddock Admiral Benbow and other portraits of Admirals–A figure or representation of the Victory man-of-War of 100 Guns, commanded by Admiral Sir John Balchen, & fully manned with 1100 picked Seamen & volunteers, all of whom & this uncommonly fine Ship were lost–*sunk to the bottom of the Sea*–this was accompanied with a poetical lament of the catastrophe–part of which was "ah hapless Victory, what avails thy towering masts thy spreading sails".[3] Some of the Portraits I recollect, were now & then to be met with, which were very well done in this way, on Wood–in Mr Gregson's kitchen one of this character hung against the wall many years, it was a remarkably good likeness of Captn Coram—In cottages every where were to be seen, the sailor's farewell & his happy return–youthfull sports, & the feats of Manhood–the bold Archers shooting at a mark–the four Seasons &c–some subjects were of a funny & others of a grave character–I think the last portraits I remember of, were those of some of the Rebel Lords & "Duke Willy"[4]–These kind of Wood Cut pictures, are long since quite gone-out of fashion, which I feel very sorry for & most heartily wish they could be revived again–it is desirable indeed, that the subjects should be well chosen, for it must be of great importance that such should be the case–as whatever can serve to instill morality & patriotism into the minds of the whole people, must tend greatly to promote their own happiness, & the good of the community, for all Men, however poor they may be, ought to feel that *this* is their country, as well as it is, that of the first noblemen in the land, & if so, they will be equally as interested in its happiness and prosperity—There is another way, not yet indeed entered upon, of similar import as the foregoing, in which prints might with good effect be made, of subjects fit to embellish almost every house throughout our country, & that is from Wood blocks, printed in colours, like paper hangings–having seen some such, done by paper stainers, so as almost to equal good paintings–this leads me to wish that this method could be pursued, for the same ends as those already noticed–the most remarkable productions of Art, of this kind, from blocks done to print in colours, like beautifull little paintings, were sent to me by Mr Gubitz of Berlin, they might indeed be said to be perfection. Several impressions from duplicate, or triplicate blocks, done & printed in this way, of a very large size, were also given to me, as well as a drawing of the press from which they were printed, many years ago, by an old Man of the name of Jackson ("Jean Baptiste Jackson") who had been patronized by the King of France, but whether these prints had been done with the design of embellishing the walls of houses in that country I know not–they had been taken from paintings of the eminent old Masters & were mostly scripture pieces–they were well drawn & perhaps correctly copied from the originals, yet in my opinion none of them looked well[1]–Jackson left Newcastle quite enfeebled with Age, and it was said, ended his days, in an asylum, under the charitable & protecting care of Sir Gilbert Elliot Bart, at some place on the border near the Teviot or on Tweedside–Whether the speculations, here noticed, may be thought worthy of being acted upon, or otherwise I know not— But it is not in any of the above noticed ways of woodcutting, that my attention is directed, it is in my ardent desire to see the *stroke* engraving[2] on Wood carried to the utmost perfection, & done in the way now pursued, that I hope the *World* will be gratified, & I trust the time is not distant when its superiour excellence, will be seen, particularly in Landscape scenery, so as to surpass copper engravings–the effect to be produced by Wood engraving has not (in that way) yet been tried & its powers are not made apparent–and this is, I think, to be attained by two, or even more blocks being used, on one print, that a greater & more natural effect, as to colour & softness is to be produced–I am well aware that some difficulty may arise, as to bringing off a clear impression of fine strokes from so large a surface, but in this age of mechanical improvement & invention, I think this apparent difficulty, will readily be got over–perhaps printing from a Roller, instead of an even down pull,[3] might easily accomplish this business—I have often thought, had William Woolett been a Wood engraver, he

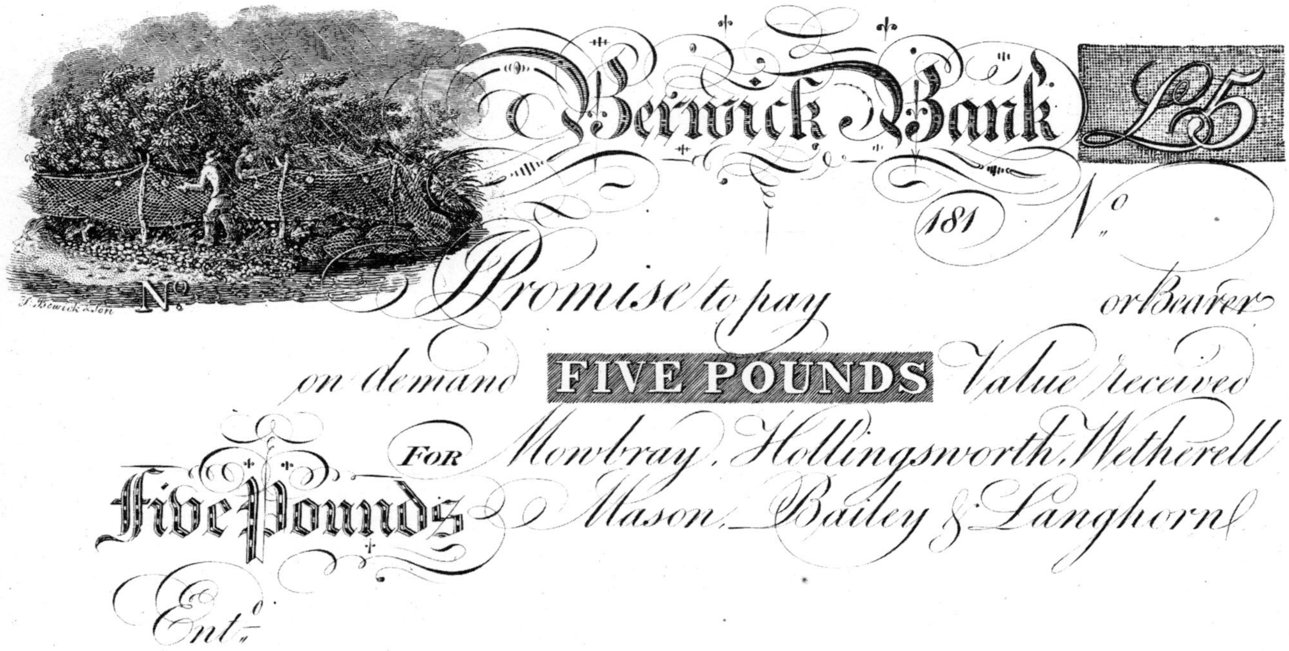

A note engraved on copper by Bewick for the Berwick Bank (original size)

51

This worthy man had been educated for a priest 30

but he would say to me "of a trouth Thomas I did not like them ways", [some] gave up the thoughts of [being a Priest] & bent his way from Aberdeen to Edinburgh, where he engaged himself to Allen Ramsay the poet, then a Bookseller, in the latter place, & in whose service he was both a shop-man & Bookbinder — from Edinburgh he came to New-castle & engaged him-[I believe]-self to Mr Slack as a Bookbinder [& careful] and as a faithfull inspector of the Books printed in the office — Mr Slack, [illegible] at [was] a woman of [uncommon] extraordinary abilities

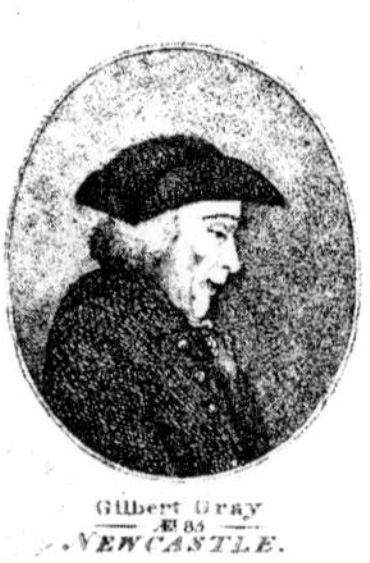

& great goodness of heart. Did not overlook Gilbert & he was her right hand man — as long as she lived — he was afterwards employed in the same [way], to the end of his life, under Solomon Hodgson, the successor to Thomas Slack —

—Gilbert had had a liberal education bestowed upon him — had read a great deal, & reflected upon what he had read, this with his retentive memory enabled him to be a pleasant & communicative man — but some thing of a prejudice against priests stuck by him as long as he lived — I was in habits of intimacy with him to the end of his life, & when he died, I with others of his friends attended his remains to the grave — at the ballast Hills — he died on the 12 Feby 1794 — in the 86th year of his age — I think his age was not known — some people said he was 84 & others [illegible]

In my attendance at the work shop of Gilbert, I got acquainted with several young men who like myself admired him — but one of the most singular of these, was Anthony Taylor, a glass maker he was a keen admirer of drawing & painting, but had no opportunity of showing his talents [in the arts] otherwise, than in this [has] painting & [illegible] in which way, [illegible] his [illegible] in the [illegible] he was a [illegible]

A page from the manuscript of the Memoir (original size $8\frac{15}{16}'' \times 7\frac{3}{8}''$)

would have shewn its excellence long ago–his prints, from copper have not been equalled,[1] but from the nature of the wood & the effect it produces, he would have advanced a step farther & on it, have outdone his excellence on copper—if I live (health & sight continued) I will make the attempt to shew that all this is not a visionary theory[2]—Should I not live to get this Memoir printed, under my own inspection, for the *benefit* of yourself, your Brother & Sisters–or whether it will ever be printed at all I know not,–but at any rate the Manuscript itself, which I leave to my dear Jane, will satisfy her (were that necessary) how ardently I have ever wished well to Arts & Artists and 'tho in my endeavours to shew this, I have often been thwarted & disappointed–yet I never lost sight of my object nor became disheartened, in my struggles to fight through & surmount numberless difficulties & barrs thrown in my way. You know a part of those I met with in the course of my business, in which my time was misspent–and also the waste of it bestow'd upon useless & wicked pupils–I know you wish me to give you a history & description of such–but to do so, would be an irksome task & I cannot now be troubled to think about it–I shall however give you a curtailed list (as a whole) & only speak of such as served out their time—I have already noticed my Brother John as my first pupil, & therefore have little further to say respecting him–but only further by adding that nature seemed to have befitted him for becoming a first rate wood engraver–but at the time he was with me, the thoughts of aiming at excellence did not enter into our heads–and he left this world, at the time when it was only begun to be looked upon as a matter of any interest—Our first apprentice, was John Laws, who was brought up as a silver engraver & I think he never touched upon the Wood–his turn was directed to the ornamental & chiefly in the branch, of what is called bright engraving[3] & at this kind of work he excelled, & is perhaps the best at this day–with it he also follows the business of a Farmer at "Heddon Laws", the place of his nativity. We greatly respected him for his honesty, sobriety, civil deportment & attention–The next for whom we had a great regard, for the like reasons was John Johnson,[4] & who we put to do engraving on Wood, as well as other kinds of work–I think he would have shone out in the former branch–but he died of a fever, at about the Age of 22 when only beginning to give great promise of his future excellence—Our next Apprentice was Robert Johnson who did not incline to do wood cutting & prefering copper plate engraving he was almost wholly employed in that way & in it attained to great excellence–and besides that, he became great as a draftsman & colourist–but as he was of so delicate a constitution, that he could not bear confinement, we for that reason, set him to work to make sketches & views, where he had both air & exercise—It may be necessary to give a more detailed history, than ordinary, of this Boy on account of the unceasing pains I bestowed upon his tuition and my reasons for doing so. His Mother had been long a Servant in fathers House, where she became a great favourite and like one of our own family.—When she married, this boy Robert was her first born; and when he was christned I was to have been his Godfather–this however did not happen, for while I was, for that purpose, on my road near to Ovingham, where the ceremony was to be performed;–but being only about 16 or 17 years old–and exceedingly bashfull, I could not think of appearing before a congregation of people–and when, on getting to the top of the "pantin brae" the Bells began to ring in for Church, I felt so abashed at the thoughts of what I had to do that I "turned tails"–went a little back, and crossed the River upon the top of the Fishermens Weir by stepping from one stob to another, which are driven in to support the wicker work & stones of which the weir is formed—I then went to Cherryburn & after getting some refreshment, returned again to Newcastle–in the mean time my father & mother stood sponsors for the child. As the boy grew up, he having been almost constantly told, he was to be my Apprentice–he looked up to me as a kind of deity–& having been, at every opportunity, kept closely employed in drawing, & "*making pictures*", which were regularly shewn to my father & mother & through them to my Self, he thus came very early into practice—As soon as he attained somewhere about his 13th year, his friends began to act upon the plan so long intended of putting these intentions in force, and in this business my father & mother stood formost, as the warm friends of the boy, & begged I would always shew the same disposition towards him & to take him under my fostering care—He was about a year too young to be bound as an Apprentice, but I took him into my house 'till the proper time arrived, when he was bound to my partner & myself for seven years–He was mostly employed in drawing, & was also at intervals practising himself in the use of the graver & in etching on copper–but being very delicate in his health, we were carefull not to confine him too closely at any thing—It may perhaps be usefull to Artists, to know how I thought it best to order & manage such a tender & pampered boy. The system I begun upon was that of a rigid temperance–he got no medicine from me–my Sister Ann, at that time kept my house, and to get her to second me in my plans, I experienced great difficulty, chiefly from her fears "that folks would raise a report that we hungered him" but I resolutely persisted in my plan and would not allow her to put in her word against it–I began by cutting off, for him, almost every thing he had given him to eat–the animal food with which I helped his plate at dinner, did not exceed in bulk, the size of three of my fingers, to this was added, a portion of vegetables–for breakfast & supper he got a pint of milk, with leavened rye bread, to which last article I did not prevent him from helping himself–he had not been kept to this kind of temperate or pinched regimen about two months, 'till such an alteration for the better took place in his looks as seemed surprizing, so much so that his Mother, when she called to see him, held up her hands in astonishment at seeing this change, from a pale pasty, sickly look, to that of his having cheeks blushed with health like a rose & this same plan was pursued while he remained under my Roof*—The methods I took to learn him his business was also of a piece with his mode of living–I did not keep him so long at work, as to tire him, with whatever job he might be put to do, but especially in drawing, but then, whatever I gave him to copy, was to be done *perfectly correct*, & he dreaded to shew me work that was not so, altho' I never scolded him, but only, if I was not pleased, I put the drawing away from me without saying a word–sometimes indeed I remember of saying O fie! & in this way of treatment he attained to great accuracy–The next thing I put him to was that of colouring, chiefly my own designs, and these occasioned me much time & labour, for I made it a point of drawing these with great accuracy, and with a very delicately pencilled outline–The practical knowledge I had attained in colouring, was imparted to him &

* Another of my plans was to make growing Boys exercise with dumb bells half an hour or so before bed time. I believe were this practised by the sedentary of both sexes–it would go a great way to banish consumption.

he saved me a great deal, of what I considered a loss of my time in being taken up in this way–and besides he soon coloured them in a stile superiour to my hasty productions of that kind–indeed, in this way he became super-excellent, & as I conceived he could hardly be equalled, in his water coloured drawings of views & landscapes, by any artist–for some time, I continued to sketch in his figures, but at length he neaded none of my help, in this way–I remember of his once coming to me & begging I would drawn or sketch in a tree for him–no Robert said I, but I will direct you to a place, where you will see such a tree as you never saw painted by any artist, in your life, and that was a tree then growing in *Adonis's Grove*–he went & endeavoured to do justice to his pattern, & I do not know that any one could have made a better likeness—As soon as the time arrived, that he became entitled to have wages[1] from us, this tempted his father & mother to leave the country & to reside in Newcastle & to have him to board with them–how he was managed, as to his diet with them I know not, but it soon appeared to have been a wrong treatment in this respect, for he soon lost his health & was from that time, seldom out of the hands of the Doctor; and at one period, of his apprenticeship he was about a year absent from our employment, either in the country or in being nursed with watchfull care at home–he however became quite well by the time he was freed from his servitude with us, & he then commenced painting & engraving on his own account. In the former Art he seemed to be much patronized, and had, I believe, turned his attention to oil painting–The last of his efforts in this line, was done under the patronage of the Earl of Breadalbane,[2] by whom he was employed to copy some portraits & perhaps some other things at [Kenmore] where he took ill of a fever & died in the year 1796 & in the 26 of his Age–and was buried there—It always appeared to me, that he would have become great, as a painter, but a delicate constitution & want of stamina prevented this–I have often thought it was a great mistake in parents & a very common one, to fix upon some sedentary employment for their *tender delicate Boy*, when perhaps, had he been sent to Sea, or some other out door work, where he would be exposed to fresh Air & exercise–he might have become a healthy stout Man—My friends having often expressed a wish, that I would give some account of my pupils, has occasioned me to dwell thus long on that of Robert Johnson[1]–but I think it unnecessary to notice others, who were not gifted with talents & some others again who had neither one good property nor another and with whom I had much vexation & much reason to complain—The first of my pupils, who made a figure in London, after my Brother, as a Wood Engraver was Charlton Nesbit[2]–he went at a nick of time, when wood cuts seemed to claim something like universal attention & fortunately for that Art it was under the guidance of the ingenious John Thurston*[3] who pencilled his designs stroke by stroke on the Wood, with the utmost accuracy & it would appear that Nesbit was the first, by his mechanical excellence to do justice to these designs. Henry Hole†[4] & John Anderson[5] preceded Nesbit.

The next of my pupils, who chiefly turned his attention to Wood engraving was Edward Willis,[6] who while he remained with me was much upon a par with Nesbit, but did not equal him in the mechanical excellence Nesbit had attained to in London–I had a great regard for Edward Willis on account of his regular good behaviour while he was under my tuition–he has now been long a resident in London–My Nephew John Harrison,[7] was chiefly employed on Writing Engraving–he died of Epileptic Fits . . ., & was buried, at N° Shields church, between 2 trees near the foot path.—Henry White,[8] from London, was engaged to me to serve out the remainder of his apprenticeship, when his master, the late Mr Lee died.–When the term of his engagement with me was ended–he returned to London, & chiefly turned his attention, to the imitation of sketchy *cross hatching* on Wood, from the inimitable

* John Thurston was reared from a child at a place called the Leases, near Newcastle, where a burn separates a large pasture, (which goes by that name) from the "Town Moor"–his Mother, who lived at Scarbro, where the Boy was born, had married a second husband, who it appears was of a base character, & had married her solely for her property–this her friends saw & to prevent her ruin, sent her off incog: to the forenamed place, to be out of the way of the worthless fellow–and my friend, John Anderson, Surgeon, was deputed to advance her the money, necessary for her support–the boy was afterwards sent to the Academy of the ingenious Mr Hornsey at Scarbro', to finish his education & with him he also learned to draw–Mr Hornsey made the designs for the copper plate Magazine & for other things–was author of "Hornsey's Grammar and . . . ." When the youth had finished his education, he was engaged to Mr Heath as an Engraver–but left it off, & wholly devoted his time to making designs & drawing them on the Wood, for the Wood engravers.

† Henry Fulke Woolcomb Plantagenet Hole, left Newcastle & went thence to Liverpool where he was patronized by Mr Roscoe–Capel Loft, Maccreery the printer & others–he continued in Liverpool untill the death of his Grandfather–Hole Esqre of Ebberly Hall, Devonshire to whose very large property he fell heir to,–& left off pursuing the Arts any longer.

pencil of Mr Cruikshanks, & perhaps some other artists in this same way–Henry White appears to have taken the lead of others, who followed that manner of cutting, which shortly became *quite the Ton*[1]—Another of my pupils of distinguished ability, both as a draftsman and Wood Engraver, was Luke Clennell[2] whose melencholly history, will be well remembered by the Artists of London & else where, and the simpathetic feelings, which was drawn forth & shewn to him by a generous public, by their subscriptions to a Print of the battle of Waterloo, from his painting of the decisive charge of the Guards, on that eventfull day–the next of my pupils, was Isaac Nicholson,[3] who was both a good Apprentice & a good Artist–his engravings on Wood are clearly, or honestly cut, as well as being accurately done from his patterns–he did not pursue his business in London, but carries it on in Newcastle—The next of my pupils, & one of the first in excellence was William Harvey,[4] who both as an engraver & designer, stands preeminent at this day –his fellow Apprentice was William Temple (who left off Wood engraving, & commenced linnen Draper in Newcastle), he was a faithfull copyest, & his pieces were honestly or clearly cut–The last apprentice I had was John Armstrong, who is now pursuing his business in London–I have not gone down in regular succession with my pupils, but I have noticed all those who (in my estimation) were worth notice and now when the time is fast approaching for my winding up all my labours–I may be allowed to name my own Son & partner,[5] whose time has been taken up with attending to all the branches of our business & who I trust will not let Wood Engraving go down, & tho he has not shewn any partiallity towards it–yet the talent is there, if he will & I hope call it forth—

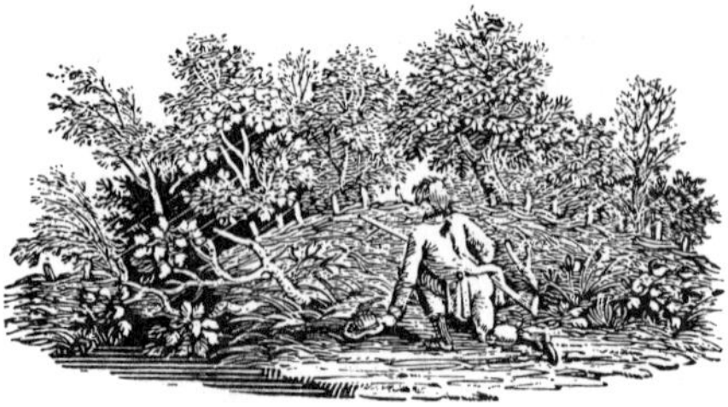

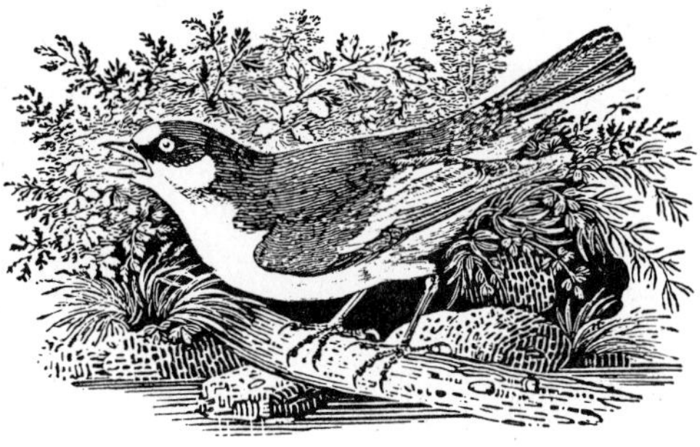

[24]

How far I may venture further to obtrude my opinions or advice on the notice of artists, particularly to engravers on Wood, I know not, but they may readily imagine, that I cannot help feeling a deep interest, and an ardent desire, that the Art may long flourish & that those who follow it may feel happy in the pursuit–perhaps, what I have already said, may be thought not uninteresting to some of them, and if I knew how I could go further in any way that might urge or stimulate them to feel an enthusiasm for this art, it should not be awanting, for this wish, 'tho tottering on the down-hill of life, is extended bejond the Grave.

The sedentary Artist ought if possible to have his dwelling in the country where he could follow his business undisturbed, surrounded by pleasing rural scenery & the fresh air and as "all work & no play, makes Jack a dull Boy", he ought not to sit at it, too long at a time, but to unbend his mind with some variety of employment–for which purpose, it is desireable, that Artists, with their *little Cots*, should also have each a Garden attached in which they might find both exercise & amusement–and only occasionally visit the City or the smokey Town & that chiefly for the purpose of meetings with their Brother Artists in which they might make an inter-change of their sentiments & commune with each other as to what-ever regarded the Arts—And were I allowed to become their M.D., my prescription shall cost them nothing & be *easily taken*–it being only attentively to observe two or three rules–the first of which is, that they will contrive to be very hungry once a day–never send a second supply to the stomach, till the first has left it, and never to indulge to satietey in eating any thing–by persisting in this, they would find their reward in great good health & a vigorous unclouded mind & [by] a little observation, they may clearly see[1] that a great portion of mankind Live to eat, not eat to live. To say more to men of sense and artists,–which a desire to contribute everything in my power towards their peace of mind and happiness prompts me to do,–I may be allowed to add, that those of them who have attained to eminence will find themselves pursued by envy; for "There is no species of hatred greater than that which a man of mediocrity bears to a man of genius; his reach of thought, his successful combinations, and his sudden felicities are never forgiven by those whom nature has fashioned in a less perfect mould."—It is the duty of parents & guardians of youth to endeavour with the utmost care to discover their capacities and their fitness for pursuing any business, before they are engaged in it, but particularly for such as are intended to be put to learn the fine arts for without they are innately gifted with the power for becoming Artists, the want of it will be found to be to them *uphill-work* & be productive of unhappiness to them 'thro life–but the fondness of parents for their ofspring is mostly such as to make them so blind as to think them fit to learn any thing & disappointment follows them like a shadow–it would be well, for such parents to read Gays Fable of The Owl, the Swan, the Cock, the Spider, the Ass & the Farmer [and the] Dodsley Fable of the Eagle & the Owl—It may indeed be conceeded that there are some rare exceptions to this general rule for a man may be so formed in body & mind–with such cimitry & health in the one, & such energy in the other, that they may attain a great way towards perfection, in any thing they ardently pursue–but an "Admirable" Chrichton & a Sir Josua Reynolds do not appear every day—Men so gifted by nature, whether as Artists or in any other way where intellectual powers are to be drawn forth, ought never to despair of rising to eminence, for it is wrong in them to take it into their heads that they can never equal, such men, *of this character*, as have excelled all others in their day–but they ought to keep in mind that the same superintending providence, which gifted these men with talents to excite wonder & to improve Society, from time to time in all Ages–still rules the World & the affairs of Mankind & will continue to do the same for ever–as often as the services of such men are wanted–and this consideration ought to act as a stimulant to their successors, to endeavour to surpass in excellence the brilliant luminaries who have only gone before them to pave the way & to enlighten their paths. Had I been a painter, I never would have copied the Works of "*Old Masters*" or others, however highly they might be esteemed–I would have gone to nature for *all my patterns*, for she exhibits an endless variety–not possible to be surpassed & scarcely ever to be equalled–I would indeed have endeavoured to find out the way how these artists of old made or compounded their excellent colours as well as the disposition of their lights & shades by which they were enabled to accomplish so much & so well–All Artists (& indeed all Men) ought when necessary to divide their time–by regularly appropriating one portion of it to one purpose, and another part of it to the varied business that may be set apart for another–in this way a deal of work may be easily got through & the Artist (after leaving off his too intense application) would see, as it were, what he had been doing with *new Eyes*–by which he would be enabled to criticise the almost endless variety of lights, shades & effects &c which awaits his pencil to produce—but the work of the painter may be said to be as endless as the objects which nature continually presents to his view, & it is his judgement that must direct him in the choice of such as may be interesting, or otherwise–in this he will see, what others have done before him & the shoals & quicksands that have retarded their progress as well as the Rocks they have at last entirely split upon—On his taking a proper survey of all this, he will see the *labour-in-vain*, that has been bestowed upon useless designs, which have & will continue to find their way to a Garret–while those well chosen & well executed subjects, will, from their excellence be preserved, with perhaps increasing value for ages to come—In performing all this, great industry will perhaps be required and it ought ever to be kept in mind, that, as in morals nothing is worth listning to but truth–so in arts nothing is worth looking at but such productions as have been faithfully copied from nature but, poetry indeed may launch out [and] take further liberties to charm the intellectual minds of its votaries–It is only such youths as providence has gifted with strong intellectual innate powers, that are perfectly fit to embark in the fine arts–and the power & propensity to do so, is often seen early to bud out & shew itself in the various ways which youth is destined to pursue—this is first seen in the young Musician, who without having even learned his ABC[s] breaks out with a random kind of unrestrained freedom to whistle and sing & how often have I been amused at the first assays of the plowboy & how charmed to find him so soon attempt to equal his whistling & singing Master at the plow-stilts, & who with avidity uneasing–never stopped 'till he thought he excelled him—The *future painter* is shewn by his strong propensity to sketch out whatever objects in nature attract his attention, & excites him to imitate them. The Poet indeed has more difficulties to contend with at first, than the others, because he must know language, or be furnished with words wherewith to enable him to express himself even in his first assays, in his dogerel metre & *singsong rhymes*—In all the varied ways, by which Naturalists & Artists are befitted to enlighten, to charm & to embellish civilized society, as they advance through life–if they entertain the true feeling that every production they behold is created not by chance, but by design–[they] will find an encreasing & endless pleasure in the exhaustless stores which *nature has provided*, to attract the attention & promote the happiness of her votaries during the term of their sojourning here.—The painter nead not roam very far from his home in any part of our beautifull Isles, to meet with plenty of charming scenes, from which to copy nature–either in an extended or limited scale & in which he may give full scope to his genious & to his pencil either in animate or inanimate subjects–whether he searches for such in the narrowed romantic Ravine–the placid Holme–the hollow dell, or the pendant foliage of the richly ornamented Dean–with the burns by which they have, by time, been scooped out & which roar or dash through their bottoms –or run murmuring from pool to pool through their pebbly beds–and all these bounded & bordered with a back ground of Ivey covered ancient hollow Oaks, with Elms, Willow & birch–thus clothed, as if to hide their Age–or kindly to offer shelter to an undergrowth of hazel–Whins, Broom, Juniper & Heather with the Wild rose & Woodbine & brambles–beset with clumps of Fern & Foxglove–while the edges of the mossy braes are covered with a profusion of wild flowers, which "blow to blush unseen" or which peep out among the creeping groundlings the bleaberry, wild strawberry, Harebell, violet & such like—but I feel a want of words to enable the pen to give an adequate description of the beauty & simplicity of these neglected spots, which dame nature has planted, as if to invite the admiration of such as have hearts & Eyes–befitted to appreciate & enjoy these her exquisite treats–while she may perhaps smile at the formal pruning efforts of the gardner as well as doubt whether the pencil of the Artist will ever accomplish a correct imitation–but be all this as it may, she has spread out her beauties to feast the eyes & to invite the admiration of all mankind & to whet them up to an ardent love of all her works–How often have I, in my Angling excursions, loitered upon the such sunny braes, lost in extacy, & wishing I could impart to others, the pleasures I felt upon such occasions–but they must see with their own Eyes to feel as I felt, & form their own opinion, how far the scenes depictured by Poets come up to or fall short–The naturalist's Poet, Thomson has done as much as he could, so have others–Allen Ramsay's "Habbies howe" where "a' thy sweets of spring & Summer grow" may have been covered with ⟨beauties⟩ such as I have noticed–but the Man smit with a fit turn of mind & inclined to search out for such *beauty Spots* will not nead the aids of poets to help him in his enthusiastic Ardour.

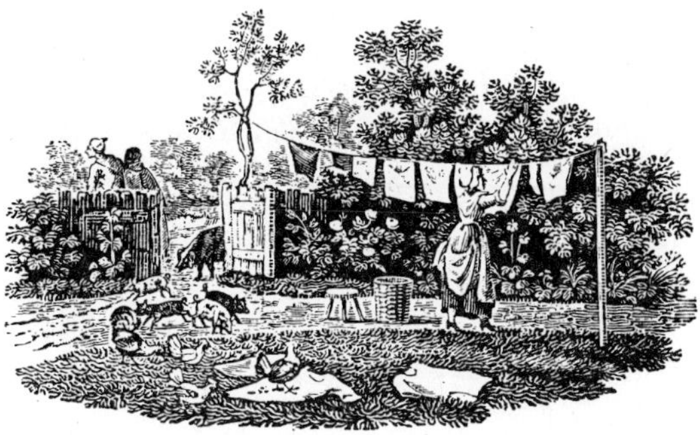

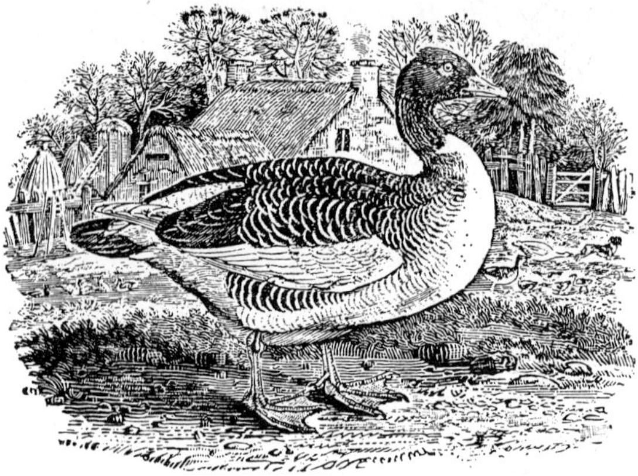

[25]

My dear Jane, will well remember the times, when on a Sunday morning, I had fixed upon spending the day at home, and of my calling it a "*Red nightcap day*"–because it was set a part for contemplation & for this purpose, I walked undisturbed in the Garden alone–and thus employed, it was always a welcome & a happy 'tho a short day to me–& yet this was not without its alloy, for when your Mother led you forth, all clean & neat, with her to Church, I felt grievd at my not making one of the party–but you know the first cause which prevented me, and that was owing to my not being able to sit in the cold Church with my Hat off, without my suffering for it, when I did so–I often wished, that the different congregations, would leave off this foolish custom & follow the good sense & the example of the Quakers, in this respect–

This however, 'tho it was the beginning, was not the sole cause or objection I had to attending regularly at Church–for I did not like to *hippocrise*–that is indeed wicked folly, for "God knows the secrets of our hearts, & our desires are not hid from him"–I knew of nothing I had to petition for–& had only to pour out my thanks for his numerous blessings–which I hoped I could do better, when alone, than when I was surrounded by a congregation–for I never could be religious at Church–I could not believe in the Miracles nor dogmas & creeds which seemed to me to have been invented by interested men to bewilder the understanding–With these preached up Sunday after Sunday to arrest the solemn attention of their hearers, I felt annoyed–& wondered how any rational being could listen to such absurdities—when very young, I read the Bible through & through–but I at that time minded it no more than other tales & Histories, with which my scanty Library was furnished–I could not then judge of it, nor properly estimate the sublime precepts it contained–I felt indeed much pleased & excited by the account of numerous battles therein described–sober reflection however, respecting these quite altered the bent of my inclination that way, and I began & continued to consider the political History of the Israelites as superlatively wicked & horrible–for their Historians have so described them, as under the direction of Moses–who, it is said always obtained the command or the sanction of "the Lord" to do so, & to set the people to work in the business of War, *alias* robbery, assasination & murders–at all of which the Israelites appear to have been both very ready & expert.—It however, is evident that in the Nation of the Israelites, there were Men of great intellectual powers & inspired with an ardent desire to trace the Author of nature through his works, as well as having a foresight of their future destiny–and in its being clear to them, that it was the intention of Omnipotince that Men should live in a state of civilised Society, & under this impression on their Minds, they set to work, as well as they could with an *uncivilised people*, to being about such a desirable order of things but in which, they *must have* felt great difficulties–the first of which was to abolish Paganism & to establish the pure religion of worshiping one God only–thus "*Thou* shalt have none other Gods but me", was the first commandment, & which was most strenuously urged upon them, in every way & in every transaction of their lives, while they were kept together, as a Nation–Science & a knowledge of nature, on which science is founded,–could not, in these early times, be expected to be known either by Moses, or their other Governors & teachers & they could not explain *such important matters*, to the people otherwise than they did. The wonders of this World, and of the magnitude of the Universe was not then contemplated upon, neither was it perhaps necessary, to attempt any explanation of them, in these dark ages–& besides it appears it was not a leading *object* with them–civilization seems to have been the first, & perhaps the only important business they *at that time* had in view—They therefore, in their endeavours to accomplish this & to govern & keep the People in awe, attempted to personify the Deity & to prescribe the boundary of time & place, as the theatre on which he acted, that they might thus understand something of the meaning of the commands, so strenuously laid upon them, not a little of which was delivered to them in allegory & fable–Moses begun by telling them of the beginning of the World–& the length of time it took to make it–& the manner in which god created Adam & Eve–as the parents of the whole human race–he then brought forth his *main* Allegory of paradise or the Garden of Eden & the disobedience of our supposed first parents, in their eating of some kind of forbidden fruit, & this original transgression is said to have entailed misery, sin & death upon the whole human race–this "original sin" however strange it appears to all thinking Men, has been kept up in terrorem with uncommon pains, by superstitious, bigotted or interested men, for hundreds of years past, and is continued with unabating fervency & pains to the present time—That mankind should suffer under this condemnation for the real or imaginary fault of these, our supposed first parents, seems impiously to set aside the justice of an Allwise & benevolent God, in decreeing that the Generations of Men, for thousands of years past, & to come, should be thought to deserve being thus criminated, for what they could not possibly help, does not seem in my humble opinion to come within the scope of either rationallity or justice—What Moses said, as to the time that God took to make this World with the whirling floating Universe of which it is comparatively as a small part, a speck–a mote, he could not see himself, nor know from any other person that might pretend to see or to know it–no no, this sublime, this amazing, this mighty work of Suns & Worlds innumerable is too much for the vision, of a finite purblind proud *little* atom of the creation, strutting or crawling about in the shape of Man–instead of this description, if Moses (or his biographers) in his or their reveries, about the creation of this world had said "as to the time it took to make it", that it required only the fiat of the great architect to will its instant production, and as to the time since it was known, to his creatures to exist, that was bejond human comprehension, & time–eternity–a beginning and an end, were still much more bejond the reach of thought–for the powers of the mind would soon become bewildered & lost, in attempting even to form any conception by figures of what is meant by *unnumberable* Millions of centuries–here on this subject we must rest! It is sufficient for the Soul of Man, in this life, to reverence and adore the omnipresent–& except thro his works the unknowable God whose wisdom & power & goodness has no bounds–and who has been pleased to enable his reasoning creatures so far to see that every thing is made by design & nothing by chance & from the display of his infinite power, that every thing in the universe is systematic–all is connection–adhesion, affinity & hence we may infer some principle of order–some moving power–some mighty Agent–but all this *still* ends in the name of Deity & dwells awefully retired–bejond the reach of mortal Eyes. What Moses has said about the Deluge & the destruction it occasioned to every living creature–we are led to conclude, must have been handed down to him in ancient Eastern traditions, for he could not otherwise know any thing about it–nor about the Ark, that was made to hold the family of Noah together with a pair, male & female, of every Genera & species of the brute creation is all bejond the comprehension of Men, at this day–who are of course left to wonder, where the timber was brought from & the carpenters found out so soon to put together a Vessel of that magnitude—there is however no harm in the credulity of men who believe in all this & who may either look upon it as a fable or as a reality, just as they please for to compel belief is an absurdity–but it requires no over stretched credulity to believe that a Deluge happened which destroyed almost every living creature on that part of the earth, over which its devastations were spread for it cannot be doubted that this Globe has undergone many such deluges convulsions & changes equally difficult to account for and Geologists at this day feel convinced of this, from the changes which they see matter has undergone–but of which they are still greatly left to conjecture as to the cause–they cannot, however, doubt the power of a Comet (if it be the will of the mighty director) to melt the Ices from the Poles & to throw the Sea out of its place–or to reduce this Globe instantly to a Cinder–a vitrification–to Ashes, or to dust, & that in its near approach to this, our place of abode, it may have occasioned the various changes & phenomina which have happened & may happen again.

The Marine productions, found embedded in the Earth, so many fathoms below its surface* supplies another source of wonder & seems either to confirm the foregoing hypothesis, or to lead Men to conclude that a great portion of the Earth has once been covered by the Sea, and it may, perhaps not be carrying conjecture too far to suppose that Nations have been overflowed & sunk to its bottom while others have arisen out of it – & that in the apparently, slow changes which are continually operating upon all matter, new nations may yet arise & be now in progress to take their turn, for from our measuring & comparing time by our own short span of life, it appears [that] every mountain & hill is becoming less & less, & is by little & little at a time (apparently slowly) sliding away into the Ocean – and this may be accounted for by the waste continually seen in the many Tons of earthy mud which every flooded River carried off & deposits in the Sea – The same kind of changes are also continually operating upon the remain[g] lakes, by this wasting or wearing away of the outlets that form the barriers by which their waters are at present stayed – and it is not unlikely that every valley & hollow dell was once a lake, till they were operated upon like those still left, preparatory to their change to dry land.—But the early history of Mankind, nor the changes – the wonders – nor these mighty events which have happened on this Globe could not be known & we may reasonably suppose Men must have long remained in darkness & ignorance, 'till rescued from such a state first by hieroglyphics & then by letters – what they were before these enabled them to communicate an exchange of thoughts to each other, preparatory to a social intercourse, is involved in darkness on which conjecture may surmise, invent & exhaust itself in vain—Nation after Nation in unknown Ages past, may have glided away, or have been by the accu[mu]lation of their own wickedness more suddenly hurled unto oblivion – Before Men drew forth their reasoning powers, or bestowed the least thought upon the duties they had to perform & the business they had to fulfill, as the will of their creator while they sojourned here.

* In my Brothers colliery, at Mickley Bank, were found (about 30 fathoms below the surface) perfect muscles, embedded in Iron stone – in appearance they differed not from those newly taken from a *Muscle scaupe* – The Shells effervessed with acid, but the insides were Iron stone, the same as that with which they were surrounded.

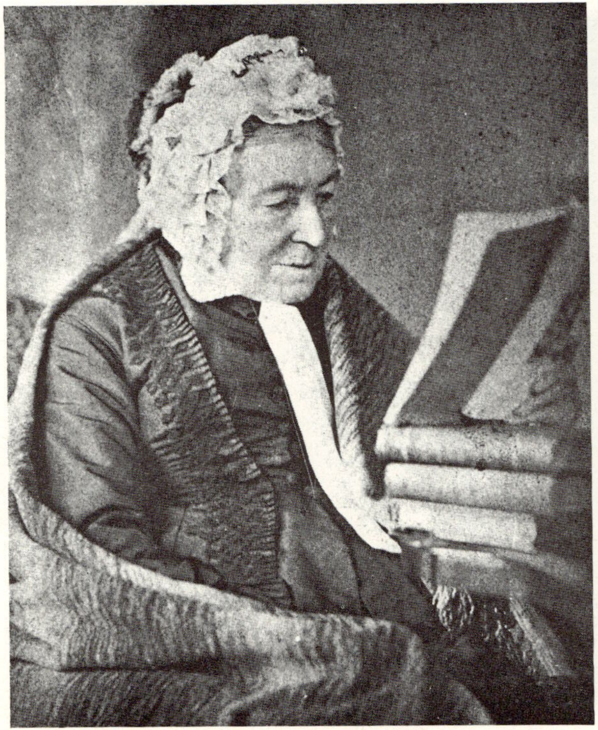

Bewick's eldest daughter Jane

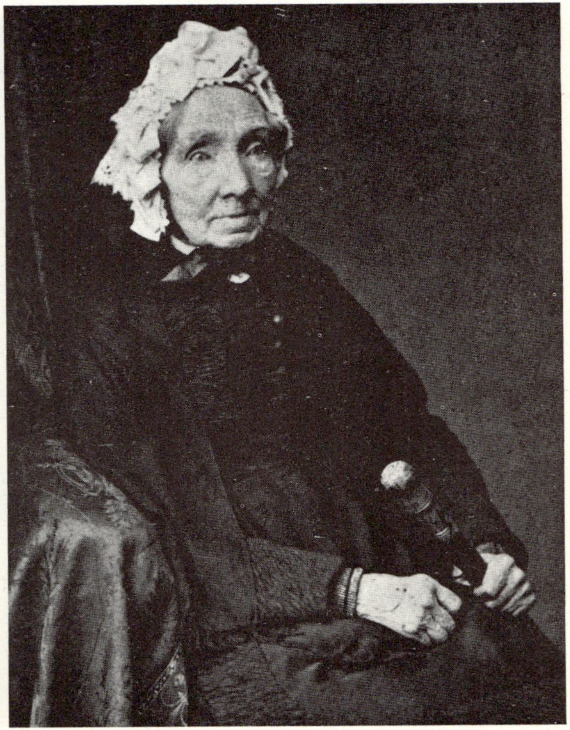

Bewick's second daughter Isabella

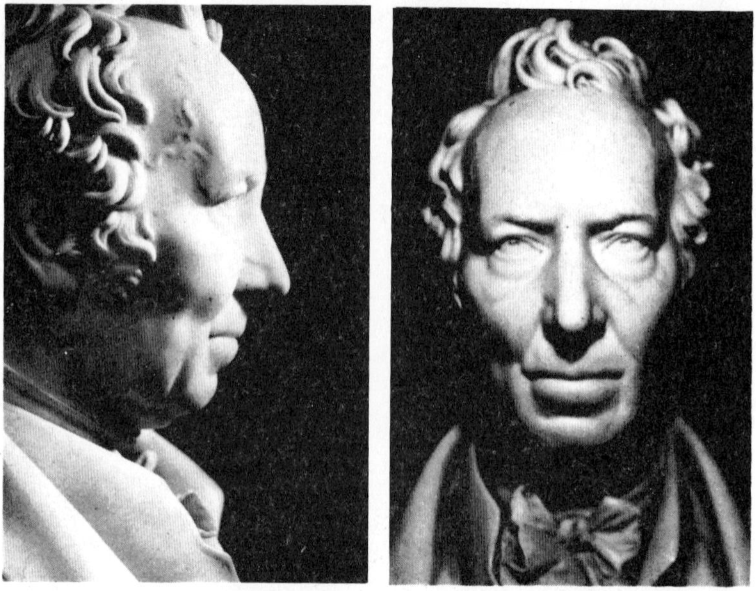

Two views of the marble bust of Thomas Bewick aged 73, taken from a life mask by E. H. Bailey in 1826

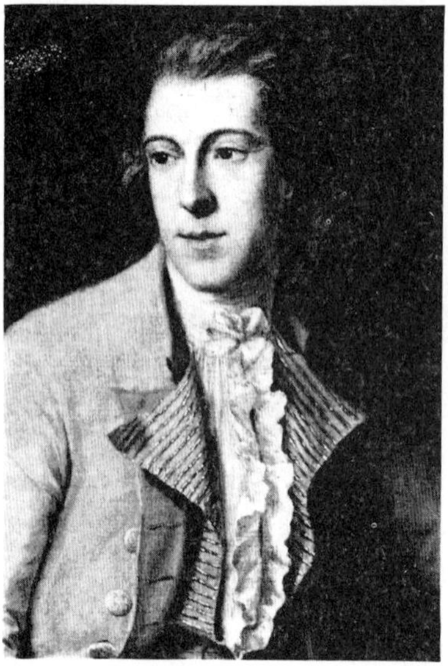

Robert Pollard, by Richard Samuel. Engraver and print-seller, fellow apprentice and life-long friend of Bewick

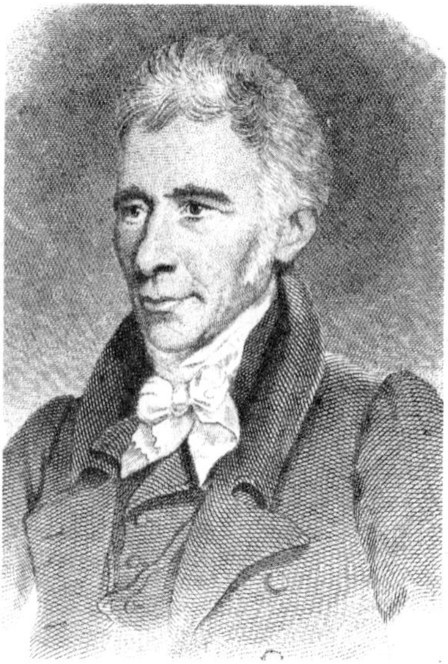

William Bulmer, fellow apprentice of Bewick and celebrated printer at the Shakspeare Press

We may, perhaps reasonably conclude that Mankind, in this savage state of useless ignorance & indolence uncontrolled by their inate but dormant reasoning powers would on the slightest excitements give vent to, and be guided only by their violent & bad passions, which may not improperly stamp them with the name of human Brutes–and we may picture to ourselves that we can (while in this state) see them with gutteral raucous voice prowling about & contending for dominion with the scarcely equally ferocious beasts of prey–or seeking revenge for real or imaginary wrongs of their fellow men & in giving utterance to their vengeance in bellowings & horrid yells against each other preparatory to murder & destruction & that this would end in fiend like growlings of satisfaction at having, in this business of blood, accomplished their purpose.—But the providence of God is over all his creatures & it pleased him that men should not remain longer dormant in this degraded state–& the provision made for the change, in the natural order of things, was placed in the latent intellectual powers gifted to man & drawn from his inspired mind, which, thus put in action drew forth as (it may be presumed) the first efforts of cause & effect that produced the Bible–which, as far as we know, seems to have been the first instrument of knowledge, that shed its rays over & revealed to Mankind the accountable station they were destined to hold on this Globe.–before the religious & moral precepts of the venerable old Book made their way over a more civilized *World*, & taught rational beings to worship one God the father of all & to consider each other as brethren; before this time it does not appear that the great Mass of Mankind had bestowed a thought upon the astonishing miracles of creation by which they were surrounded, & presented to their understanding & sight, in so visible & tangible a shape–that it required no faith to believe in them nor any thing to raise doubts in their Minds as to their reality.–The brilliantly studded canopy of Suns & Worlds above their heads and, as a part of these, the equally wonderfull Globe, of this earth & Sea which is allotted to them, they could not, with their clouded intellects & want of science see nor appreciate, & 'till the mind by research becomes illumined by these in degrees in the varied blaze of light spread abroad which, will, in some degree enable men to see the perfections of the omnipotent author of the whole–Viewing the Bible as to its moral & religious contents in this way, the good old Book ought to be held in veneration & esteem, as containing the most unequivocal marks of the most exalted piety & the purest benevolence–give it therefore a place in your regards to which it is entitled, and amidst the necessary cares of life, never lose sight of your destination for another–an infinitely more important state awaits us bejond the grave.—It may be presumed, that this original & sacred document will continue to arrest the attention of reasoning beings, so long as men continue to reason & be an eternal stimulant together with the other stimulants so abundantly presented by the wonders of the universe, to lead the soul to rest its hopes on the source from whence it derived its existence.

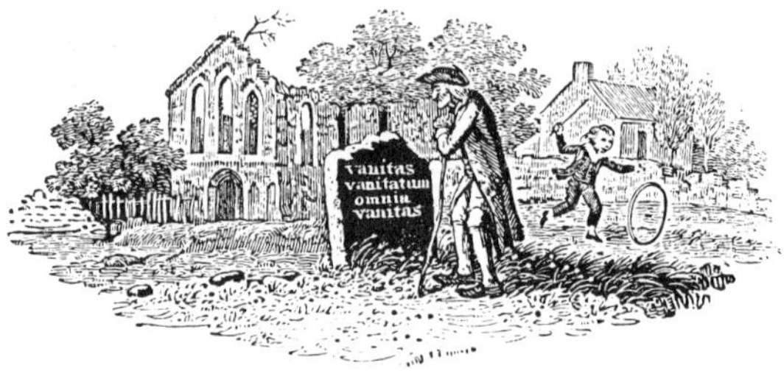

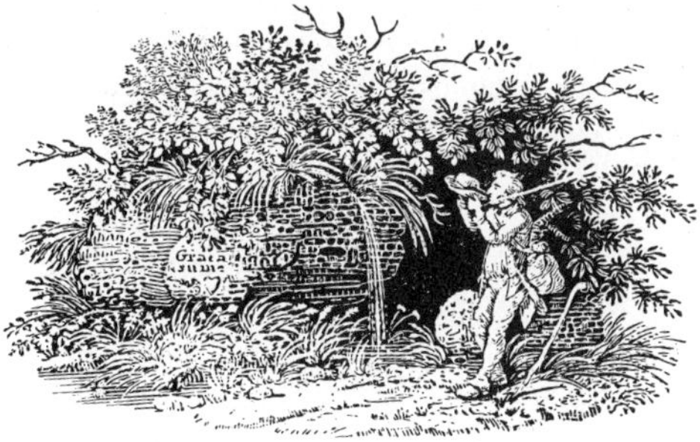

[26]

I have before ventured *my* opinion on the political history of the Israelites & their Wars, and I wish I could not believe in them, but I fear that portion of their history is too true, and also that the example thus set, has been followed since by other nations to wage the horrid wars in which they have embarked, on the most trivial pretences, whenever their rulers found it convenient to give vent to their bad passions wantonly to engage them—There are many other matters related in the Bible, which operate as stumbling blocks to those who otherwise revere it, for the clear truths set forth in its texts—the doubtfull ones consist in one part of these, contradicting, or seemingly contradicting, another part–and in some cases of making assertions which appear to be derogatory to the Majesty of omnipotence.–There may indeed be two causes assigned as reasons for these, the first is by reading many portions of the Scriptures literally, which must have been intended to be understood allegorically–It surely could never be meant to be literally understood, that the Sun & Moon *stood still* by the command of Joshua, 'till he was *avenged of his enemies*, & that the regular order of nature & the universe was to be set aside to please either Joshua or the Israelites in their man-killing pursuits, or, to say that this was the way by which omnipotence willed the destruction of whole nations of people, does not seem to accord with the reverence in which man ought to view his maker–when had it been his will that such Nations should no longer inhabit the Earth, instead of such cruel butcheries being resorted to, the whole of such a people thus devoted might have so shortly been annihilated by a puff of pestilential Wind, if omnipotence had pleased to do so–altho' it does not become us to scan what was or what was not his will, as we only judge of all such matters according to our crude & weak conceptions–The next cause for suspecting the accuracy of several parts of the texts of the sacred Book is in fearing they may not have been correctly translated*–all these seemingly contradictory passages, not to be well understood has been a most fertile source of employment, for self interested & bigotted men to attempt giving their explanations & contradictory comments and annotations upon them, & to twist them into meanings often to bewilder the common-sense of Mankind and to suit certain selfish purposes subservient to their own ends–it I think would have been much better to leave people to judge upon these texts as well as they could themselves rather than trust to such explanations, or to pin their faith upon the slieve of such men. I fear they have done more harm than good. But all these & such like doubts seem trivial & light in the ballance when weighed against the solid sublime truths & valuable instructions contained in the Ancient venerable Book—The mind of man thus prepared by the sacred Texts laid open to him by the Bible–as well as by the help of other good systems of morality, which all lend their help & serve to lead him in the paths of rectitude. In this state he sees himself surrounded by the wonders of creation–and furnished with passions given him for the wisest purposes, to spurr him on to exertions, without which, this beautifull World & its affairs would soon be at a stand-still–& then in this state of things men would soon revert back to unintellectual apathy, or savage barbarity in which Mankind would cease to adore God and seek his providential aid & protection—But when these passions are not fully kept under the reasoning guide–man feels himself to be a strange compound–a heterogenious mixture of pure metal & base alloy,—and placed in the infancy of an endless and therefore an infinitely important & mysterious but conscious existance—"Wonderfully & fearfully made" he views with amazement "this pleasing anxious being"–this spirit confined in mortality, with heavens own pilot placed

* The Revd James Murray (before mentioned) shewed me a chapter of the Book of Job, which he had translated–it was in poetry, as near the original as he was able to make it–I cannot judge of his poetry–but the sense & meaning was clear & easily understood,–but not so with the chapter from which he took it.

within, as its moral guide & with a soul fed like the flame of a lamp, supplied from the material of which he is made, to enlighten his paths to eternity–thus prepared by the hand of omnipotence–his reasoning powers commence their operations–his Mind is then his kingdom and his Will his Law, as to his deeds in this life–but for which he must render an account to the justice of his maker, in another state of existance in another World–other-wise he has lived in this, in vain–If he avails himself of this reasoning power, the choicest gift of God & by which he has revealed himself to man –then will he feel something of a fore-taste of the future happiness he is preparing for himself in another World–but if he will perversly cease to commune with his own soul or reject its admonitions, & turn away from them he thus puts himself under another guide & must then become debased–degraded–& associated with Sin–for he then suffers his bad passions & gross appetites–to overpower his reason–& thus creates for himself an evil spirit or a devil & a hell in his own breast–that consumes or annihilates his good spiritual guide and so disfigures the image of God within him before it returns to whence it came. Thus mutilated to appear before his maker–this must be a hell of itself, of fearfull import–not to be endured–and this it would appear, to be the only devil & the only Hell–and it is a sufficient one as the greatest possible punishment–the debased & polluted soul can undergo–and it may be well for us all to keep in mind that a year of pleasure can be outballanced by a day of pain—to judge simply of all this, it may be concluded that those who from pure motives have shed abroad the greatest *quantum* of happiness to mankind & to all Gods creatures, while they sojourned here, will, according to our notions of justice–besides the pleasure derived from self approbation in this life, he will be rewarded & entitled to such like, but more exalted ones in another state to all eternity—What ever weight these opinions of mine may have upon others I know not–they are given with the best intentions & they concern all men–they are on a Subject, in its own nature of a more sublime & important object of enquiry, than any to which our intellectual powers can be applied,–It is on them that Religion, the life of the soul, is built–Religion is both natural & necessary to Man–those who reject this primary sentiment of veneration for the supreme being–only shew their inferiority to other men–like those born blind they cannot perfectly understand the nature of vision & thence conclude there is no such thing as light in existance—Religion is of a pure & spotless nature, it is uniform, consistant and of the same complexion & character in all nations–languages and customs may greatly differ, but the language of the pure devotion of the heart to its maker is the same over the face of the whole earth–Religion therefore demands our utmost reverence. She is both the comfort & ornament of her true votaries & add[s] dignity to philosophy–The morality taught by the Religion of nature, & as such, that which was laid down by Jesus of Nazareth, unsophisticated by dogmas & creeds, or the misterious wonders of faith, with which interested Bigots have bespattered & disfigured it.—I admire the sublime & yet simple plain doctrines & truely charitable principles which Christ laid down & inforced only by his own example–His life was a continued scene of active benevolence–no fatigue was too hard to be born[e], no inconvenience too great to be submitted to, provided he could instruct the ignorant, reclaim the vicious, relieve the destitute & comfort the mournfull–such was the philanthropy of Jesus Christ who went about doing good. He was a Deist–he could be no other–he spoke only of one God & of him with the utmost reverence–as his heavenly father & the father of *all mankind*–but never of his *coming down* in the Shape of a Holy Ghost to beget his mother with child–that was an after contrivance of the men of those days who modelled & managed all matters connected with this business in their own way to suit their own purposes & a pretty Mess they have made of it–Christianity divested of the trash by which it is obscured, in its purity is the most liberal & best religion in the World ⟨but the numerous teachers of it who are continually worrying Mankind with their denunciations are the greatest enemies of religion⟩ Its benevolent Author preached up the chearfull doctrine–of Man's reviving again after death & of the certainty afterwards of his living to eternity, & did his utmost to persuade all mankind to live godly lives–that their souls might thereby be prepared to return to God the author of it & the giver of all good–as unblemished as possible–and thus so far as his influence reached and his advice was taken & acted upon, he may truely be said to be the Saviour of mankind–but there are questions connected with this subject which none but the Almighty God can solve–It was by the divine will & the providence of God–

that such a person appeared upon the stage of life–gifted with great intellectual & consequently inspired powers he had conquered every bad passion & gross appetite & his immaculate mind, thus made him the instrument befitting the mission he held, to teach mankind, then lost & grovelling in wickedness & corruption, the important lessons of religion & morality, & to reclaim *such of the lost flock* high & low as had grown up and established themselves in iniquity.—But the truths of his doctrines, it was soon shewn, did not accord with the Laws of the Hierarchy & the governors of the people of that day—for it would appear they had long battened at their case & did not like to be disturbed, with any plan of *amendment* or change–and nothing can shew more strongly the jealousy and the smotherd vengeance, with which they were actuated, towards him & his disciples, for preaching up their pure doctrines to the people for tho he published no writings, either on religion or politicks yet that mattered not–for when such men are awakened by their fears or alarmed & are bent upon putting a stop to any thing which appears to militate against their interest or to pull down their pride–the pleas of innocence are, & ever will be, preferred in vain; and as soon as it was determined to stop his preaching & shed his innocent blood his murderers were not long in maturing their plans to do so, for it may be remarked that tyranny deals largely in vengeance & never forgives.—The highly finished superlative cruelty, with which this tragedy through out was conducted–is too shocking to narrate–the feeling mind cannot bear the recital, & shudders with horror at the cruelty attached to it—it shews in the extreme the utter absence of the reasoning power & of justice ever having been appealed to on this occasion. When this wicked business was all over & the actors in the Drama had leisure to look about them & to think upon what was best to be done to keep *the minds* of mankind in subjection under their rule—they knew well the power that pride & selfism had over the governors–and fear over the ignorance of the governed–they then, after concocting their schemes & time after time maturing their plans–they then published them to the world—what followed is very surprizing–passing strange indeed!–for this the innocent victim of their cruelty, was then made an object of worship & adoration coequal with the Almighty God the creator & governor of the universe & the author of all nature—A list of the miracles which

Christ was said to have performed, with an account or description of them, was then made out & handed from one to another [and] was eked out with additions to prove that he was the Son of God, and of the same divine character–and of the same vast importance, which these able & designing men attached to him–What they asserted was not & is not allowed to be doubted & it was & is at the peril of those who did, & who do so–Along with all this they had the audacity to new model divinity itself & to rob (as far as in them lay) the Almighty of his attributes, as if the omnicient-omnipresent God of infinite wisdom, truth Justice & mercy, neaded an assistant, of his own creating–to supplicate & advise with him, in disposing of the Souls of his *frail* creatures, in the regions of eternity–I never could bring my mind to believe in this, nor to form any conception how all this could possibly be, otherwise than conceiving the belief of it, to be derogatory to the majesty of omnipotence—these planners of the creeds, to which mankind were compelled to assent to, or led to believe in & all the vagaries of these their own inventions, went still further, for they then affixed attributes to the God they wished to be worshipped & adored, which they made out to be, or described as jealous revengefull & unmercyful to his erring creatures, and have described him as employing a Devil as a tormentor to keep them burning in a lake of sulphur to all eternity!—in this, their object must have been to rule mankind by fear & terror, instead of adoring their maker with the utmost love & reverence. These creeds were then presently, in their way made out, & with the utmost energy & with every exertion, & they have succeeded, in spreading them over many Nations, & millions of people, which some have assented to & others have believed in, as gospel truths–by *which* some have been made happy, and many others, on their leaving this world, very unhappy.

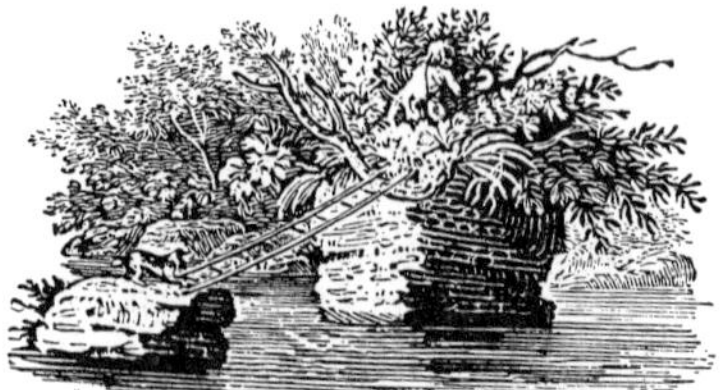

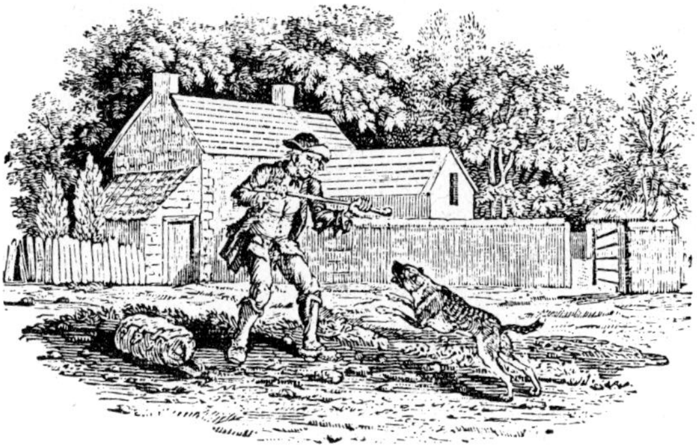

[27]

–I never read "Hume on Miracles"[1]–I did not nead to do so–but I have read an Account of the Miracles performed by "Breslau" & have seen the "Seur Herman Boaz"* perform his, as well as those by Catterfelts, & some others since his time–all these were very surprizing, very amusing and well enough in their way–but I have always thought that the man must be very bad to please with miracles, who could not be thoroughly satisfied with the one–the only true one–the unutterably great one of the Miracle of the universe–made up indeed of millions of other miracles & of its attendant component parts–which will for ever excite the astonishment of reasoning creatures, & draw forth their adoration of the Great Author of the whole–as long as it shall please him to gift them with the power to do so—Had it pleased God to shew any miracle, on the occasion before alluded to by setting aside the natural & regular order of all things, one may suppose it would have been shewn upon this pure minded Man's wicked accusers, & that their tongues, as well as that of [Caiaphas] the high priest would have

* He only assumed that name while he was performing his slight of hand tricks–his real name was James Bowes, a surgeon, belonging to Darlington–he was a most agreably pleasant & worthy gentlemanly-behaved Man–After he had restored his finances, by his performances–he then [*illeg.*] to his almost constant employment of Angling at which sport it was said he [was] the most expert of any man in England–In his fishing [*illeg.*] to do all the good he could in the way of his profession–he died at Edinburgh, greatly advanced in years.

been made to cleave to the roofs of their mouths, & that the judge, "Pontius Pilate" would have been turned to a petrefaction–a stone–& to have remained fixed to his judgement seat to this day. To those, who think for themselves, and can believe in one God only, & reverence, adore & worship him–must ever feel disgusted to dwell on the endless modes of faith with which Mankind have been pestered & stultified for ages past, and also feel grieved to think upon the evils–the persecutions, the Wars & miseries, they have, from time to time, inflicted upon the half civilized world–Brother has been set in enmity against Brother–Neighbour against Neighbour–and nation against Nation, fully charged with vengeance to destroy each other & by which rivers of blood have been spilt. Jesus Christ I believe never said one word, that could be construed into any such meaning or to countenance such doings–neither did any other man possessed of the spirit of the true religion & its attendant humanity ever view all this, otherwise than with horror.—It would be a tedious & an irksome task to give even a list of all the religions, as they are called, from the days of paganism, down to the present time–Truth long struggled with error before System after System have passed away & notwithstanding the exertions of power to keep them up, they exist now only in story–but do the laws of nature ever alter, do the Sun, moon & starrs, shine in any other way, than they did to the votaries of Jupiter–do the human passions operate in any other way than they did thousands of years ago? no indeed—Let us then rejoice that true Religion is independant of human caprice, it is founded upon the immutable principles of truth, reason & common sense & therefore must be durable as nature itself–it is not vague & mutable–it is acquired by experience–not merely the creature of chance, habit & prejudice, it is capable of demonstration like the principles of mathematics & its necessity is evinced by the very nature of man in society—There is a rational and an irrational belief, and how can we distinguish the one from the other without reference to the reason of the thing—If reason be abandoned then sense and nonsense are just the same–Religion becomes a chaos & faith has no merit–I therefore believe that no faith can be acceptable to God, which is not grounded in reason–nothing but truth is permanently pleasing and nothing at the same time brings us lasting & solid advantage. But it would appear, the teachers of mankind, in this important concern to them, have too seldom been actuated by these pure principles, and the "*caring for mens souls*", has been made only, a very secondary consideration with them–their leading objects have been the establishment of a system of revenue & agrandisement, & to ensure the accomplishment of these ends they began with children, well knowing when their creeds & catechisms were once, thus early, instilled into the infant mind, no matter howsoever absurd they might be, they then grew with their growth, and acquired a firm rooted footing in their minds, from which early impressions & prejudices, when once fixed in by ignorance can seldom or ever be removed;–in this state these victims to deception might have been made a pagan in India, a mahomedan in Turkey, a disciple of Confusious in China & been moulded into any of the various Sects of misled christians which have, like wens & carbuncles, often disfigured the comely face of natural religion & the pure & plain doctrines of christianity—After all these preparations, the next most important step as a finish to this business, was to get this their religion (of whatsoever kind it might be) interwoven deeply into all the various Governments, of the different countries, under their influence–But preparatory to this religion's becoming firmly established, the knowing ones, or heads of it, who were called Saints the fathers of the Church, were gathered together to judge & determine upon the creeds & doctrines which were to be obeyed–some of them might indeed, be actuated by good & others of them by impure motives, but it always appeared to me like *their own act of parliament* to oblige Omnipotence to listen only to the kind of worship which they had been pleased to dictate to him & which by many is consider'd as arrogant presumption—But when these [doctrines were] interwoven into all the different Governments, it then became a "part & parcel" of the law of the land—And thus fenced, barricaded and fortified, few ever dared to say that any thing these laws promulgated, was wrong—and if any man, whose mind happened to rise superior to superstitions, ventured to publish his opinions of these laws, to shew that they were absurd–then racks, tortures, Inquisitions & death, or fines & imprisonments with attendant ruin stared him in the face, in this world–and threatnings of eternal misery in the next. It is thus that the free exercise of the understanding & the full use of all the means of advancing in virtue, knowledge & religion is checked & debarred,–for unless the free use of writing & publishing the well digested opinions & plans, of the lovers of mankind, are allowed to go on without risk, all public improvement, which is, or ought to be the chief end of all governments to promote, is, for want of this liberty, taken away—but in this business, even Government itself, being entangled & bound by oaths to support present establishments, may perhaps be affraid to meddle or countenance any writing tending to a reform or that may have the appearance of militating against this order of things—The Clergy are also bound in a similar way, by old laws & oaths, which have been imposed upon them to swear to their belief in a certain string of creeds before they are allowed to enter upon the clerical office, and all this backed & encouraged by the lures of enormous stipends or livings attached to their Church–which is furthermore made sure of, by these livings, being as it were held out as a provision to the unprovided part of the younger branches of the families of all the poor gentry of the land. Thus situated, any alteration or improvement may be looked for in vain while self interest and pride continue so powerfully to guide & govern the actions of mankind.—Time indeed may bring about wonders—and the example & the influence of North America *now* the greatest Nation the world ever knew–can perhaps only be looked up to, to lead the way, as the great regenerator of the old World–There they have none of the old prejudices of Europe, Asia & South America to contend with nor the old protecting laws; and must see the follies these have fallen into.–No, America has no foolish or impure old establishments to break up & may move forward upon clear ground–"the Rites & ceremonies of all Nations" will serve them like a kind of text to point their fingers at, & be also like a beacon & a guide post to shew them the way they ought to pursue to steer clear of the absurdities, to say no worse of them, by which mankind have been so long led hoodwinked into so many solemn egregious follies—

—But to dwell on this, the gloomy side of the picture, without noticing the other side, may be unfair, for the inventors or framers of unaccountable Creeds set mankind a-thinking generally upon these & many other matters, which, perhaps, they would not otherwise have done, & besides this–it is, on all hands allowed that the Monks & Friars of old, amidst all their superstitions, preserved, in their Monastries, many records, & much valuable knowledge which, without their care would have been lost to the world—add to these their charities to the destitute & their constant best endeavours–to teach the grosly ignorant & to reclaim the equally grosly wicked part of the community–and in examining impartially into the change effected by the boasted reformation it amounts only to lessening or setting aside a small portion of the bigottry & superstition by which they enforced their old doctrines—In believing in these, the simple well meaning honest people knew no better–they were worshiping God, in a way to the best of their judgment & surely they ought not to be blamed–the fault in this case rested with their teachers—Although one may lament, that a more rational view of religion & its very important concerns had not been fully contemplated upon, yet even under its guidance, with all its defects–before the mighty change of the reformation took place it would appear the moral conduct of the common people was generally good, & they were happier & better off, than they have ever been since—For the Lands & other property belonging to the religious institutions, by which so many were supported, was suddenly cut off–they were robbed of their all as it appears to me by the greatest monster in human shape, that ever breathed & polluted the air of England—Their lands &c were sold for himself or divided amongst his Satellites & sycophants, who in a great degree partook of the character & quallity of the robber, their Master–and the Lands are now quietly enjoyed by their proud offspring, or their Heirs to this day.—The Romish Clergy, or priests, in these times, tho' they took the Tythes, (according to an old Jewish custom) yet these were then more usefully & justly divided than they are in the present time, for they, in their day, took only a third part of these to themselves & the other two thirds were expended, in building & repairing their churches & supporting all the poor—there was then no Church Cesses, nor poor laws nor the sickening, harrassing & continuall gathering of the enormous sums of the poor rate—It must furthermore be conceded on behalf of the present religious establishment of this enlightened & comparatively happy Land notwithstanding the spots & blemishes which barr the approach to rationallity & perfection,–the regular Clergy, with few exceptions, and taken as a whole–are from their learning–their acquirements and their piety are real & valuable ornaments to our country,–without whose help & the example they set, it is to be feared, the people would soon retrogarde into barbarism, or into what is nearly as bad, into fanatiscism. To keep down, or prevent this latter growing evil, from rising to a height, will require the utmost exertions of the regular Clergy, as well as the united wisdom & prudence of the legislature to discountenance it–redicule seems to me to be the best way, to check this & all follies–force would only serve to unite its votaries & increase their numbers,–for as long as ignorance is stalking abroad, multitudes will be found, in every country, who see all things with an obliquity of intellect and are thus ready prepared to adopt any thing new, however stupid–and the reveries of Johanna Southcote[1] and the ravings of Ranters, do not appear to them sufficiently absurd.

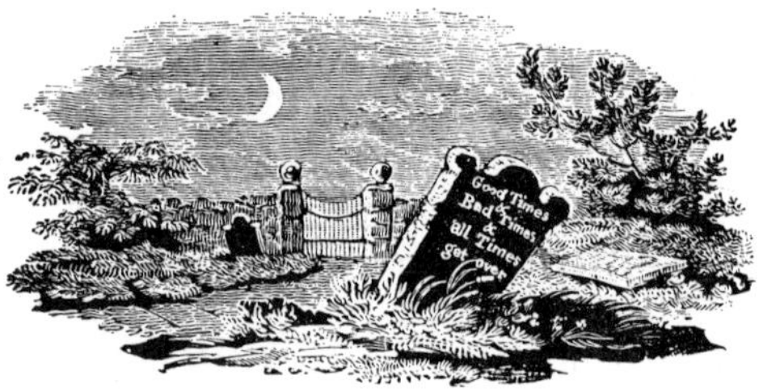

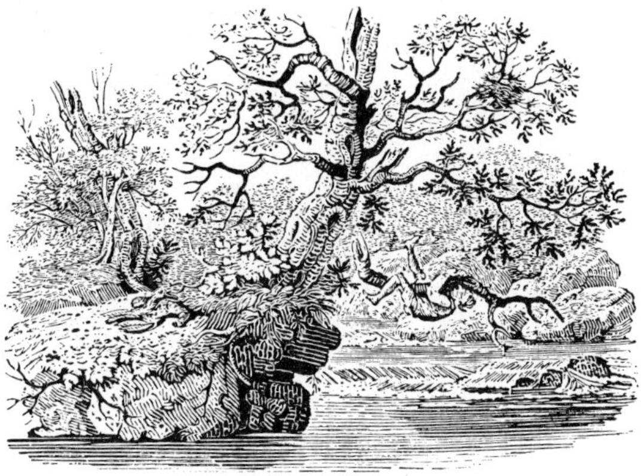

[28]

I have, with all the consideration I have been able cooly to bestow upon it–become clearly of opinion, that the highest character a Man can hope to attain to, in this life, is that of his becoming a religious Philosopher & he cannot be the latter, without the former being deeply impressed upon his mind & without these conjointly, he nead not hope to feel all the happiness in this World, attendant upon his thus approaching towards perfection—The happiness derived from ignorance is like that of unreasoning animals, & in carrying this a little further or, to the extreme, it is, comparitively, like the happiness enjoyed by a Gate post.

It is from amongst Men of this enlightened character only that all & every clergyman ought to be selected, without permitting in the most distant way the least interference of *private patronage*, for that has been, & will continue to be, if not stopped! an evil of the most benumbing magnitude which will upset the best laid plans & render such nugatory or null & void. Could such a stride towards purity as this ever be accomplished–then every Village ought to have its Church & would then become a moral religious & patriotic little community–in which its preceptors ought to teach youth the usual routine of their education five days in the Week, & those of all ages, on the Sunday. This Clergy ought not to be sworn to any belief, nor tramelled with any creeds–but only to promise, with the help of God, to instill into the minds of their hearers the best maxims of morality & the purest religious adoration of the omnipotent–In this the Scriptures would supply them with its pure & sublime precepts, & above all the still more sublime & amazing works contained in the great Book of the Creation, so amply spread out before them, & made up of the living the visible Words of God–so plainly to be seen–read & felt–that however miraculous & astonishing they are, it would require no stretch of faith to believe in them all–from these, such a Clergy, one after another, in succession for ages, might take their texts, ever new, & preach from them to all eternity, for as to the numbers of subjects to preach from & explain–they would be found to be endless even on this Globe only we dwell upon–(without soaring to those in the regions of immensity) & if its wonders were productive of disease–enlightened Men would die of wondering—Were a Clergy, of this description established there could be no fears entertained of their teaching any nonsense nor any thing bad–they would, on the contrary, from their knowledge & virtue be the pillars of the state & the main stays & ornaments of civilization. Every Church ought to have its Library of good Books & its philosophical apparatus, to illustrate, or explain the various Phenomena of Nature & the amazing magnitude & distances, of "the heavenly bodies" or rather the incalculable number of Suns & Worlds, floating about, with the velocity of light in immeasurable endless space–it is from these that something like the truest conception of the adorable Author of the whole, can be formed, & it would soon be found that men of common capacities & without even haveing been learned either to read or write, would be at no loss to understand the clear lectures delivered on this latter subject, and I think it would be folly, or worse than folly to entertain any suspicions that poor men, thus enlightened would forget the station in which they are placed & cease to work honestly to maintain themselves, or to become bad members of Society—on the contrary it is reasonable to conclude they would by such a universal spread of knowledge which would follow this system of education & this kind of religious worship as would stamp the character of a whole people, as intellegent good subjects, and it appears to me certain that untill such a mode of enlightened religion is adopted & acted upon, mankind will continue to be torn assunder, as they have too long been–and that, if it could quickly be spread over, the partly civilised world, there would then never more be any religious bickerings, or animosities on that score, and that then, but not 'till then, all mankind would become with each other in a short time as bretheren–those who from early prejudices dissented from this worship & order of things ought to be allowed to take their own way, & maintain their priests themselves–untill they coud see into their own follies, & I think they would not be very long in doing so—Such a change as this, which with diffidence I humbly offer, to those whose business, it ought to be to take it into their serious consideration & coolly & impartially examine & weigh it in all its bearings–& make use, as far as they please, of these hints & these opinions of a humble individual who wishes them well—I am well aware, that the pride & the fears, of what are called the dignified Clergy, might operate powerfully against the purity & simplicity of such a change–if so, they will then, thus clearly & decisively shew, that it is, a System of revenue only, & not religion that they can be fearfull of upsetting–but if none of these are deprived of their present livings (or an equivalent to their value) which they hold only during their lives, what have they to be affraid of?—To sell their present enormous revenues & fund the amount–& then divide the interest equally among the newly established clergy would be only fair & just, and they above all other men ought [to] be made perfectly independant, amply provided for (without being obliged to collect any other revenue) and made as happy as men can be in this World–And whatever salary might be deemed sufficient, a certain Sum taken from this income, ought also to be funded as a provision to support them in their declining years. Such a body of men as this clergy could not fail of being revered & held in the greatest respect & estimation by all good & wise men and what more any good man can wish for in this World, one may be at a loss to know—It is from Government with the aid of our own enlightened & liberal minded Clergy & other such like men that this important business in my opinion ought to be openly & boldly taken up–they ought to have the honour to shew the way, & not leave any other nation to take the lead of them in such a mighty & momentous concern–in which the happiness of the whole human race would become most deeply interested & from the change in Mens minds which is now taking place & widely spreading–this change by its own weight will most certainly happen & perhaps at no very distant day—Were our own Government inclined to make this improvement in religion & politics they would assuredly soon see the happiest results from it–it would soon be found, that there would then be no nead to keep Ireland in subjection like a conquered country by an expensive military force—The Irish, naturally acute, lively, generous & brave, would soon feel themselves (under our excellent constitution) become as happy & loyal a people as any in the World, and as much attached to their country, which for its healthy climate & fertility of soil may match with any other on this Globe–and one would hope that the native gentry would at length see into the very reprehensible injustice of becoming absentees—Landowners, in all countries, as well as in Ireland, ought, as far as possible to spend their Rents where they receive them–where they do not do so, any country is certain to become poor.–Ireland ought instantly to be put on a par, in every respect, with their fellow subjects of the British Isles.* To withold Catholic emancepation from them, appears to me to be invidious & unjust, and it would, at no very distant period, (if emancipated) be found that they would (under the foregoing tuition) individually become enlightened, think for themselves, adopt a rational religious belief, and throw off the bigotry & superstition, taught them with such sedulous care, from their infancy, & by which fooleries they had so long been led blind fold–If they could be brought to think & to muster up as much of the reasoning powers as to do all this, they would soon thus emancipate themselves—But even on this business, it ought to be observed & acknowledged, that the protestant Establishment does not interfere with the Catholic modes of faith–they may preach up & believe in what they please–in this they are not only fully tolerated, but also are protected in their worship, so that on this score they can have nothing to complain of—But bejond this, the protestant assendity, having got all the rich Church Livings secured to themselves, are fearfull that the Catholics, ever

* In my ardent wish for the perfect happiness & union of the sister Isles, I have suffered my sanguine imagination to wish & hope that some great convulsion of nature might some day happen to throw up the bed of the sea between them–or to encroach upon the Bay of Biscay & Atlantic, so as to unite them both in one & to present a south western Rocky front to the Ocean–I see no harm in indulging in such reveries–they may indeed be visionary but they are innocent ones.

watchfull & never ceasing in their struggles to be at the head of all church affairs, the protestants have become extremely jealous of them, lest this emancipation, they now seem so eagerly to wish for, may if granted only be a prelude to future further strides & that their latent object, in view, is to partake in these rich livings or to get them wholly to themselves—To dwell longer on these matters, seems to me useless, for so long as rich livings are set apart as a provision to those, whose creeds continue in fashion, all the various numerous Sects who dissent, will always be barking at them, untill the purity and simplicity of worshiping One God only, can be established, and which to a certainty will some day happen–'till then all arguments, on this subject may seem to be in vain—Having given my opinion on religious matters, freely & sincerely, and with the best intentions–in which I do not wish to dictate, but only wish mankind to think for themselves on such a momentous & important an affair as that of their present & their future eternal happiness–I thus leave them to their own reflections, and shall only furthermore attempt to shew some of the salutary effects which I suppose would follow from mine—I first picture to myself that I see such a body of learned, rationally religious, moral & patriotic men as this clergy spread over our already matchless country, & that the effect of their tuition & example, founded on honour & virtue would very soon be seen & felt among all ranks of society, as would further exalt the character of our Countrymen all over the Globe & make them be held up as patterns of imitation to the rest of mankind—and it is only by an education like this, that any country can hope that its institutions can remain unbroken up, and endure as a nation for ever, but so it will be, if the Government is founded in Wisdom & virtue, & backed by a whole people of the same character. To rear up & establish such a renovated order of things, as I have taken the liberty to recommend, & cooly & deliberately do away [with] old errors, will not perhaps, soon or easily be done–for there are so many interests to consult, & so many men of the character who doubt & dispair of accomplishing any thing however good, that if they have influence over weak minds to back them out in this disposition to despondency it will have the direct tendancy to realize such doubts & to throw a cold damp over the best & wisest plans–but we ought never to dispond of accomplishing any thing, where our objects in view are good ones–To minds thus gifted & such as this Clergy it is hoped would possess, there could be little nead to dictate, their own good sense would enable them aided by the Gentry of the land constantly to see when any thing was going wrong in this little community & to be speedily rectified. Such a number of little Colleges spread over the land would excellently prepare such youths as might be intended to finish their education in Colleges of a higher character so as to fit them to fulfill the various offices of the State, in any [of] its several departments, as well as the many other employments they might be destined to pursue; and in this, the Teachers would have it greatly in their power to discover the talents or innate powers of mind of their pupils as well as the bent of their inclinations, so as to be inabled to advise or direct, their inexperienced youth as to what might best suit their several capacities & to point out to them the proper course of education that led to the calling or occupation in which they might make the most respectable figure when they were launched into the World. This duty of every teacher, is an important business & would require the keenest observation to make the true discovery–for after all, we may be assured of this, that it is impossible to set bounds to the improvement of the human mind, and it is almost equally so to limit the capabilities of the human frame, when duly cultivated.

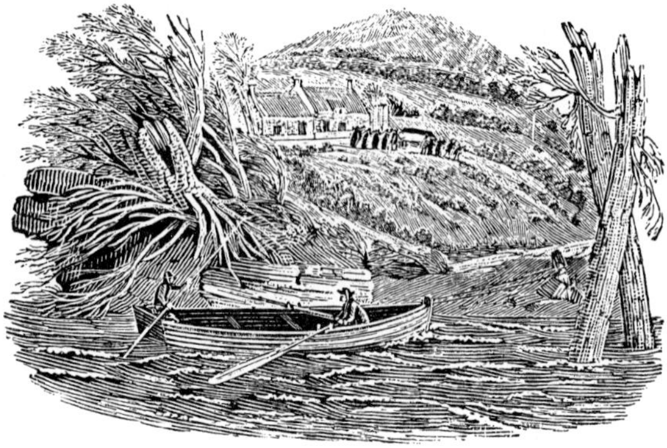

FINAL

In offering these my sentiments & opinions, derived from the observations I have made on my passage thro' life, I have never intended to give offence to good men.–with these sentiments some may be pleased & others displeased—but conscious of the rectitude of my intentions I do not covet the praise of the one, nor fear the censures of the other—it is to another tribunal that I, as well as all other men are to account for their conduct.

EXPLANATORY NOTES

Page 2. *I was born:* Bewick is said to have believed that he was born on the 10th or 11th of August, but the 12th was the date that was always celebrated. He was baptized on the 19th of the same month.

Page 3. *Rowns:* to roun, to speak much and often about the same thing; to whisper.

Page 6. (1) *across it to school:* There were ferries at Eltringham and Prudhoe, but no bridge until one was built between Prudhoe and Ovingham in 1886.

(2) *Foumart:* polecat.

Page 7. (1) *Brea:* hill.

(2) *Whins:* common furze bushes.

(3) *shive:* slice.

(4) *beild:* shelter or refuge.

Page 8. (1) *muck the Byer:* to clean out the cowshed or stable.

(2) *Earl of Derwent-Water:* 'Derwentwater's Farewell' remains a well-loved melody for the Northumbrian pipes.

(3) *Dilston Hall:* Dilston is some 7 miles up river from Cherryburn, near Corbridge.

Page 9. (1) *Dyking Mitten:* glove for wall building.

(2) *cree:* soften.

(3) *Mall:* hammer.

Page 10. (1) *little window at my bed head:* this can be seen at the gable end of Cherryburn in the engraving by John Bewick of 1781 on p. 23.

(2) *lown:* sheltered side.

(3) *Set Gads:* stakes for fixing a fishing set or fixed net; or standing fishing rods. See Bewick's tail-piece on p. 181.

Page 11. *sykes:* ditches.

Page 13. *Boat Stower:* boat hook or punt pole.

Page 16. (1) *Silkey:* (Northumberland) supernatural being popularly called silkey from the nature of her robes. See James Hardy, 'Silky: A Northumbrian Tradition', *Alnwick Mercury,* 1 March 1862.

(2) *Hedley Kow:* the name of a 'bogle' or sprite connected with the Northumberland village of Hedley.

Page 17. *Sods:* rough saddle made of coarse cloth or skin, stuffed with straw.

Page 18. (1) *Jackleg Knife:* pocket knife, large clasp knife with single, broad, square-edged blade. Possibly derived from the name of the cutler inventor, Jacques de Liège.
(2) *Kirn Supper:* harvest home, supper held on completion of harvest.
(3) *guiseing:* masquerade, dressed for a mumming.
(4) *Messet Dog:* pet or lap dog.

Page 23. (1) *Gills:* ravines, narrow valleys or wooded glens with streams.
(2) *Kylo:* small breed of Highland cattle.

Page 24. (1) *Garth:* small piece of enclosed ground near the home, paddock.
(2) *Lonnings:* lanes or by-roads.

Page 25. *Click-hook:* large salmon hooks bound together shaft to shaft. Poachers used them to strike fish in the belly. Click: to snatch, seize, steal (Northumberland).

Page 26. (1) *flipes:* hat brim.
(2) *revolution:* of 1688.
(3) *flaid:* frightened.

Page 27. *smout hole:* smout, the fry of salmon.

Page 28. (1) *Sinker:* digger of mine shafts.
(2) *lave:* to bale or draw water.

Page 29. *Glasshouse at Bill Quay:* Newcastle glass bottle manufactory, established 1694 (Brand).

Page 30. *Gin driver:* the colliery gin was a rope-winding device to which horses were harnessed, situated at the head of pit shafts for raising the coal.

Page 31. (1) *Ovington:* a village about two miles west of Ovingham.
(2) *Prudhoe:* a village on the high south bank of the Tyne opposite Ovingham. The castle at Prudhoe was formerly a stronghold of the Percy family.

Page 32. (1) *Glead:* the common kite.
(2) *Gorfoot:* the carrion crow.

Page 33. (1) *the late Duke of Northumberland:* although the second Duke had died in 1817, before Bewick began writing, the reference is to Hugh, the first Duke, 1712–86.
(2) "*Admirable Crichtons*": a reference to the accomplishments of James Crichton (1560–?1585), Scottish scholar and poet, whose title of Admirable originated in Sir Thomas Urquart's account of his career, 1652.

Page 36. (1) *haugh:* level ground by riverside.

(2) *the great flood of the 17 November 1771:* Ovingham boat house was entirely destroyed, only two of the ten occupants surviving. At Bywell a horse belonging to TB's father-in-law was saved only by getting onto the altar table in the Black Church (Sykes, *Local Records*, 1833, i. 283–9).

Page 39. (1) *enamel painting:* see James Rush, *The Ingenious Beilbys*, 1973, for fine colour plates of Beilby painted glass.

(2) *Copeland's Ornaments:* Copeland's *New Book of Ornaments*, 1746, or the same by Lock and Copeland, 1752. Both editions were in the Bewick family sale of 1884. Copeland and Lock produced most of the designs for Chippendale's *Cabinet Maker's Directory*, 1754.

(3) *William Beilby:* he appears as the only drawing master in the first issue of Whitehead's *Newcastle Directory*, 1778.

Page 40. (1) *Ladies Diaries:* the earliest copy in the British Museum is dated 1706. Hutton edited them between 1773 and 1818. Hutton's *Mensuration* began publication in parts in 1768 and it is this work rather than the *Ladies Diaries* which must have occupied Bewick when first apprenticed. Certainly on Hutton's own evidence it was: see *Newcastle Magazine* June 1822, and Note on Bewick's Engraving, p. 257.

(2) *no employment in this way in Newcastle:* Beilby etched and engraved two copper plates for Hutton's *Mensuration* in 1768–70, but these were heraldic and architectural and it may not have been until 1786 and the publication of Consett's *Tour through Sweden* . . . that the partnership was at all involved in landscape work.

(3) *copper plates:* these were bought from the coppersmiths in large sheets by the pound. Extra-beaten copper would be specified if the plates were likely to be much used: more time spent in beating the metal had the effect of hardening it. Polishing involved the laborious use of charcoal and was presumably done by Beilby to save expense.

Page 41. (1) *nicer work given me to execute:* in 1772, during the fifth year of his apprenticeship, Bewick wrote his master a memorandum saying that he was a stranger to copper plates, seal cutting, '. . . and not half master of engraving' and continued that there would be no likelihood of his being so 'if you continue to do the finer parts and I the coarse.' (V & A MSS).

(2) *barr bill:* for the George Inn, Penrith (Hugo).

(3) *Thomas Saint:* the work for Saint did not develop until the end of Bewick's apprenticeship. In 1771, his fourth year, the workshop produced 151 wood blocks, four of which were for Saint. Dr Hutton had 49 and the bookseller William Charnley (for whom Saint was printer) 69 (Weekly Engraving Book No. 3, V & A MSS).

(4) "*the Storey Teller*": *Youth's Instructive and Entertaining Story-Teller*, Saint, Newcastle, 1774.

(5) "*Gays Fables*": *Fables by the late Mr Gay*, Saint, Newcastle, 1779.

(6) "*the Select Fables*": *Select Fables*, Saint, Newcastle, 1772 appeared as part of *Moral Instructions of a Father to his Son*. The *Select Fables* were published alone in an edition of 1776 and later elaborated in the edition of 1784.

Page 42. *the news first arrived:* 12 February 1776. Gregson's son Christopher who was training as an apothecary in London, collected the bounty awarded (Hack MSS). Twenty guineas were divided as follows: William Coleman, seven; Bewick, seven; Thomas Hodgson, six. Hodgson's award was for his work on Sir John Hawkins's *History of Music* (R.S.A. Minute Books).

Page 43. (1) *Aunt Blackett:* his father's sister Sarah who married Thomas Blackett, Silversmith in Newcastle.

(2) *Chare:* narrow lane or alley.

Page 44 (1) *at a cheap rate:* such titles as *The Countryman's Treasure, Multum in Parvo*, and *The Compleat Fabulist*, which he sold at the market on Saturdays (Dobson).

(2) *Ballast Hills:* Ballast Hill burial ground about half a mile east of the old town wall.

(3) *others called him 90:* an MS extract from the *Newcastle Advertiser* inserted in the *Memoir* MS but not in TB's hand gives Gray's age as 84.

Page 45. *Hoppings:* country wakes, annual festivals in Northumberland.

Page 47n. *went to London & did the same:* John Bewick wrote to his brother 9 April 1788: 'Your old Friend Mr Wm Gr[ay] from Notm has been in London some time . . . he is the most industerous & active man I've seen since I came to Lon^{n} he is as sharp as a whitechapple Needle & runs about the streets as if a Pack of Hounds were after him . . . he has done all that laid in his poor to serve me while he has been in Town . . .' (Hack MSS).

Page 49. *Lewis Cornaro:* Luigi Cornaro, *Sure and Certain Methods of attaining a Long and Heathful Life*, 1724 (Fourth Edition). A copy of this edition was in the Bewick family sale of 1884.

Page 50. (1) *went to Elswick:* now a district of Newcastle but in Bewick's time outside the town wall, about a mile west of the workshop in St Nicholas Church Yard.

(2) *for bread and milk:* with Bewick went his friend William Bulmer whose letter to TB of 20 August 1825 refers to their 'former anxious and early visits to Goody Coxon's to partake of her sour milk and hot brown cakes at a place generally known (in our day) by the polite designation of the "Hog's Tavern" at Elswick' (Dobson: original not traced).

Page 53 (1) *a Sir Walter Blackett:* a political turncoat.

(2) *many curious books:* e.g. *The Teacher of Common Sense*, 1779;

The Rights of Swine, 1796; *The Meridian Sun of Liberty*, 1776; *Pennyworth of Pigmeat*, 1793. Several of these were in the Bewick family sale of 1884.

(3) *sincere and honest:* On 9 April 1788, John Bewick wrote to his brother from London: '. . . your old Friend M[r] Spence has been in Town some time, not in the most affluent circumstances you may be shure, he has frequently called upon me. I generally fild his Belly & gave him something to drink when so, is as hearty as a Cracket & as full of his Coally Tyne Poetry as ever, he refers people to me for his Caracture Poor fellow & I say as much in his favour as I possible can. I spoke to M[r] Cook, Publisher Pater Noster-roe–he has been a friend to him & Employ's him at present in doing little od jobs . . .' (Hack MSS).

Page 54. (1) *gallow pots:* small earthenware pots, possibly with handles for hanging.

(2) *Charles Hutton:* see note to p. 42 (2) and Note on Bewick's Engraving, p. 259.

Page 58. *she long after this:* in 1778, only four years later. The manuscript line ends with 'she' and the construction suggests that Bewick intended to write 'she *not* long after . . .' but inadvertently dropped the negative. Mary Beilby died in 1797.

Page 59. *Northumberland pipes:* see note to p. 97/1.

Page 62. *M[r] Robertson, Silversmith:* John Robertson, a Scot, and partner to John Langlands, silversmith in Newcastle. See note to p. 92 (1).

Page 63. (1) *the print fields:* where the printed cloth was laid out to dry. 'In Scotland . . . the print fields were centred almost exclusively round four streams, the Cart, the Glazert, the Leven, the Blane, and also the Clyde.' Turnbull, *A History of Calico Printing in Great Britain*, 1951, p. 110.

(2) *long latin inscription:* written by Professor George Stewart and Ramsay of Ochtertyre with finishing touches by Dr Samuel Johnson. The text is given in Chambers's *Smollett*, 1867, p. 199.

(3) *having done so:* i.e. having acted so.

(4) *leish:* well-made, lithe.

Page 65. *hoppings:* country wakes, annual festivals in Northumberland.

Page 67. *Carron Works:* the Carron Company established in 1760, the first modern iron works in Scotland.

Page 68. *my way through Scotland:* Bewick's journey on foot could not have been less than 500 miles. His own estimate of the Scottish section of the walk was 300 miles. See p. 72.

Page 70n. *Thomas Hodgson:* one of the three awarded a bounty for wood engraving by the Society for the Promotion of the Arts in 1776. See note to p. 42 (1). For John Bewick's reference to him see note to p. 80 (1).

Page 71. *working for myself:* G. C. Atkinson's *Sketch of the Life and Work of Thomas Bewick*, 1831, refers to TB's working with an engraver by the name of Cole. Although Chatto and Jackson in their *Treatise on Wood Engraving*, 1839, could find no trace of a wood-engraver of this name, there was a contemporary copper-engraver B. Cole who engraved most of the large plates for Maitland's *London* (Dobson). It may be that Atkinson confused Cole with Coleman, the engraver who shared the 1776 premium awarded by the Society for the Promotion of Arts.

Page 75. (1) *the Hole in the Wall,* &c: a tavern in St Dunstan's Court, Fleet Street; demolished in 1860. Much frequented by Newcastle men who there regularly celebrated Carlin Sunday, the fifth Sunday in Lent. Carlings or grey peas were prepared for this feast which celebrated the relief of a famine in Newcastle during the Middle Ages when a ship carrying a load of peas entered the port (Brand, Mackenzie).

(2) *determined to return home:* TB's friend and fellow apprentice, David Martin, wrote to him 29 January 1777: '. . . not much surprised when I consider your natural love of Sincerity & Simple Honesty that you despise the luxury Pomp and splendour of the Town. I can't say but I have been much deceived with regard to the encouragement they give to wood cutting in London for I tho't as there was not any body there in that way who could do anything worth looking at & yours being so much superior thereto that you would get any price you asked . . .' (Hack MSS).

(3) *Duke of Richmond's gallery:* Charles Lennox, 3rd Duke of Richmond, 1735–1806, in 1758 opened a gallery in the garden of his house in Whitehall as a free school of painting and sculpture. Cipriani and Joseph Wilton the sculptor were the instructors.

Page 76. (1) *to live in London:* See Introduction, p. xii.

(2) *Annalitical Magazine at the time:* the Memoir of Taylor actually appears in the *Literary Panorama*, iii. (January 1808).

(3) *which he never answered:* TB's letter was dated 18 April 1806 and accompanied a gift of the two volumes of his *British Birds*.

(4) *Cunningham's Poems:* first published 1766.

Page 77. *the "Theban Harp":* the engraving for this appeared in the *Pismire Journal*, Newcastle, 1777.

Page 78. *one of the most impudent–malignant & worst apprentices we ever had:* possibly Charles Hickson, apprenticed 18 April 1795, who absconded in February 1800 (Hack MSS).

Page 79. (1) *a coward & a scoundrel:* costs of £9. 10s. 7d. and damages of £11. 5s. 6d. were awarded against Beilby and Bewick, 29 April 1795. A clear reference to the affair of Robert Johnson of whose skill and talent Bewick writes most generously on p. 196. (See note 1 to p. 199). Bewick was also brought up to court for redress of grievances by another apprentice William Seth. A letter from TB to the Mayor and Aldermen of Newcastle, 28 June 1780, describes Seth's misdemeanours (Laing MSS).

(2) *taken an Apprentice:* probably John Laws, who trained as a silver engraver (see p. 195). An album of impressions from his work is in the Laing Gallery, Newcastle.

Page 80. (1) *at a very low rate for them:* TB wrote to his brother John on 9 January 1788: 'I am much pleased with the cuts for 'Death's Dance' [*Emblems of Mortality*] . . . I am surprised that you would do them for 6s each. You have been spending your time and grinding out your eyes to little purpose indeed. I would not have done them for a farthing less than double that sum'. (Pease Collection). To which John replied on 19 February: 'The price I had for the Cuts was too litt[le] to be shure, but at that time I could not do better & Mr [Hodg]son tho Pregnant with Religion, & pretended goodness, yet is ready to snatch at all advantages, . . .–your prices in N Castle, do not seem to agree with the people in Lond[n] at all, these last cuts you did for Mr Hodgson, he tells me he was out of pocket by them & has never done any work for the People since, their are so many wood-cutters in London, & the Publishers are mighty fond of having things done cheap' (Hack MSS).

(2) "*Fabliaux or Tales*" *by Le Grand: Fabliaux or Tales, abridged from French Manuscripts of the XIIth and XIIIth Centuries by M. Le Grand selected and translated into English Verse* by Gregory Lewis Way, 2 vols, 1796 and 1800. John Bewick completed at least six of the required fifty blocks before he died. His brother worked a similar number and finished others. The remainder were given to TB's former apprentice Charlton Nesbit. Correspondence between Way, the translator-publisher, and Bulmer his printer, proofs, sketches and original blocks are now in the possession of Mr David Chambers and the editor.

(3) *blocks for the chase: The Chase. A Poem. by William Somerville* printed and published by William Bulmer at his Shakspeare Printing Office in 1796. Second edition 1804. The original blocks are now in the Pease Collection, Newcastle. See Introduction, p. xix.

(4) *after his decease:* he died of tuberculosis. In March 1793 he had written to his brother: 'I have for these few days past spit a good deal of Blood . . .' (Pease Collection).

Page 86. *Cot at the Forth:* the house was in Circus Lane at the Forth, a district just to the south-west of the old town wall.

Page 87. (1) *fother:* cartload.

(2) *Galloway:* a pony, small saddle horse of a strong breed formerly peculiar to Galloway in south-west Scotland.

(3) *pinfold:* enclosure for strayed cattle.

Page 88. (1) *Gin:* see note to p. 30 (1).

(2) "*seddle boards*"*:* the boards or frame work at the top of a coal pit.

(3) *dreg:* bar of iron put between spokes of a wheel to act as a brake.

Page 91. *retail:* should read wholesale.

Page 92. (1) *Langlands & his partner John Robertson:* there are many references to the firm and a complete ledger reserved for the account is among the Bewick papers in the care of the Laing Gallery. A fine example of Bewick's work for them is now in the Victoria & Albert Museum: a silver salver carrying a fine etched vignette of a hunting scene dated 1808.

(2) *disposition as his partner:* Jane Bewick in her notes on her father's acquaintances had this to say of the two silversmiths: 'Langlands was a Gentleman but his partner Robertson (of the family of Strowan), was a cunning Scot–under the appearance of great friendship he took every advantage–he was for some time a partner with Beilby, & planned every thing relating thereto–He I believe once incited Ralph to begin the Button trade in the Engraving premises–but my Father *kicked*–Beilby never persisted in such cases–always knowing how to back out with perfect tact–Robertsons nephew & heir–took my father in for £1000–as bad a fellow as ever lived, & as plausible–a fiend in human guise' (Laing MSS).

Page 97. *my efforts were not lost:* The Northumbrian small-pipes, a bellows-blown bagpipe. A delightful sweet-sounding chamber instrument, probably derived from the French musette, it lost much of its popularity during the later 19th century with the advent of the concertina. But it has never been without its small group of gifted players. A feature unique in bagpipes is the closed end of its chanter which makes possible a brilliant articulation in fast passages. The present time sees a remarkable revival in the number of performers and there are now at least three active makers of the instrument in Northumberland. Peacock wrote the earliest manual of instruction and was responsible, about 1800, for adding keys to extend the range of the chanter. Bewick was particularly fond of its music and paid Peacock to teach his son Robert, whose skill as a player was remarked upon by J. F. M. Dovaston and by Audubon (see p. xxii).

Page 100. *Bible in Numbers:* i.e. for sale in periodical parts.

Page 101. *one of my Tramps:* the manuscript diary of this journey is now in the Pease Collection.

Page 103. (1) "*History of Durham*"*:* Hutchinson's *History and Antiquities of the County Palatine of Durham*, 1785.

(2) *Goldsmiths deserted Village: The Poetical Works of Oliver Goldsmith*, Hereford, 1794.

Page 104. (1) *what I did for him:* Nicholson's *Literary Miscellany*, several volumes in various years, *c*. 1799.

(2) *Parnels Hermit: Poems by Goldsmith and Parnell* printed and

published by William Bulmer at his Shakspeare Printing Office, 1795.

(3) *tour of Lapland:* Liddell and Consett, *A Tour through Sweden, Swedish-Lapland, Finland and Denmark*, 1789.

Page 105. "*Three hundred Animals*": *A Description of Three Hundred Animals viz., Beasts, Birds, Fishes, Serpents, and Insects* appeared in many editions in the second half of the 18th century. A. D. McQuin's edition of 1812 contains direct copies of TB's cuts by Samuel Williams.

Page 107. (1) *after the days work of the shop was over:* TB wrote to Isaac Taylor, 18 April 1806: '. . . the greater part of the cuts was done by candlelight, when left in my workshop alone, and chiefly on account of my being uninterrupted at that time' (quoted in Memoir of Taylor, *Literary Panorama*, iii. (January 1808).

(2) *Rev[d] Richard Oliphant:* Jane Bewick wrote of him in her memoir notes on her father's acquaintances: 'my father said of him that he was "a bundle of knowledge".' (Laing MSS.). Oliphant was Jane's godfather.

Page 110. (1) *John Bailey:* of Chillingham, steward to Lord Tankerville and agriculturalist. Later a banker at Berwick. TB made several visits to Chillingham; several letters survive relating to his times there.

(2) *drawing on the Wood:* the engraving of the Chillingham Bull was completed in 1789. A large block, $5\frac{1}{2}'' \times 7''$, TB was believed to have considered it his masterpiece. The Work Book (January 1787–December 1790) (Laing MSS) records: 'M.Tunstall Esq[r] The Wild Bull on wood £7.7.0.' By leaving the block in the sun over the weekend, TB allowed it to split, and the accident has since caused much speculation amongst collectors as to the number of impressions taken off beforehand. Certainly there were only a handful, and these reached a very high value. The block was clamped together and in 1817 further impressions of very good quality were achieved although the hairline crack could never be quite concealed. A full account can be found in D. C. Thomson's *The Life and Works of Thomas Bewick*, 1882.

(3) *Newfoundland Dog, kept there:* the visit to Eslington is celebrated in the finished engraving (*History of Quadrupeds*, 1790, p. 306) with the following legend: 'TB Eslington 1789 P·V·B·B'. The initials were of the four figures to be seen in the background: William Preston, Vint of Whittingham, John Bell, and Bewick himself.

Page 116. (1) *Brookes and Miller's "Natural History":* R. Brookes, *A System of Natural History*, 6 vols, 1763; John F. Miller, *Various Subjects of Natural History*, . . . 1785.

(2) *D[r] Smellies abridgement of Buffon:* George Louis Le Clerc, Count de Buffon, *Natural History general and particular . . . with occasional notes by the translator*, [William Smellie] 9 vols, Edinburgh, 1781–5.

(3) *Pennants Works:* Thomas Pennant, *British Zoology*, 1766; *A Synopsis of Quadrupeds*, Chester, 1771; *History of Quadrupeds*, 2 vols, 1781; *Genera of Birds*, Edinburgh, 1773; *Arctic Zoology*, 1784.

(4) *Albins "History of Birds":* Eleazar Albin, *Natural History of Birds*, 3 vols, 1731–4–8.

(5) *Belon's very old Book:* Pierre Belon, *L'Histoire de la Nature des Oyseaux avec leurs Descriptions, & Naifs Portraits retirez du Naturel*, Paris, 1555.

(6) *"Willughby & Ray":* Francis Willughby, *Ornithology, translated into English and enlarged by John Ray*, 1678.

(7) *Gesner's Natural History:* Conrad Gesner, *History of four-footed Beasts and Serpents, translated by E. Topsell*, 1658.

Page 117. (1) *Edwards "Natural History":* George Edwards, *A Natural History of Uncommon Birds . . . Gleanings of Natural History*, 7 vols, 1743–64.

(2) *"Whites History of Selburn":* Revd Gilbert White, *The Natural History and Antiquities of Selborne in the County of Southampton*, 1789.

(3) *Latham:* John Latham, *A General Synopsis of Birds*, 6 vols, 1781–5, with various supplements.

(4) *Ornithological Dictionary:* Col. George Montague, *Ornithological Dictionary; or Alphabetical Synopsis of British Birds*, 2 vols, 1802.

(5) *the extensive Museum there:* The Wycliffe collection was eventually acquired by the Literary and Philosophical Society of Newcastle after the death in 1800 of its second owner, George Allan of The Grange, Darlington. See G. T. Fox, *Synopsis of the Newcastle Museum*, 1827.

(6) *drawings of the Birds:* On 8 August 1791, TB wrote to his wife from Wycliffe: 'I have dulled myself with sticking too close to it . . . I am tired out already & wish it was over . . . tell Jane & Robert that if they behave well I will let them see a vast of little pictures of Birds when I come home . . .' (Hack MSS).

Page 121. *hirpling:* limping.

Page 122. (1) *"Beilby & Bewick" as the Editors:* this was never done explicitly; only Bewick's name appeared prominently on the title as engraver of the illustrations. The introduction was unsigned and Beilby's name appeared with Bewick's, but insignificantly, at the foot of the title among the publishers and distributors. See Introduction, pp. xix–xxi.

(2) *Revd. Thomas Hornby:* Jane Bewick wrote of him: 'He frequently sat over my Father when at work upon the cuts in the Evenings–He was Godfather to my young Sister . . . I have heard my Father say that the Revd Hornby used to annoy him with talking about religious High Church opinions–which by TB's Letter to Revd seems to have ended very abruptly these visitations . . .' (Laing MSS).

Page 123. *our separate cases in writing directed to him:*

Mr Charnley   Saturday 9 Sepr 1797

As I do not wish to conceal from the Public the part Mr Beilby has taken in compiling the History of Birds, and require nothing but truth and candour, a very short statement will be sufficient to shew my Motives for opposing his taking upon himself the Parade of Authorship and representing me merely employ'd as a workman to engrave Figures to embellish a Work of his composing–making himself the Mr Pennant and me the Moses Griffith–

I grant that he has spent much Time in compiling the Description of Birds from several Authors, but as it was chiefly during the Hours when I was constantly employed in the Cuts, I have as much right to his time as he has to mine, and to shew the Folly of his making any Claims of being an Author I can safely declare that he has not furnished one original anecdote nor from himself described one Property of a Bird in the whole Book.–He has laid much Stress upon the Communications, made to *him*, but all those Communications were either made directly to *me* or to him & me jointly.–The Knowlege he had of the Subject was so trifling that on copying accounts from Authors who have published the most glaring falsities & absurdities he never cou'd discriminate between Truth and Falshood, I have been obliged to cross out a great quantity of trash as may be seen by the Manuscript Copy; on these occasions he always appeared to me to be quite ignorant and he cannot deny that if I had not constantly looked over what he had copied, many of the Discriptions woud have been at variance with the Figs of the Birds which I had drawn & cut, as faithfully as I cou'd, from Nature–If he thinks himself entitled to be called the Author because he has compiled an Introduction & a Preface, I can only say that I did not desire to have either, and as the World wou'd have thought it great Presumption in either of us to have published a Book on the Subject if there had not been a stronger Motive than the mere Vanity of being Authors.–The discription of the Subjects was all that could be expected or was looked for in the Book, and the Introduction being mostly a Compilation it wou'd make any person appear rediculous who shou'd pretend it was original' (TB's copy of his statement to William Charnley, V & A MSS).

Page 125. (1) *ruinous concerns:* see Introduction, p. xx.

(2) *the Printing of the Quadrupeds:* see Introduction, p. xviii.

(3) *the second Volume:* contrary to TB's statement, Beilby had already done some of the work on this. On 9 December 1799 TB wrote to Beilby: 'In these long winter Evgs & while I am a kind of Cripple I am employing myself in writing the descriptions of the Water Birds, and as you have many already sketch'd out which were taken from the Birds sent us by our friends, I will be much obliged by your looking them out for me when convenient–for I have no expectation of having these Birds sent to me a second time' (Hack MSS).

Page 127. (1) *writing Engraving:* very often a specialist occupation. In the London trade it was customary for the illustration engravers to send their plates to the specialists for the addition of captions and titles. TB's nephew and apprentice, John Harrison, was trained in this line.

(2) *ruling Machine:* invented by Wilson Lowry in about 1790. A diamond point (for working through an etching ground) traversed a bar placed over the plate to be engraved. It was capable of very fine adjustment and enabled the engraver to lay his lines very close together and at regularly controlled intervals. Lowry undertook work for the trade and his device was employed by TB and Pollard (V&A MSS).

(3) *Engine turning:* Jacob Perkins, Gideon Fairman, and Charles Heath in partnership, were responsible for bringing steel-plate engraving into the London book trade in 1819–20. Perkins was a bank-note engraver from Philadelphia who had a number of inventions to his credit. Engine turning involved the use of a geometric lathe capable of producing extremely complex patterns, impossible to imitate exactly.

Page 128. *forgeries:* probably traced and transferred to lithographic stones. See TB's Berwick banknote facing p. 194.

Page 130. *his own private account:* for a full account of Sir William Congreve's activities in security printing see Elizabeth Harris, 'Experimental Graphic Processes in England, 1800–59', *Journal of the Printing Historical Society*, iv. (1968). Jane Bewick's MS memoranda (Laing MSS) records the following 'curious circumstance' relating to her father's forgery prevention experiments: 'My Father rec^{d} a Letter sign^{d} W. B. Wollaston intimating that my F^{rs} plan was likely to be adopted–&c & requesting an ans^{r} with *explanations* of his method &c & very *flamming* Compliments respect^{g} the Nat: Hist^{y} & a promise that the writer w^{d} call on him shortly on his way thro' N Castle–the ans^{r} was to be sent to Pentonville–where, no doubt it w^{d} have been taken in; but on enquiry we found that there was no *W B* Wollaston & the Letter was evidently a Trap–& must have been written by some rascal–for a bad purpose–I think I know the hand writing–tho' disguised–my Father was "as innocent as the Dove & not always as wise as the Serpent". . .' (W. *H.* Wollaston 1766–1828, chemist and physicist, was known by artists for his camera lucida, patented in 1807).

Page 131. "*Croxalls Esops Fables*"*:* the *Select Fables* of 1784, published by Saint of Newcastle with engravings by TB, has designs based on Croxall many of whose illustrations were in turn derived from Le Clerc and Francis Barlow.

Page 132. (1) *Wm Harvey & Wm Temple:* there has been much discussion of the responsibility for the designs and engravings in this book. Certainly a large proportion were supervised by TB in the manner described by him in a letter to Robert Pollard of 29 January 1816 (Laing MSS): '. . . during the day I am employd in designing & drawing the subjects on the Wood–& this is rather a laborious kind of work–I am obliged [to finish] the drawing with miniature like minutia, otherwise my Boys cou'd not cut them–This also requires my close superintendance & help and when the Cuts are done I then go over the Whole . . .' He also wrote to John Bailey on 5 February 1818: 'I hope to derive some assistance in the cutting [of] the Fables from a young man [Harvey] who left me last September. As he expressed a wish to continue to work at them for me, I gave him a number of designs with him to London, which I had, on his acct drawn on the wood with a finish and accuracy of fine miniature paintings, and flattered myself that I cou'd put a finishing hand to them when he returned them; but he has sent me none of them back, and I fear he only intends to make a *blaze* about the Fables being of his doing, *at my expense*, in London. These are my conjectures, for I have often been served so before . . . (Boyd). It seems highly unlikely that TB made use of designs by Robert Johnson (who died in 1796), as claimed by Chatto and Jackson in their *Treatise on Wood Engraving*, 1839, p. 594. See note 1 to p. 199.

(2) *much too strong, black & thick:* On 5 January 1819, TB wrote to the Bishop of Bristol: '. . . I am sorry to find that too many of the Impressions of the Cuts of Esops Fables are ragged and grey and have none of the softness & smoothness which Wood Cuts will exhibit, when properly printed. I think the radical defect is in the paper which was unfortunately too hard sized–and although M[r] Walker was at great pains to get the best ink, I think his Men, from their not being used to print from Ink of so thick a quality, were at a loss how to distribute it properly upon their Balls [large wooden-handled leather pads for applying ink to the printing surface] . . .' (Collection of Hugh Gibson Esq.).

Page 133. *White Smith:* pewterer or worker of other light coloured alloys.

Page 137. *gaging bills:* bills that powerfully restricted, such as the Act of 12 July 1799 requiring the registration of all printing presses.

Page 138. "*Yeomanry Cavelry*"*:* perhaps the Peterloo Massacre of 1819 when people assembling in St Peter's Fields, Manchester, to petition for parliamentary reform, were charged down by the yeomanry.

Page 139. *Agricultural reports:* for example: J. Bailey & G. Culley, *A General View of the Agriculture of the County of Northumberland with Observations on the Means of its Improvement. Drawn up for the Consideration of the Board of Agriculture*, 1798.

Page 142. (1) "*Englands Grievance*"*:* Ralph Gardner, *England's Grievance discovered in Relation to the Coal Trade*, 1655.

(2) *General* (*Leslie? Hobson?*): General Alexander Leslie, first Earl of Leven, 1580?–1661.

Page 161. (1) *J. F. M. Dovaston Esq[r]:* the friendship of John Dovaston is recorded in the series of twenty-eight letters written to him by TB and now in the British Museum. See *Bewick to Dovaston, Letters 1824–1828*, ed. Gordon Williams 1968; and Introduction, pp. xxiii–xxiv.

(2) *ornithoscope:* Dovaston's name for his telescope.

Page 166. (1) *dry stone dykes:* stone built walls constructed without mortar and common to the north country and Scotland.

(2) *Whin hedges:* hedges of common furze.

(3) *beild:* shelter or refuge.

Page 173. (1) *Strike:* possibly boards or timbers set in the river bed to divert a deep water flow at a ford; or simply a fishermen's station.

(2) *nice:* exact.

(3) *abundance in the Tyne:* See Sykes, *Local Records*, 1833, i. 221, 246, and 281: 20 July 1750, 2000 salmon taken in the Tyne, sold at 1d. and 1½d. per lb.; 15 July 1771, 4000 salmon . . . at 1¼d. per lb.

Page 174. *along the shores:* a memorandum by TB on the taking of spawn is in the Pease Collection.

Page 176. *Pought Nets:* nets fastened to poles with which fishermen poked the river banks to force out the fish.

Page 177. *Saughs:* sallow or willow.

Page 179. *fitters:* coal-brokers who sold and loaded coals.

Page 181. *John Rastrick of Morpeth:* 'a very clever, highly talented Mechanical Genius–a perpetual talker–blabbed all his inventions which were as readily picked up & acted on–he made himself enemies by freely commenting on the Jobberies & stupidities which were perpetrated from time to time under his eyes and in his neighbourhood–I remember once, at the Forth (where he frequently was bro^t^ to Tea by my Father) the remarks he made respect^g^ a Crane on the Quay which, he said, would, like those previously set up there–soon be snapped–My F^r^ watched, & sure enough–such was the case–he explained why. The County Court–he freely abused–& the Goal–Mickle took out a patent for Rastricks Threshing Machine. Rastrick defended the farmers in the use of it, & beat his opponent–but the Gentlemen & their Tenants gave poor R. nothing towards his Law expenses. If he could have held his tongue he might (altho' not a rich man) have been a happy one but no one (except my Father & he did not mind) can be happy who is continually robbed–' (Jane Bewick's Memoranda, Laing MSS).

Page 182. *Eidograph . . . which he invented:* in 1801, serving the same purpose as the pantograph more generally used by engravers.

Page 184. *capable of performing:* about twenty impressions were taken of this, TB's only essay in lithography. TB wrote to John Dovaston, 26 February 1824: '. . . my reason for fixing upon that particular design was to pourtray, as well as I could, the motion of a Horse in the long or full trot, & to shew it to a very ingenious painter (in Edinburgh)

& excentric man of the name of Stowe, who had been labouring in vain like thousands, perhaps, of other painters to give a representation of motion in Animals, this led to a close conversation, or lecture on the subject, in which I convinced him thoroughly of his being quite wrong, & indeed of the absurdity of his drawings, in this respect . . . I told him I had always endeavoured to give the proper motion to animals, but was never satisfied with my own performances . . . –It may perhaps amuse you to look at a Horse either galloping or trotting–in the first, you will find he does not, nor can he, throw his feet so far forward as his nose–in the latter action you will see that his knees do not appear further forward than his breast . . .'.

Page 186. *every vacant spot:* several of TB's tail-piece engravings illustrate his idea. See pp. 50, 186, and 213.

Page 188. *to find out this themselves:* the most detailed account of the niceties of presswork and surface lowering in engraving, is to be found in the final chapter of Chatto and Jackson's *Treatise on Wood Engraving*, 1839.

Page 190. *balls:* the wooden-handled leather pads used for applying ink before the invention of the inking roller in the early 19th century.

Page 191. (1) *a fac:* a small block displaying an initial letter and a view of Newcastle and St Nicholas's church lantern spire.

(2) *to which they are exposed:* most of TB's still surviving blocks, now widely scattered, still print as well as ever. Careful inking and choice of paper produces astonishingly fine results.

Page 192. *the plank way:* as opposed to being cut across the grain.

Page 193. (1) "*king Charles's twelve good rules*"*:* these were: 1. Urge no healths; 2. Profane no divine ordinances; 3. Touch no state matters; 4. Reveal no secrets; 5. Pick no quarrels; 6. Make no comparisons; 7. Maintain no ill opinions; 8. Keep no bad company; 9. Encourage no vice; 10. Make no long meals; 11. Repeat no grievances; 12. Lay no wagers. A broadsheet of these rules was in the Bewick family sale of 1884.

(2) *the valiant Granadier:* Tom Brown's portrait engraved by L. P. Boitard. He was a private in Bland's Dragoons and recaptured the standard at the battle of Dettingen, being many times wounded.

(3) *thy spreading sails:* the Victory sank off Alderney, 8 October 1744.

(4) . . . "*Duke Willy*"*:* the Duke of Cumberland and the Highland chiefs defeated at Culloden in 1746.

Page 194. (1) *none of them looked well:* these prints were in the Bewick family sale of 1884. They were published by Jackson in 1742 when in Venice. He later published *An Essay on the Invention of Engraving and Printing in Chiaro Oscuro . . . and The Application of it to the Making*

[*of*] *Paper Hangings* . . . 1754, which had samples of work of this kind.

(2) *stroke engraving:* Engraving with fine burins rather than the coarser gouges and chisels used for woodcuts.

(3) *from a Roller, instead of an even down pull:* The 'even down pull' refers to the action of the platen on the hand-press where the whole printing surface makes contact with the paper at the same instant. The action of a cylinder has a distinct advantage in that the impression progresses in a line across the printing surface. Charles Knight publisher of the *Penny Magazine* used wood-engravings extensively during the 1830s and '40s and much of his printing was done on the new cylinder machines. Chatto and Jackson's *Treatise on Wood Engraving* (also published by Knight) describes the techniques.

Page 195. (1) . . . *have not been equalled:* a number of Woollett's engravings were in the Bewick family sale of 1884. His plate after Stubbs's 'Spanish Pointer' served as the model for TB's engraving of this dog for his *History of Quadrupeds.*

(2) *theory:* see TB's uncompleted print 'Waiting for Death'.

(3) *bright engraving:* bright work, silversmith's term for a style of graver cutting that had a particularly sparkling effect.

(4) *John Johnson:* a cousin to Robert Johnson and apprenticed to Beilby and Bewick, Christmas 1782. Some of the engravings in TB's *Birds* have been credited to him by Chatto & Jackson.

Page 198. (1) *entitled to have wages:* after the first four years, as seen in TB's Weekly Engraving Books (V & A and Laing MSS).

(2) *Breadalbane:* MS reads incorrectly Earl of Buchan.

Page 199. (1) *Robert Johnson:* Born Shotley, Northumberland, 1770, the son of a joiner and cabinet-maker, he died 29 October 1796. His work in Scotland at the time of his death had been commissioned by the firm of Morrison, the Perth booksellers, who were publishing Pinkerton's *Gallery of Scottish Portraits.* Of the nineteen copies of portraits by George Jamesone (1586–1644) that were required, he had completed fifteen when he was taken ill. His delirious fever was taken to be madness and the unfortunate young man was bound with ropes and beaten. In his introduction to the book Pinkerton stated that it was Johnson who had drawn the figures on the wood for the *Quadrupeds*, and to refute this TB wrote to the Morrisons on 3 March 1798: '. . .–You must know then, that I feel myself much hurt at the falshoods which through your information to Mr Pinkerton, have made their appearance so publicly in the world–Mr P gives you up as his authority for saying, that my late unfortunate Apprentice, poor Johnson–had been employ'd by me to trace the figures on the Wood for the History of Quadrupeds &c–however trivial this may appear to you–it does not by any means appear so to me, & my friends–it is making me look rediculous (or worse) in the eyes of them & the Public, & must continue to do so, untill it is contradicted & they are informed of the truth.–I do not suspect that you are the Authors of the falshoods, of which I complain– but I do *strongly suspect that your informant* from the most malicious motives, has been prompted to deceive you . . .' (Copy MS by TB in the collection of Mr Bewick Hack). Johnson was apprenticed between 1787 and 1794. Some of his surviving watercolours in the Laing Gallery display a skill that fully warrants Bewick's praise. Johnson is also credited by Chatto and Jackson with all the drawings for the *Fables of Aesop* of 1818: while a handful of accomplished water-colours of some of the subjects survive in the collection of the Natural History Society of Northumbria (unsigned, but certainly in a different and individual style), to say that all the *Fables* designs were done by him, so many years in advance of the work, is clearly untrue.

(2) *Charlton Nesbit:* Born 1775, the son of a keelman, at Swalwell, Durham, he was apprenticed to Beilby and Bewick *c.* 1789. He contributed a number of cuts to the *Birds* 1797, the *Poems of Goldsmith and Parnell*, 1795, and *Le Grand's Fabliaux*, 1796 and 1800, before leaving for the London trade in 1799. There his work appeared in Ackermann's *Religious Emblems*, 1809, *Puckle's Club*, 1817, and *Northcote's Fables*, 1828 and 1833. He returned to the north in 1815 having come into an inheritance. He died in 1838 at Brompton, having come back to London in 1830.

(3) *John Thurston:* Born Scarborough 1774, he died at Holloway in 1822. Innumerable books of the early nineteenth century had engraved illustrations based on designs which Thurston had drawn on the wood. Two in which TB's workshop was involved were Thomson's *Seasons*, 1805, and Burns's *Poems*, 1808.

(4) *Henry Hole:* The son of a captain in the Lancashire militia, Hole was apprenticed to TB between 1795 and 1801, which is after and not before Nesbit as stated by TB. The fortune and the Devon estate he came into led him to dissipation and 'the bottle'. After ending his apprenticeship he kept in touch with his master and commissioned his aid on a large work he contracted to do in Liverpool. His anxious letters relating to TB's long delays still survive (Hack MSS) as do TB's copies of his letters to Hole chasing a long outstanding debt. He executed a few of the engravings in the *Birds* and he also contributed to Ackermann's *Religious Emblems*, 1809. See p. 264.

(5) *John Anderson:* The son of Dr James Anderson of Edinburgh, editor of *The Bee*, and one of TB's customers. He engraved the illustrations for the first edition of Robert Bloomfield's *The Farmer's Boy*, 1800 (attributed to TB by almost every bookseller) and Maurice's *Grove Hill*, 1799. Some time in 1803 or 4 he went to South America (according to Dobson) or Botany Bay (according to Henry Hole in a letter to TB of 21 October 1804) and was lost to wood-engraving. He has no connection with the well known American engraver Dr Alexander Anderson who reproduced several of TB's works.

(6) *Edward Willis:* A cousin of George Stephenson the engineer, he

was apprenticed to TB between 1798 and 1805. A note in the workshop engraving book records the end of his time: 'never a cross word passed between us' (Laing MSS). He communicated a certain amount of detail relating to the workshop to W. A. Chatto for his *Treatise on Wood Engraving*.

(7) *John Harrison:* Thirty-five of TB's letters to him are now in the Pease Collection (271), and some contain much interesting detail relating to the skills of writing engraving on metal.

(8) *Henry White:* White came to TB from London in 1804 to complete his apprenticeship after the death of his first master, Lee. He engraved the designs of Thurston for Burns's *Poems* published by Catnach & Davison of Alnwick in 1808. His work can also be seen in *Puckle's Club*, 1817, in William Yarrell's *A History of British Fishes*, 1836, and in Major's edition of *Walton's Angler*, 1824.

Page 200. (1) *became quite the Ton:* i.e. 'black-line' engraving which faithfully reproduces the drawn line. See pp. 258 and 259.

(2) *Luke Clennell:* Born at Ulgham near Morpeth in 1781, he was apprenticed between 1797 and 1804. Many tail-pieces in the second volume of the *Birds* are attributed to him, and his work can also be seen in Hodgson's *The Hive*, 1806. He moved south to London in 1804 and worked on many books such as the *Antiquarian Itinerary*, 1815, *Recreations in Natural History*, 1815, Samuel Rogers's *Pleasures of Memory* (cut in the black-line manner after Stothard), and Cowper's *Poems*, 1808 (after Thurston's designs). The Society of Arts awarded him their Gold Palette in 1806 and he was one of the few of TB's pupils truly 'gifted with a painter's eye' (TB p. 190) and his rare watercolours are now much prized. He became insane in 1817 and tragically remained so until his death in 1840. Both his wife and son suffered the same affliction.

(3) *Isaac Nicholson:* Born Melmerby, Cumberland, 1789 and died 1848. Apprenticed to TB in about 1802. A skilled engraver but wanting in artistic talent and originality. TB had to take him to task for copying his work when out of his apprenticeship and working on his own account in Newcastle. See D. C. Thomson, *Life and Works of TB*, p. 229.

(4) *William Harvey:* 1796–1866. Born Newcastle and apprenticed to TB between 1810 and 1817. At the end of his time he set up in business in London (see p. 134, note 2 above) eventually becoming Thurston's successor as the principal designer for the wood-engraving trade. His work appears in innumerable books, some of the best of which is to be seen in *Northcote's Fables*, 1828 and 1833, Lane's *Arabian Nights*, 1838–40 and *The Gardens and Menagerie of the Zoological Society*, 1829. His engraving was exquisitely fine but his figures have a certain dainty unreality and his animals' feet never seem to be planted firmly on the ground. With William Temple he worked extensively on TB's *Fables of Aesop*, 1818.

(5) *Son & partner:* Robert Elliot Bewick, 1788–1849. TB's only son suffered much from his ill-health, retiring nature and the powerful personality of his father. His work has much unrecognized talent, evidence of which can be seen in surviving drawings and water-colours in the collections of the Natural History Society of Northumbria and the British Museum. The *History of British Fishes,* for which he prepared many fine water-colour drawings and several engravings, was never published.

Page 202. *may clearly see:* a small sketch of the shining sun in the original MS has not been reproduced here.

Page 219. "Hume on Miracles": David Hume's essay 'Of Miracles' in his *Philosophical Essays concerning Human Understanding,* 1748.

Page 224. *Johanna Southcote:* Joanna Southcott, 1750–1814, daughter of a Devon farmer who began to write doggerel prophesies in 1792. A religious fanatic and impostor, she attracted a considerable following before dying of brain disease.

NOTE ON THE TEXT

The text has been taken directly from the original manuscript now in the British Museum (Add. MS 41,481). There have been five previous editions but this is the first presentation of a full literatim transcript and there have been considerable emendations throughout in word and phrase. Bewick's daughter Jane prepared the first edition of 1862 with the unwelcome aid of its printer Robert Ward. The writing was smoothed out and occasionally the revised punctuation quite altered the sense of a passage. Jane Bewick's page proofs of the *Memoir*, now in the possession of the Editor, show many manuscript corrections that were not incorporated, and in several places she recorded her concern at Ward's lack of understanding and his rudeness to her. Of the missing references to her father's friends and acquaintances at the end of chapter 18 she wrote: 'I insisted that these passages should not be left out–& got well bullied by the printer'; and 'When this sheet was sent to Press, I said, now Mr Ward every word, just as it is, *shall* be printed. It had been a constant fight, sheet by sheet, to alter.—I s^d^ if so, it is your Memoir not my Father's, do let him speak for himself . . .'. Very few of her corrections were heeded. But by chapter 20 no further marks appear and there is a note in chapter 19: 'The M.S. now free'd from interference, threat of "disgrace" for no longer suffering it to be meddled with!!' Jane Bewick was nevertheless plainly willing to make some adjustments: a word in chapter 15 was marked 'JB's suggestion to soften the MS'; and she made no remark about the missing references to her father's apprentices and here we must assume she was a party to the omission. All subsequent editions used the first edition text as a basis, with two of them adding previously omitted material: Dobson (1887) and Weekley (1961), although the latter at the same time abridged the work substantially.

The manuscript was put up for sale by Ralph Bewick, great-great-grandson of Thomas Bewick's brother William, and was acquired by the British Museum at the Sotheby auction of 11–13 April 1927. It contains 243 closely written quarto pages on several of which are pasted newspaper cuttings and engravings. These, together with two small thumbnail sketches drawn within the manuscript line, have been included in this edition.

Although Bewick wrote with a view to publication, he never fully prepared the manuscript for the printer and it contains many undecided alternatives of word and phrase: in cases where no word is clearly superior, the first written has been chosen. Deleted matter of any significance has been shown within pointed brackets and the remainder silently dropped. All capitals and contractions have been retained. Occasionally names have been capitalized silently; the old style ſ has been modernized. The punctuation has been followed, except where to do so would lead to the reader's confusion. Idiosyncrasies of spelling have been retained, but repetitions of single words have been omitted without note. Very obvious slips of the pen have been silently corrected. The occasionally omitted but obvious word has been supplied within square brackets. Quotation marks were not always closed: where missing they have been inserted without remark. Bewick's paragraphing was haphazard and he would frequently employ a long dash rather than waste space by starting a new line: this has been followed. There are numerous underlinings throughout the text which were employed for three purposes, though not always obviously: often for emphasis, sometimes in place of inverted commas round colloquialisms, and often in a tentative manner as an indication of uncertainty of expression. The first two groups have been italicized and the third left in roman. Bewick's own footnotes appear here at the foot of their relative pages. Many have blanks which had been left for the later addition of dates and other matter; these have been indicated with square brackets and the information has been supplied wherever possible. Two short passages on pp. 163 and 202 which occur in the first edition of 1862, and for which there is now no manuscript original, have been taken from the printed version. These were probably on separate slips similar to several now bound in at the back of the main manuscript, one of which now provides a paragraph on pp. 45–6.

Bewick gave his memoir no title and that of the present edition is the one used by his daughter in 1862. There are no chapter breaks in the original and again those followed here are those of 1862. The chapter summaries compiled for that edition have now been dropped in favour of an index.

NOTE ON THE ILLUSTRATIONS

The vignettes which Bewick engraved for his unpublished and uncompleted *History of British Fishes* and which decorated the first and second editions of his *Memoir*, have here been replaced by a selection from his best work for the *History of British Birds* and *General History of Quadrupeds*. While no reproduction can match the quality of fine impressions direct from Bewick's blocks, care has been taken to work from the best possible originals.

Bewick originally intended to illustrate his *Memoir* with portraits of his friends. In November 1823 he wrote to John Dovaston: '. . . favor me with your *likeness in shade*, to place in a Book I am in hands with, and that is a Memoir of my own life . . . I have got shade likenesses of several friends to place in the Book, where I have had occasion to mention them & I hope to have yours among the rest . . .'. For the first time, seven of these which Bewick engraved on wood, have now been placed in the text as he wished. All but the silhouette of Dovaston (which is in the editor's possession) have been reproduced from impressions in Julia Boyd's *Bewick Gleanings* (1886). The opportunity has been taken to add to these by reproducing a few portraits of friends and family. Those of his daughters, son, and brother, are of particular interest and have not been published before. Other illustrations within the text have been reproduced from material which Bewick pasted into, or drew in, the manuscript.

Bewick's engravings and other line drawings reproduced in the text are about 12½ per cent smaller than the originals.

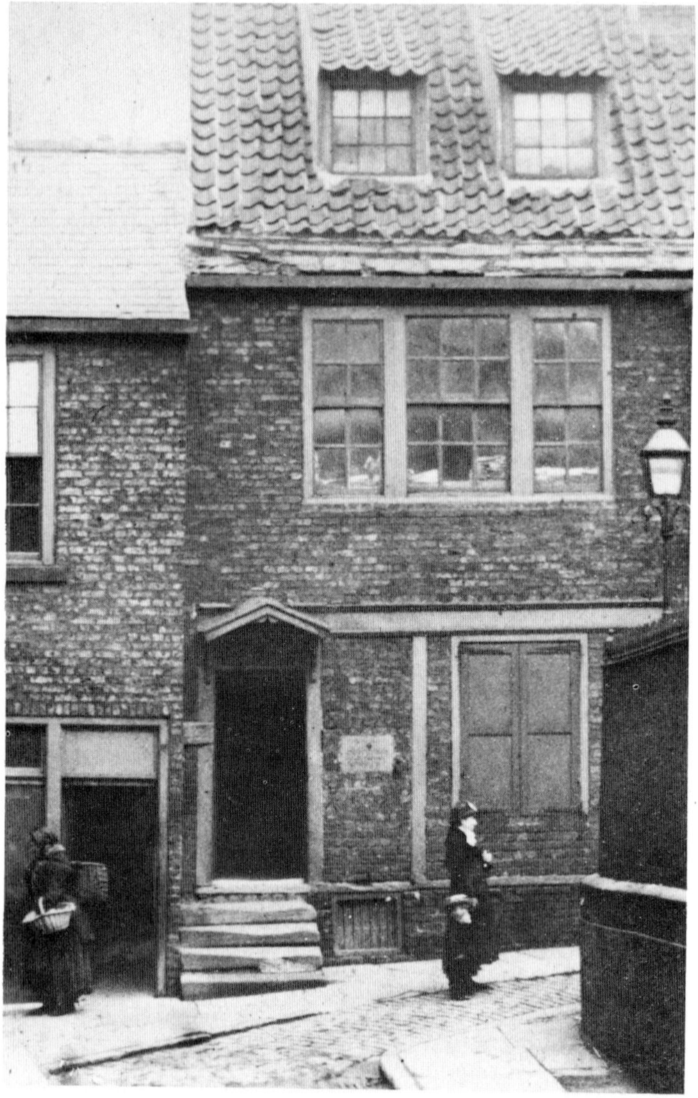

A recently discovered photograph of Bewick's workshop taken during the second half of the last century. The workshop was pulled down in 1902

NOTE ON BEWICK'S ENGRAVING

For those who have no previous knowledge of wood engraving and its history, those sections of the *Memoir* that deal with technique and trade practice may not be easy to appreciate;[1] for those who already have an interest in such matters they present much fascinating detail but detail which is still lacking in some essentials. The following observations may therefore be helpful to both.

When Bewick came to Beilby's workshop, the business was concerned with metal engraving of every sort: decorative–for silver, clock faces, and swords, and practical–for bottle and button moulds, seals, trade cards, and banknotes. Engraving on metal continued to predominate throughout Bewick's life and, as is often overlooked, the celebrated wood engravings were, relatively, a small part of the day's work. Indeed the emphasis was evident on the sign outside the premises and in the description on his billheads which always read 'Engravers & Copper-plate Printers'. For metal engraving of the sort that was designed for printing, facilities of a special kind were necessary. The image was recessed into a thin plate of copper either by engraving with cutting tools or by etching with acid–and sometimes with a mixture of both methods. To take a print, the lines thus made had first to be charged with ink and the surrounding surface wiped clean with a variety of coarse and fine muslins and the palm of the hand. The plate was then covered with dampened paper and passed, under specially resilient blankets, between the cylinders of a rolling press built rather like a mangle. The very heavy pressure forced the damp paper into the lines to pick up the ink. The whole operation was a slow one, and therefore if associated with book production was relatively more expensive than the use of a relief-cut wood block which could be inked with ease, and which could be printed at the same time, and in the same press, as its accompanying text.

In the 1770s Newcastle had a thriving book trade, particularly

[1] pp. 39–41 and 187–200.

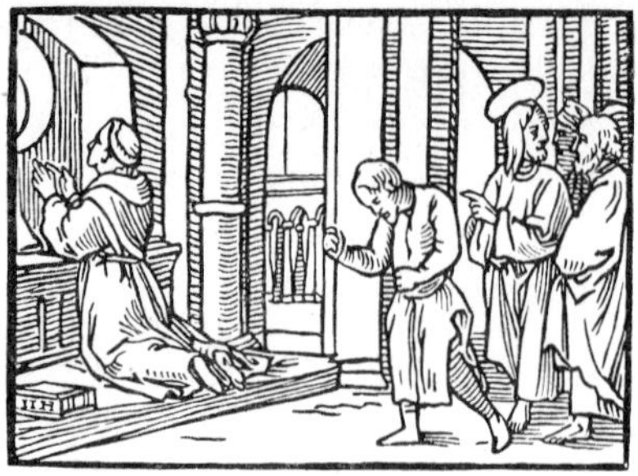

Facsimile woodcut after Holbein by John Jackson
showing the early black-line style

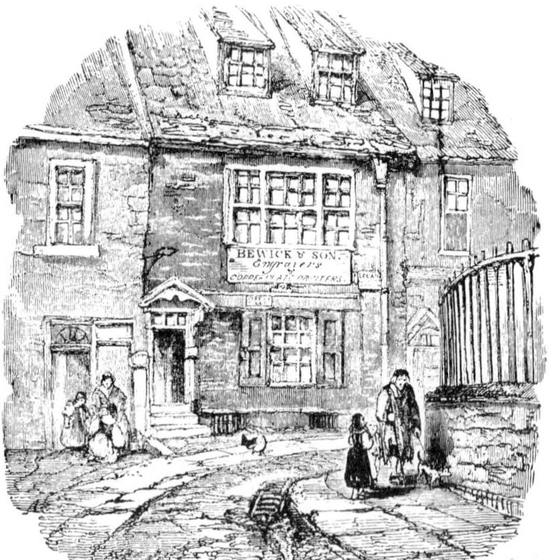

A view of Bewick's workshop in St Nicholas church-
yard. Engraved by John Jackson in the finer black-line
style adopted by later 19th-century engravers

in children's books, but it was quite unsophisticated in its production methods. If wood was used for the illustrations it was cut with a knife along the grain in the coarse manner seen in old ballad broadsheets. That the process was cheaper was a fact that did little to keep up standards in engraving, and crude hack work was the norm. It was in fact possible to get far finer results by using the burin of the metal engraver on the end grain of a hard slow-growing material such as boxwood, and in England such work is known to have been done as early as 1673.[1] Soon after Bewick was apprenticed, Dr Charles Hutton came to Beilby to suggest that he cut the diagrams for his forthcoming *Treatise on Mensuration* and on his own evidence 'there was not then in that part of the country any artist who had ever seen such engraving executed'. But Hutton had made himself acquainted with the techniques already established in the south and accordingly 'procured the necessary blocks of box-wood from London with the tools proper for cutting or carving on them, instructing those persons [Beilby and Bewick] how to cut out and square the blocks, and to cut or engrave on the smooth surface of them the necessary lines and letters in the diagrams, by which, in frequently attending them for their instruction, we got the cuts tolerably well executed . . .'[2] Although the association is twice referred to in the *Memoir*[3] there is no explicit acknowledgment of Hutton's preliminary instruction –and if Hutton is to be believed it was perhaps a human enough omission from one who had been so much fêted in his own lifetime as the sole originator of the art. But the true significance of the matter lies in the fact that Bewick was an artist of genius whose hand, eventually vastly skilled and trained in fine work on metal, was by this happy chance brought to a sympathetic medium, and that he later developed to full perfection a creative manner of engraving that could never be satisfactorily employed by a craftsman trained only in reproductive skills. Instead of cutting away non-printing areas of wood surrounding the previously drawn lines of a design (the 'black line' technique that can be observed in the

[1] Original end-grain wood blocks for initials used in books of that date printed at the Oxford University Press still survive, and it is thought that some of them may be as much as 100 years earlier in origin. See Stanley Morison, *John Fell, the University Press and the Fell Types*, 1967, pp. 187–94.

[2] Dr Charles Hutton, 'Some Account of Mr. Thomas Bewick . . .', *The Newcastle Magazine*, June 1822, pp. 321–2.

[3] pp. 40 and 54.

works of Dürer and Holbein), Bewick saw the surface of the virgin block as solid black and every stroke of his graver as a white line. All his best work contains the most exquisite touches of light and shade, not in a naturalistic manner, but as Ruskin observed, to express form and dark local colour.[1] The isolated black lines that do occur in the lighter areas are achieved with broad freehand white-line cutting, rather than with laborious 'facsimile' work cut round drawn lines.

As the delicacy of his work increased, so did the difficulty of printing it well. But it is not true to say that he engraved beyond the capacity of his printers because he was not a printer himself.[2] He was immensely practical and had the closest contact with the means of production. He had copper-plate rolling presses in his own workshop always, and while his books were in progress we know it was his usual custom every morning 'to proceed to the printer's to see what progress they were making, and to give directions to the pressmen about printing the cuts'.[3] In the early days that he complains of in the *Memoir*,[4] the wooden press for printing types was seldom a very precise instrument; ink was of indifferent quality as was the manner of applying it; and the generality of pressmen were unaccustomed to work of any degree of excellence. Bewick writes of his various devices for counteracting these deficiencies. The lowering of certain areas of distance and fine texture to ease the printing pressure on them, thus at the same time to protect their delicacy and allow them to print lightly, was his own discovery, although not original, for it was a technique that had been practised as early as the sixteenth century.[5] He also lowered the edges of his blocks in order to prevent the crude leather balls or dabbers from overloading them with ink. It was usual at this time to print with a soft impression – the tympan on the press, which carried the paper to the printing surface and stood between it and the impression platen, being packed with a fine close-woven blanket. This was largely to compensate for the possible irregularities in worn type and in the surface of the platen and press bed,

[1] John Ruskin, *Ariadne Florentina*, 1876, p. 71.
[2] James M. Wells, introduction to *A Portfolio of Thomas Bewick Wood Engravings*, Chicago, 1970, p. 9.
[3] W. A. Chatto and John Jackson, *A Treatise on Wood Engraving*, 1839, p. 600.
[4] p. 188.
[5] Chatto and Jackson, *A Treatise on Wood Engraving*, p. 548.

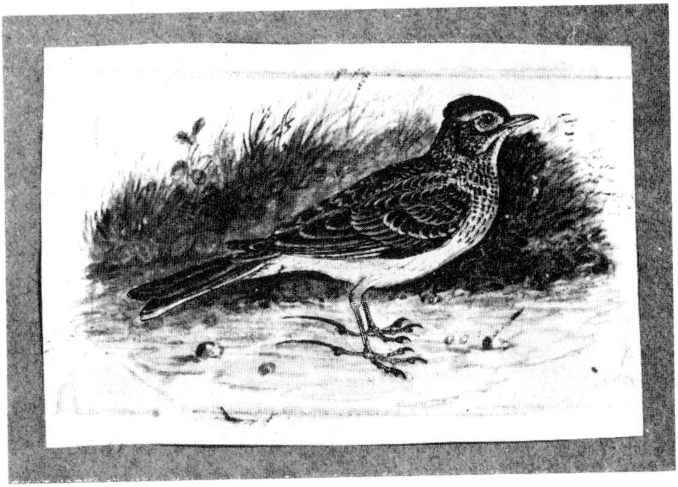

Bewick's preliminary water-colour drawing (original size) for the engraving of the Skylark in his *History of British Birds*. See opposite and p. xxiii

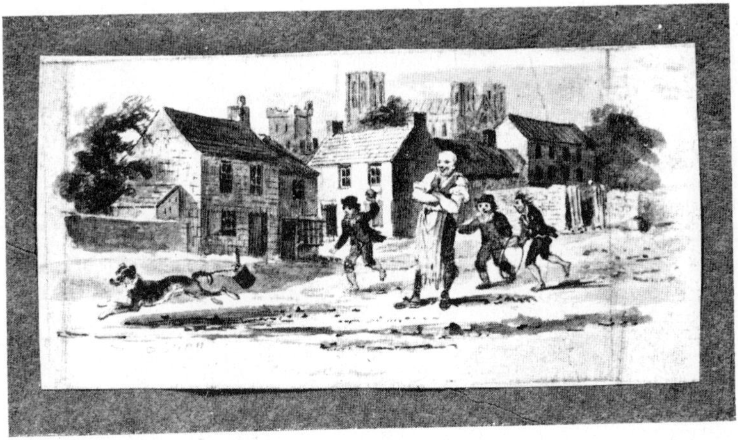

The water-colour drawing for a tail-piece engraved in Bewick's *British Birds*. The crease on the right of the subject shows that the drawing was too wide for the piece of boxwood selected for engraving

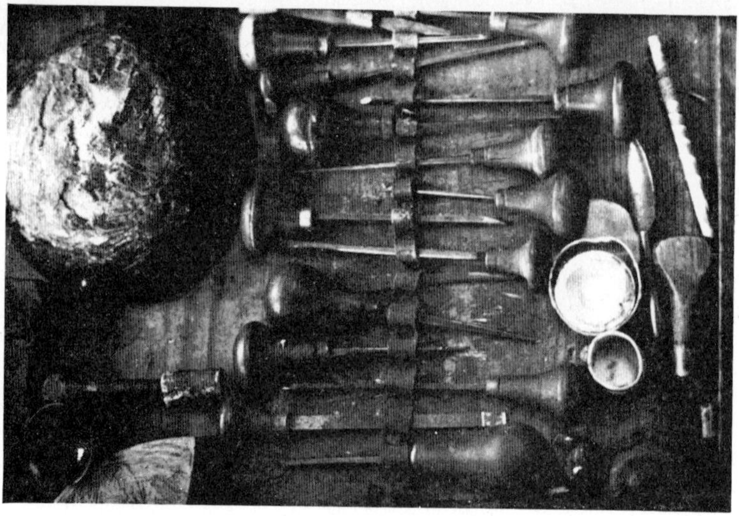

Bewick's tool box as it was left at the time of his death

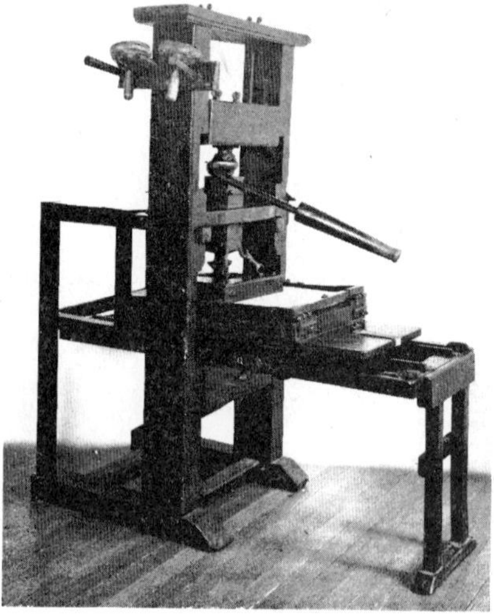

An 18th-century wooden press of the type on which Bewick's blocks were first printed

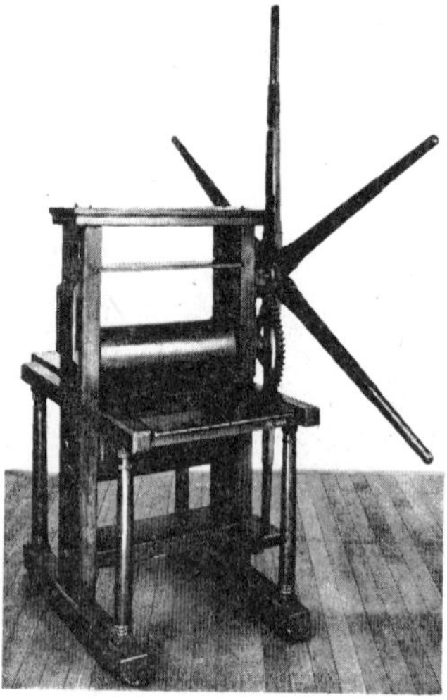

An 18th-century wooden rolling press for printing engraved copper-plates, modified with 19th-century gearing

and it was for these conditions that Bewick engraved. With the advent of the iron press and the inking roller in the early years of the nineteenth century it became less necessary to 'lower' blocks: the variety of pressures for the darks and lights were now achieved by pasting small tissues of paper to the tympan to increase pressure on the darks and this in turn relieved the pressure on the surrounding highlights. By 1826, when Bewick's earlier blocks were being printed in improved conditions, he found it necessary to apply tissue overlays to the tympan, not to bring up the darks but to help reach the detail in their lowered areas.[1]

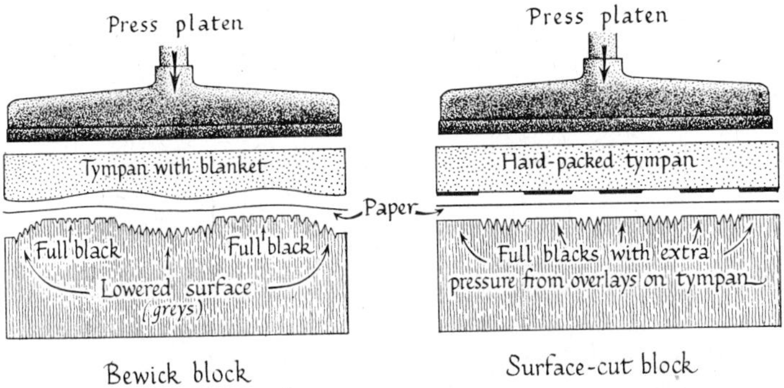

Cross-sections of 'lowered' and 'surface-cut' blocks showing how variations in pressure are achieved

Much of the trouble he had with the quality of printing stemmed from the poor inks that were used (not to mention the effect of frost on them during the winter months) as well as the inattention of the pressmen. It is usually necessary to see several copies of an edition before the true quality of all Bewick's blocks can be observed, and it was common for him to suggest to his special customers that they should select the sheets of the books for the best impressions before having them bound. When the *Fables of Aesop* was printed in 1818, although a fine quality stiff ink was bought in for the job, the pressmen in Walker's newspaper office were quite unused to it and applied it far too thickly. To this difficulty was added the hardness of the paper which had too much

[1] TB's MS notes in his copy of the 1826 edition of the *Birds* (Natural History Society of Northumbria).

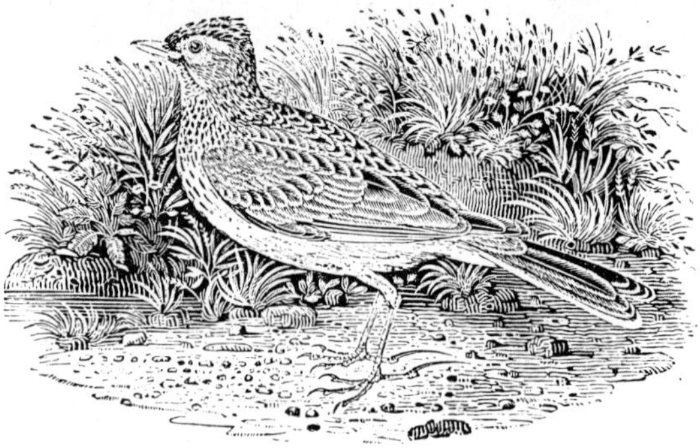

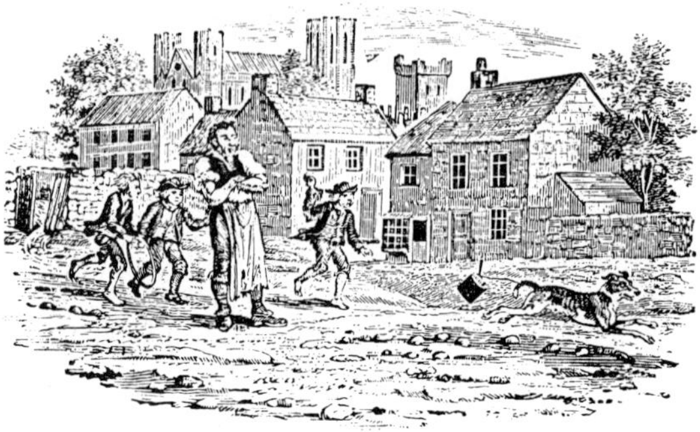

size in it, so that in spite of the usual softening effect of damping it refused to take the ink satisfactorily.[1]

Nothing is said in the *Memoir* to explain exactly how Bewick prepared his blocks for engraving, for of course at the time the process was general and well understood. It is fortunate that several hundred of his drawings and water-colours have survived and are now in the care of the British Museum and the Natural History Society of Northumbria. From these we can see that it was generally his custom to prepare the most minutely accurate pen and pencil drawings which frequently were finished in delicate colour. (Many are superb works of art in their own right and deserve to be far better known.) These were then heavily leaded on the back with soft pencil, after which the paper was placed over the selected piece of boxwood and the edges folded over to

[1] See p. 132 and n. 2.

steady the position. The crease marks from this folding are usually clearly visible and are the means of distinguishing final from preliminary drawings. A fine hard point was then used to trace the basic outlines of the designs. Under the pressure these were transferred to the surface of the block which had previously been prepared with brick dust so that it would pick up the pencil carbon more readily. On John Dovaston's evidence it was not Bewick's custom to draw much detail on the block; he described his 'filling up the foregrounds, landscapes, and light foliage of trees, at once with the tool, without being previously pencilled'.[1] By inference this is confirmed in Bewick's account of his preparation of the engravings for the *Fables of Aesop* where he complained of having to draw the designs in the greatest detail for his apprentices.[2]

The boxwood was bought in logs from London at 24 shillings a hundredweight and while Bewick's brother John was in the south he acted as agent for its purchase.[3] Since it is slow-growing the diameter seldom exceeded eight or nine inches, so for large blocks two or more pieces had to be jointed together. It was sliced like a cucumber, across the grain, and had to be left to season for some time before it could be used. The tools Bewick used were of his own making and as Dovaston records 'were various in sizes and sorts. Some broad gouges for wide excavations; some narrow, for fine white lines; and some many pointed for parallels, which, either straight or wavy, he cut with great rapidity, by catching the first tooth in the last stroke, which guided it equidistant with the former'.[4] Something of the variety and quantity can be judged from the illustration opposite which shows Bewick's tool box. His eyeglass (probably only used in later years) and the curved leather-covered block on which he placed the piece to be engraved, can also be seen.

The *Memoir* has a good deal to say of Bewick's apprentices; he remarks that he often wondered whether, if he had his life to live over again, he would not have done without the burden of pupils.[5]

[1] J. F. M. Dovaston, 'Some Account of the Life . . . of the late Thomas Bewick', *Magazine of Natural History*, 1829, p. 430.
[2] TB to Robert Pollard, 29 January 1816 (Laing MSS). See p. 132, n. 1.
[3] John Bewick to TB, 24 July 1787 (Hack MSS).
[4] J. F. M. Dovaston in the *Magazine of Natural History*, 1829, p. 429.
[5] p. 77.

They gave him much trouble and much assistance. There are several references to their good or bad behaviour in the workshop engraving books, and to Henry Hole (who had himself been bailed out of jail by his master when taken in for fathering a bastard child) Bewick wrote: 'I find it expected that I will give some account of my pupils–this I feel to be an unpleasant task, as some of them were beneath contempt either as Men or Artists, such therefore have been passed by without being noticed . . . you yourself might probably know some, to whom I acted as a father or a Brother & when I had done all–every thing I could think of to promote their happiness & prosperity–they shewed in the end a disposition that would have strangled me.'[1] Nevertheless he was proud of his part in the achievement of a number of them and the fact that they had won prizes and taken up leading positions in the London trade. It is much to be regretted that he says nothing of the part some of them took in the engravings in his major works, for there was and still is much speculation on the subject. At the end of his life he replied to G. C. Atkinson that not more than six of his Birds had been worked by his assistants. No mention was made of the tail-pieces at this time,[2] but John Jackson (who was with him between about 1819 and 1824 but was not considered worthy of notice in the *Memoir*) gave a detailed list of the prentice hands concerned with them.[3] As already remarked, we have specific evidence that the apprentices cut, although they did not design, most of the blocks in the *Fables of Aesop* of 1818,[4] but much could yet be done to secure more information from the work books of the business where often apprentice initials appear against named blocks. Naturally Bewick, as master, considered the matter of no consequence–although he was much exercised when he suspected a pupil of passing off some of his master's drawings as his own.[5] He had the overseeing eye and it is quite clear that his was the

[1] TB to Henry Hole, 11 October 1826 (Hack MSS).
[2] 'Sketch of the Life and Works of the late Thomas Bewick', *Transactions of the Natural History Society of . . . Newcastle upon Tyne*, i, (1831).
[3] Chatto and Jackson, *A Treatise on Wood Engraving*, pp. 587–8. Chatto's draft manuscript for this is now in the London Library. Much of it was based on information provided by Edward Willis who had left the workshop thirty years earlier and whose memory was not always accurate.
[4] TB to Robert Pollard, 29 January 1816 (Laing MSS).
[5] TB to John Bailey, 5 February 1818 (Julia Boyd, *Bewick Gleanings*, 1886, p. 65).

driving inspiration. From the point of view of the publishers, a book that carried Bewick's name on its title would have a greater chance of success. As master he would see no objection to a work such as the edition of Burns's Poems published by Davison of Alnwick being titled as having 'engravings on wood by Mr Bewick': here in fact all the principal designs were drawn on the wood by John Thurston (as was acknowledged) and were engraved by Henry White, while many of the tail-pieces were from the hands of the apprentices Isaac Nicholson and Edward Willis as well as their colleague White.[1] But they were of the workshop and nothing would have gone out without the check and guidance of its proprietor. Whatever may have been said by Bewick's detractors and those who attempted to diminish his reputation as an engraver, it is remarkable that, when independent, not one of his pupils—with the possible exception of Clennell—came anywhere near to approaching his achievement, nor indeed did they match him in the distinction of character so clearly displayed in his writing.

[1] Evidence from the workshop ledgers (Laing MSS).

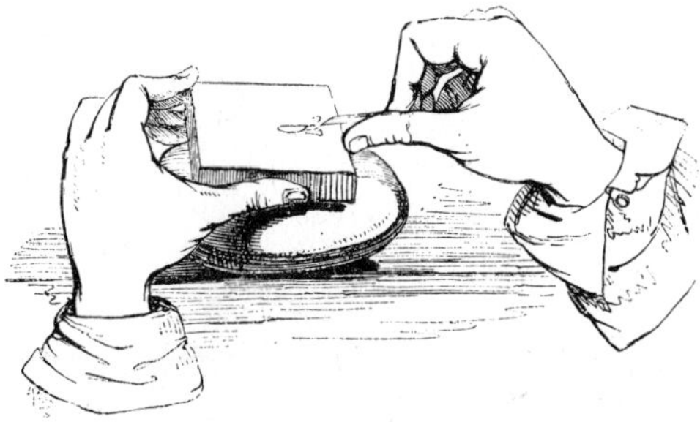

A sketch of an engraver's hands at work, from Chatto & Jackson's *Treatise on Wood Engraving*, 1839

SELECT BIBLIOGRAPHY

EDITIONS OF THE MEMOIR

After the first edition of 1862, referred to in the Note on the Text, a new edition with an introduction was produced by Austin Dobson in 1877 as part of the five-volume Memorial Edition of Bewick's works, printed and published between 1885 and 1887 by Robert Ward & Son of Newcastle. A certain amount of previously omitted matter was taken in from the original manuscript, although the text remained substantially as reworked by Robert Ward and Jane Bewick. Later editions were published by The Bodley Head, 1928, introduced by Selwyn Image who used the 1862 text; the Cresset Press, 1961, edited with an introduction and abridged by Montague Weekley; and the Centaur Press, 1961–a lithographic reprint of the 1928 edition with a new introduction by Edmund Blunden.

BIBLIOGRAPHY

S. Roscoe's *Thomas Bewick, a Bibliography Raisonné* of the principal works issued in Bewick's lifetime, Oxford, 1953; reprinted 1973, is the most thorough work available, although it does not make use of the extensive collection of ledgers and workshop papers formerly in the possession of the Ward family and now in the care of the Laing Gallery, Newcastle upon Tyne. The Revd Thomas Hugo's *The Bewick Collector*, 1866, and supplement, 1868, contains a vast amount of material but much has to be used with care, being of doubtful attribution. *A Descriptive and Critical Catalogue of Works illustrated by Thomas and John Bewick* by John Gray Bell, 1851 contains much useful annotation based on personal knowledge. The extensive collection of Bewick's books, blocks, and manuscripts assembled by J. W. Pease and now in the Central Library, Newcastle upon Tyne, is recorded in substantial form in the *Catalogue of the Bewick Collection* (*Pease Bequest*) by Basil Anderton and W. H. Gibson, 1904. *A Checklist of the Manuscripts of Thomas Bewick* compiled by Iain Bain, reprinted from *The Private Library* with addenda, 1970, presents the first listing of Bewick's surviving correspondence and other papers, amounting to more than 1000 items.

BIOGRAPHY AND CRITICISM

The principal sources based on personal acquaintance are: G. C. Atkinson, 'Sketch of the Life and Works of the late Thomas Bewick' in the

Transactions of the Natural History Society of Northumberland, Durham and Newcastle upon Tyne, i. 1831; read before the Society in June 1830; J. F. M. Dovaston, 'Some Account of the Life, Genius and Personal Habits of the late Thomas Bewick' in Loudon's *Magazine of Natural History*, nos. 9–12, 1829–30, which for all its hyperbole contains valuable original observations which supplement the fascinating letters Bewick wrote to Dovaston in his later years: *Bewick to Dovaston, Letters 1824–1828*, (ed.) Gordon Williams, 1968; J. J. Audubon's memoir in his *Ornithological Biography*, 1831; Dr Charles Hutton, 'Some Account of Mr. Thomas Bewick, and Other Artists, in Newcastle upon Tyne', *The Newcastle Magazine*, June 1822; Revd William Turner, 'Memoir of Thomas Bewick, Eminent Engraver on Wood', in Jardine's *Naturalists Library*, vi. 1836; Thomas Doubleday, 'Life and Works of Bewick', in the *British Quarterly Review*, ii.4, 1845; and W. A. Chatto and John Jackson's account of Bewick in chapter VII of their *A Treatise on Wood Engraving*, 1839.

The earliest substantial appreciation appeared in the *Annual Review for 1804*, iii, 733, 1805, by Arthur Aikin. Professor Wilson's long notice 'Thomas Bewick, Engraver on Wood' was published in *Blackwood's Magazine* for July 1825. William Howitt published a 'Memoir of Thomas Bewick' in his own *Howitt's Journal*, ii. 38, 18 September 1846.

Among the later nineteenth-century studies the following are the most valuable: F. G. Stephens, *Notes on a Collection of Drawings and Woodcuts by Thomas Bewick. . . .*, Fine Art Society, 1881; D. C. Thomson, *The Life and Works of Thomas Bewick*, 1882; Austin Dobson, *Thomas Bewick and His Pupils*, 1884; Robert Robinson, in his introduction to the *Bewick Memento* (the reprinted catalogue of the sale of Bewick family effects), 1884; Julia Boyd, *Bewick Gleanings: being impressions from Copperplates and Wood Blocks engraved in the Bewick Workshops . . .* edited with notes, 1886; Robert Robinson, *Thomas Bewick, His Life and Times*, 1887; and W. J. Linton in Part II, chapter II of his *The Masters of Wood Engraving*, 1889.

In the present century, Montague Weekley's *Thomas Bewick* (1953) gives us the only modern biography. D. C. Thomson's *The Water-Colour Drawings of Thomas Bewick*, 1930 surveys this surprisingly little-known aspect of Bewick's art. Other shorter studies are given in John Rayner's *A Selection of Engravings on Wood by Thomas Bewick*, 1947; Graham Reynolds's *Thomas Bewick: a résumé of his Life and Work*, 1949; and Reynolds Stone's *Wood Engravings of Thomas Bewick: selected with a biographical introduction*, 1953, which is valuable for having been written by a practising wood engraver.

The various editions of Bewick's principal works are recorded in the Chronology.

INDEX